ZAIRE

ZAIRE

The Political Economy of Underdevelopment

edited by **Guy Gran**

with the assistance of Galen Hull

PRAEGER SPECIAL STUDIES • PRAEGER SCIENTIFIC

Library of Congress Cataloging in Publication Data

Main entry under title:

Zaire, the political economy of underdevelopment.

    Bibliography: p.
    Includes index.
    1. Zaire--Economic policy--Addresses, essays,
lectures. 2. Zaire--Politics and government--
Addresses, essays, lectures. 3. Zaire--Social
conditions--Addresses, essays, lectures. 4. Zaire
--Rural conditions--Addresses, essays, lectures.
5. Zaire--Foreign relations--Addresses, essays,
lectures. I. Gran, Guy. II. Hull, Galen.
HC591.C6Z37   330.9'675'103   79-19512

ISBN 0-03-048916-4

Zaire

Published in 1979 by Praeger Publishers
A Division of Holt, Rinehart and Winston/CBS, Inc.
383 Madison Avenue, New York, New York 10017 U.S.A.

© 1979 by Guy Gran

123456789 038 9876543
Printed in the United States of America

to my mother

for teaching so well
what is wrong
and what is right

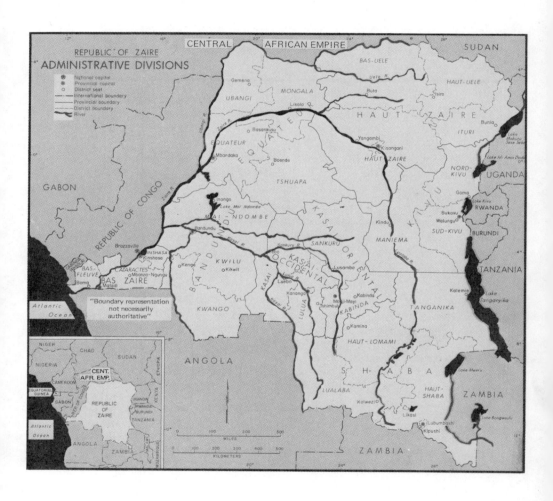

PREFACE

This book grew out of several overlapping concerns. There has not been for many years a broad and analytical introduction to modern Zaire for the English-reading audience. Thus a prime concern of the contributing specialists is to fill this void.

Normative judgment is inescapable in any human endeavor. Most, if not all, of the contributors have concluded that the path followed by the Zairian government since 1965, indeed since 1885, has entailed an awesome and unacceptable magnitude of poverty, deprivation, and suffering for most Zairians. Conventional analyses in the media and from so-called responsible official sources have explained and rationalized this situation with surface phenomenon as the expectable pangs of Third World development. This book will demonstrate a far different and more somber set of processes at work.

What first impelled the editor was the sheer magnitude of the development disaster that accumulated for Zaire as the 1970s drew to a close. By early 1979, Zaire was more than $1.3 billion in arrears on long-term debts and the International Monetary Fund was poised to offer its third restabilization plan in four years, both without precedent in recent history. Doctors reported in 1979, the International Year of the Child, that half the children in rural Zaire were dying by the age of five. Malnutrition was also obvious in urban areas. The managers of the world system, however, still supported the government of Mobutu Sese Seko because they were unable to conceive that the costs of going without change are greater than the costs of having change.

Because of the extreme nature of this particular Third World development experience, the basic contradictions of export-led growth, the historical path sponsored by the International Monetary Fund, the World Bank, and the West revealed themselves more clearly. This was a central and initial concern, as indicated in the first and last chapters.

It has, in addition, grown more and more apparent to the editor, from a previous decade in Southeast Asian studies and forays into Latin American issues as well as this African example, that most of the core premises of the conventional understanding of modern world history and of the modernization process are misconceived. The banal discussions of capitalism versus Marxism are not illuminating or constructive. The basic problem facing humans everywhere is the conflict between people, on the one hand, and large concentrations of power, public and private, on the other. As a direct result of the powerlessness of people, the development choices made by Zaire and by most other societies are not producing jobs, social services, and other human needs in any relation to the present magnitude of human wants. Nor are they going to in the foreseeable future.

To understand this situation, its causes, and its potential cure, new theoretical paradigms and practical alternatives are required. I have been working to synthesize a field termed <u>international development systems analysis</u>. Published samples of this appear in Chapter 1 and my October-December 1978 article on Zaire in <u>Africa Today</u>. Benefiting from advances by Wallerstein, Amin, Elliott, Samoff, and others, I would propose the following: systems analysis applied to contemporary historical processes; far more multidisciplinary frameworks than are now in use; much more empathic and perceptive cross-cultural research; and longer term, more theoretically grounded, historical foundations to contemporary policy analysis. Each contributor was challenged to use the specific issues of the Zairian situation to struggle with and improve the state of the art of historical and developmental understanding along these lines. Readers will, I hope, be as challenged by the results and find here a useful model to approach the study of any Third World society and its development dilemma in the world system today.

Putting together any study of this magnitude is naturally a collective experience. Several people deserve special thanks. My colleague Galen Hull gave much wise counsel, stepped into the breach to complete the unforeseen tasks of a second chapter and a major translation, and justly deserves the more formalized share of public recognition. Beyond his chapter, David Gould also contributed ideas and tangible aid throughout, which was most helpful. Crawford Young shared funding for some collaborative research in the summer of 1978, facilitating my own work considerably. Friends at the Centre d'Etude et de Documentation Africaine in Brussels and anonymous colleagues in Zaire were most helpful in acquiring a variety of current publications. My brother Douglas provided much tangible and intangible aid throughout. Ann Kuhn gave invaluable support in the same generous spirit that she has shown so many African human problems for so long. My colleagues and I share naturally the final responsibility for this effort. We hope it will make some contribution toward a day when the people of Zaire enjoy in reality the basic human rights the world system proclaims it promotes for all.

CONTENTS

PART II

ZAIRE: THE MODERN AND URBAN WORLDS

PART III

ZAIRE: RURAL WORLDS AT THE SYSTEM'S PERIPHERY

LIST OF TABLES AND MAPS

LIST OF ACRONYMS

ABAKO	Alliance des Bakango
AGEL	Association Générale des Etudiants de Lovanium
AIA	International African Association
AID	Agency for International Development (United States)
ANC	Armée Nationale Congolaise
CCCI	Compagnie du Congo pour le Commerce et l'Industrie
CCP	Compagnie de Commerce et de Plantations
CEDAF	Centre d'Etude et de Documentation Africaine
CGTC	Confédération Générale des Travailleurs Congolais
CIA	Central Intelligence Agency (United States)
CIDEP	Centre Inter-disciplinaire pour le Développement et l'Education Permanente
CND	Centre National de Documentation
CNECI	Nation Saving Bank for Housing
CNKi	Comité Nationale du Kivu
CODESCO	Convention des Democrates Socialistes
CONACO	Convention Nationale Congolaise
CRIDE	Centre de Recherches Interdisciplinaires pour le Développement de l'Education
CRISP	Centre de Recherche et l'Information Socio-Politiques
CSK	Comité Spécial du Katanga
CVR	Corps des Volontaires de la République
EDF	European Development Fund
EIC	Independent State of the Congo
EXIMBANK	Export-Import Bank (United States)
FAO	Food and Agricultural Organization (United Nations)
FAZ	Forces Armées Zairoises
FDC	Front Democratic Congolais
FLEC	Front for the Liberation of the Cabinda Enclave
FLNC	Front for the National Liberation of the Congo
FNLA	Frente Nacional de Libertação de Angola

FNLC	Front de Libération National du Congo
FODELICO	Forces Democratiques pour la Liberation du Congo
FSA	Front Socialiste Africain
GDP	gross domestic product
GECAMINES	Général de Carrières et des Mines du Zaire
GECOMIN	Société Générale Congolaise des Mines
HEW	Department of Health, Education and Welfare (United States)
IBRD	International Bank for Reconstruction and Development
IDA	International Development Association
IMF	International Monetary Fund
INERA	National Institute for Agricultural Research
INS	Institut National de la Statistique
IRES	Institut de Recherches Economiques et Sociales
JMPR	Jeunesse du Mouvement Populaire de la Révolution
LME	London Market Exchange
MARC	Mouvement d'Action pour la Resurrection du Congo
MNC	Mouvement National Congolais
MNC/K	Mouvement National Congolais/Kalonji
MNC/L	Mouvement National Congolais/Lumumba
MNUR	Mouvement National pour l'Unité et la Reconciliation
MPLA	Movimento Popular de Libertação de Angola
MPR	Mouvement Populaire de la Révolution
OAU	Organization of African Unity
OCAM	Organization Commune Africaine et Malagache
OECD	Organization of Economic Cooperation and Development
ONAFITEX	Office National des Fibres Textiles
ONDE	National Ranching Development Authority
ONL	National Housing Office
OTRAG	Orbital Transport und Raketen A.G.
PLZ	Plantations Lever au Zaire
PNP	Parti National du Progrès

PPA	Parti Populaire Africain
PRONAM	National Cassava Program
PRP	Parti de la Révolution Populaire
RCP	Rassemblement des Congolais Progressistes
REGIDESO	National Electricity and Water Supply Corporation
SGB	Société Général de Belgique
SGM	Société Général de Minérais
SIMZ	Société Internationale des Mines du Zaire
SMTF	Société Minière de Tenke Fungurume
SODIMIZA	Société du Développement Industriel et des Mines du Zaire
SOFIDE	Société Financiere de Développement
TA	territorial administrator
TFC	land in customary tenure
UGEC	Union Générale des Etudiants Congolais
UMHK	Union Minière du Haut-Katanga
UNAZA	Université Nationale du Zaire
UNDP	United Nations Development Program
UNITA	União Nacional para Independência Total de Angola
UNTZa	Union National des Travailleurs Zairois

1

AN INTRODUCTION TO ZAIRE'S PERMANENT DEVELOPMENT CRISIS

Guy Gran

INTRODUCTION

The extreme poverty of the vast majority of people of Zaire at the end of the 1970s is not primarily an accident of geography and history. It is instead the logical result of deliberately designed historical processes that are implemented by and through a system of local, national, and international institutions. This book proposes to analyze aspects of Zaire's struggle for economic and political development in the world system and to define the links between the institutions that guide Zaire and the processes that have and will continue to impoverish the majority of its citizens. The thesis is that this is a potentially permanent situation. The vast majority of Zairians have no effective political or economic institutions acting on their behalf, and the human results of their dilemma pose a moral imperative to the world community of scholars and citizens to seek fundamental change.

For more than a generation the conventional wisdom of the West has been that money and advice from international aid institutions (the World Bank group, the Agency for International Development, and others), combined with the investment and trade activities of multinational corporations and the Westernized leadership of Third World governments, fostered development and improved the lives of people. In Zaire, like most developing societies, the vast majority of people, however, remain at, or even below, subsistence levels. If one departs from mainstream economics and looks at this result as a systems analysis problem, the reason for such conditions is suddenly and disturbingly clear. Systems analyst Stafford Beer (1974, p. 319) wrote:

> Institutions are systems for being what they are and for doing what they do. No one believes this: it is incredible, yet true. People think that institutions are systems for being and doing what they were set up to be and do, or what they say they are and do, or what they wish they were and did.

1

But they are not. This book is an exercise in looking at what the development system does.

Zaire began as a nation in 1960 with handicaps that would have made miracles difficult. A five-year civil war immediately exacerbated conditions. The rudimentary health and transportation systems deteriorated. Absence of educated personnel throughout government and industry led to continued reliance on foreigners. Significant foreign control over the nation's major economic resources and a profound dependence on the world copper price persisted. Progress by any human measurement has been minimal, even over the last 14 years of comparative peace, whether chronicled by official observers (IMF 1971, 1975b; IBRD 1975) or by more independent sources (for example, Peemans 1975; Kamitatu-Massemba 1977).

Zaire's development problems are far more complex than the current budgetary, debt, and trade imbalances officially ascribed to the recent collapse of the world copper price, which began in 1974. Ironically, it is the continued export of copper—long praised and promoted as Zaire's primary engine of growth—that lets loose the processes that prevent the creation of an economy that functions for people. The export of copper and other minerals, to the general exclusion of all but subsidiary industrial activities, has created and sustained a profoundly unbalanced economy. Such an economy cannot significantly aid the three quarters of the people of Zaire who endure through subsistence, or less than subsistence, agricultural pursuits at a per capita yearly income of between $25 and $50. Export dependence has instead unleashed a complex series of forces that prevent balanced growth and push Zaire toward ever greater external borrowing and ever larger imports.

Underlying this process are the most fundamental causes of impoverishment, the unequal exchanges that characterize both urban-rural and national-international trade for Zaire. For it is these transfers of value from the agricultural sector to the urban and from the mining and urban sectors to the international market that permanently stifle the rich potential of Zaire to provide a healthy and meaningful existence for its 26 to 27 million people.

This discussion will not enter into the theoretical debate (for example, Emmanuel et al. 1975) surrounding the concept of unequal exchange. Exchanges here will be termed unequal when the sale of goods or labor means the transfer of surplus value that leaves one group or sector consistently poorer or weaker than another. Some of the types of exchanges chronicled are common to Marxist discussions; others, such as deteriorating terms of trade, are common to capitalist discussions. What is relevant here is the relationship of perpetual impoverishment to particular policies and processes occurring at each level of economic activity from the village world to debt renegotiations overseen by the International Monetary Fund (IMF).

THE RURAL SECTOR

In 1978, an estimated 18 to 20 million people, about 75 percent of all Zairians, lived in rural areas and practiced predominantly subsistence agriculture. Subsistence, however, implies subsisting. Many of these people are slowly starving. Life expectancy is about 41 years. Daily protein intake is far below minimum standards set by the UN Food and Agricultural Organization (FAO) or the U.S. Department of Agriculture. The International Bank for Reconstruction and Development (IBRD 1975, 2:4) put it this way: "About one-third of the rural population suffer from deficiencies in caloric intake; and more seriously, a grave shortage of protein is characteristic of most of the population of the country." There is approximately one physician per 30,000 inhabitants. "Overall, an estimated 75% of the population remain outside the formal health care delivery system. For many, traditional medicine dispensed by local practitioners is the only type of health care available" (U.S., HEW, 1975, p. 4). Conventional understanding of human rights here as elsewhere has not yet grown to include health.

It is orthodox to analyze the origin and perpetuation of such an economic reality with the concept of a dual economy. Zaire has a traditional agricultural sector with a low gross national product and per capita income, a sector that supplies food to the cities. Zaire's modern sector, defined as mines, plantations, manufacturing, and the urban world of government and services, has a much higher gross national product and per capita income than do the rural areas. Such a dichotomy, however, hides more than it reveals. Most important, it obscures the fundamentally parasitic relationship between the two sectors that only becomes clear from a systems analysis of the creation and distribution of value. One must view the ongoing rural poverty and Zaire's growing inability to feed itself as manifestations of deeper, more complex historical processes.

Western social science would point not to process or system but to specific government policies that work against increasing agricultural production and rural wealth. The U.S. General Accounting Office (1975) succinctly chronicled a representative worldwide sample of disincentives that have been institutionalized by societies ruled by urban or absentee elites more interested in industrial or export advance. These elites control consumer and producer rights, export taxes, exchange rates, movement of products, credit, and land tenure to their own advantage. Further disincentives are noncompetitive buying, import subsidies, and disruptive administrative changes. The Zairian government has used all of these mechanisms on one crop or another against the farmer during the last decade. The sum of these policies makes a system. Given space limitations, primary data on just one part of the system must suffice.

Controls on prices have been a singularly effective mechanism in transferring wealth from the countryside and, at the same time, stagnating agricultural production. Zairian national research groups, such as Institut de Recherches Economiques et Sociales (IRES) and Institut National de la Statistique (INS), have done frequent surveys. In one, prices paid producers in Bas-Zaire for items destined for Kinshasa declined from 40 percent of retail prices in 1960 to about 25 percent in 1970. IMF observers (1975b, p. 9) concluded that most farmers believe the minimum price is the maximum price, and rarely receive more. With the exception of cotton, government prices were left unchanged from October 1967 to 1972; incremental changes thereafter did not come close to compensating for inflation. By looking at the 15-year index in Table 1.1, the full magnitude of loss can begin to be understood.

The farmer loses initially in the basic act of exchange. The amount of labor going into his product is far more than is represented in the goods his money can buy. This is the core unequal exchange.* He loses again as one of many and comparatively poor sellers in a market situation dominated by a few wealthy middlemen. For crops marketed through the Offices Agricoles, the situation can be even worse when officials demand bribes and commissions and cannot perform their duties competently. If, then, one translates the resulting market price into the situation described in Table 1.1, the additional losses are apparent. The farmer who grew bananas, for example, over the last 15 years found that the real value of his return on a given unit in December 1974 was about 25 percent of his 1960 earnings.

If President Mobutu Sese Seko, as he is promising, is going to improve agriculture's terms of trade to any degree approaching either efficiency or equity, he has multiple problems. Anything more than incremental change is perceived to portend both political and economic costs that his urban supporters will not accept. Mobutu's fear of market forces may or may not be unfounded. Logic also impels one to question whether there exist the technical skill and political will to make substantive changes simply because the national leader proclaims them. It is one thing to recognize problems or produce motion that appears like action. It is quite another thing to attain socially responsible and meaningful solutions. A quick look at the problems of one specific crop suggests how large that gap is for Zaire.

In recent years palm oil has been Zaire's second leading agricultural export. Here, as elsewhere, production and marketing historically have been dominated by the multinational firm Unilever. In the mid-1960s, Unilever itself produced about one-third of the exports. As the decade ended, Unilever still controlled 80 to 90 percent of total exports through a cooperative selling arrangement (Kabala Kabunda 1976, p. 308). The industry, however, was in decline. European planters left, in part because of falling profits. Labor shortages helped to decrease tree replanting and thus yields. Significant additional damage was done by nationalization measures imposed in 1973 and 1975.

A look at unclassified U.S. government cable traffic during 1975 reveals through a brief slice of Zairian economic history the profound flaws in the political economy and acute official awareness of those flaws. These U.S. observers predicted that the 1975 rate of decline would force Zaire to import

---

*Those who do not wish to correlate labor and value in any way may contemplate this issue from the framework of the basic incommensurability of four categories of goods: primary (renewable and nonrenewable) and secondary (manufactures and services). Contrary to conventional economics, the creation of value and concept of cost would appear to be quite different among the four categories (see Schumacher 1975, pp. 49-51).

TABLE 1.1

Zaire: Index of Real Agricultural Minimum Producer Prices, 1960–74
(June 1967 = 100)*

	June 1960	June 1970	December 1974
Domestic crops			
Maize			
Shaba-Kasai	114.9	100.7	96.0
Other	94.8	85.0	81.0
Groundnuts (unshelled)	103.4–120.7	90.7	86.4
Cassava			
Shaba-Kasai	98.5–114.3	64.8	30.8
Bandundu	126.4	75.6	36.0
Rice (paddy)	157.9	109.2	104.0
Banana plantain	160.9	90.7	43.2
Beans	137.9	90.7	43.2
Cotton			
First quality	172.4	85.0	63.0
Second quality	172.4	85.0	67.5
Export crops			
Palm			
Bas-Zaire	191.6	44.1	36.0
Other	241.4	79.3	64.8
Coffee			
Robusta			
Central, Bandundu, Equateur	195.4	90.7	64.8
Bari	193.1	99.7	77.7
Sankuru	193.1	90.7	77.7
Other	195.4	75.6	64.8
Arabica	202.0	93.9	52.4
Tea (first quality)	91.0	90.7	43.2

*Deflated by the index of retail prices in the markets of Kinshasa; Institut de Recherches Economiques et Sociales series for the period June 1960–June 1968 and Institut National de la Statistique series thereafter.

Source: International Monetary Fund, "Zaire—Recent Economic Developments," SM/75/225, August 26, 1975, p. 16.

5

palm oil by 1977 or 1978. They noted these processes at work: The November 1973 nationalization measures drove third-country middlemen out of the interior, hastening the decay of the marketing infrastructure; this greatly diminished the supply of goods available for sale in rural areas; workers then moved back to subsistence agriculture or toward urban possibilities.

Problems in management were also severe. Zairian-appointed plantation managers proved to be disinterested and incompetent. In January 1975, the government "radicalized" the previously nationalized plantations. In effect, this represented a move from Zairianization of ownership to Zairianization of control. As government employees, the new managers added to the cost of government. One U.S. observer who assessed the results in a November 1975 cable pointed out:

> Radicalization has no legal status. It was simply a decree by the President or better said, an effort in desperation to reverse a declining industry. What it has meant in fact is that many of the men put in charge of large plantations have systematically depleted the working capital in an effort to rescue their financial position, in the fear that the radicalization decree which put them in power could just as quickly take them out of power.

Marketing problems were varied and severe throughout the year. The world market price for palm oil was more than twice the domestic price in March 1975. A February decree required 70 percent of production to stay in the country. At that time the producer received $43.80 per barrel for what sold on a retail level at $120. Palm oil was set at 32¢ per liter in stores; quantities were limited or nonexistent. On July 21, 1975, the government prohibited all export because of widespread black marketing; it continued unabated. All urban and rural storage facilities quickly filled. With oil going rancid, the government finally allowed the export of 10,000 tons in October. A decree of September 19 raised exfactory, wholesale, and retail prices in Kinshasa, revealing again the considerable disparities in efficiency among plantations and processing facilities. External factors were at work as well. Shortage of steel led to a shortage of drums, hurting local distribution. The Angolan war disrupted fuel supplies for the copper industry; a production slowdown there cut that industry's significant use of palm oil in the extraction process.

This brief excursion into one recent year of Zaire's palm oil industry demonstrates significant limits to both political will and potential reforms within the present framework. A comparable portrait could be drawn for the state of the other major export crop, coffee. Plantations, however, produce only about 15 percent of Zaire's export value, and plantation workers represent fewer than one-third of the million or so wage earners. The most significant test of whether a central government could begin to rebalance rural-urban economic disparities and provide a basis for growth toward self-sufficiency is its performance in increasing the size of and reward for domestic food production.

Zaire was a net exporter of maize before independence. Total imports of wheat, rice, and maize in 1959 were 47,000 tons. By 1968, imports were 125,000 tons and in 1973 they were up to an estimated 306,000 tons (IBRD 1975, vol. 3, Table 7.6). In 1976, grain imports were still at that level, and, as of late 1978, there was still no sign that Zaire was making any real strides toward grain self-sufficiency (Gran 1978). Indeed, manioc, notoriously low in protein, has become in the last two to three decades the primary food for the considerable majority of Zairians. (The health implications of this are specifically addressed in the last chapter of this book.)

All parties concerned have recognized the human and economic results; the burden of food imports, about 20 percent in 1973/74 and probably higher thereafter, represents a considerable drain on foreign exchange. The last few years have seen a singular number of commissions, reports, proposals, speeches, bureaucratic reshufflings, and pledges of change. The creation and perpetuation of such poverty was not, however, accidental. Unequal exchanges were institutionalized at several levels by the stronger urban and foreign interests against the weaker rural ones. It is illogical to expect that the central government, handmaiden to the creation of these inequalities, will be willing of its own accord to move freely toward equitable relations. As the actions of the late 1970s show, the government is unlikely to do more than modestly rebalance the terms of trade and raise slightly the magnitude of investment in agriculture (for example, Marché Tropicaux, May 7, 1976, pp. 1199-1202 or Gran 1978). It is not simply a matter of limited altruism or political will but also one of sheer inability. The forces that created the enormous imbalance are still at work pushing in the other direction, preventing rethinking or reshaping of the transfers of value. To understand why agriculture cannot be significantly reformed in isolation, one must deal with the basic creation of disharmony, the export process, and its chief commodity, copper.

THE MODERN SECTOR AND
ITS INTERNATIONAL NEXUS

Zaire is situated on the periphery of the world economic system. Its role in the system is to supply copper, cobalt, and other minerals and agricultural products to the industrial countries in return primarily for consumer goods and the multiple needs of the mining sector. Zaire's modern sector is not focused on or seeking to energize the subsistence sector. It is instead conditioned by its international links to use resources and distribute surpluses through multiple exchanges so that value flows out of Zaire. The purity of such a thesis is marred by the existence of groups in the modern sector, such as the civil service, the army, and the multiethnic economic elites, that compete for that quantum of wealth remaining in the society and seek in certain ways to enlarge their piece of the pie.

Before discussion of particular forms of unequal exchange, it is important to sketch the overall economic processes at work in order to understand specifically how international trade shapes domestic development. The over-

all analytical model crystallized by Samir Amin (1974, see pp. 359-94 especially) and Norman Girvan (1976) very neatly summarizes Zaire's experience.
Modern mineral exporting like copper requires modern infrastructure and facilities; a Third World government like Zaire is drawn into putting a disproportionate capital investment into what facilitates this exporting. Contact
with the West in general and the needs of the multinational corporations and
banks in particular put pressure on the government to modernize to a degree
far beyond the financial ability and needs of the society as a whole.

The result is high-salaried bureaucrats and workers in the export industries. They naturally seek to spend their wages, but many desire goods
that are not available locally. Instead of altering policies to facilitate local
production, they follow the easier path of importing consumer goods whose
prices are controlled by market forces far from Zaire; the loss of value in
such unequal exchange is considerable. Moreover, new wealth creates new
local processing and service industries, but, without the appropriate preexisting light industry, these lead to even more imports and a stifling of balanced growth. Burgeoning government and new industry combine to push the
urbanization process too rapidly; the food supply cannot keep up and imports
grow. New employment is not large in modern, comparatively capital-intensive industries, and new imports ruin local craftsmen. The cumulative result is very high urban unemployment and low wages. All of these processes
are visible in Zaire, as the following discussion will try to demonstrate.

What is at work throughout the Zairian economy is the interface of actors at greatly different stages of modernity and with disproportionate power.
This is institutionalized unequal exchange with value flowing toward the more
modern sector. Quantification of this transfer of value, particularly between
Zaire and the international market, must be postponed. Neither the appropriate data nor commonly accepted analytical tools are yet available. Logic suggests, however, that an exchange of machine-produced consumer items from
Belgium for a quantity of copper from Zaire by a market price determined by
a complex of forces beyond the control of and far stronger than the Zairian
market necessarily results in an unequal exchange. This is a transfer of
value out of Zaire that perpetuates its poverty.

What can be more precisely documented are the gross magnitudes at
stake and how the export process forces both intrinsic structural changes
and cultural norms on a society that places great pressure on a central administration, whether or not it nationalizes the firms doing the exporting, to allocate the financial rewards of exports in particular ways that are inherently
not in the interest of the society as a whole. This section will examine the
copper sector in some detail (see Chapter 7 for a fuller portrait), sketch
briefly the plantation and industrial sectors, and then explore how the Zairian
government has been allocating the proceeds from these sectors.

Zaire, the former Belgian Congo, began mining copper in 1910. Today
it is the world's seventh ranking copper producer, with 1974 production reaching a modern high of 500,000 tons (IBRD 1977a, Table 2.3). In the mid-
1970s, mineral production provided between 80 and 85 percent of Zaire's export value and at least 45 to 50 percent of its tax revenues, but only an esti-

mated 13 percent of its gross domestic product (GDP) and 6 percent of its wage employment. Copper accounted for between 60 and 66 percent of total exports. Zaire is the world's largest producer of cobalt and of industrial diamonds, but copper is by far the largest source of its revenue (IBRD 1975, vol. 2).

The companies that produce copper (and most other minerals) are largely or entirely government owned. By far the largest is Général de Carrières et des Mines du Zaire (GECAMINES), which before 1967 was the major Belgian concern, Union Minière de Haut-Katanga. Until 1973, GECAMINES produced more than 90 percent of Zaire's copper and cobalt and through subsidiaries most of its zinc and tin, as well as the chemicals and coal necessary for refining operations. Steady efforts are reducing the number of European personnel involved in these activities, but Société Général de Minérais (SGM), the former Belgian parent company, still provides technical aid and marketing facilities. A 1974 agreement changed the compensation agreement of 1967 from 6 percent of annual sales through 1982 to a flat sum of $100 million. SGM is supposed to aid GECAMINES in becoming more self-sufficient in marketing and refining (IBRD 1975, vol. 2).

The government also has entered into joint ventures with foreign firms. The first was Société du Développement Minier du Zaire (SODIMIZA), which was established in April 1969. It began producing copper in 1973. It is 85 percent owned by a consortium of Japanese firms and the yearly output (potential capacity, 50,000 tons by 1975—yet to be reached through 1978) will be exported to Japan. SODIMIZA was to pay no export tax until 1978 (now likely deferred) and would not pay a full rate until 1993. Another joint venture is Société Minière de Tenke Fungurume (SMTF), which, with an exploration company, SIMZ, began in 1970. It had hoped to be in operation by 1978, but was mothballed in 1975. SMTF-SIMZ is 20 percent government owned. The rest was apportioned in this fashion: AMOCO Mines Company (United States), 28 percent; Charter Consolidated, Ltd. (England), 28 percent; Mitsui and Company (Japan), 14 percent; Omnium Mines (France), 7 percent; and Leon Tempelsman & Son (United States), 3 percent. SMTF was scheduled to pay no taxes until five years after start of production and then a 50 percent tax rate for an additional 15-year period (IBRD 1975, 2:28-30). Such investment terms go a long way to explain the present government's survival and the degree of Western support it can command.

SMTF was by far the largest part of current or pending U.S. investment. In a brief State Department memorandum to the Congress dated September 1975, the U.S. financial stake in Zaire was shown to be between $150 and $200 million in direct investment (SMTF, Gulf, General Motors, Goodyear, IHC Hotel, Continental Grain, IBM, and Singer), $35 and $40 million in nationalized assets (Mobil and Texaco), $600 million in loans and contracts (five-sixths covered by the Export-Import Bank), $275 million in pending copper investments, and another $1,600 million (Reynolds Aluminum, Kennecott, and so on) on the horizon. Zaire's parlous national economic situation (see Part III) has cooled most of these plans; but the U.S. financial stake in Zaire at that accounting was second in Africa only to its holdings in South Africa.

It is, however, GECAMINES, not SMTF or SODIMIZA, which is central to the financial and development crisis that Zaire faces. Even without entirely current data it is possible to see with figures from 1969 to 1973 how copper dominates national accounts and trade patterns. Over these five years, GECAMINES's share of Zaire's total export of goods and services fluctuated from 50 to 64 percent; its share of goods alone was 61 to 79 percent. Over this same period taxes on foreign trade ranged from 58 to 67 percent of total government revenue; GECAMINES paid directly 24 to 39 percent of that figure and paid indirectly most of the rest. At the same time GECAMINES annually was using up between $150 and $250 million in foreign exchange earnings for materials, spare parts, capital goods, salaries, financial charges, and technical agreements (IBRD 1975, 2:35-39).

The modern sector of Zaire is thus dominated by the export of minerals. International ties also dominate the subsidiary elements of economic activity. As of 1970, an estimated 260,000 people, or 30 percent of wage labor in Zaire, worked on large plantations. Total agricultural exports have earned $110 to $140 million a year since 1970, or 10 to 17 percent of total exports. Palm oil, coffee, and rubber have been the principal export crops. The IBRD is encouraging revitalization of this sector (see Chapter 14) and expansion of timber production for export as a more efficient initial use of agricultural funds. Major studies (for example, Beckford 1972) of the world record of plantations have not found this method of production a very effective way to develop human resources.

An additional 150,000 Zairians worked in diverse manufacturing industries in 1970. Direct government controls on employment and wages permit enterprises to avoid paying the benefits due to permanent workers by hiring for periods of less than six months and then paying the cost of training new labor. "Industrial policies in Zaire have discouraged the growth of industries based on local raw materials . . . and have resulted in an industry which may be financially profitable but has the following pitfalls: (a) high import dependency; (b) high capital intensity; and (c) large excess capacity" (IBRD 1975, 2:57).

The result of an export-dominated modern sector is a disarticulated or disjointed economy. The various sectors do not face each other as relative equals whose growths are mutually stimulated, as happened in the internal economic growth of the United States or some of the countries of Western Europe. Instead, the primary stimulation comes from abroad. Much of the new value created is exported through profit remittances, less visible mechanisms like transfer pricing, and, most important, by unequal exchange. The effects for Zaire cannot be simply defined in terms of budget deficits and a growing national debt, both to be remedied by an IMF stabilization program.

Growth requires investment. Private investment, both domestic and foreign, seeks areas of greatest profit. It does not address itself to the rural agriculture, health, and education needs of Zaire, investments that over the long run would enhance its economic potential by upgrading its human resources. That leaves human needs to the attention of the government. One measure of performance may be seen in the disposition of the central government's investment budget, roughly 7 to 8 percent of the GDP. Best estimates for 1970 to 1975 show agriculture, health, and education together re-

ceiving 6 to 10 percent of the total (IMF 1977, p. 29). Adding foreign investment does not appear to shift the visible priorities appreciably.

Agriculture, to take a specific case, received 2 to 3 percent of government investment from 1970 to 1974. In 1975, that figure rose to from 5 to 6
percent, most of which went to a few high-priority projects with limited relevance to most of the 75 percent of the population in rural areas. Multiple institutional changes in the mid-1970s have not improved the security of land
tenure or stemmed migration to the towns. Internal deterioration of terms of
trade has been coupled with external deterioration, a fall of some 25 percent
between 1968-70 and 1971-74 (IMF 1975b, p. 49). It will thus take far more
than the recent promises of raising the absolute or relative amount of financial investment in agriculture to return to food self-sufficiency, much less
produce a surplus that could be the basis for rural development.

The preponderance of public and private investment goes into copper
production and its needs. In 1973, mining and processing industries used
about 70 percent of all electricity. Despite its availability to the urban 22 percent of the population, less than 2 percent of all Zairians actually have the
wealth or means for its use (IBRD 1975, 2:61). Rural transportation has been
decaying since 1960. The needs of mineral exports, and thus the Inga-Shaba
region, receive the major portions of both maintenance funding and new investment. IBRD observers found that only 15 percent of the roads were being kept
up. The distribution of health and education investment was equally distorted
in favor of urban and Western sector needs. Even if the government should
reverse its priorities, the resources available are orders of magnitude away
from anyone's definition of the task.

The needs of copper have affected not simply investment but the entire
pattern of government spending. The national budget rose by 108 percent
from 1971 to 1974. As Table 1.2 shows, the size of unclassified expenditures
under the direct control of President Mobutu defeats any precise functional
analysis. A number of reasons can be cited for the considerable recent cost
rises beyond the apparent deficits of newly acquired state enterprises and the
salaries that that involved. Sense of national dignity and pride provided public justification for a considerable expansion of new embassies abroad, and
the sheer cost of travel rose appreciably. Efforts at national integration
were expensive: extension and upkeep of national television and radio networks, new regional political structures, an army reorganization, and the
openly proclaimed glorification of Mobutu and the state. The net result, however, was to put an ever-increasing number of Zairians on the government
payroll. There they consume national resources while adding little to the national product.

Contact with the West and its material lures combined with the needs
of mineral exporting, so that by mid-1973 the 211,000 government salaries
looked like this: 51 percent earned $600 dollars or less a year, another 25
percent earned between $600 and $840, another 10 percent earned from $840
to $1,080, and the rest made more (IBRD 1975, vol. 3, Table 9.7). Adding
perquisites, matabiche, and revenue from business acquired free of charge
via nationalization measures (see Chapter 5) raised the actual figure consid-

TABLE 1.2

Zaire: Composition of Current Government Expenditures, 1970–75
(millions of zaires; 1 zaire = U.S. $2)

	1970	1971	1972	1973	1974	1975
General services	124.7	129.9	135.0	152.8	226.2	207.5
Defense	38.3	38.1	35.2	34.5	75.7	67.3
Justice and police	23.9	17.0	16.2	10.9	21.7	18.2
Foreign affairs	7.7	9.6	6.8	12.0	14.8	16.2
Regional administration	29.7	26.2	19.8	18.3	19.4	20.7
Social services	62.7	71.7	76.5	89.1	104.1	120.3
Education	52.1	62.8	64.1	75.1	84.6	109.5
Health	6.8	5.4	9.9	11.3	14.6	8.0
Economic services	9.2	12.2	25.9	28.3	41.2	40.6
Agriculture	1.5	2.5	3.6	5.6	9.8	4.3
Transport	2.7	3.3	3.2	4.1	6.1	10.2
Subsidies to state enterprises	2.0	8.7	8.4	23.1	80.2	n.a.
Interest on public debt	8.4	10.6	11.7	22.1	30.8	n.a.
Domestic	7.4	8.7	6.9	6.7	7.0	n.a.
Foreign	1.0	1.9	4.7	15.4	23.8	31.0
Unclassified expenditure	50.6	39.5	16.6	16.6	40.5	n.a.
Total	257.6	272.6	274.1	332.0	523.0	493.7

n.a. = not available

Source: International Monetary Fund, "Zaire—Recent Economic Developments," SM/77/113, May 18, 1977,
p. 70.

erably. Wages for skilled workers in private industry averaged not significantly less. Neighboring Tanzania, after implementing pay reductions that
limited income disparities to no more than ten to one, found markedly less
corruption. Whether many of the 2,350 top-ranking Zairians who together
average more than $10,000 a year can identify with or act upon the needs of
the majority of their countrymen who subsist on the equivalent of $25 to $50
a year is a problem not unique to Zaire. Austerity measures, however, are
not going to make much of a dent in the kinds of outlays described above or in
those needed to redress the economic imbalances. Any measure that will
greatly alter these spending patterns must overturn the vested interest they
represent.

It is not enough, however, to explore where money is spent. One must
see how the Zairian government operates on a daily level, for only then will
it be realized why many of the neat Western social science models and categories collapse. Local government, modeled after the strongly centralized
colonial government, plays that role. The disparities between stated and
operative goals, detailed by Gould (1976) are striking (see also Chapter 5).
Development of human services is left largely to the church. Government
maintains law and order and performs routine administration and political indoctrination. As described in eloquent detail by Nzongola Ntalaja (1975),
government's prime activity is revenue collecting to pay its salaries; such
routine administration involves high entrepreneurial skills and much "price
indeterminancy." That means corruption.

The modern sector of Zaire contains more than economic and political
processes. It contains people. With very few words one can obtain a sense
of the human reality for those who left the subsistence sector. Here is a
single portrait from official sources (IBRD 1975, 1:15) of urban unemployment,
of exploding cities in an unexploded economy:

> Urban unemployment is widespread, and a large percentage of ur-
> ban males has not a set job. There is least unemployment in Lu-
> bumbashi and in Kolwezi, the two cities which grew in response
> to the labor needs of the copper mining industry and whose hinter-
> land is extremely sparsely populated. However, even in Kinshasa,
> where work opportunities are numerous and growing, thirteen per-
> cent of working males were found to be unemployed in 1967, while
> 33 percent had no set occupation. In Zaire's other cities, the situ-
> ation is much worse. A sample survey carried out in Bukavu in
> 1971 revealed that 22 percent of household heads were unemployed.
> The population of Bukavu is estimated at 134,000 and there are re-
> portedly only 9,700 wage jobs in the city. In Mbuji-Mayi, the num-
> ber of wage jobs is estimated at 10,700 for a total population of
> 256,000. In Kananga there are 15,000 to 20,000 such jobs, so
> that about one fifth of the male labor force has wage unemployment.

No matter how one views the operation of casual employment and of an
extended family or how one Africanizes the concept of employment, there is

simply no relation between human need and economic possibility within the prevailing economic policies and processes. A complete analysis should investigate the psychological and cultural results as well, as, for example, V. S. Naipaul (1975) and others have; but enough has been laid bare to see how the export process structures the society for the use and gain of foreigners and their local assistants. It is now appropriate to introduce the remaining key policy makers in the overall development system—the international actors.

THE WORLD SYSTEM IN THE GUIDANCE OF ZAIRE

A very few copies of a highly confidential document rest in certain offices close to downtown Washington's skyline. That document is an overall five-year country development plan for Zaire. It is drawn up and revised yearly by a small number of officials high in the IMF and the IBRD. Such documents are not discussed in any available literature on the world economy, yet they are apparently prepared for every country in the world that receives World Bank or IMF assistance. In fact, secrecy might have meant oblivion if the Mexico plan had not leaked to the press in the mid-1970s and caused a furor.

This document does not, however, deserve oblivion, for it is the highest level of policy making for the Zairian economy. A small number of high IMF and IBRD officials, profoundly limited by mainstream neoclassical economics, make the basic decisions that create much of the economic environment and framework within which the national government acts. These decisions facilitate or permit the processes set forth in Parts I and II of this book. These officials are not substantively challenged either within or outside their organizations; there does not even exist a feasible institutional framework through which to mount such a challenge. Thus, until uncontrollable disaster arises, the policies of a generation will continue. One does not need the primary document, for the policy is manifest.

The official development community of the West shares with the multinational corporations the basic thesis that the welfare of people is most effectively served by the expansion of trade through the prevailing market mechanisms. What that means for the Zairian people can be seen most graphically by the mid-1970s projection of Zaire's export growth and its potential human results presented in Table 1.3. A peek into history to find out who produced and who used copper in the last quarter-century ably portends the future as well. From 1950 to 1972, the developed countries mined between 49 and 56 percent of the world's copper and used between 94 and 96 percent; the developing countries produced between 44 and 51 percent and used between 4 and 6 percent (IBRD 1974, vol. 2, Annex 2, Table 5.6).

The development plan for Zaire must, of course, be far more sophisticated than this portrait. The political and economic elite in Zaire must be permitted to share enough of the profits to be willing to allocate resources as the export process requires. The evidence (see Part II) suggests that they

TABLE 1.3

The Future of a Disarticulated Economy: Resource Production and per Capita Gross National Product

	1970	1972	1974	1976	1978	1980	1985	1990
Copper (thousand tons)	385	428	491	530	740*	815*	950	1,185
Cobalt (thousand tons)	13.9	13	16.4	17	20.5*	25	31	39
Zinc (thousand tons)	—	72	72	72	72	72	72	72
Tin and cassiterite (tons)	—	5,892	5,500	5,200	4,900	4,600	4,000	—
Manganese ore (thousand tons)	347.1	369.5	330	330	330	330	330	—
Gold (kilograms)	—	4,300	4,000	3,600	3,000	3,000	2,200	—
Diamonds (millions of carats)	14.1	13.4	—	15	15	15	16.6	—
Oil (billions of barrels)	—	—	—	9	—	—	—	—
Per capita gross national product	—	100	85	87	100	103	117	126

*Actual projections are now lower as investment has slowed because of political and economic instability.

Source: International Bank for Reconstruction and Development, "The Economy of Zaire," Report no. 821-ZR, vol. 2 (Washington, D.C., July 1975), compiled from various tables.

15

have been. The elite must also be able to maintain overall financial stability,
protect the integrity of foreign investments, and pay debts on time. When
they appear unable, the international agencies step in. Such actions, unsurprisingly, also serve the interests of the other world system directors, the
multinational banks and corporations; indeed, the coterminous perceptions
and goals of these public and private institutions can be seen by their mutually
supporting activities when "stability" in Zaire is threatened.

A discussion of the initial steps during 1975 and 1976 in the handling of
Zaire's long-term debt crisis will provide a demonstration of this archetypal
pattern of the system's maintenance. It will also show the cooperative subsidiary role of national governments, particularly, of late, the United States,
in the process of perpetuating the status quo in this region.

Zaire's dilemma at the end of 1975 was a short-term debt of about $550
million, most of which needed to be repaid or rolled over in the first half of
1976. This debt came to public attention in the summer of 1975 when Zaire
defaulted on interest payments due on those loans. The genesis of the debt
and of the concurrent budget and trade deficits were commonly ascribed (for
example, U.S., AID 1976b, pp. 8-9) to three developments during 1973/74.
The 1972-74 rise in copper prices encouraged a rapid expansion of the government budget. At the same time, world prices in food and fuel were rising.
In 1974, the copper price began a sudden collapse. Both imports and exports
were hurt at the same time. Moreover, in November 1973, President Mobutu
began another series of "Zairianization Measures," giving the state and Zairian
personnel control over more and more economic sectors.

Zaire raises about two-thirds of its domestic revenue from taxes on international trade. Revenue from copper accounted for 45 to 50 percent of
total revenue. The recovery from a 1972 low of 48¢ per pound on the London
Metal Exchange to a 1973 average of 81¢ and a 1974 average of 93¢ greatly
encouraged a rapid expansion of government expenditures—by 30 percent in
1973 and nearly 60 percent in 1974 (see Table 1.2). When the crunch came
in 1975, the government could not renege on investment commitments or overcome bureaucratic opposition to make cuts in line with declining revenues.

At the same time, import costs were going up steadily. In 1972 Zaire
was paying $4.80 per barrel for oil, but by 1974 the price had risen to $13.63.
This, after adding exports of bunker oil, left a net increase in imported oil
cost from $36 million in 1972 to about $140 million in 1974. Thanks largely
to world trends, the cost of imported food also more than doubled from 1972
to 1974 (IBRD 1975, 1:53-54). Adding to these burdens on domestic resources
were the economic costs of Zairianization. Both IBRD and U.S. observers
noted inconsistent implementation patterns that disrupted production. This
was especially true in the agricultural plantation sector, which produced
about 15 percent of total export value. Oversight added expensive new layers
of bureaucracy, particularly where the state decided to retain more formal
control. Revenue was lost because new owners were able to avoid paying
taxes and import duties.

All of these processes combined to raise the yearly overall central government deficit from about $150 million in 1971 to $272 million in 1973 and

$328 million in 1975 (Bank of Zaire 1976b, p. 9). The government's major response was to borrow. The growth of both long- and short-term public debt was rapid; long-term debt rose from $632 million in 1971 to $2,738.5 million (of which $1,684.2 million was disbursed) by the end of 1975 (IBRD 1977b). Debt service payments of about $170 million in 1974 were met. Nevertheless, 1975 obligations of $240 million in long-term obligations and substantial ($550 million in the spring of 1975 was one estimate) short-term obligations were too much. During 1975, international reserves were drawn down and Zaire went an estimated $100 million in arrears (U.S., AID 1976b, p. 9).

The international process of system maintenance swung into action during 1975 and 1976 to shore up Zaire's national economy. The major components were initial efforts by the United States to provide stopgap financing and an overall package of austerity measures and debt renegotiation in March 1976 by the IMF. First to act was the U.S. State Department, which in May 1975 sent to Congress its bilateral aid request for fiscal year 1976. It appeared on the surface to be $9.3 million plus $7.95 million for the transitional quarter (July-September 1976—a changing of the fiscal year). A careful reading of multiple executive branch communications to the Congress, however, revealed that the total prospective package for Zaire was closer to $80 million. Potentially controversial requests were divided to make the total appear smaller. Multiple legislative channels were used. In this case Food for Peace commodities, Export-Import Bank credits, military credit sales, and security supporting assistance were sought.

The U.S. executive branch (U.S., AID 1975, p. 91) was not subtle to the Congress about why this money and the even larger requests for fiscal year 1977 were wanted:

> To prevent Zaire's severe short-term financial problems from causing economic disruption and undermining political stability.
> To prevent Zaire's economy from further deterioration while steps are being taken to improve financial management and the anticipated upswing occurs in world copper prices, Zaire's primary export earner.
> To prevent substantial American investment and resource development projects from floundering for lack of essential commodities and equipment, or of banking confidence.
> To indicate through our example that other donors should also respond to Zaire's immediate financial needs.

In a later document, the U.S. Agency for International Development (1976b, pp. 3-4) described U.S. objectives as "to contribute to economic development and economic stability in a key African country, to foster trade and facilitate U.S. investment, to maintain access on favorable terms to Zaire's rich mineral resources" and to encourage Zaire's cooperation in international forums. The Defense Department (1976, p. 182) sought military aid from a similar perspective. Events in Angola pose "a significant potential external threat," and, "although Zaire's internal threat is low, subsequent

events could encourage internal latent dissident elements to become active."
This world model speaks for itself, and continues to thrive in the Carter administration as events of the spring of 1977 and of 1978 demonstrated.

During 1975 and 1976, Congress (U.S., Senate, Foreign Relations Committee 1975, 1976) received these arguments with typical ambivalence. Zaire
was a country of only moderate import. It could not claim too much attention.
Having just escaped from Angola, Congress was naturally wary of what these
vast increases from a total program of $9.2 million for fiscal year 1975 por-
tended in the way of a comparable situation. There was, however, no one on
hand with the national stature of a John Marcum to lead an educational process.
Congress itself had minimal access to professionally trained Africanists within
its staff and supporting agencies; its self-perception of an expert is still
largely defined as one who made a recent visit to an area. Thus the executive
branch, waving the patina of IMF authority that Zaire's troubles would improve, met some skepticism but no vigorous opposition. Congress slowly
learned a bit about Zaire as it appropriated most of what was sought. The
spending for fiscal year 1976 grew to $50.6 million (plus $20 million in Export-
Import Bank credits), and $18.7 million went in the transitional quarter.
Spending for fiscal year 1977 was $60.5 million in bilateral aid, a level main-
tained in the next two fiscal years. Such sums represented a significant commitment and were surely read as such in Kinshasa and Europe.

In addition to bilateral U.S. government efforts, private banks, led by
Chase Manhattan, went to Zaire's assistance. They have a vested interest in
maintaining Zaire's creditworthiness in general and their own notes in particular. Zaire's high percentage of debt to private sources and the higher interest rate that the debt implies were worrisome factors. During 1973 Zaire,
South Korea, and the Ivory Coast together received 75 percent of all private
bank long-term lending among mid- (per capita income $200 to $375) and
lower-income countries. Zaire alone received $720 million. At the end of
1973, loans from commercial sources were 47.7 percent of Zaire's total.
A year later, they were 57 percent (IBRD 1975, 1:47-50; 1977b). Chase Manhattan and Citicorp could not afford to let the taxpayer realize that public funds
might be going through bilateral and multilateral channels to bail out not Zaire
but her creditors, namely, the multinational banks. Wary of President Mobutu's slowness to accept IMF remedies, however, the banks lent primarily
psychological rather than tangible support during 1975 and early 1976.

In the meantime the IBRD and IMF were at work. It took five missions
and eight months of negotiating to put together an attempted system maintenance package. Their 1975/76 effort began with the discovery that Zaire
really had no idea how much it owed. They first found positive signs of cooperation in the work of Zaire's Stabilization Commission and the November
25, 1975, Anniversary Day speech by President Mobutu. In March 1976 the
IMF plan prevailed. In return for $160 million in stopgap loans, Zaire agreed
to the following: a 42 percent devaluation of its currency, a lid on imports,
cuts in the cost of government, and changes in investment priorities and price
policy to favor agriculture (U.S., AID 1976b, pp. 9-12). In mid-June, debt
renegotiations were worked out; 85 percent of Zaire's unpaid 1975-77 obliga-

tions to bilateral creditors was deferred for three years (Washington Post, June 15, 1976; New York Times, June 18, 1976).

Zaire's perceived creditworthiness was thus momentarily restored. Private international banks then sought to settle Zaire's unpaid obligations to them. Meetings in the fall produced a November 1976 settlement in which Zaire agreed to a predictable series of 1976/77 payments to catch up on its debt arrears, while Citibank N.A. agreed to lead a "best-effort" to syndicate a medium-term $250 million credit that would meet most of Zaire's known 1976-78 obligations to the multinational banks (Belliveau 1977; Urbach 1976; IBRD 1977a).

It was an interesting exercise in statistical juggling and short-term crisis management. Unfortunately for the IMF and the New York banks, such an exercise had little impact on the real fiscal processes of Zaire. At the end of 1978, and after several more comparable efforts, Zaire was $1.334 billion in arrears on its known public debts and the world system was seeking more extreme remedies for an ever more disintegrating situation (Gran 1979). Official sources have been conspicuously quiet about this systemic debacle, as criticism would destroy the psychological substance of the term creditworthy. Internal reports do, however, make occasional comments; the World Bank in April 1977 (IBRD 1977a, p. 20) reviewed the efforts of 1975 and 1976 and found that "no fundamental improvements were achieved in the management of public finances." From an historical as well as a contemporary view, the 1975/76 restabilization effort also appeared flawed. In 1967 the IMF went through a virtually identical exercise with President Mobutu. Then, as now, the stopgap measures did nothing about the basic processes of destabilization let loose by export-led growth.

LOOKING TOWARD THE FUTURE

The processes of impoverishment and the policies and institutions that guide them thus constitute a system. The Zairian farmer who cannot obtain sufficient reward on his crop to pay for the medicine or protein that his sick child needs is contributing a measure of value that ultimately helps to make possible the steak dinner cooked in a copper-bottom pan by the suburban U.S. housewife. Given the evidence at hand, one can draw a preliminary systems analysis conclusion. The international economic institutions and the national government of Zaire both say they exist to improve human welfare, but both do something else. They perpetuate poverty for 70 to 80 percent of the society and assist the multinationals to transfer wealth to the industrial countries.

It is not reasonable to expect those with the privileges, power, and wealth to abandon the policies that brought such rewards merely because the system is perceived to be a bit unstable at the moment. It is, however, a little curious to watch the restabilization efforts of 1975 and 1976 when one knows that the internal IBRD assessment is that the system, as IBRD itself perceives it, is not viable in its present form even for the 15 to 25 percent of the Zairian people who could be viewed as benefiting to some minimal extent.

In early 1975, the IBRD (1975, vol. 4) extrapolated upon the admittedly incomplete and often shaky data it had available. It concluded from such an undertaking that the current Zairian development patterns would not produce a workable economy. In IBRD's terms, growth in manufacturing would neither meet the society's job needs nor significantly affect the balance-of-payments situation. Continued expansion of the mining sector would not address the needs of the traditional sector (no real explanation was given) but would increase vulnerability to the world market and dependence on external resources.

Behind such an unpromising forecast was a complex variation of the standard "two-gap" model of an optimal policy for the period 1973-90. Its base run was pegged to a world copper price termed medium, a low of 68¢ per pound in 1975 rising continuously to $1.24 per pound by 1980. The advantage of hindsight shows a 1975 average in the 53¢ to 55¢ per pound range. Even with a price 13¢ higher, the base run showed the following negative results. With optimal policies, poor domestic savings would still not be overcome by extensive external borrowing, even given its possibility. Enlarging imports to foster domestic growth would be expensive and likely to be counterproductive.

Another option considered for the projected necessary capital was using the domestic banking system. That would, however, produce a presumed unbearable rate of domestic inflation averaging 17 percent a year until 1980, a rate far below what actually occurred in the late 1970s. Most of the 1974 budget deficit was made up in this manner, and the degree of recent inflation evident must bear some relation to the continued growth of the monetary supply chronicled monthly and annually by the Bank of Zaire.

If one goes beyond these general conclusions and relates the statistics of the base run to some of the model's implicit assumptions, the picture for Zaire looks considerably more bleak. To make even a minimal per capita raise in wealth to a projected $126 million a year would, the IBRD found in its mythical 1975 portrait of an apolitical and noncorrupt society, require substantial external resources on the order of $480 million a year until 1980. Despite some recent rise in U.S. investment and bilateral aid, this figure has never become a real possibility. Given the reality of much lower copper prices and thus earnings, the hypothetical $480 million figure inevitably rises. Long-term industry use trends for copper in the West also do not bode well; copper is being replaced by other materials in many applications (IBRD 1976a, 1976b).

Thus, face to face with the ugly and ongoing historical reality of Zaire and comparable societies, the citizen and scholar must not accept the moral myopia and intellectual poverty of conventional views, but strike out in search of alternatives. There is no reason to accept the constituent elements of the prevailing development system as monolithic and immutable. There are people inside all of the institutions discussed who oppose the human results of the current historical processes. They are reachable, and they need and want the assistance of world citizens. Several sorts of aid seem appropriate.

The assumptions underlying conventional history and economics badly need reformulation. In Washington, history is still often viewed as a narrative of discrete events. As this book intends to demonstrate, however, history is more meaningfully seen as interweaving and unfolding processes that yield coherent patterns, given some moderately rigorous analytical method. This is not to argue for historical determinism. Nor is it to argue that individuals cannot upset or alter processes unfolding. President Mobutu is not a puppet. Nevertheless, it does suggest that individual decisions and constraints upon particular policy making must be analyzed in a systems manner as part of an entire world system in operation.

If conventional history misleads, the effects of conventional economics on human welfare are all too obvious. Neoclassical capitalist economics argues that the best system for society is the one that maximizes production and profits, namely, the free market. The experience of Zaire, and of poor people and poor nations everywhere, has been that the market is often relatively indifferent or actively hostile to their needs. Unlimited freedom to produce has not created a society where people matter. Too much liberty has led easily to license. What economic assumptions must begin with is a better balance between freedom and social responsibility. There may always be some disparities in income and opportunity, but overall socioeconomic policy must start with the welfare of people, not with abstract models of macroeconomic efficiency. E. F. Schumacher (1975) and Charles Elliott (1975) have made reasonable starts in formulating this path.

Such philosophic growth does not come easily to most people, particularly those who have used traditional intellectual tools to gain professional stature, wealth, and power. The Vietnam War remains a graphic reminder of the human ability to prolong error in order to preserve one's sense of position and self-worth. This chapter quoted official sources at length precisely in order to show how the neoclassical economist or bureaucrat is able to perceive human disaster in the abstract while simultaneously divorcing it from macroeconomic models and decision making. On some levels one could charitably term such behavior unenlightened self-interest.*

Criticizing Zaire's current development path as basically antihuman demands a concrete alternative. Discussions by spokesmen of the new international economic order provide some possibilities. Chapter 15 will discuss an overall theoretical model. Ironically, it is a high IBRD official who has published one of the most articulate versions to date. Mahbub ul Haq (1976) ar-

---

*A more solution-oriented book would have to explore in detail the philosophical and cultural basis for this world model and its perpetuation in Washington. One of Washington's strongest internal norms, for example, permits one to criticize a policy abstractly but never to comment on a proponent's motives or values. Nor is it fashionable to question the profoundly self-serving line that is used to divide what is termed political from what is seen as apolitical or "objective." The reader wishing to explore these issues would profit from several recent pieces in Washington Monthly and Harper's, especially that of Roger Morris (1977).

gues for a strategy of self-reliance aimed at equalizing opportunity. At a national level he suggests that a developing country like Zaire must pursue at least these four policies: "not introduce any consumption goods which cannot be shared by the vast majority of the population at that particular stage of development"; make maximum use of local resources and technology; make minimum use of foreign assistance; and deliberately unlink itself from past dependent relationships (pp. 71-74). Such policies need to be combined with fundamental institutional changes in the international market and monetary systems, topics Haq addresses somewhat less cogently.

Underlying the pursuit of such a people-centered economy must be a conscious recognition of how value is created, measured, and transferred. For without an alternative vision, both theoretically and practically sound, Zaire cannot end the addictions of export dependence and will not easily regain even minimal financial stability. Even if such a minimal stability could be attained through partial IMF remedies, Zaire remains, with 75 percent of its population deprived of elementary human needs, caught in a final and irresolvable dilemma. Dependence on large-scale export of copper means ultimately dependence on the continued good health of the world economy and on its use of copper. In the best of times, Zaire, as a peripheral state, can grow no faster than the average rate of the consuming economies. Thus international specialization makes it impossible for Zaire to catch up on its historical handicap. That means that by accepting its present role, it will remain permanently a fourth-class economic citizen in the world system. It is with the historical creation of this dilemma that this book begins.

REFERENCES

Amin, Samir. 1976. Unequal Development. New York: Monthly Review.

_____. 1974. Accumulation on a World Scale. New York: Monthly Review.

Bank of Zaire. 1976a. Annual Report. Kinshasa.

_____. 1976b. Bulletin mensuel de la statistique. Kinshasa. February, p. 9.

_____. 1975. Annual Report. Kinshasa.

Beckford, George. 1972. Persistent Poverty. New York: Oxford University Press.

Beer, Stafford. 1974. "Immanent Forms of Imminent Crisis." INFOR 12 (October): 318-30.

Belliveau, Nancy. 1977. "Heading off Zaire's Default." Institutional Investor, March, pp. 23-28.

Elliott, Charles. 1975. Patterns of Poverty in the Third World. New York: Praeger.

Emmanuel, Arghiri, et al. 1975. Le Débat sur l'échange inégal. Paris: Maspero.

Girvan, Norman. 1976. Corporate Imperialism: Conflict and Expropriation. White Plains, N.Y.: M. E. Sharpe.

Gould, David S. 1976. "The Role of Dependent Public Administration in Underdevelopment and Its Impact on Decision Making and Administrative Reform in Local Zairian Administration." Paper presented at the African Studies Association 1976 Annual Meeting.

Gran, Guy. 1978. "Zaire 1978: The Ethical and Intellectual Bankruptcy of the World System." Africa Today 25, no. 4:5-24.

_____. 1979. "Zaire 1979: The IMF at Waterloo." In Foreign Assistance Legislation for Fiscal Years 1980-1981, House Foreign Affairs Committee, pt. 6, pp. 406-17. Washington, D.C.: Government Printing Office.

Gutkind, Peter C. W., and Immanuel Wallerstein, eds. 1976. The Political Economy of Contemporary Africa. Beverly Hills, Calif.: Sage.

Haq, Mahbub ul. 1976. The Poverty Curtain. New York: Columbia University Press.

International Bank for Reconstruction and Development. 1977a. "Economic Conditions and Prospects of Zaire." Report no. 1407-ZR. Washington, D.C., April.

_____. 1977b. World Debt Tables—Supplements. EC-167/76/S-1. Washington, D.C., June 6.

_____. 1976a. "Copper: Current Situation and Outlook for 1976." Commodity Paper no. 18. Washington, D.C., January 23.

_____. 1976b. "Price Prospects for Major Primary Commodities." Report no. 814/76. Washington, D.C., June.

_____. 1975. "The Economy of Zaire." Report no. 821-ZR. 4 vols. Washington, D.C., July 23.

_____. 1974. "Special Report on the Chilean Economic Outlook." Report no. 551-CH. 3 vols. Washington, D.C., October.

International Monetary Fund. 1977. "Zaire—Recent Economic Developments." SM/77/113. May 18.

_____. 1976. Zaire—Use of Fund Resources-Stand-by Arrangement." EBS/76/129. March 13.

_____. 1975a. "Staff Report for the 1975 Article XIV Consultation." SM/75/189. July 17.

_____. 1975b. "Zaire—Recent Economic Developments." SM/75/225. August 26.

_____. 1971. Surveys of African Economies, vol. 4. Washington, D.C.

Kabala Kabunda, M. K. K. 1976. "Multinational Corporations and the Installation of Externally-Oriented Economic Structures in Contemporary Africa: The Example of Unilever-Zaire Group." In Multinational Corporations in Africa, edited by Carl Widstrand, pp. 303-22. New York: Africana.

Kamitatu-Massemba, Cléophas. 1977. Zaire, le Pouvoir à la portée du peuple. Paris: Editions l'Harmattan.

Marché Tropicaux. 1976. May 7, pp. 1199-202

Morris, Roger. 1977. "Jimmy Carter's Ruling Class," Harper's, October, pp. 37-45.

Naipul, V. S. 1975. "A New King for the Congo." New York Review of Books, June 26, pp. 19-25.

Nzongola, Ntalaja. 1975. "Urban Administration in Zaire: A Study of Kananga, 1971-73." Ph.D. dissertation, University of Wisconsin.

Peemans, J. Ph. 1975. "The Social and Economic Development of Zaire since Independence: An Historical Outline." African Affairs 74, no. 295:148-79.

Rymenam, Jean. 1977. "Comment le régime Mobutu a sapé ses propres fondements." Le Monde Diplomatique 278 (May): 8-9.

Schumacher, E. F. 1975. Small Is Beautiful. New York: Harper & Row.

United Nations. Development Program. 1976. Country Program for Zaire. DP/GC/ZAI/R.2. February 25.

U.S., Agency for International Development. 1976a. Fiscal Year 1977 Submission to the Congress—Security Supporting Assistance—Zaire, Zambia, Southern Africa. Washington, D.C., June.

_____. 1976b. Zaire Commodity Import Loan. Project Paper. AID–DLC–2145/1. Washington, D.C., June 30.

_____. 1975. FY 76 Submission to the Congress—Middle East Peace and Security Supporting Assistance. Washington, D.C., May.

U.S., Congress, Senate. Appropriations Committee. 1977. Foreign Assistance and Related Programs Appropriations FY 78. Hearings.

U.S., Congress, Senate. Foreign Relations Committee. 1976. The Political and Economic Crisis in Southern Africa. Staff Report. September.

_____. 1975. Security Supporting Assistance for Zaire. Hearing. October 24.

U.S., Department of Defense. 1976. Congressional Presentation Security Assistance Program FY 77. March.

U.S., General Accounting Office. 1975. "Disincentives to Agricultural Production in Developing Countries." Report no. ID–76–2. Washington, D.C., November 26.

U.S., Department of Health, Education, and Welfare, Office of International Health. 1975. Syncrisis: The Dynamics of Health—XIV: Zaire. Washington, D.C.

Urbach, Alan. 1977. "Lessons to Be Learnt from Zaire Debt Settlement." New African Development, January, pp. 69–73.

_____. 1976. "Zaire's $2.000m. Debt Spells Trouble for Africa." New African Development, November, pp. 1107–9.

PART I

ZAIRE'S ENTRANCE INTO THE WORLD SYSTEM

2

ZAIRE ENTERS THE WORLD SYSTEM: ITS COLONIAL INCORPORATION AS THE BELGIAN CONGO, 1885-1960

Bogumil Jewsiewicki

A THEORETICAL INTRODUCTION

Historical studies of all varieties on the colonial period in sub-Saharan Africa suffer the same intellectual isolation as does African historiography in general. Perhaps it is because in the historiography of this period there are few multidisciplinary, broadly designed historical works. Nor are there many efforts at comparative history. The evolution and guiding mechanisms of African societies have not been confronted; ignored as well have been processes such as the transition to an industrial (capitalist or socialist) mode of production.* Because of this, the colonial character (that is, control over the transition by the state apparatus functioning in the name of and interests of foreign groups and locally incorporated commercial firms) of primitive accumulation is little, or at best partially, perceived.

---

*It is necessary to discard all ideas of linear progress in history either in the guise of an emerging "modernity" or in the form of a predetermined progression of modes of production. There is no universally valid theoretical scheme of evolution. It is possible, however, to describe through concrete analysis a historical reality, its principal tendencies toward change and toward stability, and their mechanisms. History does not verify the realization of an idea that was conceived of in the past and came to pass in the present. It does allow one, however, to understand evolution leading from the past to the present that is not necessarily the dominant tendency of the future. Often historical discussion gives the impression of presenting the accomplishment of a design leading from past to present, the fruition of a conspiracy.

The text that follows, wishing to be brief in its historical explanation, presents only the events and processes that, in the author's opinion, contributed to the elaboration of a system that ensures Zaire today its spectacular underdevelopment. It is not a question, however, of a scheme designed 50 years ago by some naughty capitalists nor of one of a century ago created by the capitalist genius of Leopold II.

As far as the Belgian Congo is concerned, only J. P. Peemans (1973) has clearly shown the role of the state in the economic aspects of accumulation. The works inspired by the theory of unequal exchange and of unequal development have too normative and too global a vision to establish a solid basis for comparative history. However they certainly open doors. Finally, the work of C. Peerings (1979) contributes valuable insights and offers an example to follow in studying the constraints upon the process of primitive colonial accumulation by the evolving conditions of the capitalist world economy: changes in market prices, qualitative demands, technological change, and evolution of the capital market.

In previous works the author has tried to show the totalitarian character of the colonial state that ensured political control over the primitive colonial accumulation. Colonial planning (Jewsiewicki 1976c) had to allow for and manage the impact of accumulation on the social and political evolution of local societies, both black and white. The author has also had occasion to analyze the role of primitive colonial accumulation in the transformation of village economy and society (Jewsiewicki 1979c). Finally, as in the work of J. Stengers (1974) and J. L. Vellut (1978), the author has shown that the famous colonial triumvirate (state, capital, church) resulted more from a profound community of interest among these three groups than from the direct control and the corruption carried out by the grand bourgeoisie.

The lines that follow are a brief synthesis, an essay of global history in the colonial period. In order not to overextend the bibliography, only some of the author's own works and a few other recent titles are cited. The reader will find there much more detailed discussions. The economic perspective predominates, which seems amply justified; colonization in the twentieth century was first and foremost an economic activity, even if in a number of cases its initial goals were of another nature and even if the initial balance of expenses and profits was often negative for the average European taxpayer.*

The birth of a mode of production is surely most difficult to describe; it is a question of one of a number of avenues open to the world system at a given moment and the reinforcement of that one because it permits the dominant groups to attain their basic goals. In the operation of a mode of production, the attainment of objectives and the logic of its internal operation, reinforcing a system, both work as a filter retaining certain solutions and rejecting others. To save the reader time, only the solutions retained will be presented herein; one might not deduce from this, however, that what follows is an essay in teleogical history.

*The history of the metropole in colonialism remains to be done. If there is considerable historical literature devoted to imperialism in the nineteenth and twentieth centuries, we know still little of the "secret" history of colonialism in the sense of the real participation by diverse interest groups of the metropole in colonial propaganda and in military, political, and economic decision making. The use of public funds of the metropole to ensure a profitable colonization for private capital remains to be studied, as does

Primitive colonial accumulation constitutes the central theme of this synthesis. The adjective "colonial" seems indispensable. The same basic process that precedes all industrialization, be it capitalist or socialist, has a particular character. The colonial state, which was, on the one hand, guarantor and controller of the development of primitive accumulation, played also the principal role as distributor of the gains from this process. As much for its state planning as for the necessity of realizing primitive accumulation entirely at the expense of the societies directly incorporated into the territory of the state, primitive colonial accumulation more closely resembles primitive socialist accumulation. (The resemblance is only of a methodological sort; their results are functionally different in their impact on internal development, understood as state or colonial appropriation of physical product.) Moreover, the two types took place almost at the same time, contrary to the kind of primitive accumulation that preceded the establishment of liberal capitalism in Western Europe, North America, and Australia. The two are probably reactions, in opposite directions, to the world expansion (imperialism) of liberal industrial capital.

Primitive accumulation is not only the initial accumulation of capital necessary for the material start of industrial production. Basic social and political conditions have to be created. By the expropriation of the mass of small producers and by the destruction of the economic basis of rural communities, the separation of capital and labor takes place. Consider the theoreticians of the birth and development of liberal capitalism: "the historic movement which divorced labor from its external conditions, thus spelling the end of the accumulation termed 'primitive' because it pertained to the prehistoric age of the bourgeois world" (Marx, p. 154). Marx specified also that "the methods of primitive accumulation are all that one would wish except for the material basis for an idyll" (Marx, p. 154). Rosa Luxembourg distinguished the following phases of accumulation: "The struggle of capital against the natural economy, its struggle against the market economy, and its struggle on the world scene amidst the enduring conditions of accumulation" (Luxembourg, p. 40).

The exchange established between agents of the industrial economy and the zones at "the fringes of the capitalist system" was designed with three goals: extraction of primary materials, utilization of the work force, and disposition of the surplus. Contrary to Rosa Luxembourg, it seems that during the entire period of European expansion from the fifteenth to the twentieth centuries, the first two goals dominated relations with Africa. The colonial occupation at the end of the ninteenth century was basically a function of the need for political control to realize these three goals in a coordinated manner,

---

the accounting of profits and losses for the average taxpayer in the metropole. Belgium without the Congo would certainly not be the Belgium it is today. The exact role of the Congo in the Belgian economy remains to be determined at all levels, from the politics of banking to the creation of specialized Belgian manpower.

a need created by changing conditions in the capitalist world market (Coquery-Vidrovitch and Moniot 1974, pp. 149, 297-98).

Colonial policies following the conquest phase were marked above all by the search for a delicate equilibrium between, on the one hand, the use of local labor, reproduced outside the industrial economy, for the extraction of resources and, on the other, the growth of the real capacity to absorb goods and investment capital coming from the metropole. The need to conciliate these two drives explains the preference, which grew over time, for economic mechanisms to encourage less than willing labor forces. The expansion of the markets, which the colonial economies represented, was, however, continually slowed by the need to assure the reproduction of labor forces outside the capitalist system, the basic condition of cheap labor.

The result was a basic contradiction in the colonial system between the need to accelerate primitive accumulation and the need to prevent the complete transformation from the nonindustrial to the capitalist mode of production. To make this deep contradiction clearer, remember Luxembourg's four elements in the struggle of capitalism against the "natural economy": the direct appropriation of considerable resources of productive forces; the liberation of labor to create a reserve proletarian army; the introduction of the market economy in place of the subsistence economy, creating a market for goods even while impoverishing people; and the separation of agriculture and handicrafts.

It is important to add here that true industrialization, the creation of what are often and not ironically termed poles of development, accomplishes principally the latter two goals; it also offers the metropolitan economy new markets for finished goods, as well as for capital and technology.

Realization of primitive colonial accumulation first requires attainment of a certain number of preliminary conditions. The most important are imposition of political power capable of ensuring the maintenance of a legal system and a repressive apparatus guaranteeing the functioning of primitive accumulation for the profit of the metropole, that is, its colonial character; the creation of subordinate economic zones and the funnel to drain resources toward the world market; control over the evolution of local social and political structures to guarantee their stability halfway between what they were in precolonial social and economic formations and the atomizing effects of proletarianization and individualization; and the creation and maintenance of the symbolic power* of the industrial world (Jewsiewicki 1978b). The composition

---

*The importance of this power, "proper" because it is nonviolent, on the physical universe has not been emphasized enough yet. Only P. Bourdieu (1977) offers a theoretically valid analysis of this problem, however in another context. The role of all ideologies of "authenticity" in black Africa was central in the creation of a double scale of values: good-modern-white and bad-traditional-black. The symbolic power of modernity has recently replaced that of race, permitting a "soft" transition from the colonial phase to the postcolonial. Studies of indigenization are rare in Latin America and almost non-

of this power changes significantly the length of the colonization: Civilization as a way of life and system of education, Christianization, racial superiority, technological superiority, modes of consumption, styles of political life, and so on all come to bear. The symbolic power of the Western world plays a great role in the practices of colonial domination and spares the colonial state such disagreeable and costly options as a more intense use of direct physical force.

LEVELING THE DIFFERENCES AND UNIFYING THE TERRITORY

Having gotten his territorial pretensions recognized at the Berlin Conference, Leopold II, king of Belgium, applied himself to give his African empire an existence in reality. This had not been evident either in the official proclamation of an Independent State of the Congo (EIC) at Boma in 1885 or in the successive recognitions of his political sovereignty by the Western world and not least in the operatic game of treaty signing by African chiefs that allowed all this. Leopold II had to create an economic and political territorial organization capable not only of financing itself (paying for its own conquest and exploitation) but also furnishing a profitable surplus from colonial activity. To manage this, he had to impose the real political, that is to say, military, control of an EIC administration on the African territory that was his only according to the international law of the conquerors in Berlin.

The economic and political realities quickly forced Leopold II to abandon his utopian facade of a coalition of states (or rather chiefs) of Central Africa in the shadow of his throne. The treaties with the African chiefs were not worth the paper they were signed on. Each signatory had considered them as his own political success and discounted obligations to the other. It was quickly obvious in less than five years that the mercantilist exploitation (the spread of banks of the European merchant societies dealing with the networks of African traders) was not profitable either for the European commercial groups or the state.

To be sure, the Brussels Conference authorized the EIC to collect a 10 percent entry tax, but the trade was too small to create significant revenues. Neither the conditions in the world market nor those in the African market were those of the 1850s or 1860s. Because of world price movements the profit on single transactions had fallen for the Europeans, which heightened competition and forced them to enlarge the volume of trade. The African traders resisted the substantial deterioration in the terms of trade. Moreover, production conditions had not changed in black Africa, and a very substantial price fall risked affecting the volume of production.

This new economic situation provoked the European traders in the 1870s and 1880s to push toward the center of the continent in the hopes of destroying

---

existent in Africa. I have on occasion mentioned this problem in some of my other works.

the interior monopoly held by African traders, lowering the net cost, and increasing the volume. Conflicts grew among the European trading societies, between Europeans and African chiefs protecting their monopolies, and among Africans protecting old and new trading routes. At the same time, as their capital resources grew larger, the predominant trading firms in the metropole gained a greater and greater political voice at home.

The political advances of colonization by the European industrial powers were thus basically economic in nature. Sometimes political control was directly assumed and sometimes it took the form of a temporary delegation of concessionary or chartered companies. It was necessary to take political control to ensure the extraction of the surplus produced by exploiting local labor. This surplus financed all, as in the case of the Belgian Congo, or a major part of the transformation in Africa of the conditions of production and distribution, the transition to an industrial mode of production. In most cases this transition was primed by the noneconomic pressures of the colonial state and/or the trading companies. The situation for the Belgian Congo was special. Political recognition at Berlin gave free access to the exploitation of the Congo basin region, which limited the interest of specifically Belgian capital. As a "royal personal possession" the EIC found it difficult to profit from public Belgian capital for the initial mise en valeur.

If the complexity, as much political as economic, of the map of the Congo basin facilitated the first phase of the imposition of Leopold's sovereignty, it made very difficult, in contrast, the organization of a state within the boundaries set at Berlin. Nearly everywhere in the Congo the arrival of pax belgica and the destruction of preexistent political and economic arrangements froze a world in transition. The second half of the nineteenth century in Central Africa was marked by dramatic changes in local political structures and probably social ones as well. Political systems, based on cultural and familial links and those of the extended family, buttressed by ideologies of symbolic power, and deeply rooted in the prestige of oral traditions and in the symbolic control of the life cycle, progressively gave way to new sociopolitical forms.

The merchant adventurers, strengthened—yet in ways weakened—by a heterogeneous group of auxiliaries, superimposed themselves with the aid of modern weapons on the sociopolitical institutions of clan and village. At the end of the century they began to organize new political systems. To be sure, to legitimize their power, with such a fragile base depending on the integrity of an armed band, the new chiefs took up local traditions, gave themselves ancestors, and appropriated symbols of prestige. They rose and fell, however, according to the quality and expeditiousness of the justice enforced by their armed bands. The rights of succession did not solidify in this manner. In Central Africa, a distant but illustrative analogy to this nineteenth-century revolution was the Jaga "revolution" (Birmingham 1977, p. 552).

The rush of new powers thus undermined the foundations of both empires and modest local governments. But the profound economic changes can be explained only in part by the political and social revolution. New commodities resulting from agricultural and hunting activities began to supplant slaves as

African contributions to the world market. The latter, certainly, did not disappear as objects of exchange, but in great measure their end destination changed. More and more they were absorbed by the interior market as a productive investment in new economic structures. Slaves enhanced the human potential of the unit of production and improved food production and the transportation of goods. Their status was, moreover, not clearly defined in societies where social mobility was rapidly improving.

This tributary commerce, interweaving markets, way stations, and networks, gave way rapidly before the commercial offensive of the Tshokwe, the Swahili, the Sudanese Arabs, the Ovimbundu, the Bangala, and the whites of various nationalities. We do not know what new production dynamic corresponded to the new exchange dynamics and political systems. The ever greater influx of industrial goods into the trade of prestige goods is only one sign. It is possible that the North American crops maize and manioc were finally assimilated enough to spark a new population boom, that firearms increased the returns for hunting, and that the new commerce opened new productive possibilities locally. We still know next to nothing of the dynamics of these transitional societies. We hardly begin to know their place in human history and how they treated the colonial state as a priority. It will be necessary to create for each its own place and therein ensure it its own sovereignty.

Without understanding the Kivu of that day, essentially linked to the political and economic systems of the lake region and isolated from the Congo until the 1920s, the EIC proceeded to carve out its political and economic territories by merging into separate parts from four district regions (Jewsiewicki 1972, 1974a). Beginning in the north, one finds the northern savanna and fringe forests, which clearly belonged to the savanna region of Egyptian-Sudan. The Swahili area, symbolically but abusively termed the "empire of Tipo Tip," covered the region east of Lomani and was separated on the south from Luso-African territory by the kingdom of Msiri. To the west was a considerable area of the central basin, giving way to the Atlantic region and having the Congo River as its vertebra. These regions, so contrived and so intermixed at their specified borders, nevertheless possessed, ever more clearly after the 1880s, the character of autonomous markets with distinct centers and their own currency either of standard weight goods or accounting money.

The history of the EIC, in sum, was, in terms of the administrative and military effort, the extraction of immediately salable resources and the creation of "national" territory by the military and economic destruction of preexisting polities. This effort, of which only the military dimension and the political superstructure were completed by the EIC, came to an end with the economic planning of the Belgians in the 1920s.

The installation after 1890 of a state monopoly on natural resources and the management, directly or through concessionary companies, of their exploitation furnished the financial base necessary for the military effort. At the same time the state monopoly, by its suppression of all commercial activity, drove into ruin the old trading posts and networks. It was typical that where the state was not able to impose its monopoly immediately, as in the Arab area after crushing the Swahili, it still banned all commercial activity.

The EIC thus assumed its role at the expense of local economic, social, and political institutions and prepared the way for a new organization of the territory delimited by the political frontiers drawn at Berlin. One should not overestimate the overall efficiency of these efforts. The strength of the Swahili elite in opposition and the revolt at Luluabourg and that of the soldiers of the Dhanis expedition offer one proof of this. The profound ecological, demographic, and economic crises resulting from the savage overexploitation of certain regions, particularly the central basin and western Kasai, implied a system with limits. The exhaustion of local resources like rubber and ivory and the evolution of world market conditions imposed such limits to the system of administered exploitation. From the moment industrial capital began to penetrate the Belgian Congo, the EIC began to lose its reason for being. The transfer of the Congo to Belgium and the reforms that followed prepared the country for a new type of link with the Belgian economy and the world.

BUILDING THE BASE FOR
IMPLANTING AN INDUSTRIAL ECONOMY

The period 1906-20 was one of creating new institutions, sketching a new organization, and putting into place the basis for colonial industrialization. It was characterized above all by the creation of the great mining companies, Union Minière du Haut-Katanga and Forminière in 1906, and the companies for commercialization and transformation of vegetable products, Lever in 1911 and Cotonco in 1920, with international capital and state (except for Lever) participation. The experiences of foreign capital and of the state in this period demonstrated the profitability of industrial production based on local resources and aided by African labor.

Considerable changes in world market conditions and the international situation of Belgian capital at the end of World War I became the basis for a boom in the Congolese economy of the 1920s. During this period the colonial administration was able to gain effective control almost everywhere against both African chiefs and diverse European usurpers such as missionaries, traders, and even colonial agents acting like local lords. The legal cadre and corps of magistrates, necessary for the creation of the framework for a capitalist economy based on private property and the Napoleonic Code, were put in place as well during this period.

One of the essential tasks of the Belgian administration was the replacement of administrative and military incentives for labor by economic, moral, and symbolic incentives. Direct extraction of resources by or with legal assistance of officials was progressively replaced in the years after 1910 by a head tax paid only in money and accompanied by profound commercial inroads and forced labor. The state budget still relied in great part directly on the African producer. Nevertheless, taxes on revenue and customs duties grew progressively (Leclerq 1965).

In this stage of implanting the preliminary framework of colonial industrialization, the role of the grand bourgeoisie was limited to the enjoyment of a few, particularly rich, concessions. It was the small trader who, almost without convertible capital, created the initial trade links between the units of production and the agents of the capitalist market. These small merchants were Portuguese, Greek, Belgian, and African, in part former employees of trading companies. They revived commercial networks, built local mini-monopolies, and associated themselves with clan and village political structures. However, they were generally loath to use money in transactions with African clients. Barter and a complex system of dependent social relations worked well to limit the impact of competition.

Acceptable at the beginning because it furnished Africans a minimum amount of money for tax payments and ensured their entrance, however indirect, into the trading of the capitalist market, this system could only be transitory. Its impact on local social and economic structures was weak, and its role in the processes of primitive colonial accumulation was very limited. Reproducing the game of mini-monopoly in association with local political power, it impeded the expansion of the large trading firms and the concentration of economic activities. It modified very little the mode of production of the clan economy, nor did it create a labor market for industrialization. All of these considerations explain why the years following 1920, when the grand bourgeoisie took political control of the colony in Belgium, saw the elimination of the small traders, sanctioned by a decree of 1925 that had already been prepared by Governor General Maurice Lippens in 1921.

The extraction of resources in the years after 1910 was carried out by a dual system of noneconomic compulsion, particularly for manual labor, and of exchanges, part monetary and part barter. State agents still continued to intervene directly, in part legally and in part out of venal motives, to "encourage" material production especially to extract salaried labor. In the last case, one must qualify the period of industrial slavery. Conscription for certain infrastructure projects, railroad construction for the Great African Lakes Company, for example, and the supplying of recruits by chiefs on order of the colonial administration were the methods of recruitment for salaried workers.

The transportation conditions between the place of recruitment and that of work (a long caravan march), the difficulties of provisioning them and the poverty of the rations, the miserable working conditions and lodging, the lack of hygiene, and the psychological shock of the forced labor environment were responsible for very high death rates, illness, and desertion, not to mention evasions. The method of recruitment itself, by which the recruiters were burdened with slaves and village undesirables, resulted in a very low rate of return to villages after the term of the contract. All of these factors encouraged a growing resistance to participation in the work force.

Several signs indicated that the production of fresh agricultural goods was profitable, especially near the commercial, industrial, and administrative centers along the routes of communication, thus ensuring the level of exchange desired by rural communities. The response to initial commercial demand seems to have been positive, in the Bas-Congo region as well as in Kasai and Katanga. However, limits to the production of traditional shifting agriculture were quickly reached, and the pressure of demand could only bring about a sharp increase in prices. The difficulties of transportation considerably limited the geographic extension of commercial agricultural produce. The economic and social transformation of traditional society, under the impact of the accumulation of primitive capitalism uncontrolled by colonial authorities, was a possibility envisaged but soon rejected during the 1920s (Jewsiewicki 1977a; Vellut 1977). Economic and political factors inhibited the formation of a bourgeoisie and rural African proletariat, with the exception of the zone of action of Union Minière.

By 1910 the Belgian administration had managed to penetrate the major pockets of resistance and to command acknowledgment of its authority in the regions that previously had escaped European influence. The imposition of a legal system, the reorganization of an administrative structure along territorial, district, and provincial lines, and the organization of the colonial army (Force Publique) all paved the way for the development of a modern bureaucracy. The European population was finally subjected to the colonial administration also, with the exception of the giant enterprises, which retained control of their "empires." The last of the great chiefs, such as Kasongo Niembo, who had held out against the Belgians, were neutralized. Those who had attempted to play the role of allies rather than simply executors of the colonial authority, such as Lumpungu, were forced into submission or ejected.

Ironically, at the time when the "national road" linking Katanga and the Congo River was finished, the colony was broken down into four provinces. The national network consisted of a railroad from Matadi to Leopoldville (now Kinshasa), river transport from Leopoldville to Stanleyville (now Kisangani), rail and water transport from Stanleyville to Bukuma, and rail from Bukuma to Elizabethville (now Lubumbashi). Two of the four provinces, Katanga and Orientale, enjoyed considerable autonomy on the strength of powerful provincial authorities. This posed an important threat to the future economic and administrative unity of the colony. However, this paradox proved ephemeral, reflecting the discontinuity between the economic absurdity of the national communication network and the real situation. These two provinces were more directly connected with British Africa during the early 1900s than with Matadi and Anvers. Katanga was linked with Rhodesia and South Africa through the recruitment of workers and as an evacuation route, while Orientale Province was tied to Uganda. These economic relations were greatly weakened from the beginning of the dependency of the Congolese franc on the Belgian franc (1919). Depreciation of the Belgian franc made the cost of living in the Congo more expensive. External economic relations were further weakened by the intensive Belgianization of Union Minière and the gold mines of Kilo-Moto, as well as the closing of the cotton market to nonapproved companies.

With respect to the internal political structure, the decree of 1910 systematized King Leopold's policy of recognizing indigenous chiefdoms as the first echelon of colonial administration. The colonial authorities proceeded to recognize the chiefdoms and subchiefdoms by rewarding their chiefs with medals as symbols of their legitimate colonial function. This policy began to produce a new elite consisting of former soldiers, children educated in colonial schools, shop foremen, and domestic servants. Former subchiefs and auxiliaries, such as the Nyampara in former Swahili regions, also earned entry into the elite. Colonial administrators were more concerned with loyalty to the system than with legitimacy, in the traditional sense, of the chiefs. The legal practices of the subchiefdoms also led to the fragmentation of power exercised by chiefs and weakened their authority. Most chiefs became puppets of the colonial administration, but the more clever ones were able to manipulate the system to their own ends. Those local traditional leaders who refused to collaborate with the colonial order were subdued or simply swept away by the social evolution of the preceding quarter century (Jewsiewicki 1974b).

At the beginning of the twentieth century the economic and social map of the Congo was very complex, and it still remains rather obscure for the historian. The one fact that seems certain, however, was that the demographic dynamics of the last half of the nineteenth century had been severed. The military conflicts and raids in the Swahili zone during the past 50 years and the subsequent rupture in commercial lines created a precarious situation in the east, aggravated by the hostilities arising from World War I. The recruitment of workers and manufacturing industries and the production of agricultural goods profoundly changed Katanga. Certain regions, such as Tanganyika, were nearly emptied of their inhabitants. The Central Congo basin and the Kasai were ravaged by systematic exploitation and at the same time stricken with sleeping sickness. The Bas-Congo saw a sizable portion of its population reduced by the forced recruitment of porters for the caravan route from Matadi to Leopoldville before the construction of the railroad. Sleeping sickness continued to plague the Congo during the early 1900s. With the return of soldiers who had fought in the Central African theater of World War I, a variety of Spanish influenza also was introduced into the Congo.

Nothing can quite measure the disastrous effects of these factors on the social and economic fabric of the Congo. It seems, however, that the internal dynamism of the country was not entirely destroyed. Evidence of this was to be found in the palm oil industry boom in the Kasai and Equateur provinces toward the end of the war and substantial local improvements in traditional agricultural production.

THE ORIGINS OF THE COLONIAL
MODE OF INDUSTRIAL PRODUCTION

Other than the necessity of furnishing certain products to the colonial administration, the involvement of Europeans in the agricultural sector was still negligible. After the costly failure of the European agricultural colonization in Katanga, the director of the Ministry of Agriculture, E. Leplae, initiated in 1917 a system of obligatory rice and cotton production in Orientale Province to serve war needs. The administration also successfully terminated experiments in African cotton cultures by the U.S. expert, Ficher, before the war. The construction of palm oil factories and the system of forced labor further hindered the development of the African agricultural sector. The

Congo was thus prepared for total submission to exploitation by the industrial economy. The minor commercial crisis of 1920-21 led to the elimination of a portion of small businesses seen as undesirable and to the takeover of Union Minière by the Société Générale de Belgique, which represented the first phase of financial centralization.

The sudden interest of Belgian investors in the Congo can be explained by the losses they incurred during the war. Belgian capital and personnel were henceforth directed toward enterprises in the Belgian colony. The Congo also became the object of interest of the Belgian middle class in search of employment in the postwar economic crisis. Investment in the colony was a windfall. Because the Congolese currency was tied to the Belgian, it was possible to invest with depreciated Belgian francs in order to produce goods sold on the world market against stronger currencies.

At the beginning of the 1920s, the new Congo project was already in operation, as were the economy and society of the colonial mode of industrial production. Before proceeding to an analysis of its formation and function, let us first examine the conceptual basis of economic realities. Often the countries of the periphery, or the developing nations, are seen as experiencing a temporary illness capable of being healed. In fact, they represent a type of economy and society whose structures are subject to systematic exploitation by the industrialized world. They exhibit the following basic economic, social, and political features.

Following colonial expropriations, the industrial economy was implanted in its entirety in nonindustrial modes of production that remained essentially rural. There was a strong horizontal and vertical concentration of industrial activities and their localization in the nonindustrial environment. Noneconomic measures ensured the maintenance of the industrial order.

Localization of foreign capital, technology, and personnel ensured a high degree of independence in comparison with local structures, leading to increased dependence of the economy on the world market. International economic conditions became the primary determinant of long-term decisions regarding investment in the colony. There was a strong concentration of capital controlled by foreign holdings with diversified economic activities. Their zones of influence occasioned a policy of extortion and deception.

There was as well interpenetration of interests between the colonial administration and the technocracy of the large industrial groups, which allowed the latter the extensive utilization of local, metropolitan, and international public capital. Because the colonial and postcolonial state represented the democratic industrial type of bureaucracy, its financial and political operation was dependent upon the industrial economy. The participation of the state in the large industrial enterprises led, not to their control by the state, but to just the opposite. And at the bottom village economies were held in place by extraeconomic means: as producers of raw materials, both animal and vegetable, and by a salaried labor force increasingly "indigenized," but excluded from the investment goods market and from the right to private property.

The colonial society was divided into two different social orders according to separate principles. The "civilized" order was characterized by an individualist life-style and was subject to the Napoleonic Civil Code, which guaranteed full rights to private property. This group derived its status of individual participation in the exercise of power of the colonial administration and its revenue. Its social prestige was also derived from its function within the colonial apparatus. In light of the fact that the holders of capital lived outside the colonial society, it was the participation in the bureaucratic order that determined social position. From 1920 onward, this order was essentially Western, strictly identified by the skin color of its members.

The indigenous order included all the "noncivilized" colonial subjects and was characterized by its nonindividualist life-style. Africans were subject to traditional law rather than the Napoleonic Code. Their primary identity was with the village world and their obligation to work for the industrial sector. This order was horizontally rather than vertically structured, according to "race" or ethnic identification. Except for their utilization by the industrial sector, members of this order were bound by obligations to their traditional chief and the necessity of cultivating the soil. The relations between two orders were regulated by Christian morality, the consumption of manufactured goods, the workplace, and selective human values. These factors formed the base of the symbolic power of the bureaucracy of the state and capitalist interests.

The welfare state was buttressed by bureaucratic authority and reinforced by the principle of co-optation in the absence of all political life apart from the state. The public administration was ideologically presented as being a neutral arbiter. The network of consultative organisms and the participation of large companies in the state ensured capitalist interests a direct role in the exercise of public power.

Political power was exercised by the interpenetration of three entities: the bureaucracy that controlled the colonial administration and the army, the capitalists who controlled the industrial sector, and the church. The ideology of the Catholic church ensured the long-term efficiency of the system. Because none of these institutions had any solid local social basis, capital interests enjoyed considerable independence from the bureaucracy. The budget of the state was more and more a financial tributary of company revenues from the industrial economy. The state could therefore only constitute a foreign and coercive power for the indigenous order. Despite the appearance of economic independence projected by the church, it was directly tied to the industrial system and the state through free land concessions, subsidies for the educational system it controlled, and the recognition of nonprofit status of church enterprises.

The African political order was subordinate to the state bureaucracy and separated from it in order to guarantee its specifically "indigenous" nature. The indigenous system of administration exercised by traditional chiefs ensured a distinct separation between African and European bureaucracies. On the other hand, the execution of colonial orders in an often odious manner was the responsibility of traditional chiefs.

Let us then offer a brief analysis of the formation of the system described above. It was during the economic and social crisis of 1920/21 that the system received its initial impetus and during the depression that it culminated. From 1919 to 1925, four factors came into play. There was a massive influx of Belgian investments from three main holding companies: Société Générale de Belgique, the Empain group, and Compagnie du Congo pour le Commerce et l'Industrie (CCCI). This was accompanied by increased Belgian immigration to the Congo and the alignment of the colonial currency with that of the metropole. Second, a new policy toward the indigenous population submitted all Africans to the direct control of the state. By 1925 the "indigenization" process was complete and the social orders were entirely separated. Third, the administration introduced an experimental compulsory system of traditional African agriculture, including both humans and land as village capital, thereby guaranteeing the large monopoly enterprises the supply of raw materials with limited investment. Last, the system of control of African labor between the industrial sector and the village economy was established on a long-term basis through family recruitment. Work camps, which became the long-term habitation of a portion of the labor force, provided the biological replenishment of workers according to the needs of the company.

Social stability in the cities was relative, however. Administration control of work contracts usually resulted in sending the infirm, the aged, and all others unfit for work back to the villages. Whenever the camps failed to reproduce a sufficient number of workers, youths in the villages were conscripted. The working class "elites" consisted of proletarian "professionals" who had acquired familial stability in the city or work camps. In 1931 African townships received legal recognition. However, they were "indigenized" that year by a "traditional"-based political and legal structure, avoiding any confusion with the European social order despite the initial similarity in lifestyle, places of work, and habitation.

Attempts to capitalize traditional African agriculture proved costly to the colonial administration, and their social impact was difficult to predict (Jewsiewicki 1975). While distorting the policy of indigenization, these efforts risked creating a proletarian class and at the same time causing the disappearance of the system of communal property. There was as yet no indication that a capitalist type of peasant agriculture would work in Africa. The organization of peasant-worker enclaves only threatened to reinforce the industrial empires to the point where they became entirely autonomous in terms of labor and production. The colonial administration, fearing an imbalance of power with capitalist interests, refused to allow the implementation of this type of project in Katanga.

Thus the decade of the 1920s witnessed various types of experiments in administrative planning at the provincial level. They involved representatives from the large companies, the church, and the colonial administration. In addition to the unification of regulations governing the African sector, central planning overrode the passive opposition of the provinces. Deprived of any budgetary autonomy, the provinces could not manage to escape control by the central administration. Finally, in 1928, they accepted a plan to exploit human resources jointly according to economic zones. The reason for this was the increasing tensions of the labor market created by the poorly controlled influx of capital and by the extensive utilization of local forced labor. In order to preserve a demographic equilibrium and to guarantee human resources to already existing enterprises, it was decided that new installations should be planned. The planning of economic zones was made possible by the considerable development of the transportation infrastructure.

Thus the construction of new transportation routes and the reorganization of the old ones entailed the massive intervention of the state. Substantial capital from the metropole, borrowed from the public, was injected into the colony, thereby affirming the will of the colonial administration to control the organization and financing of transportation. This policy required public financing of the route to the ocean, which entailed building the portion of the railway from Bukama to Port Franqui (1928) in the south and fortifying rail and road links in the north. This facilitated the economic network linking the interior of the Congo to Belgium via Matadi. Before the opening of the Benguela railroad from Katanga to Luanda (Angola) in 1931, the road from Orientale Province to Dar es Salaam via Kigoma played an important role in the east. While these routes were economically important, they were not the threat to colonial unity that the link between Katanga and Rhodesia and South Africa posed. The opening of the Bukama-Port Franqui railroad helped to stimulate the development of Katanga and maintain its link with the rest of the Congo.

At the beginning of the 1920s, the movement of social demands among white workers and functionaries in Katanga and the isolated strikes of certain segments of black workers were arrested. The colonial administration managed to still the aspirations of "detribalized" blacks—clerks, small traders, former soldiers, and nontraditional farmers—who had aimed at creating a "creole" society that did not meet with colonial objectives (Jewsiewicki 1976a, 1976b).

TOWARD THE MATURITY OF THE SYSTEM

Bureaucratic centralization was ensured as the network of communications in the Congo was completed. The administrative reorganization of 1931-33, prompted by the economic crisis, resulted in the dissolution of the four vice-governorships and their replacement by six provinces. Henceforth, the governor-general and his staff controlled the country. The chief administrator of the province became the executor of central administrative orders and the coordinator of specialized provincial services. At the same time, the role of the district commissioner was considerably reduced (Jewsiewicki 1977c).

Between 1933 and 1935, a strict system of economic planning was introduced in order to guarantee maximum productivity of the indigenous population. This was necessary to counter the drastic reduction in investments and the sharp decline in the price of raw materials on the world market. The Congo ensured the economic survival of colonial industrial economy, thanks to the efforts of its rural population, which was forced to produce obligatory crops such as cotton and palm oil. Prices for some of these commodities had fallen as much as 80 percent from levels before the world economic crisis. The result was not only the continued survival of commerce and the transformation of the large agricultural enterprises but of the mining industry as well. The cost of labor fell sharply following the decline in the prices of agricultural produce. Workers who became unemployed were simply sent back to the villages and put to work on the mandatory crops.

In the years following the Great Depression, Belgian capitalists began to consider that the time was ripe for the Congo to pay the price of their investments in the 1920s. During the 1930s, and even after World War II, the functioning of the industrial economy in the Congo was made possible largely by massive demands on the land and human capital of the traditional economy. The system of mandatory crops, the monopoly of the transformation of agricultural goods, and the fixing of minimum prices (in practice, the real prices paid) for the marketing of industrial vegetable products were combined with the de facto monopoly of the purchase of agricultural goods. Rural zones gradually came to approximate labor camps. The head tax and other taxes levied by the administration on the African population accounted for at least a fifth of the total annual revenue, without considering legal fines. Social life was controlled by a variety of regulations with a view toward obtaining a maximum work effort. During the depression upkeep of the local transportation infrastructure (secondary roads) was placed in the hands of village communities (Jewsiewicki 1977c).

Prudence in the management of human resources brought the "rational" utilization of industrial labor. This was a preoccupation of the large enterprises and accompanied technological change. It allowed the partial replacement of white workers by less costly skilled black laborers during the depression. The basis of an African skilled industrial proletariat was thus laid, reproduced in the urban centers and in camps maintained by the large enterprises. Nonskilled workers would still come predominantly from the villages. The purchasing power of salaried urban workers was maintained, and the cleavage between rural and city life-styles became more pronounced. After World War II an African elite of bureaucrats and skilled workers emerged. Professional organizations were formed by religious missions, reinforcing their corporate nature. By the end of the war, strikes by white workers had revealed the first rupture in the monolithic social order and the emergence of class structures, while an African proletariat and bureaucratic elite had begun to take shape (Jewsiewicki, Vellut, and Kilola 1973).

THE FIRST SYSTEM CHANGE:
TOWARD A DUAL ECONOMY

The situation in the Congo after World War II imposed several modifications on the model described. They were determined by three principal factors: the exhaustion of both land and human capital in the rural economies, accentuated by the war effort; the slow replacement of the structure of order by that of classes, thereby necessitating a rearrangement of symbols of order and principles of identity and belonging; and the change in the structure of the Congolese and Belgian economies as well as the world market, resulting in an increase in the consumption of manufactured goods in the Congo.

The impact of the war on the colonial society and the economy of the Congo brought about the necessity for internal financing at all levels, especially in the consumer goods sector. This in turn contributed to the acceleration of industrialization of small and medium-sized enterprises. State control of these enterprises was at once technically difficult and politically undesirable, resulting in open conflicts. After the war, control was quickly abandoned except in the European agricultural sector. During the war, the necessity of exploiting all the human resources available and the difficulty of increasing European personnel for growing industrialization resulted in the utilization of a specialized African labor force. Indeed, available European personnel actually declined, owing to military needs.

This movement had begun during the crisis of the 1930s, but it took on another dimension during the war. The demand was such that the schools increased their preparation of Africans for specialized work, notably for office jobs. The violent conflicts that split the monolithic white society gave the budding African bureaucracy a glimpse of its importance to the colonial order. These "elites" therefore began to claim a larger share of the benefits, which their potential position as an intermediary bourgeoisie should ensure them. By the Declaration of Luluabourg (1944) these black elites separated themselves from the "noncivilized" African society in order to claim their place among the bourgeoisie. It became increasingly evident, as seen in the revolts at Masisi, Matadi, and Luluabourg, that the maintenance of the prewar order would be suicidal. That order was characterized by three features: racial criterion—skin color; legal criterion—exclusion of Congolese from the industrial mode of production by their legal incapacity to acquire individual property; and discriminatory economic or institutional criterion—the position in the system of social redistribution of the national product (level of salaries, access to employment, and so forth).

Between 1948 and 1959, there was therefore an attempt to restructure the order, guaranteeing class solidarity between white-collar Europeans (employers, qualified workers, and professionals) and the African bureaucratic bourgeoisie. The process was mainly empirical, but politically very delicate. The upper class (grand bourgeoisie) remained essentially outside the impassioned debates, unaffected by the proposed changes. The pragmatic technique of stifling social dissent among the newly emerging class allowed the Congo to regain quickly what appeared to be social stability. Both the working class and intellectual Europeans, the source of strikes in Katanga during 1941-44, and the African bureaucratic elites were rapidly submerged by the newcomers. Their movements were directed toward new institutions such as labor unions and cultural associations based upon ethnic solidarity that were horizontal in organization and therefore retained the potential for internal conflict.

The African working class was similarly disarmed. Although its role in opposition movements such as the revolts at Luluabourg and Matadi was not very clear, the black proletariat did give the impression of being on the threshold of class consciousness (Jewsiewicki, Vellut, and Kilola 1973). In the rural areas there was an attempt to create a petite bourgeoisie (small producers) whose economic interests were opposed to those of both chiefs and the village masses in order to resolve social conflict. However, the Masisi revolt revealed the danger to the interests of the colonial power posed by exploited rural masses deprived of a collaborating elite. Only a few administrative auxiliaries represented the interests associated with the colonial order and they were the target of the Masisi revolt.

It is remarkable that the Congo escaped serious social troubles until 1959 through a program of projects and counterprojects in the new society, marked by the co-optation of the African bureaucratic bourgeoisie and a favorable convergence of economic interests with whites. At the core of this success was a dualist political and social philosophy and economic policy that sacrificed the white-collar and middle class (the colonial administration) to the interests of big business. Mutual mistrust and fear progressively paralyzed the white bourgeoisie (farmers, workers, and employers) and the rising African bureaucratic bourgeoisie. The state increasingly became the sole arbiter, especially after Colonial Minister Buisseret partially cut off the Catholic church. Despite appearances of liberalization, owing above all to the proliferation of institutions and projects in which the white community and the black bureaucratic bourgeoisie were mutually involved, the authority of the state came more and more to resemble an iron fist in a velvet glove.

J. H. Boeke's "rational" principle of economic dualism became the philosophical cornerstone of Belgian as well as Dutch colonial action. The ten-year plan of 1949, which for the Congo represented the program for a new society and economy to be achieved at substantial public expense, was profoundly modified (Jewsiewicki 1977b, pp. 236-37). Thus "traditional" society, which was presumed to be incapable of being modernized, found itself subjected to a "modern" and "rational" society that served as its model. Henceforth this transformation was to be according to a principle of "modernization" rather than culture in the strict sense of skin color as it had been in colonial society. It is obvious that during the 1950s the coincidence between the principle of modernity and that of racial distinction was still very distinct. Nevertheless, it was possible to abandon the color bar progressively and to admit certain Africans to the legal realm of individual property in order to grant them certain political rights. The assimilation of the new African bourgeoisie thus became possible toward the end of the 1940s. The dualist principle did not, however, signal in any sense the rapid absorption of the entire black population into the modern sector. On the contrary, the principle of assimilation was used to justify and reinforce the arbitration of the state in the relations between the two sectors, strengthening the role of the bureaucracy and technocracy.

Official policy toward the peasant sector, both in terms of annual and perennial crops, followed this principle: The creation of an agricultural petite bourgeoisie offered a political and social base for collaboration between the modern industrial sector and the modern rural African. Legal and practical changes followed the same pattern, leading to the progressive transfer of small commercial concerns to Africans in both rural and urban areas. However, the great majority of the population remained in the paysannat sector or in traditional villages to be "guided and protected" and used in planned labor programs. The most evident example of the application of this principle was the use of the paysannat for crop rotation schemes where cotton was the primary product. Colonial authorities established a general marketing cooperative under the para-statal agency known as COGERCO, rather than organize peasants into a system of small cooperatives. At the production level, the system of mandatory crops was replaced by obligatory crop rotation in the paysannat, supposedly scientifically studied and freely accepted by individual peasants.

A technocratic principle was progressively replaced by a bureaucratic one with a bureaucratic administration. At the same time the production cooperatives functioned by grouping peasants in communal control of land and crops rather than in groups of owner-producers. They were submitted to a bureaucratic administration aligned with the modern sector, generally tied to a European farmer or small enterprise that ensured their production and marketing operations (Jewsiewicki 1975).

The principle of integrating village economies nevertheless continued to be the same as in the 1930s. The African peasant was considered to be "qualitatively different," both psychologically and socially, and incapable of accomplishing the transition to the "rational" individual economy before several more generations. It was thought necessary that the state guide and direct his relations with the "modern" industrial economy. If the villages remained anchored in nonindustrial modes of production, they risked (according to the principle of their economic nonrationality) being incapable of investing in agricultural production. Everyone, however, especially the cotton lobby, agreed that the renewal of land capital was necessary. This could be only partially ensured through agrarian reform, including new technology and crop rotation, and through modification of working conditions. At the local level at least, it remained essential that investments permit the utilization of selected seeds, insecticides, pesticides, and agricultural machines.

In light of the presumed inability of the peasant to assume this task, the state intervened once again to centralize the surplus of peasant laborers and redistribute them. One portion of the collective modernization was financed by public investment, another by obligatory private investment of the large cotton and palm oil companies, and another by the reinvestment of the profits of the cooperatives.

The administration of rural communities was increasingly considered to be the responsibility of the African petite bourgeoisie. The policy changes introduced by the decree of 1958 concerning the native districts (conscriptions indigènes) were intended to bring about this transformation. The "traditional" authorities were eventually sacrificed in the course of the long process of modernization. In the process the state ceded a portion of its power of arbitration and coercion to the white and black bourgeoisie.

If the African remained always the producer of raw materials and the source of forced labor, his second economic function—that of consumer—

took on even greater importance after World War II. The competition between the industries of transformation that had emerged in the Congo and those in the metropole that had an eye on the Congolese market could not be resolved except through difficult economic arbitration, particularly in a sector where there was little concentration. Still, the development of a local consumer market was a salutary solution for all. It increased the dependence of Africans on the modern sector, limiting them further to the extraction of raw materials and "rationalizing" their production through increased specialization. This in turn facilitated the circulation of capital between Belgium and the colony, weakening social tensions while building a demand for consumer goods. The policy of regular and substantial increases in African taxes found a consensus between the capitalists and the colonial administration. On the other hand, the policy was considered, and often was, ruinous for small businesses. Benefits accrued by the state bureaucracy from this policy need not be underscored: "It is the State that causes people to earn more." The erosion of purchasing power considerably moderated the real effects of the policy of establishing a legal minimum wage and the pressures in favor of increasing nominal rural taxes.

African consumption nevertheless rose sharply, spurring the economic growth of the period from 1950 to 1956. The unequal increase in consumption between wage laborers and peasants and between rural and urban dwellers served to increase the already existing divisions (Jewsiewicki 1975). The city dominated and controlled and was the focus of modern life-styles. This domination, economic as well as ideological, fed the fetish of modernity, one of the key concepts of the symbolic power of the industrial state. The city breathed an air of modern consumption and of "liberty": freedom from cultural obligations, the annoyance of traditional authorities, and colonial administrators.

Education, the key to the modern world, also reinforced its ideological position. Entry into the bureaucracy, where the African could fulfill more and more lower-order functions, meant entry into the sanctuary of power. Even a tiny portion of bureaucratic authority, no matter whether or not it was legally manipulated, provided the possibility of elevation to a position of status within the African society. This was true for teachers and clerks, as well as for nurses and subalterns.

The formation of this new African bourgeoisie, which was by and large white-collar workers, posed a problem of rupturing relations between the traditional masses and an elite that was becoming increasingly modern. The latter manifested a desire to separate itself from the "savage" masses and to be able to find a place in the white social order. Although this separation was judged dangerous in political and social terms, as it left the masses without direction or guidance, it was partially avoided by the rapid emergence of associations based on ethnic identity that tended to regroup elites and masses if only in a fragmentary manner. It was in this way that ethnicity began to play an important role in politics. Even so, its economic and social bases were rooted in the instability of the city. It was still impossible for a worker to guarantee survival for himself and his family without falling back on assistance from his original village community (Jewsiewicki 1976a, 1978b).

The integration of the African bourgeoisie into the system of economic and social benefits enjoyed by whites was too slow, formal, and void of real consequences to contain dissent. Integration into the modern economic sector entailed access to private property, to bank credit, and equality of salary with whites at the same level. Leadership of the culturally based ethnic movements gave the bourgeoisie a political base, even if it was fragmentary and subject to internal conflicts. Disenchanted with the hypocrisy of the white bourgeoisie who refused them equal social standing, the African elites began to look toward ethnic solidarity for their revolution from 1956 onward.

Economic difficulties and the decline in social progress that followed in their wake created conditions favorable to urban revolt. For their part, the peasants as a group had seldom if ever experienced any real increase in their standard of living whether as rural or urban laborers. Suspended by the colonial system between the desire for modern consumer goods and the economic capacity to obtain them, between grievances with traditional authorities and the demands of production, rural society showed mounting signs of conflict. The exodus toward the cities was for most peasants the only solution to a hopeless dilemma in the rural areas between an increasingly dominant ideology of modernity and rural traditions maintained by the colonial bureaucracy.

From 1956/57 onward, this gate to the urban world began to be closed as unemployed workers in the cities were gathered up and sent back to their villages of origin. Urban revolt became more and more inevitable. The uprising in Leopoldville surprised not only the colonial authorities but probably a large portion of the African elites. However, the elites were quick to exploit the situation, this time not in order to obtain assimilation with the white bourgeoisie but to replace it. The tense situation in the rural areas, aggravated by the economic crisis that began to be felt after the application of the new 1958 law on native districts, did not provoke any response from the colonial authorities. Ethnic conflicts such as between Luba and Lunda at Luluabourg further hinted at a difficult period. Thus the rapid abandonment of the Congo at independence to the black bureaucratic bourgeoisie was not surprising when viewed from the perspective of the big business interests that had dominated the colony since 1920 (Jewsiewicki 1979a).

CONCLUSION: "PLUS ÇA CHANGE,
PLUS C'EST LA MÊME CHOSE"

It is not necessary here to present a summary analysis of the period that followed. That is the task of the chapters that follow and, besides, the postcolonial state did not really differ from the colonial state. The replacement of the white bureaucratic bourgeoisie by a black one did not change the state, nor could it have. The colonial mode of production ended in an absurd manner. The deterioration of the conditions for economic exploitation of the colony and for political control was the result of internal conflicts of interests within the bureaucratic bourgeoisie and violent social conflicts between unorganized and desperate peasants, on the one hand, and the petite bourgeoisie, on the other. The authoritarian and centralized structure of the state and the ideology that sustained it were taken over by the African bureaucratic bourgeoisie and used for its own ends. The Zairian state continued the policy of distrust toward small and middle-sized enterprises and was ever aware of the political danger of the development of a national business bourgeoisie that would be capable of assuming control of the political apparatus of the state. Control of that apparatus remained essential for the redistribution of the national product and for relations with foreign investors. These were the two basic sources of revenue.

The ideological role of modernity in the maintenance of the system was reinforced after independence. The city and education opened the door to modernity in a seemingly democratic manner. Nevertheless they served to justify the arbitrary domination of the bureaucracy and the unequal distribution of the national income between the modern and traditional sectors. After the rebellions of the mid-1960s, the villages were in a certain sense "laid to rest." The deterioration of the road system, and therefore of commerce, separated the rural areas from the benefits of modernity. The temporary prosperity of the mining sector allowed the state to remain disinterested in the development of the rural economy.

Although the rural areas had been profoundly disturbed by the decolonization process, they remained the reserve of peasants who participated less and less in the economic, social, and political life of the country. As long as the situation in the cities allowed for the absorption of the rural exodus and the prosperity of the mining industry provided the economic base for the purchase of imported goods, a fragile political equilibrium could be maintained. This was managed through a game of intrigue within the bureaucratic bourgeoisie, through the consistent co-optation of young technocrats into the system, and through the threat of armed force. However, the economic problems of the 1970s placed this delicate equilibrium in question. The general exhaustion of public resources obliged a large portion of the bureaucratic subalterns to live off the land, to pillage peasants through legal as well as illegal extractions. At the same time the state attempted to find exportable material in the village economy. International rural development organizations were called on to sustain the dualist ideology of modernization. Even old cultural obligations, so detested by peasants, were invoked to justify their "revolutionary" reeducation.

If Western attitudes toward the past have begun to change recently (Garaudy 1975; Chesneaux 1976), it remains nevertheless generally admitted that the future will invent itself and will be discovered by studying the past. To create the future, one conjugates history (Morel 1975) or, in other words, perpetuates the system. Possibly it is now time to pose the problem of changing the system, not from inside but from without. Changing the system is not making adjustments from inside (Jewsiewicki 1978a). This latter operation, so efficiently accomplished for so many years by bilateral and multilateral aid, guarantees the growth of the colonial mode of industrial production, including its internal contradictions.

Despite the abundance of good intentions and goodwill that so often ac-
companies such efforts, international aid intends to and can accomplish only
changes in the interior of the system, prolong its material survival, and increase its structural contradictions, as Chapter 15 demonstrates in detail.
In a vicious circle of continuity and change, international aid continues to assume the transfer of a fraction of public "metropolitan" capital to ensure that
private capital operations remain profitable, and that the equilibrium of the
global creation of industrial production is maintained. Historians, like all
Africanists, are the accomplices of the group that, by means of scientific
theories and cooperative goodwill, continues to entice the whole world to pump
water desperately out of a boat that not only has been sinking for quite some
time but whose planks are beginning to rot. And the world pumps so much,
it barely has time to ascertain that the boat does not steer anymore, even if
the waves continue to jostle it along, and that a good port does not appear on
the horizon.

REFERENCES

Birmingham, D. 1977. "Central Africa from Cameroun to Zambezi." In
The Cambridge History of Africa. 5 vols. Cambridge: At the University Press, 3:519-66.

Bourdieu, P. 1977. "Sur le pouvoir symbolique." Annales, économies,
sociétés, civilisations 32:405-11.

Chesneaux, J. 1976. Du passé faisons table rase? Paris: Maspero.

Coquery-Vidrovitch, C., and H. Moniot. 1974. L'Afrique noire de 1800 à
nos jours. Paris: PUF.

Garaudy, R. 1975. Paroles d'hommes. Paris: Laffont.

Jewsiewicki, B. 1979a. "Le colonat agricole européen au Congo belge, 1910-
1960, problèmes politiques et économiques." Journal of African History, no. 3.

_____. 1979b. "L'histoire ou le commerce des idées usagées en Afrique."
In L'africanisme en crise, edited by A. Schwarz. Montreal.

_____. 1979c. "African Peasants and Totalitarian Colonial Society in the
Belgian Congo 1917-1960." In Peasants in Africa: Historical and Con-
temporary Perspectives, edited by M. Klein. Beverly Hills, Calif.:
Sage.

_____. 1978a. "L'histoire africaine et la prospective: Une refléxion sur
l'idéologie de la connaissance historique et son usage en Afrique."
Paper presented at the Eighth Annual Conference of the Canadian Association of African Studies.

_____. 1978b. "Refléxions historiques sur la prise de conscience politique par la paysannerie africaine au Zaire a l'époque coloniale." Paper presented at the Twenty-First Meeting of the African Studies Association, Baltimore.

_____. 1978c. "Historie économique d'une ville coloniale. Kisangani 1877-1960." Cahiers du CEDAF, ser. 2, no. 5.

_____. 1977a. "Unequal Development: Capitalism and the Katanga Economy, 1919-1940." In The Roots of Rural Poverty in Central and Southern Africa, edited by R. Palmer and N. Parson. London: Heinemann.

_____. 1977b. "Anthropologie économique et les 'modes de production.'" Cultures et développement 9, no. 2:195-246.

_____. 1977c. "The Great Depression and the Making of the Colonial Economic System in the Belgian Congo." African Economic History, no. 4, pp. 153-76.

_____. 1976a. "La contestation sociale et la naissance du prolétariat africain au cours de la première moitié du XXiem siècle." Revue canadienne des études africaines, no. 1, pp. 47-70.

_____. 1976b. "Contestation sociale au Zaire. Grève administrative de 1920 (ex-Congo belge)." Africa-Tervurn, no. 2/3/4, pp. 57-67.

_____. 1976c. "L'expérience d'un Etat-Providence en Afrique noire." Refléxions historiques, no. 2, pp. 78-103.

_____. 1975. Agriculture nomade et économie capitaliste. Histoire des essais de modernisation de l'agriculture africaine au Zaire à l'époque coloniale. 2 vols. Lubumbashi: UNAZA, ronéo.

_____. 1974a. "Histoire économique et sociale du Zaire moderne. Une conception." Likundoli, ser. A, no. 1, pp. 205-20.

_____. 1974b. "L'administration coloniale et la tradition." Cultures et développement, no. 3, pp. 589-604.

_____. 1972. "Notes sur l'histoire socio-économique du Congo (1880-1960)." Etudes d'histoire africaine 3:209-41.

Jewsiewicki, B., J. L. Vellut, and Kilola Lema. 1973. "Documents pour servir à l'histoire sociale du Zaire. Grèves du Bas Congo en 1945." Etudes d'histoire africaine 5:155-88.

Leclerq, H. 1965. "Un mode de mobilisation des ressources: Le système fiscal. Le cas du Congo pendant la periode coloniale." Cahiers économiques et sociaux 3:99-105.

Luxembourg, R. Oeuvres IV: L'accumulation du capital (II). Paris: Maspero.

Marx, K. Le capital, III. Paris: Editions Sociales.

Morel, B. 1975. "Conjuger l'histoire. Conjoncture et prospective." L'actualité économique, pp. 194-208.

Peemans, J. P. 1973. Le rôle de l'état dans la formation du capital au Congo pendant la période coloniale (1885-1960). Louvain: Etudes et Documents, ronéo. (Abridged English version: L. H. Gann and P. Duignan, eds. Colonialism in Africa 1870-1960. Vol. 4. Cambridge: At the University Press.)

_____. 1970. Diffusion du progrès et convergence des prix. Congo-Belgique, 1900-1960. Paris, Louvain: Nauwelaerts.

Peerings, C. 1979. Black Mineworkers in Central Africa. London: Heinemann.

Stengers, J. 1974. "La Belgique et le Congo. Politique coloniale et décolonisation." In Histoire de la Belgique contemporaine 1914-1970, pp. 391-440. Brussels: La Renaissance du livre.

Vellut, J. L. 1978. "The 'Classical' Age of Belgian Colonialism: Outline for a Social History (1910-1940)." Seminar on Zaire. Center for African Studies, SOAS, London.

_____. 1977. "Rural Poverty in Western Shaba, c. 1890-1930." In The Roots of Rural Poverty in Central and Southern Africa, edited by R. Palmer and N. Parsons, pp. 294-316. London: Heinemann.

_____. 1975. "Le Zaire a la périphérie du capitalisme: Quelques perspectives historiques." Enquêtes et documents d'histoire africaine 1:114-51.

3

POSTCOLONIAL POLITICS IN ZAIRE, 1960-79

Edward Kannyo

INTRODUCTION

The near-total collapse of Zaire's political structures and the disruption of its economic institutions soon after the attainment of political independence (Institut de Recherches Economiques et Sociales 1968) provided a fortuitous opportunity for the Zairian political system to alter and renegotiate the colonial terms of its incorporation into the "world system." (For a discussion of the concept of the "world system," see Immanuel Wallerstein [1976].) However, this opportunity was not taken. Instead, the economic and political forces of the international capitalist system were able to exploit internal weaknesses and complicity to halt the process of disengagement and restore the basic role of Zaire as a peripheral underdeveloped subsystem of the world system. It is to the internal political dynamics of this process of "recuperation" that this chapter addresses itself.

INDEPENDENCE, INSTITUTIONAL
COLLAPSE, AND CIVIL STRIFE (1960-65)

The most important internal factor in the genesis of Zairian nationalism was the evolution of a distinct stratum of Zairians who had acquired the intellectual and technical skills to challenge the colonial order. This stratum, generally referred to as the évolués,* was essentially an urban phenomenon. It was composed of the subordinate African employees of the Belgian colonial administration, private enterprises, and a smattering of self-employed Zairians.

---

*The concept of évolué was always vague. It implied a person who had approached the cultural and material life-style of the typical European. However, no clear criteria for this model person were ever worked out.

What were the social characteristics of this social group? They were clerks (commis), schoolteachers, noncommissioned officers in the Force Publique, exseminarians, and other minor cogs in the Belgian order. They were necessary products of Christian evangelization and the needs of the colonial enterprise. If it is true that the primary goal of the Catholic and Protestant missions was to convert Zairians to Christianity, it is no less true that the intellectual skills that they imparted created a useful pool of potential recruits for auxiliary service in the colonial governmental and economic institutions. As a result, the costs of the colonial enterprise were reduced and, simultaneously, the superordinate stratum of the African population was firmly attached to the colonial structures. For a long time, the évolués were to accommodate themselves to the colonial situation and seek material and cultural advancement within the colonial system (as Chapter 2 chronicled).

The situation of the Zairian colonial elite illustrates the inherent contradictions of colonial rule that led to its eventual demise everywhere. Acceptance of the colonial system also involved acceptance of the material and ideological beliefs and aspirations of the metropolitan society, a version of which was reproduced in the colonized country in the white part of colonial society. These aspirations sprung from the ideology of unfettered material and cultural progress that is tied up with the culture of modern industrial societies. And yet such progress was limited by racial discrimination and other disabilities inherent to the colonial situation.

As the évolués realized that they could not achieve full material and cultural advancement within the framework of the colonial system, they began to challenge the colonial order; to do this effectively, they mobilized the "masses." This mobilization was relatively easy because both the elite of the African population and the peasants and workers suffered from low pay, racial discrimination, lack of control over their own political life, and generalized subordination within the colonial system (Young 1965; Lemarchand 1964; de Schrevel 1970).

Internal protests against colonial injustices alone would not have led to the easy grant of political independence that was affected. In the long run, external events, many of which had occurred before the 1950s, played a more decisive role in Zairian decolonization. The independence of the Asian colonies—of which the dynamics can be traced to the rise of Japan as a world power and the French defeat at Dien Bien Phu*—the Algerian War of Independence, and the independence movements in the British and French colonies were all factors that reduced the legitimacy of the colonial system and also indicated to the Belgian colonizers as well as the Zairian political leaders that the colonial system could be challenged with external moral and material support.

---

*"The great victory of the Vietnamese people at Dien Bien Phu is no longer, strictly speaking, a Vietnamese victory. Since July, 1954, the question which the colonized peoples have asked themselves has been, 'What must be done to bring about another Dien Bien Phu? How can we manage it?'" (Fanon 1968, p. 70).

Unlike the British and the French colonial regimes, the Belgians had not prepared Zaire for a more or less gradual transition to independent statehood. Political parties were prohibited until the last two years of the colonial regime; it has been said that many of the Zairian politicians only met for the first time when they went to Brussels for the Table Ronde discussions just a few months prior to the attainment of political independence.

Until the last two years of Belgian colonial rule, the energies of the évolués had been diverted into the organization of ethnic or cultural organizations rather than political parties. It is therefore not surprising that, when greater freedom to organize politically was granted in 1957 during the first municipal elections, ethnic animosity and conflict were the result. By early 1960, ethnic warfare had broken out in Kasai and a few other places.

The struggle for control of the postcolonial Zairian state among the former évolué stratum soon erupted into armed confrontation, secessions, and assassinations. In this struggle, the Zairian politicians mobilized ethnic followers (Willame 1972) and foreign political and military support. The forms and degree of external intervention were determined by the manner in which foreign interests perceived the relationships between their economic and political stakes and the political character of the contending Zairian groups and factions. It is only from this perspective that we can understand such phenomena as the Katanga secession (Gérard-Libois 1966) and the assassination of Patrice Lumumba in 1961.

Belgian colonial rule had brought the Zairian political system into the international capitalist system as a supplier of vital strategic raw materials. One of the fundamental questions that the imminence of Zairian political independence raised for foreign economic and political interests was the country's continued status as a member of this system. Would the country opt out? Would foreign investments be "safe"? These questions were of great concern to the major capitalist powers—the United States, Britain, France, West Germany—and especially Belgium, which had extensive economic interests.

A proper analysis of postcolonial Zairian politics must focus on the confluence of the economic and ideological concerns of foreign powers and the ideological cleavages within the Zairian political groups. And although the latter were not profound, they were sufficiently important to determine the nature and extent of the subsequent foreign intervention and the outcome of the struggle for control of the Zairian state.

Benoît Verhaegen (1974) has suggested that in the 1960–65 period of Zairian political history, three modes of the "structuration of social reality" coexisted at the same time that they interpenetrated and conflicted with each other with different degrees of intensity: a tribal-regional mode, a "national" mode, and a socioeconomic stratification mode. At the level of the political elite, another, broadly defined "mode" of political consciousness was significant. This was the politico-normative distinction between the "radicals," whose most important representative was Patrice Lumumba, and the "conservatives." (In the political lexicon of the early 1960s, the two camps were known as the "nationalists" and the "moderates," respectively.)

The radicals and the conservatives were both loose groupings whose respective components did not always act in concert or consistently. In addition, whereas the radicals were identified with advocacy of a strong central-ized state, the conservatives were divided between the advocates of a unitary state and those who preferred a federal arrangement or even secession, as in the case of Moise Tshombe (Young 1965).

Another significant distinction between the two camps was their percep-tion of the implications of national independence. The radicals advocated rapid decolonization of the country's political and socioeconomic structures and more populist and egalitarian policies than those that the colonial regime had pursued. The conservatives, on the other hand, preferred a more grad-ual approach to decolonization and continued association with the former colonial power and its allies, and they were immensely suspicious of "com-munist" states.

It was of decisive importance for the later evolution of Zairian history that the United States and other Western foreign policy makers and private interests came to regard Patrice Lumumba and his followers as some kind of Trojan horse for "international communism." As a result, they came to see the continued control of Zairian affairs by the Lumumbist coalition as inimical to their interests (Weissman 1974).

In retrospect, Mobutu's first coup d'etat of September 14, 1960 was even more significant for the eventual socioeconomic and political history of Zaire than his coup of November 24, 1965. With the overthrow of the Lu-mumba government, the chances of establishing a populist regime that might eventually have restructured Zaire's international and external socioeconomic relations and linkages were eliminated.

In the period between the downfall of Patrice Lumumba and the rise of the Mobutu regime, the most important events involved the reincorporation of Katanga into a "sanitized" Zaire in 1963, the populist insurrections of 1964-66 (Verhaegen 1966, 1969), and their suppression. This was the period of the consolidation of the victory of the conservative coalition and their for-eign backers over their radical and populist opponents.

THE ORIGINS AND CHARACTER OF THE MOBUTU REGIME

The immediate beneficiaries of the political and socioeconomic oppor-tunities opened up by the attainment of political independence were the bu-reaucratic members of the colonial African elite who had formed political parties and occupied the newly created posts of minister, member of Parlia-ment, diplomat, and so on. A large number of this group had moved into the formerly European positions in the state administration that had become sud-denly vacant with the flight of thousands of Belgians in the wake of the mutiny of the Force Publique on July 5, 1960. This stratum was the forerunner of the Zairian politico-administrative class that was to become prominent under the Mobutu regime. The rise of the Mobutu regime contributed to the stabili-zation of the conditions that facilitated the consolidation of the economic re-sources of the emergent politico-administrative class. Since 1965, a techno-cratic elite of the politico-administrative class has emerged as the immediate holder of political power and the primary beneficiary of the Mobuto regime's economic policies (Peemans 1975). This development is significant for Zaire's postcolonial history and deserves more detailed examination.

General Mobutu had been a member of Lumumba's Mouvement National Congolais/Lumumba (MNC/L) and had been appointed secretary of state in the first independence government. Following the outbreak of the mutiny of the Force Publique, Mobutu, who had been a sergeant in the army during the 1950s, was appointed chief of staff as part of the effort to Africanize the officer corps and mollify the mutineers. However, by September 1960, Mobutu had become Lumumba's most powerful enemy; it was his coup d'etat of September 14, 1960, that effectively broke Lumumba's political power.

From 1960 to 1965, General Mobutu's control of the troops based around Kinshasa and others scattered around the country made him the most important member of the conservative coalition after Joseph Kasavubu. From the time of the 1960 army mutiny, the political role of the military grew. This slide toward "praetorianism" was accentuated by the increasing use of force to keep power and the use of the military to put down the military rebellions of the 1960-66 period (Verhaegen 1966, 1969).

From the time of his 1960 coup d'etat, General Mobutu's public actions were marked by strong opposition to whatever he regarded as being "communist." In this respect, it is significant to note that the first important measure that he took on the day of his 1960 putsch was to order the expulsion of the Soviet and Czechoslovak diplomatic missions. Since then, "anticommunism" has been a consistent aspect of Mobutu's political posture.

THE MOBUTU REGIME (1965-73)

The 1965 coup d'etat was, among other things, the expression of the failure of the emergent politico-administrative class and other elite elements of postcolonial Zaire to find a consensual political and ideological formula. This failure was demonstrated in the form of governmental instability and coercive practices and violence in the period before 1965 (Young 1965; Willame 1972). It was under these conditions that General Mobutu seized power on November 24, 1965.

The major immediate problem that General Mobutu faced on seizing control was how to legitimize this power in a highly politicized situation. He therefore had to proceed cautiously until he had built up his own base within the politico-bureaucratic sectors that had an economic stake in the new regime. General Mobutu was also aided in his task by the low esteem with which many Zairians had come to view the civilian politicians. Initially, Mobutu appeared to represent a radical departure from frivolous and venal politics to a more nationalist and honest political style.

It was not until 1973 that the Mobutu regime overcame all sorts of public opposition or expressions of dissent. These oppositions had taken several different forms and had been dealt with in different ways. Armed opposition was put down with military force; nonviolent opposition was dealt with through administrative measures. In 1966, units of the former Katanga Gendarmerie, who had been serving with the national army in the east of Zaire, revolted; they were ruthlessly suppressed and their leader was executed. The same fate befell the mercenaries who had been recruited to fight the rebellions of 1964–66 when they revolted in 1967.

Violent repression was also meted out to civilian opponents. In June 1966, four prominent politicians of the old civilian political regime were publicly hanged in Kinshasa for allegedly plotting against the Mobutu government. They were Evariste Kimba, former foreign minister of the Katanga secessionist government, who had been appointed prime minister by President Kasavubu just prior to Mobutu's coup d'etat; Jerome Anany; Alexandre Mahamba; and Emmanuel Bamba—all of whom had held ministerial positions in the pre-1965 central governments.

In October 1968, Pierre Mulele, who had led the Kwilu rebellion (in western Zaire), returned to Kinshasa from Brazzaville (in the Congo Republic) in the belief that he had been amnestied; however, he was arrested and summarily put to death. Two other leaders of the rebellion in the east, "General" Ngalo and Ildefonse Masengo, were executed in 1969.

Along with these repressive measures, steps were taken to appease and even co-opt the opposition. In 1966, General Mobutu declared Patrice Lumumba a national hero and avowed that he was following the political ideals of the fallen leader. Moreover, some prominent former supporters of Lumumba were co-opted by the Mobutu regime. One of these was Antoine Kiwewa, former parliamentary leader of the MNC/L; he eventually became a member of the Political Bureau of the regime's Mouvement Populaire de la Révolution (MPR).

The most significant measure of reconciliation was the general amnesty that was declared in 1971 in favor of all exiled opponents. As a result, two of the most prominent leaders of the eastern rebellion, Christophe Gbenye and "General" Nicolas Olenga, returned to Zaire. Overall, some 9,150 exiles returned to the country following this amnesty (Cornevin 1974).

From the point of view of the social and ideological bases of the Mobutu regime, the most important form of opposition, apart from the armed insurrections, was that presented by the Zairian student movement organized in the Union Générale des Etudiants Congolais (UGEC) in the 1966–68 period. Although the movement never posed an immediate military threat to the Mobutu regime, its opposition was significant because, unlike the insurrectionary movements, it went beyond mere populism and questioned the status of Zaire as an underdeveloped peripheral capitalist society. The opposition of the student movement and the more serious challenge offered by the hierarchy of the Roman Catholic church in the early 1970s are considered in more detail in Chapter 14.

THE INSTITUTIONAL BASIS OF THE MOBUTU REGIME

The three most important institutional supports of the Mobutu regime are the military, the civil administration, and the official MPR. It is on the centralized and arbitrary domination of these three institutions that the authoritarian and personalist regime is based. (For a useful discussion of the concept of "authoritarianism," see Juan Linz [1975].)

The domination of bureaucratic rule is the direct result of the elimination of participatory political institutions such as freely organized political parties, a freely elected legislature, and local elective institutions since 1965. The main stages in the bureaucratization of Zairian political life have involved the proscription of the multiparty system, which was installed in the terminal period of Belgian colonial rule, the abolition of the semiautonomous provincial institutions, and the imposition of the MPR. All these measures were initiated in the 1965-67 period (Gatarayiha, Gudumbagana, and de Lannoy 1976).

The MPR traces its origins to the Corps des Volontaires de la République (CVR), which was a quasi-political organization set up by young and nationalistic individuals in Kinshasa in December 1965 to support the political goals of the newly installed Mobutu regime. In April 1967, the CVR dissolved itself and joined the MPR, which had just been created on the initiative of General Mobutu (Institut Makanda Kabobi, n.d.).

The CVR was the last spontaneous political organization to be formed under the Mobutu regime. The MPR soon became simply an extension of the administration and in effect disappeared as a separate institution. Regional commissioners (provincial administrative heads), subregional commissioners (district commissioners), and all heads of administrative units down to the village level were made ex officio heads of the local party organizations. Because all these officials are appointed, it is difficult to see how their role as administrative officials could be distinguished from their role as party officials.

It is significant that the coordination of party activities was put under the minister charged with territorial administration (Commissaire d'Etat aux Affaires Politiques chargé de la Coordination du Parti, later changed to Commissaire d'Etat à l'Administration du Territoire). It is clear that the party was perceived as being nothing more than an auxiliary arm of the administration. Moreover, according to the Zairian constitution, every Zairian is ipso facto a member of the party; there is no formal party membership. This raises the fundamental question of whether there is such a thing as a political party in Zaire. The only visible party organs that are not part of the administration are the Political Bureau, which, until the reforms of 1977, was appointed by the president, and the youth wing of the party, that is, the Jeunesse du Mouvement Populaire de la Révolution (JMPR), which plays some law-and-order auxiliary roles and engages in the singing of songs praising the president at public functions (Willame 1975; Schatzberg 1978).

The manifesto of the MPR is unabashedly explicit in its defense of authoritarian government. After declaring respect for basic individual liberties, it adds the rider that individual freedom must not lead to anarchy. The manifesto specifically states that "the authority of the State cannot be questioned. [State] Power does not retreat before groups" (Manifeste de la N'sele, p. 15).

As part of its struggle with the various oppositions, and in order to justify its political and socioeconomic options, the Mobutu regime has over the years evolved a set of propositions and assertions that pass for the official ideology. These propositions and assertions are not contained in any one document; instead, they are scattered in numerous speeches, declarations, and comments put out by President Mobutu and his officials.

The ideological assertions of the Mobutu regime have been termed nationalism, authentic Zairian nationalism, authenticity, and Mobutism at various periods. Whatever the terminological variations, the core of the ideology is essentially conservative anticolonial nationalism. The aims of this orientation involve the "indigenization" of the political and socioeconomic structures of Zaire without altering them to provide for a more egalitarian and democratic socioeconomic system. A striking example of the practical application of this ideology was the Zairianization Measures of 1973, which were exploited by the politico-administrative class to increase their economic resources (Schatzberg 1977; Kannyo 1979).

The ideology opposes anything that is deemed to threaten the existing socioeconomic organization of Zairian society. It therefore combats "communism," socialism, and populism. In foreign affairs, the ideology is invoked to justify the alleged policy of "nonalignment"; in reality, the experience of the Mobutu regime has been that whenever cold war issues were concerned, it has always sided with the West.

The theory of authenticity has also been invoked to justify the authoritarian political system (see Chapter 4). To this end, an effort has been made to create the myth of Zaire as an image of some idealistic, precolonial African village living in harmony and arcadian bliss under the benevolent authority of a strong-willed chief represented by General Mobutu. According to this theory, the more Zairian political institutions approximate this image, the more authentic they are. This image totally excludes any notion of opposition or dissent. General Mobutu has said:

> In our traditional societies . . . there has never been two chiefs in the same village, the true chief and the opposition chief. There have, perhaps been conflicts between villages, even bloody clashes. But once they were unified, only one chief emerged democratically: the chief of all. That is African authenticity. [1975, p. 349]

Another important dimension of the ideology of authenticity pertains to cultural nationalism and nativism. In this aspect, authenticity seeks to combat the sense of cultural inferiority that was inculcated by colonial domination. It is in pursuit of this goal that General Mobutu Africanized personal and place names of European origin and invented new terms to replace those passed on from Belgian practices, for example, Commissaire d'état for minister, Commissaire du peuple for député, and so on (Adelman 1975b; Wrzesinska 1975).

In all its various applications, the ideology of authenticity exalts the authoritarian state and the president as the agencies of national renovation, national independence, and peace.* Insofar as it puts emphasis on the common and shared domination and (past) contempt for Zairians by foreigners, it seeks to underplay the contradictions and conflicts that exist among the different social groups in Zairian society: the urban dwellers versus the peasantry, the workers versus the employers, the politically powerful versus the politically weak (Tutashinda 1974; Sine 1975).

THE CRISIS OF THE MOBUTU REGIME (1974-79)

The Mobutu regime arose out of the crisis that was caused by the breakdown of the Belgian colonial system and the need of the economic and political interests of the international capitalist system to keep Zaire firmly entrenched within that system. Although the rise of the regime stabilized the subsystem at the institutional level, the deeper crisis that revolved around the capacity of the postcolonial socioeconomic system to satisfy the basic needs of the majority of the population, such as food, education, and health care, was not faced. What the current economic crisis has done is to bring the underlying structural issues once again to the surface (Gran 1978).

Between 1965 and 1974, the Mobutu regime had managed to reestablish law and order in all parts of the country (except for an isolated pocket of remnants of the eastern rebellion in the Kivu highlands) and had defeated all opposition and public dissent. In international affairs, President Mobutu had succeeded in reconciling himself to virtually all those states that had at one time or another supported the radical opposition.

From 1971, when he started the campaign of cultural decolonization, President Mobutu increasingly struck a "radical" stance in international affairs (see Chapter 12). At the end of 1972, he recognized the People's Republic of China and in January 1973 he paid his first visit to Peking. (It is noteworthy that Mobutu's reconciliation with China only occurred after U.S. President Richard Nixon's opening to China.) In October 1973, he addressed the General Assembly of the United Nations in New York and used the occasion to condemn the "exploitation" of the poor by the rich countries. On November 30, 1973, President Mobutu announced the Zairianization Measures, which were designed to eject foreigners from the agricultural, commercial, and related sectors of the Zairian economy and replace them with nationals (Schatzberg 1977; Kannyo 1979).

The year 1974 can be regarded as the beginning of the current political crisis of the Mobutu regime. In that year, two factors combined to undermine the Zairian economy. The first factor stemmed from the external environment. Beginning in 1974, the price of copper on the international market dropped from BF 118,025 (approximately $3,370) per metric ton in April

---

*It is the goal of national economic, political, and cultural renovation that the Mobutu regime seeks to express by the term revolution in its political lexicon.

1974 to BF 47,402 (approximately $1,350) in December 1974 to BF 45,482 (approximately $1,280) in December 1975 (Banque du Zaire 1976b).

At the same time, the inflationary trends that had begun to affect the capitalist economies on which Zaire is almost totally dependent began to have an impact on its economy in 1974. The rate of growth of the commercialized gross domestic product dropped from 7.6 percent in 1973 to 5.4 percent in 1974 (Banque du Zaire 1975). Taking 1970 as the base (1970 = 100), the wholesale price index rose from 126.7 points in 1973 to 165.2 in 1974, an increase of 30.4 percent as against an increase of 9.3 percent in 1973 (Banque du Zaire 1975, p. 38).

An important internal factor that caused a serious decline of the Zairian economy was the disruptions resulting from the implementation of the Zairianization Measures. Given the reality that these measures had not been preceded by any serious planning and study (Kannyo 1979), there was a decline in the performance of the agricultural and commercial sectors. This process was first alluded to by the 1974 Bank of Zaire Report (Banque du Zaire 1975) and, as Chapter 1 shows, has been much analyzed since. The 1974 Radicalization Measures only increased the disruptive effect of the previous measures (Banque du Zaire 1976a).

In the course of 1975, the outbreak of the Angolan Civil War compounded the economic and political crises of the Mobutu regime. One of the serious consequences of the fighting in Angola was the closure of the Benguela railroad, which had been a vital lifeline of the Shaba mining and industrial region. On the political plane, Mobutu committed himself totally to the Frente Nacional de Libertação de Angola (FNLA) to the extent of sending in regular Zairian troops against the Movimento Popular de Libertação de Angola (MPLA) (Stockwell 1978).

The rout of the FNLA, as well as the loosely allied União Nacional para Independência Total de Angola (UNITA) and the Zairian expeditionary units, dealt a big blow to the political prestige of General Mobutu. Moreover, his alliance (directly or indirectly) with South African and Western interests wiped out his carefully nurtured image of a Third World leader (Young 1976).

The political problems of the Mobutu regime gave courage to its internal and external opponents. Whatever the actual truth of the alleged attempted coup d'etat of 1975, the imposition of a sentence of death on seven officers (including three generals) of the Forces Armées Zairoises (FAZ) reflected new tensions within the Zairian army. In 1976 and 1977, wildcat strikes in the Shaba and Kinshasa industrial centers indicated the terrible economic plight of Zairian workers and a new will to challenge the regime in the light of its weakened political position.

The most serious challenge to the Mobutu regime since its inception, however, has been posed by the exiled opponents who are generally, but misleadingly, termed the ex-Katanga gendarmes.* They crossed over from An-

---

*According to press reports, a large number of the soldiers of Front de Libération National du Congo (FNLC) were too young to have been part

gola in 1977 and 1978 only to be driven back by French and Moroccan troops. The 1978 invasion was preceded by the execution of some 13 people, mainly army officers, who were accused of having plotted yet another coup d'etat.

THE 1977 POLITICAL REFORMS

In the wake of the first invasion of Shaba (Shaba I), President Mobutu announced the important reforms of July 1, 1977. These reforms, which provided for the direct election from a multitude of candidates of members of the Political Bureau, the Legislative Council, and municipal councils, had the potential for the liberalization of the personalist and authoritarian regime. However, significantly, these reforms did not threaten the existence of the single-party domination of the MPR. (For a full text of the July 1, 1977, presidential speech, see Etudes Zairoises, June–September 1977, pp. 358–79.)

An important innovation of the 1977 reforms was the creation of the office of Premier Commissaire d'Etat (prime minister). Another innovation involved not only the election of members of the Political Bureau, who had previously been appointed by the president, but also their designation from specific regions. Previously, they were not explicitly considered to represent any geographical areas.

In October 1977, elections were held for 270 members of the National Legislative Council and 18 (out of 30)* members of the Political Bureau as well as municipal councillors. For the first time since the inception of the Mobutu regime, Zairians had political institutions that reflected a certain degree of genuine representation. The choice was, however, only relative.

The 1977 political reforms had not been won by the Zairian people; they had been granted, in monarchical fashion, by General Mobutu. As a result, candidates for the 1977 elections could neither challenge the authoritarian system nor present the electorate with any political program or alternative political leadership. The election campaign revolved around personalities and involved the distribution of money for publicity, and was to that extent irrelevant for the solution of the prevailing political crisis. There can be little doubt that the main beneficiaries of this exercise were the members of the emergent Zairian bourgeoisie who filled the elected political institutions (see Van Der Steen 1978).

Two years after the 1977 reforms, there is no sign that the political crisis is any nearer to solution than it was before. Nevertheless, a significant factor has been the greater role of the Legislative Council as a forum

---

of the original Katanga Gendarmerie, which was the "army" of the Katanga secessionist regime of 1960-63.

*In February 1978, six more members were appointed to the Political Bureau, thus bringing the total to 36.

for some muffled criticism of government policy.* At the beginning of 1979, the council went to the extent of rejecting the government's budget for 1979.

CONCLUSION

The maintenance of the Zairian political system within the international capitalist system as a peripheral underdeveloped polity was ensured through the triumph of the conservative coalition of Zairian politicians in the first five years of Zaire's political independence. In terms of the internal social structures, the victory of the conservatives was accompanied by the untrammeled ascent of the ex-évolué stratum to socioeconomic preeminence in the form of an emergent politico-administrative class. Since the mid-1960s, this emergent class has been reinforced and altered in its social composition by the addition of younger, technocratic elements drawn from Zairian and foreign institutions of higher learning. It is the latter that now form the strategic basis of support for the Mobutu regime.

At the same time, the triumph of the politico-administrative class has been accompanied by the concurrent impoverishment of the majority of the Zairian population. It is the increasing marginalization of the Zairian workers, peasants, and the mass of residual social groups of the Zairian social structure that threatens to bring about another massive upheaval akin to the "Congo crisis" of the early 1960s. Aspects of this marginalization are described in the chapters that follow.

REFERENCES

Adelman, Kenneth Lee. 1975a. "The Church-State Conflict in Zaire: 1969-1974." African Studies Review 18, no. 1:102-16.

_____. 1975b. "The Recourse to Authenticity and Negritude in Zaire." Journal of Modern African Studies 13, no. 1:134-39.

Banque du Zaire. 1976a. Rapport annuel 1975.

_____. 1976b. Bulletin mensuel de la statistique. 2eme Année, 6 (June).

_____. 1975. Rapport annuel 1974.

---

*Since the 1977 reforms, government policy is the immediate responsibility of the Premier Commissaire d'Etat. Criticism in the Legislative Council is therefore ostensibly directed at cabinet ministers and the Premier Commissaire d'Etat rather than the president. Moreover, such criticism has not involved any fundamental matters of principle.

Centre de Recherche et d'Information Socio-Politiques. 1972. Les relations entre l'Eglise et l'Etat au Zaire. Travaux Africains, Brussels, 145, December 28.

_____. 1969. Le régime Mobutu et le syndicat des travailleurs. Travaux Africains, 95, September 10.

_____. 1968a. L'UGEC et le nouveau régime. Travaux Africains, 77, March 28.

_____. 1968b. Contestation ou stagnation etudiante au Congo. Travaux Africains, 79, September 29.

_____. 1966. Congo 1964. Princeton, N.J.: Princeton University Press.

_____. n.d. Congo 1960, vol. 2.

Cornevin, Robert. 1974. "La politique interiéure du Zaire." Revue française d'etudes politiques africaines 108:30-48.

de Schrevel, M. 1970. Les forces politiques de la décolonisation congolaise. Louvain: Université Catholique de Louvain.

Demunter, Paul. 1976. Les relations entre le mouvement etudiant et le régime politique congolais: Le colloque de Goma. Centre de Recherche et d'Information Socio-Politiques, Travaux Africains, 126, April 30.

_____. 1972. "Structure de classe et luttes de classes dans le Congo colonial." Contradictions (Brussels) 1 (January-June): 67-109.

_____. 1971. Analyse de la contestation etudiante du Congo-Kinshasa et ses séquelles. Centre de Recherche et d'Information Socio-Politiques, Travaux Africains, 132, December 30.

Fanon, Frantz. 1968. The Wretched of the Earth. New York: Grove Press.

Gatarayiha, Majinya, Kangafu Gudumbagana, and Didier de Lannoy. 1976. "Aspects de la réforme administrative au Zaire." Cahiers du CEDAF (Brussels), pp. 4-5.

Gérard-Libois, Jules. 1966. Katanga Secession. Madison: University of Wisconsin Press.

Gran, Guy. 1978. "Zaire 1978: The Ethical and Intellectual Bankruptcy of the World System." Africa Today 25, no. 4 (October-December): 5-24.

Institut de Recherches Economiques et Sociales. 1968. Indépendence, inflation, développement. Paris: Editions Mouton.

Institut Makanda Kabobi. n.d. Histoire du mouvement populaire de la révolution.

Kannyo, Edward. 1979. "Political Power and Class-Formation in Zaire: The 'Zairianization Measures,' 1973-75." Ph.D. dissertation, Yale University.

Lemarchand, Rene. 1964. Political Awakening in the Belgian Congo. Berkeley: University of California Press.

Linz, Juan. 1975. "Totalitarian and Authoritarian Regimes." In Handbook of Political Science, edited by Fred I. Greenstein and Nelson W. Polsby, vol. 3, pp. 175-244. Reading, Mass.: Addison-Wesley.

Mobutu Sese Seko. 1975. Discours, allocutions et messages, vols. 1 and 2. Paris: Editions J.A.

Nzongola, Georges (Ntalaja). 1970. "The Bourgeoisie and Revolution in the Congo." Journal of Modern African Studies 8, no. 4 (December): 511-30.

Nzongola, Ntalaja. 1975. "Urban Administration in Zaire: A Study of Kananga, 1971-73." Ph.D. dissertation, University of Wisconsin.

Peemans, Jean-Philippe. 1975. "L'etat fort et la croissance economique." La revue nouvelle (Brussels) 62, no. 12 (December): 515-27.

Schatzberg, Michael G. 1978. "Fidelité au Guide: The J.M.P.R. in Zairian Schools." Journal of Modern African Studies 16, no. 3 (September): 417-31.

_____. 1977. "Bureaucracy, Business, Beer: The Political Dynamics of Class Formation in Lisala, Zaire." Ph.D. dissertation, University of Wisconsin.

Sine, Babakar. 1975. Impérialisme et théories sociologigues du développement. Paris: Editions Anthropos-Idep.

Stockwell, John. 1978. In Search of Enemies. New York: Norton.

Tutashinda, N. 1974. "Les mystifications de l'authenticité." La pensée (Paris) 175 (May-June): 68-84.

U.S., Congress, Senate. Select Committee on Intelligence. 1975. Alleged Assassination Plots Involving Foreign Leaders. Report no. 94-465, pp. 13-70.

Van Der Steen, Daniel. 1978. "Elections et réformes politiques au Zaire en 1977, analyse de la composition des organes politiques." Les cahiers du CEDAF, pp. 2-3.

Van Lierde, Jean. 1967. "L'union générale des etudiants congolais." In Congo 1966, Centre de Recherche et d'Information Socio-Politiques, pp. 84-94.

Verhaegen, Benoît. 1974. Introduction à l'histoire immédiate. Brussels: Editions J. Cuculot, S.A.

_____. 1966, 1969. Rébellions au Congo, vols. 1 and 2. Brussels: Centre de Recherche et d'Information Socio-Politiques, and Kinshasa: Institut de Recherches Economiques et Sociales.

_____. 1964. "Social Classes in the Congo." Révolution (Paris) 1, no. 12 (April): 115-28.

Wallerstein, Immanuel. 1976. "A World-System Perspective on the Social Sciences." British Journal of Sociology 27, no. 3 (September): 343-53.

Weissman, Stephen R. 1974. American Foreign Policy in the Congo. Ithaca, N.Y.: Cornell University Press.

Williame, Jean-Claude. 1975. "Les 'clés' de la politique zairoise." La revue nouvelle (Brussels) 62, no. 12 (December): 528-33.

_____. 1972. Patrimonialism and Political Change in the Congo. Stanford, Calif.: Stanford University Press.

_____. 1968. "The Congo." In Students and Politics in Developing Countries, edited by Donald K. Emmerson, pp. 37-63. New York: Praeger.

Wrzesinska, Alicja. 1975. "Problème de l'authenticité zairoise presenté sur exemple des noms propres." Africana Bulletin (Warsaw) 22:41-54.

Young, Crawford. 1976. "The Portuguese Coup and Zaire's Southern Africa Policy." Mimeographed.

_____. 1965. Politics in the Congo. Princeton, N.J.: Princeton University Press.

4

CLOUDS OF SMOKE:
CULTURAL AND PSYCHOLOGICAL
MODERNIZATION IN ZAIRE

Thomas Turner

INTRODUCTION

The typical African leader, suggests Manfred Halpern, is like the Wizard of Oz, presenting himself as a miracle worker, "busy working smoke-machines and amplifying his voice." By such techniques, the leader masks from the people the real choices that confront them in a changing world. The risk and opportunity of choice result from what Halpern calls "incoherence," a shorthand term for "the spiritual, intellectual, social, political, economic, and personal loss for all of deeply rooted relationships." Political leaders either can "attend to the overcoming of incoherence in their society," or as most often happens) can "seek to profit from incoherence and from its mere repression while they enjoy willfulness, prestige and luxury as long as they can" (Halpern 1976, pp. 12-19).

Whatever the applicability of the latter description to other African leaders (and it would seem to fit many of them), Mobutu Sese Soko is an archetypal example of this sort of leader who "seek[s] to profit from inco-herence." A modern Zaire is struggling to be born, but its emergence has little to do with the manifest efforts at political socialization carried out by the Mobutu regime, such as the promotion of "authentic Zairian nationalism." Rather, the process of emerging modernization is primarily the consequence of the past century of politico-economic change—in the political sphere, the conquest and decolonization of Zaire and, more basic than these, Zaire's incorporation into the world capitalist economy. In response to these pro-found changes, the world models of the Zairian population are changing. Rather than promote the emergence of a modern outlook, however, Mobutu the Wizard sends forth clouds to obscure the people's view.

One of the great merits of Halpern's approach is its provision of a more refined set of tools for discussing psychological change, including psychological modernization. In the past, most authors have used the blunt instrument of "tradition" (and the related "traditional society," "traditional-ism," and so on), and have argued or implied that moving away from "tradition" is the same thing as moving toward "modernity." Halpern, in contrast, conceives of modernization as the escape from "emanation," which corresponds to one of the many meanings of tradition. He explains that this concept "will allow us to come to terms with all relationships that any people regard as sacred. Sacred in the larger sense that each individual yields entirely to collaborating" with this power source, accepting or rejecting change as that source wills, and receiving "total security for one's self" in return.

Emanation, thus defined, is not restricted to traditional society. One example of such a relationship would be that of the "traditional African [who] sees himself as an extension, not only of his own kinship group, but of the land and spirits and gods that constitute the cosmos of his tribe and his ethnic community." Halpern suggests nontraditional examples as well: "This is also the relationship that links the loyal Algerian or Mozambican to his nation for whose birth and preservation so many have already died" (Halpern 1976, pp. 9-10).

In either case, whether for "tribesman" or "patriot," modernization means escape from emanation. People must free themselves for the first time to create any new relationship with themselves, others, or nature that they have never known before but that they now recognize as valuable. People must also feel free and make themselves capable of evaluating any old or new relationship, and therefore, of choosing whether to nourish or else end it (Halpern 1976, p. 11). In other words, individual-level empathy (Lerner 1958) is seen as linked to the community with which the individual identifies; to become empathic or modern the individual must come to see himself as a member of humanity, able to draw on all human experience.

Halpern's definition of modernity is a demanding one, according to which few nations and few individuals would ever be entirely modern; nonetheless, one can conceive of individuals and groups moving toward it, and the actions of political leaders encouraging or hindering their movement.

To understand how difficult the path of psychological modernization has been for the Zairians in the two decades since independence, some sense of their precolonial and colonial world models is in order. The precolonial Zairian was bound by sacred ties to a small-scale community. Despite multiple apparent political divisions, there was considerable cultural uniformity. Anthropologist Renée Fox (1968) summarized the individual's view of self and society in this sweeping manner:

> Congolese set a high value on thought, knowledge, wisdom, intelligence, insight, and feeling states. They are viewed as a positive source of creation; they contribute to protection, survival, and success. But thoughts and feelings are also considered to be fundamental determinants of the misfortune and evil that befall a man, his family, the larger community of which he and they are a part. Illness, sterility, failure, death—all the negative, disappointing, tragic experiences of life—are presumed to be caused by evil thoughts, feelings and intentions of a significant other person. . . . [T]he thoughts and feelings of the malefactor have the

capacity to harm because they are believed to harness the power of one of the numerous kinds of spirits that move back and forth between the spheres of the dead and the living, filling the cosmic space between the Supreme Being or the Creator, and man, Muntu.

From these views follow, notably, a belief in the possibility of magico-religious protection from danger and a belief that wealth is a consequence of good fortune.

The subsistence village economy prevailed, based on communally held land. Although the precolonial Zairian had a relationship of emanation to his community, his local economy was not traditional in the sense of irrational. As Perinbam (1977) argues, the precolonial African (including the precolonial Zairian) "was oeconomicus because, as a function of his existence, he was, for the most part, embedded in an integrated socio-economic structure that was anchored in the means and modes of material production" (pp. 156-57). Local economies were open to innovation, as can be seen by the progressive adoption of cassava (manioc), introduced by the Portuguese in the sixteenth century. For many if not most of the societies of precolonial Zaire, a second economic sector of long-distance trade coexisted with the subsistence sector.

The establishment of colonial rule was carried out by coercion, both physical and psychological. Little attempt was made to create a positive identification with the state in the minds of its subjects. Rather, the state was presented as a leviathan, ready to crush any resistance. This concept was eloquently expressed by the name the Zairians gave the state, Bula Matari, the "rock crusher."

Chapter 2 described the political and economic transformation wrought by colonial rule and the differential social change begun by the Belgian recruitment of local auxiliaries. Significant cultural as well as class changes took place. Ethnic and regional identifications were transformed under colonial rule as a result of the activities of the state, the church, and the companies. The state, for example, required that its subjects carry identification cards labeling them as to tribe; administrative agents, carrying out research on local political organization, succession to the post of chief, and so on, were instructed to identify the communities studied by race, peuplade, and tribu.* These administrative measures had the effect of standardizing ethnic labels and spreading them to groups that previously had not adopted them.

The differential impact of social change led to the overrepresentation of certain ethnic groups and subgroups in the army, in the proletariat, and among the évolués. Favored groups tended to dominate nationalist organizations as these emerged, and in turn became the target of resentment on the

---

*For example, the Rapport d'enquête on the Mondja (a Tetela subgroup of Lubefu zone, Kasai Oriental region), dated April 25, 1936, identifies them as being of "Race: Bantoue," "Peuplade: Okutshu," and "Tribu: Gandu."

part of the less favored groups. The Belgians, seeking first to postpone decolonization, then to influence its outcome, exploited such resentment.

The leading role of ethnic and regional parties during the decolonization period was due not only to the differential modernization just described
(and the Belgian divide and rule tactic) but also to the weakness of alternative forms of organization. While permitting and in fact encouraging ethnically and regionally defined cultural associations, the Belgians discouraged
trade unions and political parties. In the absence of such organizations, aspiring politicians based themselves heavily upon the ethnic and regional
bodies. In the atmosphere of insecurity generated by decolonization, relations of emanation came to the fore. Thus ethnically defined political conflict
predominated. The predominance of the ethnic factor, the inexperience of
the politicians, and the interference of outside forces all contributed to the
chaos that accompanied Congo/Zaire's accession to independence in 1960.

ETHNICITY, CLASS, AND NATIONALISM, 1960-65

Once elections had been held and a national government formed, that
government served as a reference point for each region, ethnic group, and
subgroup. Distribution of positions demonstrated whether or not a group was
fairly represented in that government and could expect fair treatment from it.
The provincial governments served as reference points in the same manner
on a lower level. The first Congolese government was formed by Patrice
Lumumba, head of the most successful party, the Mouvement National Con-
golais/Lumumba, or MNC/L. This government was somewhat unbalanced in
regional terms, Leopoldville and Kasai provinces being overrepresented.
All parties of great or moderate importance were represented with the exception of the Kalonji wing of the MNC (MNC/K), ethnic party of the Luba-Kasai.
Thus the Luba-Kasai were the most disaffected in the sense of feeling unrep-
resented and unprotected. Their disaffection, reinforced by the exclusion
from power on the provincial level and their bloody expulsion from Kananga,
led them to form a breakaway government, the so-called Mining State.

In September 1960, President Kasavubu revoked Lumumba and named
Joseph Ileo to form a new government. Ileo did so. In his government, representation of Equateur and of the moderate (pro-Belgian) Parti National du
Progrès (PNP) party increased sharply. The number of representatives of
Lumumba's nationalist, centralist MNC/L was much lower. "Certain of the
ministers nominated, belonging to MNC-Lumumba and CEREA, had not effectively marked their intention of breaking with Mr. Lumumba and assuming
new tasks under the direction of Mr. Ileo" (Gérard-Libois and Verhaegen
1961, 2:855). This first Ileo government was, however, only of symbolic importance, as it never sought confirmation from the Parliament and never took
office.

Two days after Ileo announced formation of his government, Colonel
Mobutu "neutralized" Lumumba, Kasavubu, and the Parliament, and called
on "our students, our African technicians" to take over direction of the coun-

try (Gérard-Libois and Verhaegen 1961, 2:869). This intervention foreshadowed Mobutu's coup of 1965, and the theme of "technicians" would be prominent under the Second Republic.

The result of Mobutu's 1960 intervention was the College of Commissioners, inaccurately described by Young as being composed of university students, of whom "few . . . had any marked party identification" (Young 1965, pp. 329, 347). In fact, 7 of the 14 commissioners-general had degrees but were not currently enrolled in postgraduate programs; only 5 of the 14 clearly were students as of September 1960. A more realistic view of effective voices in the college takes account also of deputy commissioners-general and commissioners and of the fact that some members were more active than others. For example, at the first meeting at which the functioning of the college was discussed, there were ten nonstudents and only five students present. Nor does the "apolitical" characterization hold up; college-member Bomboko had been one of two ministers (along with Delvaux of the PNP) to countersign Kasavubu's revocation of Lumumba. College members Ndele, Mbeka, and Ngwete had been chefs de cabinet of Lumumba's ministers, while Kandolo had been Lumumba's own chef de cabinet. One member, Kazadi (a Luba), was in prison when named; five others had just arrived in Brazzaville and were "considered clearly hostile to Mr. Lumumba." In ethnic terms, the College of Commissioners was heavily Kongo and Luba-Kasai, which means it was very unrepresentative of the total population but quite representative of the educated elite. The Kongo and Luba-Kasai were two of the leading anti-Lumumbist ethnic groups, politically active as the ABAKO and the MNC/K, respectively.

Early in 1961 the College of Commissioners gave way to a second government headed by Ileo. Nationalist forces supported a rival government under Antoine Gizenga, based in Kisangani (Stanleyville). Almost by definition neither the "moderate" Ileo government nor the "radical" Gizenga government was ethnically or ideologically representative of the entire country.

In contrast, the three governments headed by Cyrille Adoula (following the Leopoldville-Stanleyville compromise of August 1961) were all relatively representative in ethnoregional terms. The 1960 election results no longer constituted a very good guide to ideological orientation. Revulsion was growing against politicians in general, and participation in the central government was taken as evidence that one had sold out. The popular perception of the Adoula government can be gauged by a joke, according to which U. S.-supplied frozen chickens (which Zairians find soft and tasteless) were "the corpse of Adoula."

Probably the least representative government of 1960-65 was the so-called "government of public safety" headed by Moise Tshombe of Katanga, who was called in to serve as prime minister after Adoula had failed to cope with the resurgent nationalists. Tshombe's government included only 12 members; Premier Tshombe held five ministerial portfolios himself, his fellow south Katangan, Godefroid Munongo, two more, and their cosecessionist Kalonji, one. Only two ministers, Lubaya and Kidicho, had any credentials as centralist nationalists (Gérard-Libois et al. 1965, pp. 189-90).

Throughout 1960–65, effective power in Kinshasa was held by the Binza Group, politicians associated with the U. S. Central Intelligence Agency. The Binza Group operated behind the scenes at first, but became increasingly visible. Given the informal nature of the Binza Group, it is difficult to pin down the membership. All sources agree that the core was three men: Mobutu, Nendaka (head of the security police), and Bomboko (foreign minister, then justice minister). Others mentioned include National Bank head Ndele and Interior Ministry permanent secretary Kandolo (Gérard-Libois et al. 1965, pp. 124–74; 1966, p. 9; Willame 1972, p. 113; Lefever 1970, p. 98; Young 1965, pp. 379–80). The group overrepresented the north of the country; beyond that, it shared a common set of perceptions as to the desirability of close ties to the United States and Belgium, which led it to turn its back on Lumumba's radical nationalism.

Below the national level, the period 1960–65 was a heyday for cultural entrepreneurialism. Congolese politicians not only appealed to ethnic and regional sentiments to get elected and then attempted to represent those ethnoregional interests but also tried to reshape ethnic and regional groupings. In 1961, the Congo Geographic Institute published an ethnographic map that reflected both the concerns of the elite and the limitations of their ethnographic knowledge. The map designates peuplades (Bantu, Nilotics, and so on), ethnics (Kongo, Mongo, Baluba, and so on), and tribus (Solongo, Bawoyo, Bayombe, Bamanianga, and others, among the Kongo). Peculiarities included the attempt to identify "approximate limits" of the Mongo (annexing non-Mongo areas in the south, omitting Mongo areas in the east). The "approximate limits of the Luba" included the Luba of Kasai and those of Shaba (Katanga), but omitted other Luba-related peoples, such as the Lulua and Luntu. Probably most bizarre was the attempt to trace "approximate limits of the Mai-Ndombe," corresponding to the multiethnic district of Lac Leopold II (the Present subregion of Mai-Ndombe), which became a separate province in 1962. Some of the anomalies in this map probably reflect conscious attempts to shape events, others a fusion of objective and subjective ethnic definitions.

In 1961/62, the various Congolese factions, ranging from the Katanga secessionists to some of the centralist heirs of Lumumba, came to agree on the need for new provinces and a federal structure. Division of the provinces was made inevitable by three events: first, and probably most influential, the European-sponsored secession of Katanga; second, the exclusion of the Luba from power in Kasai Province; and third, the exclusion of the Kongo from power in Leopoldville Province (Young 1965, pp. 525–52). Other regional and/or ethnic groups actively sought new provinces; those that were less enthusiastic found themselves left with smaller provinces when other areas had opted out. For example, in Leopoldville Province, the secession of Kongo Central, Kwango, and Lac Leopold II left Kwilu as a separate province despite the centralist orientation of its leaders. In all, there were created 21 new provinces in place of the 6 of the colonial era.

The 1960 elections, the ousting of the Lumumba government, and the division of the six original provinces each produced winners and losers among the Congolese politicians and their followers. Similarly, the disruption of the Congolese economy affected some parts of the country much more than others. As Crawford Young puts it, the result was a fusion of the "identity and distribution crises . . . through the phenomenon of fragmented perception of deprivation." He explains:

> The degree to which the maldistribution of benefits of independence affected lower strata differed markedly; the Lower Congo (i.e. the Kongo area, Bas-Zaire) and Southern Katanga remained relatively affluent, whereas the heartland of the central basin, North Katanga, and Northeastern Congo were particularly affected. The sentiment of deprivation was especially acute among groups which felt themselves excluded from political power. [1967, p. 398]

As they emerged from the disorganized legislative process of 1962/63, the "provincettes" reflected no coherent set of criteria. Of the 21 provincettes, 8 were ethnically homogeneous (homogeneity being defined as "existence of a clearly dominant ethnic group"), 8 possessed party homogeneity (defined in terms of the 1960 elections and subsequent splits), and 12 possessed "administrative continuity" (defined as coincidence of provincial boundaries with those of one, or two, colonial districts (Young 1965, pp. 552-53; Verhaegen 1963, p. 4). So, although creation of new provinces was justified mainly in terms of the aspirations of ethnic groups, colonial administrative subdivisions proved more influential than ethnic boundaries in shaping the new units; the weight of Bula Matari had been felt.

There had been some expectation that the smaller provinces would be stronger than the larger ones of 1960, because they were more homogeneous. Virtually the reverse proved to be the case, for several reasons. First, creation of a large number of new governments had the effect of spreading very thin the meager resources of trained manpower. Second, as the provincettes were created, loose ends were left in the form of "contested areas" whose fate was to be settled by referendum; when the central government failed to organize these referenda, police forces and armed youth groups fought for control of the areas. Third, and probably most basic, creation of new provinces was unsatisfactory as a means of satisfying the grievances of groups that felt themselves excluded from political power and its rewards, because ethnic and regional identities are so fluid; creation of a given province typically activated subethnic or subregional rivalries, for example, between forest and savanna Tetela in Sankuru, submerged until then. In case after case, power struggles ended with the defeated side demanding division of the provincette into two still smaller units. The weakness of the provincettes and of the central government in Kinshasa was demonstrated during 1964/65, when popular insurrections led by Lumumbists spread over approximately half of the country.

The rebellions revealed clearly the cultural and psychological orientations of the mass of the Zairian population under the First Republic. Despite ideological deficiencies, the movement is best understood as an example of class conflict. In the Kwilu theater, Lumumba's former minister, Pierre Mulele, gave the "rebel" movement an ideology of watered-down Maoism:

In a country of this kind, the people are divided into two classes:
(1) the rich, the capitalists, who profit from the work of others
"like the mosquito sucks the blood of men." (2) Workers and
peasants: the poor, or the "popular masses." . . . All the
wealth of the country is in the hands of "étrangers," "foreigners,"
who can be classified in three categories: (1) Foreigners or imperialists who steal the wealth of the country. (2) Persons of the
bad government who help them steal the wealth of the country.
. . . (3) All the rest of the people who live in misery: the poor,
the peasants, the workers. [Fox, de Craemer, and Ribeaucourt
1965, pp. 95-96]

In the eastern theater, the MNC/L leadership promoted an ideology of
Lumumbism or nationalism, conceived of as a third way distinct from capitalism and from communism. Its "Catechism of the Revolutionary" began
with rather incoherent definitions of colonialism and imperialism, then asked:

5. Is the Congo independent?
    __Yes, the Congo is nominally independent since June 30,
    1960.
6. Has there been an effort to ameliorate this situation of semi-
    colonialism?
    —Yes.
7. By whom was this tentative made?
    —This tentative was made by Patrice-Emery Lumumba,
    Prime Minister of the first legal Congolese government.
8. What became of Patrice-Emery Lumumba?
    —The enemies of the Congolese people cowardly assassinated
    Patrice-Emery Lumumba.
9. Did these enemies act alone?
    —No, they used Congolese traitors to the nation.
10. Who are these traitors?
    —The principal ones, officially recognized by history, the
    United Nations, and the whole world, are 10 in number.
11. Cite them by their order of culpability.
    —Kasa-Vubu, Tshombe, Nendaka, Kandolo, Munongo, Kalon-
    dji, Bomboko, Mobutu, and Ndele. [Gérard-Libois et al.
    1965, pp. 66-67]

On the mass level, however, the ideology of the rebel movement was
rather different. Both in Kwilu and in the east, the theme of wealth (wealth
stolen, wealth to be regained) was evoked. Magico-religious power was
stressed. Mulele was said to be able to turn himself into a bird, and in the
east the rebels sang, "Forward, I shall not marry [that is, have sexual in-
tercourse], until Lumumba is resuscitated" (Verhaegen 1966, p. 126; Turner
1974, p. 201).
Given the ideological deficiencies, the targets of rebel violence provide
a more useful guide to the nature of the movement. Those killed were mainly

people connected with the postcolonial state. On occasion, however, entire ethnic groups that had sided with anti-Lumumbist parties and/or with the Kinshasa government became the targets of "rebel" violence; examples include the Mbala in Kwilu and the Lega in Kivu (Verhaegen 1966, 1969; Turner 1974).

Insurgent use of magico-religious protection contributed heavily to the rout of the Congolese National Army, as, of course, the National Army troops believed in the efficacy of such protection. A major cause of the ultimate failure of the movement was the introduction of white mercenaries to bolster the government forces, mercenaries who conversely did not believe in such magico-religious protection. In turn, President Kasavubu's threat to expel the mercenaries apparently triggered Mobutu's coup of November 1965.

PSYCHOLOGICAL AND CULTURAL
DIMENSIONS OF MOBUTU'S ZAIRE

Several apparent paradoxes characterize the psychological and cultural impact of Mobutu's rule. Considerable emphasis was placed on developing and propagating a supposedly distinctive nationalist ideology—the clouds of smoke of Halpern's metaphor—yet this effort has now been nearly abandoned. In theory, regional and ethnic sentiment, as well as class consciousness, have all been discouraged in the name of nationalism; in practice, however, they have been heightened. Depending on the point of view of the observer, one is struck either by cultural continuity or by cultural change.

This puzzling situation can be explained, in the first instance, by the characteristics of the Mobutu regime itself. It is an authoritarian regime, in the sense that Linz has defined the term, one "with limited, not responsible, political pluralism, without elaborate and guiding ideology, but with distinctive mentalities, without extensive nor intensive political mobilization, except at some points in their development, and in which a leader or occasionally a small group exercises power within formally ill-defined but actually quite predictable ones" (Linz 1964, p. 255, cited in Linz 1975, p. 264).

Mobutu has centralized power, created a single party, and fused the party with the state, creating a reasonable facsimile of the West African party-state described by Zolberg. Presumably, these actions represented both mimesis and responses to a similar situation. Whatever the relative importance of the two factors, Mobutu's party-state has been justified by an ideology similar to that of the West African party-state (as summarized in Zolberg 1966, pp. 45-46):

(1) there is a natural trend toward "unity";
(2) African societies are divided;
(3) these divisions are not to be viewed as an American thinker
(of the pluralist persuasion) might, as a healthy "pluralism,"
but rather in a negative way as "internal contradictions" . . . ;
(4) unity is manifested in support for the dominant party . . . ;

(5) the failure of unity can only stem from the actions of men who
wilfully interfere with the natural course of history.

Mobutu's version of this ideology is less coherent than Aristide Zolberg's summary, and certainly would not qualify as what Linz calls "elaborate
and guiding ideology." To the common trunk, a number of other elements
have been grafted. Mobutu "stole the clothes" or the MNC/L rebels of
1964/65 (but not those of Mulele) by adopting a number of points from their
platform, for example, nationalism as a third alternative to both capitalism
and communism. Patrice Lumumba, martyred MNC/L leader, was made a
national hero. Monuments and streets were renamed, and women given symbolic leadership posts, just as had been done during the ephemeral People's
Republic in Stanleyville (Kisangani) in 1964 (Epee, forthcoming).

Further additions were made in 1972-74 following Mobutu's visits to
China and North Korea. He adopted the Maoist titles "The Helmsman" and
"The Guide" for himself and had locations identified with significant events
in his life labeled "places of meditation."

Given the incoherence of Mobutu's ideology, labeled first "nationalism,"
then "authenticity," and finally "Mobutism," it is no wonder the population
should have felt itself enveloped in clouds of smoke. Yet, because militancy
in party affairs became a precondition for all sorts of privileges, those who
wanted to obtain the privileges had to mouth the ideology. As the party-state
intruded into more and more sectors of public life—the public administration,
the schools, the economy—it became more and more difficult to abstain from
militancy. The result was an overdeepening cynicism. (On the process in
the schools, see Schatzberg 1978).

Mobutu declared himself firmly against regionalism and tribalism and
for reinforcement of the central power (again, a borrowing from Lumumba).
The fusion of the provincettes, followed by conversion of the reunified provinces into purely administrative subdivisions of the state, deprived politicians
of ethnically and regionally defined bases. At the same time, however, Mobutu relied heavily upon people from his region of origin, Equateur. He installed a quota system at the National University so that Equateur and other
less advanced regions would be able to increase their share of graduates.
Student slang, in which Equateur became "The Holy Land" and various of its
towns "Jerusalem," "Bethlehem," and so on, indicates the reaction of a politically significant stratum to these attempts at favoritism and to the cult of
the personality in general (Tshivuadi 1974, pp. 164-67).

Mobutu's Zaire corresponds not only to Linz's model of the authoritarian
regime but also to Stanislav Andreski's "kleptocracy." Indeed, it arguably
fits Andreski's model better than any of the regimes he had in mind when he
wrote in the 1960s. It seems clear that the cultural and psychological under-
pinnings of kleptocracy are the same in Zaire as elsewhere:

Very few Africans have any deep feelings about the states to which
they belong. The ideals of impersonal service are often voiced in
deference to the higher prestige of the European countries, but

they have not been (to use a psycho-analytical term) introjected. What is regarded as dishonesty in countries well indoctrinated with political ideals, may appear as morally in order in a society where the bonds of kinship are strong and the concept of nationhood remains something very recent and artificial. [Andreski 1968, pp. 92-109]

Within the African universe, however, Zaire would appear to represent an extreme example of the situation in which "egoistic" graft prevails over "solidaristic" graft. By this distinction (borrowed from Emile Durkheim), Andreski refers to the fact that some cases seem to involve motives that are "purely selfish or at most concerned with the welfare of the nuclear family," as opposed to others "promoted primarily by the desire to help the kinsmen."

Mobutu and his immediate collaborators encourage the prevalence of graft by example (Mobutu's personal fortune allegedly is one of the world's largest), by inconsistent enforcement of the norms of "personal service" to which Andreski refers, and perhaps most basically by promoting personal insecurity.

Mobutu initially had benefited from public relief that the tremendous insecurity of 1960-65 had ended. He was able to use his confrontations with the Belgian-owned Union Minière du Haut-Katanga in 1966, and with the white mercenaries in 1967, to present himself as a nationalist. As of the early 1970s, the security and prosperity had combined to make the regime widely accepted, if not loved. In turn, the economic prosperity and the public acceptance of the regime made possible the promotion of the party-state, the cult of the personality, and a variety of "revolutionary" measures, of which the most important was Zairianization of the economy.

By 1978, in contrast, the Zairian "revolution" was in tatters. Runaway inflation and widespread shortages had severely depressed the living conditions of most Zairians. Corruption had become more extreme, driven by not just the opportunity to steal but by the necessity to steal in order to survive. Public enthusiasm for the regime was nil and repression far more evident than in previous years.

Two examples of political activity, one legal and the other illegal, underline the attitudes of the political-commercial bourgeoisie and of the peasants toward the Mobutu regime. The first concerns the political "liberalization" adopted by Mobutu after the 1977 invasion of Shaba and presumably promoted by pressure from the United States, Belgium, and other Western sources. Competitive elections were held within the single-party framework for seats on the Political Bureau and the Legislative Council; prominent among the victors were politicians (some Mobutu supporters, others opponents who seemed to want to harass him) but also businessmen whose principal motivation seems to have been the commercial advantages they hoped to secure. Both vote buying and appeals to ethnic and regional sentiments were flagrant, which is not surprising given the impossibility of presenting distinctive ideology or programs.*

The second example concerns resistance to the Mobutu regime that recently surfaced in Kwilu. A certain Kasongo, a traditional healer, set off an uprising in early 1978 that took fewer than ten lives, but that provoked army repression in which some 500 villagers were killed. The "rebels" carried machetes, bows, and spears, but believed themselves to be able to fire bullets by magic and to protect themselves from the bullets of the soldiers ("Soulèvement dit Kasongo" 1978). On the face of it, the reappearance of such a movement would seem to support the argument of Fox (1968), according to whom a traditional mentality persists and constitutes a barrier to development.

Clearly, Fox is correct concerning the form of the Kasongo movement; it represents the recurrence of a form of social action that antedates colonial rule. However, the objective of the movement was an innovation, the overthrow of the Mobutu regime. Moreover, younger and better educated Kwilu people reportedly shared the objective while rejecting the form of the movement: "We still remember too well the Mulele affair. How can one go to battle with a few bows and arrows? Our elders in the clans are really too magic, they bother us with their magic. We are no longer so naive, we did not want to go along" ("Soulèvement dit Kasongo" 1978).

Although a fully convincing demonstration would require both more evidence and more space, it seems that three factors or set of factors have shaped and are shaping the attitudes of contemporary Zairians. The first is traditional culture, that is, the culture of precolonial Zaire whether or not it conformed to a model of traditionality. Many Zairians continue to conceptualize evil and misfortune in a way that leads them to attempt to use magico-religious protection. From precolonial society, to primary resistance, to the strikes of the 1940s, to the rebellion of the 1960s, to the present—such movements are strikingly similar. Yet persistence is only one side of the coin. Change is represented by the change in the objectives of these movements.

The second factor influencing current attitudes is the nature of the incorporation of Zaire into the world capitalist economy. As a result of this incorporation, a cumulative process rather than an event, Zairians fill new economic roles; as we have seen, the various social classes possess differing degrees of class consciousness.

The third factor or set of factors that continues to affect cultural modernization is colonization and decolonization. The postcolonial Zairian party-state is both the successor to the colonial state and the instrument by which the commercial-bureaucratic bourgeoisie controls the society. Nationalism/authenticity/Mobutism is the ideology justifying this domination (Tutashinda 1974; see also Chapter 3).

---

*This passage is based on the author's interviews in Kinshasa and Lubumbashi during September–October 1978. On the 1977 election, see Daniel Van Der Steen 1978.

Ethnicity represents persistence as well as change. The element of persistence is partially attributable to traditional culture but also to the kinds of change brought about by the incorporation of Zaire into the world economy and the construction of the colonial state. Under the impact of the latter two processes, ethnic categories broadened, and Zairians acquired identification with territorial units, including the state itself, which had no precedent. They also acquired cross-cutting identities, those of social class.

The most satisfactory interpretation of ethnicity in Zaire, as elsewhere, is that of Heribert Adam, according to whom:

> Instead of reifying cultural heterogeneity as a quasi-natural state of affairs, ethnic identifications should be the result of efforts by underprivileged groups to improve their lot through collective mobilization or, conversely, the efforts of a superordinate group to preserve the privileges they enjoy by exploiting subjected groups. [1971, p. 21]

In other words, ethnic conflict, like class conflict, reflects socioeconomic change.

In the short run, the predominance of ethnicity and kleptocracy reflects insecurity generated by Zaire's peripheral position and the tactics of Mobutu. All this suggests that Fox is wrong and Halpern right, that for modernization to be possible the political situation must be conducive.

REFERENCES

Adam, Heribert. 1971. Modernizing Racial Domination. Berkeley and Los Angeles: University of California Press.

Andreski, Stanislav. 1968. The African Predicament. New York: Atherton.

Coquery-Vidrovitch, Catherine. 1969. "Recherches sur un mode de production africain." La pensée, no. 144 (April), pp. 61-78.

Dettes de guerre. 1945. Elisabethville: Editions de L'Essor du Congo.

Epee, Gambwa. Forthcoming. Ph.D. dissertation, National University of Zaire.

Fox, Renée C. 1968. "The Intelligence behind the Mask: Beliefs and Development in Contemporary Congo." Paper presented at the Eighteenth Conference on Science, Philosophy, and Religion in Their Relations the Democratic Way of Life, August.

Fox, Renée C., Willy de Craemer, and Jean-Marie Ribeaucourt. 1965. " 'The Second Independence': A Case Study of the Kwilu Rebellion in the Congo." Comparative Studies in Society and History 8:78-109.

Gérard-Libois, Jules, Jean Van Lierde et al. 1966. Congo 1965. Brussels: Centre de Recherche et d'Information Socio-Politiques.

_____. 1965. Congo 1964. Brussels: Centre de Recherche et d'Information Socio-Politiques.

Gérard-Libois, Jules, and Benoit Verhaegen. 1961. Congo 1960, vols. 1 and 2. Brussels: Centre de Recherche et d'Information Socio-Politiques.

Halpern, Manfred. 1976. "Changing Connections to Multiple Worlds: The African as Individual, Tribesman, Nationalist, Muslim, Christian, Traditionalist, Transformer and as a World Neighbor, Especially with Israel and the Arabs." In Africa: From Mystery to Maze, edited by Helen Kitchen, pp. 9-44. Boston: Lexington Books.

Jewsiewicki, Bogumil. 1974. "Histoire économique et sociale du Zaire moderne: Une conception." Lubumbashi. Mimeographed.

_____. 1972. "Notes sur l'histoire socio-économique du Congo (1880-1960)." Etudes d'histoire africaine 3:209-41.

Jewsiewicki, Bogumil, Kilolo Lema, and Jean-Luc Vellut. 1973. "Documents pour servir à l'histoire sociale du Zaire: Grèves dans le Bas Congo (Bas-Zaire) en 1945." Etudes d'histoire africaine 5:155-88.

Lefever, Ernest W. 1970. Spear and Scepter: Army, Police and Politics in Tropical Africa. Washington, D.C.: Brookings Institution.

Lemarchand, Rene. 1970. Rwanda and Burundi. London: Pall Mall Press.

_____. 1964. Political Awakening in the Belgian Congo: The Politics of Fragmentation. Berkeley and Los Angeles: University of California Press.

Lerner, Daniel. 1958. Passing of Traditional Society: Modernizing the Middle East. New York: Free Press.

Linz, Juan J. 1975. "Totalitarian and Authoritarian Regimes." In Handbook of Political Science, edited by Fred I. Greenstein and Nelson W. Polsby, vol. 3, pp. 175-411. Reading, Mass.: Addison-Wesley.

_____. 1964. "An Authoritarian Regime: The Case of Spain." In Cleavages, Ideologies, and Party Systems, edited by Erik Allard and Yrjo Littunen, pp. 291-342. Helsinki: Westermark Society.

Perinbam, B. Marie. 1977. "Home Africanus: Antiquus or Oeconomicus? Some Interpretations of African Economic History." Comparative Studies in Society and History 19, no. 2:156-78.

Schatzberg, Michael G. 1978. "Fidélité au Guide: The J.M.P.R. in Zairian Schools." Journal of Modern African Studies 16, no. 3:417-31.

"Soulèvement dit Kasongo." 1978. La vie diocésaine d'Idiofa, 2d year, no. 7 (January-April).

Tshivuadi, Katamba Kamalondo wa Kalombo. 1974. "La participation des étudiants zairois à la politique." Mémoire de licence. Lumumbashi: Political and Administrative Science, National University of Zaire.

Turner, Thomas. 1974. "Peasant Rebellion and Its Suppression in Sankuru, Zaire." Pan-African Journal 7 (Fall): 193-215.

_____. 1973. "A Century of Political Conflict in Sankuru (Congo-Zaire)." Ph.D. dissertation, University of Wisconsin.

_____. 1972. "Congo Kinshasa." In Politics of Cultural Sub-Nationalism in Africa, edited by Victor A. Olorunsola, pp. 195-283. Garden City, N.Y.: Doubleday.

Tutashinda, N. 1974. "Les mystifications de l' 'authenticité.'" La pensée, no. 175 (May-June), pp. 68-81.

Van Der Steen, Daniel. 1978. "Elections et réformes politiques au Zaire en 1977: Analyse de la composition des organes politiques." Cahiers du CEDAF, pp. 2-3.

Vansina, Jan. 1976. "L'Afrique centrale vers 1875." La conférence de géographie de 1876. Brussels: Académie Royale des Sciences d'Outre-mer.

_____. 1969. "Du reyaume kuba au territoire des Bakuba." Etudes congo-laises 12:3-54.

_____. 1965. Introduction à l'ethnographie du Congo. Leopoldville: Presse Universitaire du Congo.

Verhaegen, Benoît. 1969. Rébellions au Congo, vol. 2. Brussels: Centre de Recherche et d'Information Socio-Politiques.

_____. 1966. Rébellions au Congo, vol. 1. Brussels: Centre de Recherche et d'Information Socio-Politiques.

_____. 1963. "Présentation morphologique des nouvelles provinces." Etudes congolaises 4 (April): 1-25.

Willame, Jean-Claude. 1972. Patrimonialism and Political Change in the Congo. Stanford, Calif.: Stanford University Press.

Young, Crawford. 1967. "Congo and Uganda: A Comparative Assessment." Cahiers economiques et sociaux 3:379–400.

_____. 1965. Politics in the Congo. Princeton, N.J.: Princeton University Press.

Zolberg, Aristide R. 1966. Creating Political Order: The Party of West Africa. Chicago: Rand McNally.

PART II
ZAIRE:
THE MODERN AND
URBAN WORLDS

5

THE ADMINISTRATION OF UNDERDEVELOPMENT

David J. Gould

AN INTRODUCTION TO DISORGANIZATION THEORY

The crisis in Zaire has been amply documented by many authors. Regardless of the policy prescriptions offered, virtually all agree that Zaire is in deep trouble as it faces mounting bankruptcy, near-total breakdown of vital services, military incompetence and repression, mass impoverishment, crescendoing regime unpopularity, and increased dependence on foreign banks, other creditors, foreign technicians, and foreign soldiers. While there is agreement as to the symptoms of the Zairian crisis, however, there is little consensus on the causes. Yet this question is a vital one because a poor diagnosis of the causes of the crisis can lead to policy prescriptions that may exacerbate rather than solve the underlying problems. It is therefore important to attempt to determine the first causes of the crisis in Zaire (Young 1978; Gran 1978).

A number of the foreign donors of the present government of Zaire have conducted their own analyses of the crisis and thereupon proposed institutional reforms as a solution, stressing administrative and managerial modernization. Indeed, their analyses pinpoint mismanagement as one of the major causes, if not _the_ major cause, of the crisis. In a recent World Bank report, the problems of "waste and mismanagement of public funds" were singled out for stigmatization (IBRD 1977). Further, the International Bank for Reconstruction and Development (IBRD) was even more explicit in the mismanagement diagnosis:

> Up to [1974] the neglect and decline of agriculture, unplanned investment, lack of consistency in budget management and uncontrolled external borrowing have contributed to the mounting difficulties. The Zairianization and nationalization measures of 1973-1974, although aimed at legitimate objectives, were ill-conceived and poorly implemented. These measures only worsened one constraint on economic development which perennially plagued Zaire's

economy; the weakness of management structures. [IBRD 1977, p. 1]

This concern with mismanagement found its policy expression in recommendations made part of the various aid package conditions from 1976 on, that institutional reforms take place within the Zairian government. These were recommendations that the Zairian government, in its increasingly dependent stance of virtual beggar in the international lending marketplace, could ignore at its peril, although, as shall be seen below, the institutional reforms adopted were most often superficial facades (Kabwit 1978). Predictably, the emphasis on mismanagement was taken up by the Zairian government. In its 1976 request for UN Development Program assistance, the government stated its position as follows:

The [Zairian government] authorities hold that the major constraint to economic growth is the lack of trained technicians and top managers. (Toutefois, les autorités estiment que ce qui a le plus friené l'accroissement économique est le manque de cadres techniques, de direction et de gestion.) [Nations Unies 1976, p. 3]

President Mobutu reflected the "reformist" emphasis on management improvement when, in his November 25, 1977, speech he called for "l'instauration du management dans l'ensemble de l'appareil de l'état." This particular excerpt is now rebroadcast on Zairian television daily preceding the evening news program.

It would be foolish indeed to discount the importance of management in any country. Among Zaire's problems one would certainly have to include mismanagement. Indeed, for a long time the problems of public administration were neglected by specialists in development, and so any interest in management is to be welcomed. An excessive emphasis on mismanagement, however, founded as it is on the assumption that management reforms will lead to development, raises two serious questions:

1. Insofar as public administration is, in its structures, behavior, and impact, largely the reflection and expression of the external environment that surrounds it, to what extent can a cure applied only to the administrative apparatus and not to its external environment heal the sickness? To the extent that the external environment fosters underdevelopment, should one not call its public bureaucracy an "underdevelopment administration" rather than a "development administration?"

2. Insofar as the state apparatus has been "privatized," that is, taken over and systematically misused by a clique of national leaders so as to enrich themselves, would management improvement of such a system not amount to making "underdevelopment administration" more efficient, therefore contributing to the strengthening of underdevelopment?

This chapter seeks to demonstrate the futility of mismanagement curing reforms. To place the problem of management in its proper context, one must take into account the external environmental forces pressing for the conversion of the public bureaucracy into a tool for self-enrichment on the part of the bureaucratic bourgeoisie. For public administration is most interesting for the student of underdevelopment in countries such as Zaire in that it is a significant arena in which is played out a vital drama: the ongoing pillage of the state's resources by a small class of people with privileged access to the levers of bureaucratic power. The key to understanding this phenomenon lies in the development of an analytical framework that systematically relates public administration to its external environment.

"Mismanagement" in Zaire and elsewhere is a phenomenon that is readily apparent. Even the casual observer cannot fail to notice the apparently irrational series of decisions and practices within the administrative system, such as the "Zairianization" and nationalization measures singled out in the World Bank document quoted earlier. Later in this chapter it will be shown how the Zairianization, radicalization, and retrocession measures actually illustrate not so much mismanagement but the pursuit by a ruling class, in command of bureaucratic power, of an internally rational logic designed to maximize its own wealth. Moreover, management is part of the more or less conscious ruling strategy of those in control of the state apparatus. In an earlier study, this administrative strategy was referred to as "disorganization theory":

> What appears as disorganization may be only apparent chaos and disorder. Beneath the surface there may be an underlying rationality, organization, pursuit of a sensible purpose on the part of a group or class [composed] of a relatively few individuals to the detriment of the vast majority of the population. The administrative system [may represent] an important forum and tool in the class formation process, providing aspirants to the elite a chance to acquire, through astutely larcenous exploitation of their administrative position, the money necessary to rise. Such is, in our view, the case of Zairian [public bureaucratic] organizations. They represent <u>organized disorganization</u>: the resultant disorder and confusion are such only to those on the outside. The apparent chaos and anarchy mask a finely tuned instrument permitting those in control to capture the administration and the booty to which it gives access—and to hold it more securely, at the expense of the majority and hence of development. [Gould 1977b, p. 3]

Thus, according to this analysis, mismanagement should not necessarily be perceived as a constraint to development but rather as a symptom of underdevelopment. Viewing it as a constraint actually masks reality to the extent that mismanagement may be part of a conscious self-enrichment strategy on the part of those in control of the public bureaucracy. Adhering to such a view raises serious methodological questions and thus casts doubt on the approach used by those who do so. It is no more possible to change the fundamental direction of a society by instituting management reforms than it is to treat a festering, cancerous disease by the application of a Band-Aid.

Zaire appears to be suffering from such a disease: underdevelopment. Management improvement in such a context is not even a Band-Aid; it is tantamount to cancer enhancement. For public administration is playing an assigned role in the underdevelopment process, a particularly important one given the unique responsibility of the state and its bureaucratic apparatus in the process of extraction of resources and distribution of services. Put somewhat crudely, helping a group of people who manipulate the state structure to serve their own personal and class goals to be more "efficient" in their management is making the underlying problem worse rather than solving it.

THE ELEMENTS OF THE ADMINISTRATIVE SYSTEM

The analytical framework that best represents public administration and the dialectical relationship it has with society is a systems model, but not a mechanistic version thereof. What follows is a sketch of this theoretical approach and its application to public administration. Its component concepts include inputs, withinputs, outputs, and feedback. Applied to Zaire, these concepts take on the following colorations.

The inputs from the external environment include the demands, resources, and supports resulting from the ownership pattern of the economy, the social class configuration based thereon, the political power structure reflecting economic and social disparities, the dominant ideology, and the cultural and psychological forces characteristic of the society in question. The external environment of the administrative system consists of the dominant economic, social, political, ideological, and cultural forces in society that mobilize and articulate their demands upon the administrative system, make resources available in line with their needs and priorities, and offer support for specific policies and programs and administrative structures and behaviors (that is, those most attuned to their needs) and oppose policies and programs and administrative approaches and solutions that would threaten their interests.

The economic organization of society is the single most important variable in the external environment. It will determine in significant measure the social class stratification patterns in the society, the nature of the state, including the interests the state serves and its political power relationships, the dominant ideology, and even the cultural-psychological factors that hold sway. These forces interact with the internal environment of administration via demands, resources, and supports.

Withinputs refer to the internal environment of the administrative system, to its administrative process, per se. Here we refer to the mechanism by which the internal apparatus of the administrative system receives inputs from the external environment and converts them into outputs designed to serve that external environment. Withinputs consist of formal and informal

organizational structures, decisional procedures, and administrators' perceived class position in society and their personal attitudes and predilections.
Withinputs are in constant interaction with the external environment but develop increasingly a life of their own.

The formal structure of an organization is what appears on an organization chart. It is the hierarchical relationship that ties the various individuals
and units of an administrative system together, that establishes their respective duties and mutual relationship. Informal structure refers to the individual and group commitments within an organization or administrative unit that
is often called "the human side" of organizations, that is, how they behave
in practice. The two may be in conflict to the extent that the informal structure, that is, reality, reflects different norms and behaviors than those prescribed in the formal structure.

A common error of development assistance professionals is to ignore
the informal structure, and to act as though changes in the formal structure
(for example, promulgation of a new constitution or of an administrative reform) reflect real changes in behavior, when in fact often they do not. The
very same is true of decisional rules. There is often a conflict between the
prescribed decisional process within a given administrative structure, on the
one hand, and the "rules of the game," on the other.

An example of the conflict between formal decisional rules and the rules
of the game is the attempt to install rational, management-oriented, decision-
making structures into a public administrative system without taking the rules
of the game into account. This is certainly the case in countries such as
Zaire today, in which foreign donors insist, and national leadership promises,
that management will be the watchword and new decisional premise.

Management science, following the Scientific Management tradition,
aims at complete rationality in decision making and assumes that this is possible, through calculus, computers, and optimism about human nature. Other
authors indicate that complete rationality is limited by political bargaining
(Wildavsky and Lindblom) or by human psychology (Simon), but they still use
the rationality concept as an ideal type against which to measure deviations.
The "institution-building" approach in development administration is very
much in this tradition.

Still others, however, reject rationality as a standard, positing instead
that an inegalitarian society will forward external environmental inputs into
the internal environment of administrative systems, such that rationality will
take on a special meaning. It will not necessarily be fairness, justice, or
equality; it will be satisfying the demands of those standing to benefit from
continued structured inequality. The term underlined multirationality usefully refers to
the self-interest and class interests being pursued by administrators as opposed to the formal, public purposes of the administrative system. What
they are doing is not irrational. It is simply done in conformity to another
rationality, one linked to class, privilege, and profiteering (Gould 1977b).

Outputs to the external environment consist of the decisions, policies,
and programs achieved by the administrative system and that constitute the
impact of the internal environment on the external environment. In practice,

outputs consist of the concrete goods and services delivered to the various publics of the administrative system. They include policies (what governments choose to do or not to do in given areas of public service) and performance (the quality of the work actually produced by administrative systems).

The analyst of administrative systems will expect that its outputs will reflect systematic bias in favor of those groups that dominate society economically, socially, politically, and ideologically (inputs) and that consequently and served above all by the structure and decisional rules of the administrative system (withinputs). Outputs, in other words, reflect the configuration of society and represent the public bureaucracy's efforts to satisfy the dominant forces in its external environment by concretely favoring them in the distribution of collective goods controlled by the bureaucracy.

Feedback is the mechanism permitting the external environment to regulate the outputs of the system so as to make sure that they truly reflect the desiderata of the publics in question. Where there is deviance noted at the feedback stage, the reaction this perceived deviance provides may lead to new inputs, and the cycle continues. Feedback is the control mechanism by which the external environment reacts to the administrative system's outputs. It constitutes the reaction and the safety-valve means of regulating the outputs of a system, insofar as dissatisfaction among influential publics may result in new inputs demanding modifications and adjustments in the administrative system's policies and programs.

The analytical framework as a whole makes distinctions among inputs, withinputs, outputs, and feedback for the purpose of highlighting their main features. In reality, however, these distinctions are not at all clear-cut. One of the weaknesses of the classical or Eastonian systems theory that the analytical model employed here attempts to overcome is precisely the mechanistic implication, if not assumption, that the different levels involve distinctly different actors and processes. In fact, the dialectical, that is, permanently interacting, character of the relationship among the component parts of the administrative system often makes their differentiation problematic.

The presence among "withinputting" actors—at the level of the public bureaucracy's structures, behaviors, and indeed officials—of "inputting" actors who are strictly speaking "external environmental" forces, should not by any means confuse us, however. We should not be surprised in finding, for example, that inputs from the external environment have "colonized" the withinputs and established a permanent presence there such that the top actors and decision makers within the public bureaucracy are in fact themselves the leading property owners in a given society. Likewise, we should not be particularly surprised to find that the most salient feedback in a given administrative system comes not from the majority of a population, which may well be mute through departicipation and repression, but rather from withinputting actors high up in the bureaucracy itself. Nor indeed should we be surprised by finding that the same people act at virtually every level of the administrative system to protect their interests.

APPLICATIONS OF THE ANALYTICAL
FRAMEWORK TO ZAIRE

In this section the framework set out in the preceding section will be applied in order to demonstrate its efficacy and to gain useful insights into the relationship between public administration and underdevelopment in Zaire. In particular, it shall be shown that a mismanagement-oriented approach is inadequate to deal with the Zairian and that only a more global approach, focusing on the dynamic relationship linking the Mobutu regime and its public bureaucracy, will lead the way to appropriate solutions. First, some generalizations will be made about the four component concepts of the analytical framework in their Zairian applications and then three illustrative cases will be cited.

It will be recalled that inputs from the external environment constitute the dominant economic, social, political, ideological, and cultural forces in society, which make up the chief pressures on the administrative system and at once the chief beneficiaries of its redistributive action. In Zaire, ample studies have documented the overwhelming domination in the country by what Michael Schatzberg (1978) calls "the members of the politico-commercial bourgeoisie who control the State" (p. 481). Linkage between this class, which some have called the "bureaucratic bourgeoisie," and foreign powers (states and multinational corporations) has likewise been documented (Kamitatu-Massamba 1977).

The external environment of public administration in Zaire is made up of many forces, including ethnic and cultural factors, which influence the structures, processes, and behavior of public bureaucracy. Class is singled out over and against such other factors partly because class is a useful illustration of inputting external forces but also because it is a dominant factor. In this sense, the external environment of public administration in Zaire is seen as the effort of a dominant class to maintain and indeed enhance its status and wealth, using its privileged positions at the commanding heights of the state apparatus of which the bureaucracy is the centerpiece.

Following is a brief summary of the main social classes in Zaire today:

Bureaucratic bourgeoisie: This is the dominant ruling class in Zaire today, characterized by its command of the levers of bureaucratic power in the state apparatus and of the related parastatal and state-licensed companies, including the army, the party, and the administration. This class may be subdivided (following Jean Rymenam [1977]) into (1) the presidential clique (some 50-odd of the president's most trusted kinsmen, occupying the most sensitive and lucrative positions, such as head of the Judiciary Council, Secret Police, Interior Ministry, President's Office, and so on) and (2) the presidential brotherhood (a few hundred elite representing every major tribe and holding); after the clique, the next most lucrative and prestigious positions in the bureaucracy. As a class, the bureaucratic bourgeoisie owes its existence to past and continued foreign support.

Petite bourgeoisie: This is the chief "helper class," composed of thousands of middle-level officials, university teachers, graduates, and, in some cases, students, struggling to break into the "brotherhood." While waiting in the wings, they may enjoy more or less notable access to corruption. Their ranks also include businessmen. This class's support for the regime is critical, which is why its privileges, while inferior to those of the bureaucratic bourgeoisie, are still maintained so as to avoid disaffection and opposition.

The masses: The overwhelming majority of the Zairian population live without the privileges of either the bureaucratic or the petite bourgeoisie and thus live very badly, be they the severely underpaid urban or rural workers and their families or the lumpenproletariat, unemployed and beginning to constitute an increasingly dangerous element for regime stability in the large cities.

The class that wins the battle for control of the state apparatus, which controls the bureaucracy and the "goodies" this gives access to, will dominate society, with the secondary help of the petite bourgeoisie, cutting the masses out of the distribution of the benefits available. No observer captured the essence of the contemporary Zairian class stratification pattern better than J. Ph. Peemans (1975):

> The new "partnership" between the State and foreign capital is no longer the same as that which prevailed during the chaotic period of 1960–65. Today decisions are taken neither by the members of the administration nor even by specialized ministries, but rather by a small group of advisers and top officials gravitating around the Office of the President. They are the key economic decision-makers. A veritable political class is forming around this "base." One may indeed speak of two levels in the Zairian state structure today: a lower level which constitutes the refuge of the petty bourgeoisie and which has lost much of its privileges and economic status. As in the past, this level is characterized by inefficiency, corruption and overstaffing. The upper level is made up of those segments of the President's Office and those ministries which truly have decision-making authority. . . . Through its control of the state apparatus, this class is able to direct the process of capitalist accumulation and to determine the conditions of its relationship with the world system. Use of State power is the means used by members of this class to insert themselves in the structures of capitalist property, not only as administrators of state or mixed enterprises but also as individuals with the high income that comes with the lofty positions they hold. [P. 519]

The withinputs, it will be recalled, are the internal environment of the administrative system. These are the bureaucratic structures and decisional rules (formal and informal) and the class position and attitudes of the civil servants. In the Zairian case, what is most notable about the administrative structure and behavior is the increased absorption of the administration into the party, the two having been fused by the administrative reforms of 1972 and 1975 (Mpinga-Kassenda and Gould 1975).

Another significant feature of the Zairian case is the increased privatization of the state apparatus. The ruling bureaucratic bourgeoisie's control of the administrative structure is used so as to consolidate the class members' individual, and above all their class, interests. Whereas the formal decisional rules proscribe even suggesting, let alone receiving, bribes or any work outside one's bureaucratic functions, in practice, the watchword is yibana mayele.* Nobody has characterized the operative decisional rules better than one of Mobutu's chief lieutenants, long-time Interior Minister Engulu (cited in Thomas Callaghy 1976):

> Most administrators treat their charges as conquering occupiers, treating visitors as badly as the Belgians treated natives. Abuses proliferate misuse of official vehicles, illegal sale of gasoline, and oil and government property, poaching and illicit sale of ivory, etc. . . . It is well-known that certain administrative officials spend more time taking care of their businesses than on the job. [P. 20]

At the level of technique, earlier research (Gould 1978c) documented over 20 major corruptive techniques used at every level of the Zairian public bureaucracy. These illegalities may be outlined in the following illustrative, rather than exhaustive, catalog. Corruption in the routine course of government business includes bribes paid to have compromising documents removed from files, fraudulent use of official stationery, payment for office visits, payment for letters of recommendation, kickbacks for hiring, permanent kickbacks (no-fault bribes), phony travel documents and official travel-related peccadilloes, misuse of official housing, two salaries and neglect of public service for outside business, and embezzlement. Corruption in the exercise of substantive government programs takes many additional specific forms: false bills, income tax fraud, excise tax fraud, import tax fraud, business quota fraud, export tax fraud, tax stamp fraud, postal fraud, court tampering, and military and police shakedowns.

The outputs of the administrative system constitute its decisions, policies, and programs and the resulting goods and services that the internal administrative environment provides to the various publics in the administrative system's external environment. The flow of benefits distribution (outputs) is generally congruent with the origins of inputs from the external environment and with the patterns by which external environmental inputs are converted within the internal environment/administrative process (withinputs). The overall impact of public administration on society is underdevelopmen-

---

*In his May 20, 1976, public meeting, the president declared: "If you want to steal, steal a little carefully in a nice way. But if you steal too much to become rich overnight, you'll be caught."

talist. This can be shown (and will, on an illustrative basis, in the next section) virtually policy by policy. The administrative system serves the bureaucratic bourgeoisie.

If public policy making can be defined as the process by which governments choose to do or not to do certain things, then Zairian policy making has involved consistent "public choice" in favor of systematic distribution and redistribution of the nation's wealth to a small class of policy makers. In practice, this has meant a series of decisions (be their subject investment policy, administrative or management reforms, or nationalization of businesses) that systematically in their application favor the few over the many. While a small few benefit (using their privileged position in the bureaucracy to get richer), the vast majority of the Zairian population is not uplifted, assisted, enriched, or "developed," but rather peripheralized, repressed, impoverished, and "underdeveloped." Furthermore, while the gap between rich and poor widens, as a result of the self-serving use of the bureaucracy by the ruling bourgeoisie, the country's general dependence on the regime's Western investors, creditors, and praetorian protectors grows. Instead of the management of social change, there is the stewardship of penury, the management of mass discontent, the logic of repression.

Finally, feedback is the control mechanism by which the external environment reacts to the administrative system's outputs and, by its reactions and promises of support or opposition, brings about adjustments in line with its interests. In the Zairian case there are two significant kinds of feedback: the reaction of the population to its desperate impoverishment (for example, the Shaba I and II rebellions, the January 1978 Idiofa uprising, the March 1978 attempted coup), which in turn produces escalating repression ("the stick") alternative with promise of reforms ("carrots), and the reaction of the dominant class, domestically and internationally, when the "carrots" offered to calm mass discontent seem to threaten the privileged and ruling elite's privileges.

In the cases examined below, analysis is made of the extent to which the forces dominating the external environment of the Zairian public administrative system influence its structures and decisional rules in order to derive maximum benefit from its public policies. The three cases are the centralization of salary administration for teachers, the Zairianization Measures of 1973, and the so-called institutional reforms of 1977 and 1978.

CENTRALIZATION OF SALARIES

Since the late 1960s, and as part of the recentralization process central to President Mobutu's ruling strategy, salary lists are established in Kinshasa by computer for all 300,000 government civil servants serving everywhere in the republic. Some observers saw in this measure an example of modernization and management improvement, because, after all, computers are much more efficient than hand-prepared or typewritten lists. However, even a superficial analysis of the institution of computers in the salary centralization process suggests that this modern management technique has actually facilitated greater consolidation of class interests, via centrally controlled corruption on a mass, computerized scale, than would otherwise have been possible.

Centralized computerization has enabled the introduction of thousands of fictitious names. In a process described elsewhere (Gould 1978c), each transaction involves a multiplicity of steps, each one requiring palm greasing and substantial corruption. These steps include, at the microlevel, being placed on the computerized list (le listing), having one's pay slip (accréditif) printed up automatically (la mécanisation), and having one's pay include up to 24 months' backpay (rappel); and, at the macrolevel, various kinds of bureaucratic corruption ranging from traffic de rappels (bribery to get all or part of backpayments) to tripotage dans le reliquat (sharing of the difference between the amount sent out for all employees, real and fictitious, and the actual salaries paid to real employees).

At the input stage, the demands that were given attention in the decision to centralize were both overt and covert. The open, overt demands were from outraged payees, for the most part disgruntled because long-unpaid or irregularly paid teachers and civil servants in the provinces saw in computerization a modern management technique that would cut down on corruption. Such demands were in fact negative feedback to the precomputer salary administration policy, which had resulted in widespread fraud and manipulation of the typewritten pay lists involving ripoffs of legitimate payees. The covert demand came from those at the top, who, in proposing this technique, saw that they would be able to use their commanding-heights position to be the chief beneficiaries of the measure, at the continued expense of the outraged payees below.

At the withinput level, the centralization/computerization decision led to structures and techniques that on the surface appeared rational, but that in fact served the "rationality" of the bureaucratic bourgeoisie. Privatizing the state apparatus, top officials were able more efficiently than before to suck more and more money out of the system.

The output of the computerization policy has certainly been reinforcement of underdevelopment. Not only does the gap between rich and poor grow, but also computers provide a much more stable and ideologically unassailable technique for the bureaucratic bourgeoisie to increase its domination at the expense of the victims of computer-related fraud. For the bureaucratic bourgeoisie has acquired and turned to its own use, as was inevitable, the modern management technique ostensibly designed to modernize the country.

That this underdevelopmentalist policy is not without costs can be seen, however, in two incidents illustrating feedback. In one case, a serious student disturbance at the Lubumbashi University campus in July 1974, hundreds of students found their generalized grievances seriously aggravated by the "computer error" by which authorities had deducted "obligatory savings" from their monthly scholarship payments. Thus the misuse of modern information technology contributed to the blowup in which students actually burned two university vehicles.

In another, at the same campus in June 1977, graduate assistants actually went on strike for a few weeks to protest a series of accumulated grievances, including the fact that for several years the computer had failed to include in their monthly paychecks the housing allowances to which they were theoretically due. Here the feedback was dangerous to the regime precisely because what was attacked was not the computer but rather, indirectly, the strategy of the bureaucratic bourgeoisie of manipulating the computer (as it uses every other possible withinput) to increase its capacity to use the administrative system as a privatized tool for its own self-aggrandizement at the expense of other strata in society.

ZAIRIANIZATION

Reference has already been made to the "economic independence" measures of November 30, 1973, by which President Mobutu confiscated small and medium-sized wholesale and retail businesses, small factories, farms, and plantations from Europeans, many of whom had been in the country since independence, handing them over to Zairian "acquirers." These measures had been authorized by a series of laws passed on January 5, 1973, foreshadowing nationalization of certain business sectors. Practically overnight, some 2,000 Zairians became beneficiaries, in some cases millionaires. These measures were followed 13 months later by "radicalization" measures designed to take over slightly larger businesses. In 1975, "stabilization committees" were established to deal with the disruptive economic effects of the measures, and in 1976 "retrocession" was decreed. By 1977, most former owners had taken their businesses back (Kannyo 1979; Gould 1978a; Gould and Mwana-Elas 1979).

Applying the analytical framework to the above case, one can see that it helps to understand the relationship between the public administrative system that carried out these decisions and the external environment that influenced it.

The external environmental inputs in the Zairianization and radicalization decisions involve the demands President Mobutu felt he had to satisfy emanating from the class of people whose support had helped him come to, and stay in, power, and whose continuing loyalty he needed. As indicated earlier, "Mobutu's continuous giving top administrators access to corruption is . . . vital to his success and . . . survival."

The loyalty of this class had to be constantly bought by money or access to money. While tremendous amounts of money could be stolen from within the bureaucracy (Gould 1977b, 1978a), even more money was available from the "gold mines" that constituted the businesses and farms that were until 1973 owned by foreigners. Thus greed led top lieutenants—in the party, bureaucracy, and army—to push for these businesses. Overconfidence (buoyed by high copper prices, diplomatic "victories" in China and in the Arab world, and continued loans from the West), and perhaps a measure of desperation (these people could be dangerous if they were not satisfied), led President Mobutu to reach the decision.

Those in the commanding heights of the state apparatus simply used their influence to bring about decisions favorable to their personal interests. At the same time, a residual fear of the opposition on the part of the masses, who were getting nothing from these measures except the symbolic lift of seeing blacks instead of whites running businesses, would require that the measures be given an ideological coloration of nationalism. They would thus be so presented. This was the cover story.

The withinputs for the Zairianization/radicalization measures involve the decision itself and administrative structures and decisional rules used to carry them out and include the class attitudes and biases of civil servants charged with their implementation. Thus it illustrates the responsiveness of the internal administrative process to the external environmental inputs. In fact, clearly seen is the dominance of the external environment at the within-put level insofar as the uppermost actors and decision makers within the public bureaucracy are in fact themselves among the economically dominant class in society; thus chief inputters and withinputters are in this sense virtually identical.

The implementation of the measures was handled through the Ministries of Commerce and Agriculture, with the active participation of the regional commissioners and the Office of the President. The announced decisional rule was that the criteria for attribution were "party militantism and competence," but in fact the second of these criteria was purely incidental. The rule of thumb followed was the higher one's actual or ascribed position in the country's political-administrative bureaucracy, the larger one's "acquisitions." An earlier paper (Gould 1978a) summed this up, with extensive data support from the Shaba region:

> Who were the Zairian owners? For the most part, they were the members of the political-administrative bourgeoisie, high government officials or their "stand-in" friends or relatives. Among the largest acquéreurs in Lubumbashi, for example, were the regional commissioner and his five closest collaborators, a pattern that seems to have been followed in other regions as well. . . . Since regional commissioners are barred from serving in their native regions, reciprocal arrangements were made enabling them to acquire businesses in each others' bailiwick. Thus an assistant regional commissioner in Shaba was given businesses in his home region of Haut-Zaïre, and the regional commissioner in Haut-Zaïre was allowed to acquire in both Haut-Zaïre and his home region of Kivu. The attrition decision thus gave the political-administrative bourgeoisie an opportunity to absorb the commercial bourgeoisie by substantially "replacing" the foreigners controlling small and medium-size businesses. [P. 59]

Table 5.1 illustrates the self-serving nature of the Zairianization Measures, clearly showing that the top beneficiaries of the measures in one important region of the country, Shaba, were virtually identical with the top leadership of the ruling bureaucratic bourgeoisie.

TABLE 5.1

Zairianization/Retrocession in Lubumbashi

Rank	Largest Businesses in Lubumbashi*		
	Old Business	Type	Retroceded as of May 1977
Regional commissioner	Soco	Wholesale	Yes
	Hasson	Wholesale	Yes
	Mercado	Wholesale	No
	Boutique France	Retail luxury (lost)	Lost previously
Director, Executive Office of President	V.A.P.	Bakery	Lost previously
Bureau Politique, member and state commissioner	Covema	Hardware	Arrangement
	Mobiza	Furniture	n.a.
State commissioner for orientation	Marberie du Shaba	Quarry	Arrangement
Assistant regional commissioner	Keshav Vital	Food	Yes
Subregional commissioner	Bernstein	Jewelry	No
Exambassador	Angevan	Wholesale	No, but paid
State commissioner for justice	Franco	Wholesale	Yes
18 congressmen	18 businesses	Wholesale and retail	13/18
Regional military commander	Tarica	Wholesale	n.a.
	Menasche Velo	Bicycles	Yes
Assistant military commander	—	—	—
Retired general	Alimenza	Wholesale	n.a.
Retired general	Maessart	Retail	n.a.
Leading company director	Vendome	Boutique	n.a.
	DeReusch	Jewelry	n.a.
Leading company director	Danon	Wholesale	n.a.
	Schlitz	Spare parts	n.a.

Position	Business	Type	Returned*
Air Zaire pilot	Sporville	Menswear	n.a.
Tribal chief	Sideris	Hardware	n.a.
Brother of tribal chief	N. Stanzos	Retail	n.a.
Assistant tribal chief	—	—	—
Vice-chancellor, university	P. Stanzos	Bakery	Yes
Editor, newspaper	Mme. Toilette	Womenswear	Yes
	Radio Service	Radio	n.a.
	Maison du Disque	Records	n.a.
Editor, newspaper	Atadji, Paraytos	Wholesale	n.a.
Established businessman	Levico	Wholesale	n.a.
	Bata	Wholesale	Arrangement
Bank director	—	Retail	n.a.
Director, CND	Deftersos	Wholesale	n.a.
Exminister	Piesauto	Body shop	n.a.
Exminister	Jeanmaza	Supermarket	n.a.
Exminister	Blackwood/Hodge	—	n.a.
President, Journalists Association	—	Wholesale	n.a.
Exmayor, subregion: head, JMPR, region, and the like	Selected bars and retail shops	—	n.a.

n.a. = not available

*Distributed under Zairianization Measures of November 30, 1973, and returned to former (European) owners under retrocession, status as of May 1977.

Source: David J. Gould, "Disorganization Theory and Underdevelopment Administration: Local 'Organization' in the Framework of Zairian National 'Development'" (Paper presented at the African and Latin American Studies Association Annual Meeting, Houston, November 1977), pp. 60–61.

At the lower end of the scale, the least desirable businesses were given by the administration to the middle-level officials, another illustration of the self-serving behavior reproducing at the middle level what was done in spades at the commanding heights. In this respect, the beneficiaries of the measures followed the force lines of the Zairian ruling class referred to earlier, as developed by Rymenam (1977):

The presidential clique: Linked to the president by ties of blood and land, these trusted kinsmen can do no wrong and occupy the sensitive and lucrative positions. Generally incompetent and completely corrupt, they are linked closely to the president. They include Kengo, Litho, Seti, Mokolo, Engulu, Bokana, Ileo, Muleka, and Bumba.* They are among the wealthiest people in the country and they were among the chief beneficiaries of the measures.

The presidential brotherhood: This is a thin layer of a few hundred elite from every major area and tribe who occupy the top political-administrative posts in the country. While those from the president's tribe and region are favored more than others, there is room here for politicians and "technocratic" intellectuals from the university whose allegiance the president buys with promises of money and power. Unlike the previous category, nothing is permanent here, but the possibilities for money and access to graft are virtually limitless. The president is aware, through an elaborate network of informants, of virtually all corruption at this level, but tolerates, encourages, and virtually requires it of his appointees, holding it in effect over his top officeholders' heads, thus creating a form of blackmail. These individuals were major beneficiaries of the Zairianization Measures. A good example is the then regional commissioner of Shaba, who was able to "acquire" three of the most profitable businesses in Lubumbashi, requiring a Z 50,000 monthly kickback from the former owners to continue operating the businesses as "managers."

Aspirant bourgeoisie: This category includes thousands of middle-level officials, lower administrators, and university graduates and professors. While they cannot steal with impunity, they often have notable access to corruption, and with the proper support they can become wealthy. Thus, among the businesses acquired in Kivu and Shaba were retail shops by a university campus budget director and a subregional chef de bureau.

The outputs of the measures can be seen on two levels. In terms of distribution and redistribution of resources, the state apparatus' new-found

---

*One should also include the late Mme. Mobutu in this list. Fabulously wealthy even before the measures, she became even richer because of them, notably through her control, as sole co-owner with her husband, of the CELZA plantation empire covering virtually the entire country (including the most productive land). The CELZA empire is documented, with photostatic copies of legal papers in Monguya-Mbenge (1977).

control of the businesses in question was immediately translated in their distribution to those at the top of the bureaucratic structure. Thus the chief beneficiaries were the chief administrative decision makers, starting with the president himself. The losers were all of those who did not "acquire"; they lost both symbolically, because there had not been enough to go around for them, and economically, because the economic situation worsened, and the measures and their beneficiaries were blamed for shortage of goods and dramatically higher prices. The negative reaction and negative feedback on the part of the Zairian population were reflected not only in sullenness and threatened legitimacy but also in everyday language. Acquéreur (beneficiary of the measures) and Wabenzi (the tribe of people who drive Mercedes Benz, that is, further beneficiaries of the measures and those favored by the regime in general) became terms of opprobrium and even ridicule, which served to highlight and reinforce the inegalitarian impact of the measures.

In addition, as indicated in the World Bank quotation earlier in this chapter, foreigners were dismayed by the Zairianization Measures (which showed mismanagement and poor prioritizing by the elite) and alarmed by radicalization, in which Mobutu was striking close to their interests. They weighed in with strong recommendations to mitigate the measures' impact, which led to stabilization and retrocession (as well as, later on, devaluation and reforms). The underdevelopmental impact led to feedback—from powerful outside forces and from the Zairian population—which brought about a revision of the decision.

THE PHONY REFORMS OF 1977/78

On July 1, 1977, and subsequently, the president announced "sweeping new reforms." They included the creation of the position of prime minister, the reinvigoration of the Planning Ministry, the creation of a Rural Development Ministry and later of new offices for marketing agricultural produce, the shaping of a new constitution calling for election of some Political Bureau members and all Legislative Council members, the promise of administrative decentralization, the institution of a parliamentary question period, and the appointment of European technicians to "vital" positions within the Bank of Zaire and the Customs Service. These reforms may be understood better by applying the analytical framework to them.

The inputs to the decisions to institute reforms clearly came from exogenous and endogenous pressures. The West had become concerned with the Mobutu regime's ability to make "rational" decisions and to maintain a climate in which Western investments and indeed the regime's own security would be safeguarded. As the disastrous consequences of the Zairianization decisions became clear and the price of copper fell in 1974, Western advice to "reform" became more persistent. U.S. Ambassador Deane Hinton's expulsion by Mobutu in June 1975, on the pretext of an alleged CIA plot, was understood to be rather a reflection of Mobutu's displeasure at being told too insistently that he must reform. In March 1976 he devalued the zaire, something he had said he would never do. And, after Shaba I, Mobutu announced and subsequently carried out certain reform measures.

A January 1978 U.S. State Department colloquium on Zaire revealed that it was U.S. government policy to achieve concert of policy with other governments that had invested heavily in Zaire, along with the 126 creditor banks and multinational corporations to which Zaire owed money, with a view toward "not breaking ranks." Working through such agencies as the World Bank and the International Monetary Fund, these foreign powers could maintain a united front and impose reforms on Mobutu. In Peemans' terms, this pressure was that of foreign capital on the Zairian ruling class. In addition, Shaba I revealed not only to the world but also to the Zairian ruling class that its hold on Shaba, and on the other parts of the country that had seemed to welcome the "invaders," was shaky. Disillusionment with the regime and its accomplishments, particularly in the economic sphere, was blatantly widespread. Thus came about the 1977-78 political-administrative reforms.

In terms of inputs therefore, it can be said that the ruling class of Zaire, the bureaucratic bourgeoisie, underwent mounting pressure to adopt institutional reforms from both exogenous forces (Western governments, banks, multilateral agencies, and multinational corporations) and endogenous forces (pressure from the petite bourgeoisie and the masses within Zaire, sparked by the fear of widespread rebellion after Shaba I).

At the level of withinputs, the reforms themselves involved apparent modifications in both administrative structures and in decisional rules. The President's Office was downgraded, and the Executive Council was given new importance, with two new ministries and a prime minister. Political Bureau members and urban zone commissioners were to be elected. The Legislative Council was to have the power to question cabinet ministers. Public administration was to be decentralized.

However, although the formal structures and decisional rules changed, the informal structures and the rules of the game did not. The two new ministries (Planning and Rural Development) experienced a severe "identity crisis." Rural Development began with an imprecise mission, placing it on a collision course with the Agriculture Ministry.* Planning found that its main function (planning and plan negotiation) remained in the Office of the President in the person of Bokana. The new prime minister was limited, by the terms of his nomination and the July 6, 1977, ordinance creating the post, to "coordination, at the level of implementation of the work of the Executive Council." He had no independent power base and in practice enjoyed little margin for action independent of the president.

Administrative decentralization likewise proved a myth. The elected urban zone commissioners had no new independent tax-raising powers and were subordinate to nominated subregional commissioners. The legitimacy of the elected Political Bureau members was undercut by the constraints of

---

*On January 5, 1979, Rural Development was downgraded and placed within the jurisdiction of the Agriculture Ministry.

the elections process of the fall of 1977, during which only those with huge
campaign warchests were given serious consideration. Even then, elections
fraud was reported in six of the nine circumscriptions. The much-heralded
placement of foreigners as top officials of the Customs Service and the National Bank could only result in a slight stemming of the widespread corruption theretofore tolerated in those agencies. After all, how much can a few
individuals do, particularly if they want to get along with their colleagues and
with the regime?*

Not only did the informal structures and the rules of the game remain
the same, but so did the people. There was no massive turnover in personnel at the top to correspond with the changed structures. The same individuals whose class identification had so marked the prereform public bureaucracy and determined its massive self-serving bias remained as powerful
as ever, if not more so.

At the output level, then, small wonder that the underlying problems
of Zairian underdevelopment remained unaddressed and the symptoms worsened. Thus the measures have had no noticeable effect on modifying the redistributive bias of the Zairian public administrative system in favor of the
bureaucratic bourgeoisie. On the contrary, in giving the illusion of progress
while the underlying causes of mass impoverishment went unchecked, the
measures contributed to a worsening of the situation. Little wonder that the
feedback to these measures called their basis and indeed the regime itself
into question, thus suggesting that the population's feedback reaction to the
inegalitarian outputs of the reform measures has so far been negative. One
example of such negative feedback to the measures was Shaba II, the remarkable rebellion in mid-May 1978, which but for the speedy French Foreign
Legion response in Kolwezi, would certainly have forced Mobutu out of office.

CONCLUSION

In this study the mystique of management improvement as a strategy
for bringing about fundamental institutional reforms in Zaire, and as a general principle in the field of development administration, was questioned.
An alternative analytical framework for conceptualizing the role of public
administration in society was instead proposed. The underdevelopment administration model reveals the dynamic interpenetration of public administration and the forces dominating society as a whole. Zairian public administration illustrates the important underdevelopmentalist function of a public bureaucracy in the grip of class interests. The self-serving nature of bureau-

---

*Africa Confidential (January 3, 1979) reports on some small steps taken
by the International Monetary Fund representative in the Bank of Zaire, Er-
win Blumenthal, to stem credit to the president's cronies, including Litho,
Lengema, and Moleka. Whether such measures will work and be followed by
more stringent steps is a higher magnitude question altogether.

cratic policy decisions—salary centralization, Zairianization and institutional reforms—was shown by a series of minicase studies. While corruption, per se, is not the major focus of this particular study, * it is apparent through use of the analytical framework applied in this chapter that systemic corruption, though not in itself a structural cause of Zairian underdevelopment, is a most important operational mechanism for it.

REFERENCES

Callaghy, Thomas M. 1976. "State Formation and Centralization of Power in Zaire: Mobutu's Pre-Eminent Public Policy." Paper presented at the African Studies Association Annual Meeting, Boston, November.

Gould, David J. 1978a. "From Development Administration to Underdevelopment Administration: Zairian Public Administration in the Perspective of Paradigmatic Crisis." Cahiers du CEDAF, no. 6.

_____. 1978b. Law and the Administrative Process: Analytic Frameworks for Understanding Public Policymaking. Pittsburgh: University of Pittsburgh External Studies Program.

_____. 1978c. "Underdevelopment Administration: Systemic Corruption in the Public Bureaucracy of Zaire." Paper presented at the Conference on Political Clientelism, Patronage and Development, Bellagio, Italy, August.

_____. 1977a. "Local Administration in Zaire and Underdevelopment." Journal of Modern African Studies, September, pp. 349-78.

_____. 1977b. "Disorganization Theory and Underdevelopment Administration: Local 'Organization' in the Framework of Zairian National 'Development.'" Paper presented at the African and Latin American Studies Association Annual Meeting, Houston, November.

Gould, David J., and Mwana Elas. 1979. "Patrons, Clients and the Politics of Zairianization." In Political Clientelism, Patronage and Development, edited by S. N. Eisenstadt and René Lemarchand.

Gould, David J., and Mushi-Mugumorhagerwa. 1977. "La multirationalité et le sous-développement: L'écologie du processus décisionnel dans l'administration publique zairoise." Canadian Journal of Political Science, June, pp. 261-85.

---

*The author is at work on a book-length study seeking to grasp bureaucratic corruption in the perspective of societal underdevelopment.

Gran, Guy. 1978. "Zaire 1978: Ethical and Intellectual Bankruptcy of the World System." Paper presented at the African Studies Association Annual Meeting, Baltimore, November.

International Bank for Reconstruction and Development. 1977. "Economic Conditions and Prospects of Zaire." Report 1407-22. April 13.

Kabwit, Ghislain C. 1978. "The Aftermath of Shaba I and II Crisis: The Illusion of Political Changes and Reforms in Zaire." Paper presented at the African Studies Association Annual Meeting, Baltimore, November.

Kamitatu-Massamba, Cléophas. 1977. Zaire: le pouvoir à la portée du peuple. Paris: L'Harmattan.

Kannyo, Edward N. 1979. "Political Power and Class Formation in Zaire: The 'Zairianization Measures,' 1973-75." Ph.D. dissertation, Yale University.

Monguya-Mbenge. 1977. Histoire secrète du Zaïre. Brussels: Edtions de l'Espérance.

Mpinga-Kasenda, and David J. Gould. 1975. Les réformes administratives au Zaïre, 1972-1973. Kinshasa: Presses Universitaires du Zaïre.

Peemans, J. Ph. 1975. "L'état fort et la croissance économique." Revue nouvelle (Brussels), December, pp. 515-27.

Rymenam, Jean. 1977. "Comment le régime Mobutu a sappé ses propres fondements." Le monde diplomatique, May, pp. 8-9.

Schatzberg, Michael G. 1978. "Bureaucracy, Business, Beer: The Political Dynamics of Class Formation in Lisala, Zaire." Ph.D. dissertation, University of Wisconsin. Also published as Class and Politics in Zaire. New York: Homes and Meier, 1979.

United Nations. Zaire Program. 1976. "Assistance demandée au PNUD par le gouvernement zaïrois pour la periode 1977-1981."

Young, M. Crawford. 1978. "Zaire: The Unending Crisis." Foreign Affairs, Fall, pp. 169-85.

6

MODERNIZATION AND URBAN POVERTY: A CASE STUDY OF KINSHASA

Makala-Lizumu and Mwana Elas

> The real challenge to our Time and our Country is not growth—
> the colonizer, in that respect, was unbeatable—but development
> or growth control.
>
> Benoît Verhaegen

INTRODUCTION

The severe crisis of the Zairian political and economic system is obvious to all. Many studies, especially in the last three years, focus on the agony of a regime whose sole accomplishment has been the acceleration of the underdevelopment of a country with great potential wealth, but in concrete fact poor and getting poorer. The Zairian people, be they in the countryside or in the cities, are growing daily more impoverished. Although much has been written about this phenomenon, relatively little attention has been given to the urban dimensions of this poverty. The Zairian peasants' return to a subsistence economy, their massive migration to the cities, and the lack of a socioeconomic infrastructure and opportunities in the countryside are amply described. But, with the exception of Nzongola Ntalaja's 1975 study of Kananga, little has been written about the conditions under which most Zairian city dwellers live.

Does this mean that they are any less impoverished than the rural population or that their impoverishment is too complex to be described or analyzed? In other words, how much better is the socioeconomic situation of city dwellers to have deserved so little scholarly interest?

It appears that most of us are blinded by the "modernization" of Zairian cities and the many investments concentrated there. Thus the impression sought to be conveyed is that the entire urban population gets more and better goods and services than in the countryside. Based on this impression, a poor understanding of the conditions of urban poverty in Zaire has been developed.

This chapter accepts the challenge of depicting and analyzing the patterns of urban poverty in Zaire and attempts to show that the attendant human waste and misery in the cities is as important as it is in the countryside. Given space limitations, the study will be confined to an analysis of conditions in Kinshasa, the Zairian capital. The core realities of other urban settings in Zaire do not appear that different.

Neoclassical modernization theory is not a satisfactory tool for such an analysis. The theory of modernization thus proceeds from crude accumulation, unbalanced growth, and greedy snobbishness. By posing modernization as a close-ended point, it comes to legitimize both its basic assumptions and consequences. It plays an eminently ideological role. As such, it distorts and conceals its real objectives and goals. But it convinces people of its "goodness, while fulfilling its imitators' needs" (Gould and Mwana Elas 1979). In this chapter it is argued that the modernization syndrome—especially its theory and ideology, as well as its derived praxis—has caused and exacerbated poverty of the masses in Zairian cities.

PATTERNS OF URBAN POVERTY

The approach that considers poverty in relative terms in urban areas and in absolute terms in the case of rural areas is founded on two basic assumptions. First, it assumes that there exists a socioeconomic infrastructure designed to satisfy all the basic needs of the population in terms of health, education, housing, water, and so on. Second, the concentration of investments in the urban areas is said to generate employment and wealth.

From these two assumptions derives a way of describing Kinshasa as "a true center of exploitation of the rest of the country" (Mobutu 1977). If one may admit that an unequal exchange and allocation of resources have been established between Kinshasa and the rest of the country, by no means would this suggest the accuracy of the two assumptions. Indeed, wealth and poverty cannot be well defined unless one considers them in their relation to the existing social groups. And the existence of a socioeconomic infrastructure is not by itself a conclusive indicator of welfare. This holds true in the case of investments as well. Their importance should be determined in relation to their propensity to fulfill the basic social needs. Not only should they be seen in terms of provided jobs but also in terms of allocated wages.

As long as one does not go beyond the modernization syndrome to analyze the real socioeconomic distortions, one cannot relate the high rate of infantile mortality in the cities to families' income level; nor can one explain the high rate of dropouts, especially among high school students.

To the two assumptions outlined above, three basic theses will be opposed:

1. Rather than seeing Kinshasa as a homogeneous population exploiting the rest of the country, it is seen as structurally heterogeneous and maintaining different types of relations with the rest of the country.

2. As long as modernization is built upon the existing structures and relationships within society, it aims at legitimizing, at most, underdevelopment, that is, poverty.

3. As mentioned earlier, the socioeconomic infrastructure and investments are meaningless unless they constitute in actuality a means to fulfill
the basic needs of the population.

Needless to mention that the heterogeneous nature of the Kinshasa population is well described by the simple existence of such famous neighborhoods
as Bon-Marché and Devinière in comparison with some ghetto neighborhoods,
such as Kisenso, Masina, and Bumbu. Such differentiation based along income
lines has resulted in the concentration of wealth in the hands of particular social groups. Their having access quite exclusively, that is, in concrete
terms, to the existing socioeconomic infrastructure and to new investments
should be held responsible for the idea of an "exploitative center." President
Mobutu implicitly refuted the idea of a homogeneous exploitative center when
he stigmatized "the action of a certain bourgeoisie" concentrated in Kinshasa.
He went on to call it a "minority of idlers" who live on peasants' and laborers'
production (Mobutu 1977).
Unless somehow one has a clear idea of such a differentiation, one cannot understand the real dynamism of Kinshasa as a society. Although the
present chapter does not claim to be a comprehensive study of the economic
and social stratification in Kinshasa, it attempts, however, to provide some
elements of such an in-depth study. Such a task is a hard one given the lack
of data on some of the indicators. The gaps will be filled, when needed, by
recourse to "immediate observation." In so doing, four indicators will be
used: employment and wage policy, health care policy, housing policy, and
education.

EMPLOYMENT AND WAGE POLICY

One way of differentiating the population consists in ranging them according to their jobs. Thus three types of employment can be identified: full time
in formal and informal sectors, part time in formal and informal sectors, and
unemployment. Although such a threefold differentiation may be useful, it
hardly corresponds to the social structure. Two basic reasons can be advanced. First, it includes within the same categories all wage earners regardless of their real income level, hence distorting at the very outset the
social reality. Second, it assumes erroneously that there exists a direct
correlation between wage earners in the formal sectors and those in the informal sectors.
A second way of differentiating along employment lines has been suggested by Charles Elliot (1975). Although founding his model on the first,
Elliot somehow makes his model more dynamic. Four categories are identifiable in his model:

1. The bureaucratic and commercial bourgeoisie. This first category
includes mainly, on the one hand, the upper bureaucratic and political elite
and, on the other hand, the upper commercial and industrial elite who may
be also involved in politics.

2. Full-time wage earners in the formal sector. Four subcategories can be identified here: the bureaucratic elite comprising top managers in public or private enterprises, middle- and low-level wage earners, skilled labor, and unskilled labor.

3. Wage earners in the informal sector.

4. Unemployed.

Without rigidly following either of the two models, they will be used subsequently in part to analyze employment and wage policy in Kinshasa.*

As suggested earlier, the focus here should be the wage and salary distribution. A look at the new investments that flowed to Zaire following passage of the 1969 liberal investment code up to 1975 reveals that 12,048 job openings (89 investment projects carried out) out of 24,814 jobs (139 projects carried out) were concentrated in Kinshasa (Mulumba Lukoji 1976). As a matter of fact, such a concentration (50 percent) confirms on the surface the exploitative center thesis. However, a closer look at the existing social reality gives a much different picture of the situation, insofar as one considers Kinshasa from the heterogeneous thesis point of view. This is worth noting, as adopting the homogeneous thesis viewpoint would mean that the upper class, the wage earners, and the unemployed in Kinshasa consume and own the same amount of distributable goods.

Consider, for instance, the wage distribution in 1972. At that time, 72,000 wage earners were hired in the public sector in Kinshasa. Of this number 4,800, or 6.6 percent, held high managerial positions, and earned Z 995,000 out of Z 3.4 million in total public wages.† This corresponded to 29.2 percent of all the salaries paid to the wage earners. In the private sector, 4,919 high-level managers (2.8 percent) earned Z 24,750,791, that is, 30.8 percent of all the salaries paid to these wage earners, while 166,964 employees and workers (97.2 percent) earned only Z 56,001,927 (69.2 percent) (Kankuenda 1977, pp. 94-97). As far as consuming goods were concerned, almost 30 percent of the total demand was concentrated in the hands of 5 percent of salary earners, the top-level managers, thus leaving 95 percent of the wage earners sharing the remaining 70 percent of real demand (Kankuenda 1977).

In the seven years since the survey, the picture has changed. High managerial positions have increased at 8 percent. Their salaries have increased at 36 percent, while the working-class wages have somehow remained stagnant, and for that matter have decreased if one considers the price index and the real wage index (see Table 6.1).

If one considers the relationship among wage index, price index, and real wage index, there is a partial conclusion to be drawn. There is, in fact, an unbreakable link among income, model, propensity to consumption, and

---

*Because of a lack of reliable data on those who are hired in the informal sectors and the unemployed, attention is focused on full-time jobs.

†In 1972, Z 1 = U.S. $2; between March 1976 and the spring of 1979 the value of the zaire collapsed under International Monetary Fund tutelage.

TABLE 6.1

Wage, Price, and Real Wage Indexes, Kinshasa, 1960-76
(at official minimum wage; 1960 = 100)

Date	Wage Index	Price Index	Real Wage Index
June 1, 1960	100	100.0	100
May 1, 1964	383	575.9	67
October 1, 1971	960	1,486.2	64
September 5, 1975	1,274	3,099.5	41
March 27, 1976	1,530	5,888.1	25

Source: Union Nationale des Traveilleurs Zairois, "Positions concernant la politique des salaires" (1977).

industrialization. The latter is unlikely to meet the basic needs of society
unless dissociated from the ideology of modernization.

A global view of the population living in Kinshasa reveals two categories
of income. There are the low-income families, who represent 74.2 percent
of all the urban families, and whose expenses value at 46.9 percent. They
devote 70 percent of their budget to basic food needs, such as vegetables and
fish. They can hardly afford, therefore, to purchase modern items or to have
access to basic health care services, education, and good housing. Then
there are the high-income families, who represent 25.8 percent of the urban
families, and spend 53.1 percent of their budget in consumer goods. Unlike
the first category, this group of families can afford to purchase industrial
goods, such as cars, milk, alcoholic beverages, meat, bread, fancy clothes,
and other luxurious items (Kankuenda 1977).

As Table 6.2 indicates, in 1974 more than 50 percent (68 percent) of
the families earned less than Z 70 per month. With the shrinking purchasing
power of those families, which has been particularly aggravated by a high inflationary rate, it is worth asking whether or not the majority of urban families are better off as compared with rural families. The fact remains that,
although living under the very shadow of modernization, the majority of the
urban population share the same patterns of poverty, if not worse, as their
rural counterparts. Such a pattern of poverty as revealed by the first indicator of this study has direct and, indeed, dialectical relationship with the
other three indicators, health, housing, and education.

HEALTH

When speaking of health one should bear in mind its two aspects: the
preventive aspect and the curative aspect. Health policy should include the
two aspects, for they are complementary. The prevailing view in that respect

TABLE 6.2

Income Distribution in Kinshasa, Lubumbashi, and Kisangani, October 1974

Average Monthly Family Income (zaires)	Percent of Total Population		
	Kinshasa	Lubumbashi	Kisangani
Under 30	15	21	56
30 to 39	16	24	12
40 to 49	18	10	10
50 to 59	19	15	9
70 to 119	19	24	7
120 and over	14	6	6

Source: U.S., Agency for International Development, Office of Housing, Zaire Shelter-Sector Analysis (Washington, D.C., 1975), p. 98.

is that Kinshasa benefits more than other cities and rural areas from the national health policy and expenditures. Such a view relies on a comparative approach that takes into consideration the average distance in the rural areas from a village to the nearest facility, the quality of services in rural areas, and the partial or total lack of equipment and supplies.

As in the first indicator, it is argued here that, although rural needs assessment is accurate, the evaluation of health services in Kinshasa, and for that matter in the cities generally, proceeds from false assumptions. One of those assumptions is a "normal distribution."

As far as the preventive aspect is concerned, there is no real difference between rural areas and most overcrowded neighborhoods in Kinshasa. The unequal spatial distribution of services (founded in fact on income distribution), such as immunization, health education, water supply, and sewerage systems, does not make those neighborhoods any better than rural areas. Malnutrition, although generated by the first indicator, should also be mentioned here. This sociospatial distribution of preventive health services results in a high incidence of such diseases as malaria in most neighborhoods and in a high rate of infant mortality. Indeed, 50 percent of all the children who die in the hospital are considered to be malnourished (U.S., Department of Health, Education and Welfare 1975).

With respect to the curative aspect, the real concentration of qualified personnel in Kinshasa (more than 50 percent) does not constitute a convincing index of real health output. Apart from the fact that here again there exists an unequal sociospatial distribution, most public health facilities in Kinshasa are not any better than those in rural areas. The strong influence of the first indicator on health has been revealed by FOMECO, an Office of the President-based medical program:

Despite the fixing of prices for medical care, the highly uneven income distribution clearly delineates accessibility to medical facilities. . . . In Kinshasa of the 55 percent of the population falling into the lowest socio-economic category, only 19 percent had access to medical facilities in contrast to 100 percent of those in the highest socio-economic group having such access. [U.S., Department of Health, Education and Welfare 1975, p. 143]

TABLE 6.3

Schedule of Fixed Charges for In- and Outpatient Health Care, Kinshasa
(fees in zaires)

	Categories of Recipient				
	1	2	3	4	5
General ambulatory consultations					
First consultation	0	0.15	0.30	0.50	0
Following visits	0	0.10	0.15	0.30	0
Special consultations					
First consultation	0	0.30	0.50	1.00	0
Following visits	0	0.10	0.15	0.30	0
Hospital room fees					
One person per room	3.00	3.00	3.00	3.00	0
Two or three persons per room	2.50	2.50	2.50	2.50	0
Ward	0	0.10	0.20	0.20	0

Source: U.S., Department of Health, Education and Welfare, Syncrisis: The Dynamics of Health, vol. 14, Zaire (Washington, D.C., 1975), p. 142.

A closer look at the FOMECO figures suggests that of 1,450,000 inhabitants living in Kinshasa in 1973, more than 70 percent were excluded from modern health services. Of 19 percent of those having access, only 16 percent can be said to have access to qualitatively good services, as 2 or 3 percent of those whose employers provide medical care must go to public hospitals where the quality of services is low.

Here, again, the concentration of qualified manpower resources and the target groups in Kinshasa has resulted in decreasing the quality of the medical output. In spite of highly qualified manpower resources, the basic needs of the majority of the urban population are not met. And most of them live in worse conditions than do peasants in rural areas.

TABLE 6.4

National Health Manpower Resources, Public Sector

| | Geographic Distribution | | Nationality | | |
	Kinshasa	Other	Zairian	Foreign	Total
Physicians	280	297	305	272	577
Medical assistants	38	27	61	4	65
Dentists	4	5	3	6	9
Dental assistants	3	2	5	0	5
Trained midwives	207	34	206	35	241
Auxiliary midwives	205	580	785	0	785
Graduate nurses	504	776	1,135	145	1,280
Auxiliary nurses	572	5,071	5,643	0	5,643
Pharmacists	11	8	18	1	19
Pharmaceutical preparers	8	10	16	2	18
Veterinarians	0	0	0	0	0
Assistant veterinarians	0	0	0	0	0
Sanitation engineers	8	0	8	0	0
Environmental engineers	27	54	81	0	81
Auxiliary technicians	2	54	56	0	56
Physiotherapists	20	0	16	4	20
Laboratory technicians	6	9	7	8	15
Radiological technicians	—	—	—	—	—
Other scientific specialties	0	1	1	0	1
Other paramedical technicians	15	59	72	2	74
Health aides	681	232	913	0	913

Source: U.S., Department of Health, Education and Welfare, Syncrisis: The Dynamics of Growth, Zaire, vol. 14 (Washington, D.C., 1975), p. 170.

TABLE 6.5

National Health Manpower Resources, Private Sector

	Geographic Distribution		Nationality		
	Kinshasa	Other	Zairian	Foreign	Total
Physicians	59	182	12	229	241
Medical assistants	24	4	25	3	28
Dentists	17	1	1	17	18
Dental assistants	0	0	0	0	0
Trained midwives	17	88	23	82	105
Auxiliary midwives	12	92	104	0	104
Graduate nurses	70	604	503	171	674
Auxiliary nurses	312	1,376	1,549	139	1,688
Pharmacists	84	28	—	—	112
Pharmaceutical preparers	11	12	21	2	23
Veterinarians	0	0	0	0	0
Assistant veterinarians	0	0	0	0	0
Sanitation engineers	2	0	2	0	2
Environmental engineers	10	15	23	2	25
Auxiliary technicians	—	—	3	0	3
Physiotherapists	9	0	8	1	9
Laboratory technicians	48	14	48	14	62
Radiological technicians	0	0	0	0	0
Other scientific specialties	—	—	1	2	3
Other paramedical technicians	—	—	11	6	17
Health aides	139	117	256	0	256

Source: U.S., Department of Health, Education and Welfare, Syncrisis: The Dynamics of Growth, Zaire, vol. 14 (Washington, D.C., 1975), p. 172.

HOUSING

Any evaluation of the housing policy should take into account both the social and spatial distribution of housing services. Since 1965 three main housing offices have been created: National Housing Office (ONL), Office of the President, and Nation Saving Bank for Housing (CNECI). Two housing projects were completed by ONL in Mobutu's first decade: Limete-Sud, 200 units, upper income; and Reghini (Lemba), 450 units, economic. Development cost for the Lemba units was Z 1.2 million, and the units ranged in price from Z 3,000 to Z 6,000. The units were "sold" to the army when longer-term financing could not be found (U. S., Agency for International Development 1975).

As for the Office of the President, its initial projects have been as follows:

Year	Project	Development Cost (zaires)
1967	Cité OAU (guest housing for Organization of African Unity conference)	1.0 million
	Army housing	1.2 million
1970	Party convention, hotel, and housing complex at N'sele	5.6 million

CNECI was created in 1971 in order to initiate a national savings system and to utilize its savings to finance housing. It developed 1,100 units at Cité Salongo in Lemba in the early 1970s.

Thus, if one looks closely at a few years of government housing policy, one may conclude that there is no housing policy at all for low-income families. This proposition holds true on four points. First, as mentioned above, not only were the projects designed by ONL prohibitively expensive but they did not benefit the initial target groups, that is, low-income families. Instead, they were given to the army. Second, the Office of the President's projects were implemented to meet specific political and prestige objectives. It constitutes an illustrative example of a project designed to achieve political goals. Third, the 1,100 CNECI units, although initially built to meet the needs of low-income families, were appropriated by the middle and upper classes. This stemmed from the very fact that the rent rate exceeded by far the monthly earnings of the low-income families. While Z 3,000 per unit was the initial cost, 30 percent of the initial cost, or Z 900, was required as deposit. Thus, Z 3,900, that is, 130 times the average monthly wage of the urban worker, was required for one unit. Fourth, while the average housing allowances varied from Z 5 to Z 10 a month in 1975, the average monthly rent was estimated at Z 13 in peripheral neighborhoods, that is, the ghettos.

The housing policy contributes to a vicious circle of poverty similar to the one created by the wage policy and health care.

TABLE 6.6

Number of Persons per Room by Size of Housing Unit, Kinshasa, 1967

Zone	One-Room	Two-Room	Three-Room	Four-Room or Larger
I	—	—	—	0.58
II	3.64	2.27	2.04	1.51-1.97
III	6.56	2.65	2.28	1.43-1.82
IV	5.57	3.32	2.28	1.30-1.78
V	4.28	2.54	1.97	1.21-1.84
VI	4.52	2.55	1.73	1.37-1.51

Source: U.S., Agency for International Development, Office of Housing, Zaire Shelter-Sector Analysis (Washington, D.C., 1975), p. 88.

EDUCATION

There are two limiting factors considered to be detrimental to education in rural areas, the induced costs and the poor performance of school-teachers. Once again the mass of educational infrastructure and the high concentration of manpower resources in Kinshasa tend to legitimize the homogeneous thesis. As far as the educational system is concerned, three reasons can be advanced to invalidate the thesis.

First, because of its modernizing role, Kinshasa has attracted more rural population than any other city in Zaire. This has resulted in a contradictory situation in which the concentration of highly qualified personnel cannot meet the needs of an overcrowded city. There are now, in the late 1970s, over 2 million inhabitants in Kinshasa. This has two basic consequences. In the first place, incapable of absorbing the increasingly high number of children, the educational infrastructure produces a dramatically competitive situation. Getting one's children admitted to school becomes more the exception than the rule. In the process, the classical market law (demand-supply ratio) takes hold. But, unlike the case of a purely competitive economic market, the result is not a price increase, but corruption. President Mobutu's speech (1977) is revealing in that respect:

> Thus, an audience with an official, enrolling children in school, obtaining school certificates, access to medical care, a seat on the plane, an import license, a diploma, among other things, are all subject to this tax which is invisible, yet known to the whole world.

Once again the vicious circle reappears. One cannot be enrolled in school because one cannot compete. One cannot compete because one has low income, and one has low income because one does not have a degree enabling one to get a good job.

Two types of costs must be considered. On the one hand, there are overt costs, which consist of fees (minerval) designed to cover administrative expenses. There are, on the other hand, the covert costs. The latter are extra expenses designed to cover other needs, such as books, transportation, and uniforms. Unlike their counterparts in rural areas, who can get to school by walking, children in the cities need transportation. Moreover, their school fees are relatively higher than in rural areas. Thus, faced with these costs, most low-income families in Kinshasa find themselves excluded from adequate education.

These constraints, coupled with the spatial distribution of schools, raises the problem of performance, a third argument against the homogeneous thesis. The overcrowdedness of Kinshasa has resulted in the increasing size of its schools. A 1973 survey showed that the average number of children in both the primary and secondary school classrooms in Kinshasa was 52, while it was 37 in all rural regions.

As expected, such a phenomenon is reflected by the generally poor performance of both students and teachers in Kinshasa. This is confirmed by the reverse migration of most upper-class children to the most famous schools in rural areas. While it is possible for high-income families (less than 30 percent) to avoid the poor performance of their children through such migration or by building "big name" schools from which are excluded low-income families' children, the latter have no choice but to remain victims of the situation.

In the face of such a dramatic situation, the conclusion to be drawn in the case of education is identical to the one drawn in the case of wages, health, and housing. Although operating in a highly modern environment, the educational system in Kinshasa has not succeeded in producing a qualitatively modern output. Instead, hundreds of dropouts are being victimized by the ideology of modernization.

CONCLUSION

This brief look at the socioeconomic situation of Kinshasa has revealed, in sum, that modernization theory, and its derived praxis, is unable to discover society's real dynamism. It fails to touch upon society's relations of production, reproduction, and distribution. In so doing, it fails to reveal the relational nature of poverty. Its shortcomings have a first consequence. Poverty is said to be, if not the exclusivity of, at least much more identifiable with the rural areas.

Through the analysis of four basic indicators the vicious circle set up by the patterns of poverty in Kinshasa has been shown. In actuality, poverty as a relational phenomenon does have causal relationship with other basic social factors, and cannot be "repeated or (repeats) itself unchanged in time. . . . If there is any circular cause-effect relationship—and such certainly exists—it can only move spirally upwards or downwards, and, therefore, has a starting-point, too" (Szentes 1976, p. 54). The point being made here is that the vicious circle is, in fact, inherent in modernization theory and its derived praxis. From these two basic considerations one sees clearly the quite unscientific nature of modernization theory and its eminently ideological significance.

If the proposition holds true, then the question of whether or not urban masses are a potential revolutionary force can be raised. In other words, is there any propensity on the part of urban masses to join a rural-based revolutionary process, should the latter occur? It is contended here that such a linkage process is quite impossible, mostly because the masses in urban areas are, more than the rural population, victims of the modernizing ideology. Indeed, the real force of modernizing ideology consists in its ability to divide and rule. With but slight modification this analytical framework can be applied to other big cities in Zaire.

REFERENCES

Apter, David. 1967. The Politics of Modernization. Chicago: University of Chicago Press.

Chodak, Szymon. 1973. Societal Development. New York: Oxford University Press.

Elliot, Charles. 1975. Patterns of Poverty in the Third World. New York: Praeger.

Gould, David, and Mwana Elas. 1979. "Patrons, Clients and the Politics of Zairianization." In Political Clientelism, Patronage and Development, edited by S. N. Eisenstadt and Rene Lemarchand.

Haeger, Gerald. 1974. The Politics of Underdevelopment. New York: St. Martin's Press.

Houyoux, Joseph. 1973. Budgets, ménagers, nutrition et mode de vie à Kinshasa. Kinshasa: Presses Université du Zaire.

Huntington, Samuel, and Joan Nelson. 1976. No Easy Choice—Political Participation in Developing Countries. Cambridge, Mass.: Harvard University Press.

Inkeles, A., and D. H. Smith. 1974. Becoming Modern. Cambridge, Mass.: Harvard University Press.

Kankuenda, Mbaya. 1977. "Les industries du pole de Kinshasa." Cahiers du CEDAF (Brussels), nos. 1-2.

Lapalombora, Joseph, ed. 1963. Bureaucracy and Political Development. Princeton, N.J.: Princeton University Press.

Lerner, Daniel. 1968. "Modernization: Social Aspects." In International Encyclopedia of the Social Sciences, vol. 10. New York: Free Press.

Lewis, Arthur. 1955. The Theory of Economic Growth. London: Allen and Unwin.

Levy, Marion. 1972. Modernization: Latecomers and Survivors. New York: Basic Books.

Mobutu, Sese Seko. 1977. Discours d'ouverture de deuxième Congrès du MPR.

Mulumba Lukoji. 1976. "Investir au Zaire." Zaire afrique, 103:141-52.

Nzongola Ntalaya. 1975. "Urban Administration in Zaire: A Study of Kananga, 1971-73." Ph.D. dissertation, University of Wisconsin.

Szentes, Tamas. 1976. The Political Economy of Underdevelopment. Budapest: Akademiai Kiado.

Union Nationale des Travailleurs Zairois. 1977. "Positions concernant la politique des salaires." Kinshasa.

United Nations Education, Science, and Cultural Organization. 1976. Zaire: Etudes sectorielles de l'éducation. Report no. 151, vol. 2. Paris.

U.S., Agency for International Development. Office of Housing. 1975. Zaire Shelter-Sector Analysis. Washington, D.C.

U.S., Department of Health, Education and Welfare. 1975. Syncrisis: The Dynamics of Health. Zaire, vol. 14. Washington, D.C.

Uphoff, Norman, and Warren Ilchman, eds. 1972. The Political Economy of Development. Berkeley: University of California Press.

7

EXPORT-LED GROWTH:
THE COPPER SECTOR

Ghifem J. Katwala

INTRODUCTION

It is the curse of many developing countries that they lack the natural resources to develop in order to produce a surplus that would enable them to overcome poverty and the underdevelopment of their human resources. Of those countries that do have resources, most do not possess the means to develop them. Zaire's misfortune results from its wealth in mineral resources that, because they are needed or wanted by industrialized countries, have been developed at the expense of Zaire's human resources. This chapter will describe and analyze how the process of mineral production and export, praised as the engine of Zaire's development, has become the prime catalyst of this country's present development crisis and economic disaster.

Focusing on the chief commodity of the export sector, copper, the chapter will analyze how, since the colonial period, Zaire has been integrated into the world economy as a peripheral state and given the role of producer and exporter of primary commodities to the developed world. Following Zaire's independence, and especially since 1965, copper production and export have continued to reinforce a drastically disarticulated economy that prevents the balanced development of nonexport, human-related sectors. This process of mineral production and export, and the subsequent dependence on the developed world, have unleashed a series of complex forces resulting in structural blockage mechanisms and cultural disincentives that prevent the reshaping or rethinking of the causes of the imbalances and that work instead for the perpetuation of the present political and economic forms within the country.

In order to understand these forces and how they operate, the copper sector is analyzed as an enclave economy that absorbs the lion's share of national and multilateral economic effort, but whose surplus is either lost through unequal exchanges and loss of value or used in particular ways at particular levels that are not in the interest of most of the Zairian people. The direct and indirect consequences of dependence on production and export of copper are not only budgetary and balance-of-payments deficits but also, and most important, underdevelopment manifested through the underutilization and abuse of Zairian human resources, resulting in illiteracy, low health status, low income, and powerlessness.

HISTORICAL BACKGROUND

Most of Zaire's copper is mined in the Shaba region (formerly Katanga Province). M. A. Mahieu (1925) reported that the Africans in Katanga extracted and traded copper on a small scale and used it to make tools long before the arrival of European explorers. When the latter reached the area in the early nineteenth century, they noticed the extensive use of the mineral and recommended that prospecting be undertaken. Following the Berlin Treaty of February 23, 1885, which resulted in the creation of the Congo Free State, King Leopold II gave exclusive rights to the Compagnie du Congo pour le Commerce et l'Industrie (CCCI) to undertake colonization and exploration of Katanga. In turn, CCCI created the Compagnie du Katanga to which was given concession rights covering one-third of Katanga's territory for a period of almost a century.

Disputes between the Congo Free State and the Compagnie du Katanga over the limits of the concessed territory prevented the latter from exploiting the extensive mineral resources discovered by a team of mines prospectors led by Jules Cornet. As a result, the management and exploitation of Katangan mineral resources were given to the Comité Spécial du Katanga (CSK). The Congo Free State was to receive two-thirds of the profit from Katanga's wealth, while the Compagnie du Katanga was to be given one-third. With the financial help from the Société Générale de Belgique (SGB) and Tanganyika Concessions Limited, CSK formed in 1906 the Union Minière du Haut-Katanga (UMHK) in order to develop the extensive mineral rights and concessions in Katanga, which amounted to 7,700 square miles of copperbelt and 4,500 square miles of tinbelt.

Benefiting from the railway connection with Rhodesia and South Africa, UMHK started copper production in 1911. The company's interests lay primarily in prospecting, mining, and metallurgical processing, but in the absence of an adequate infrastructure, and as virtually the only local source of capital formation, it was led to develop in Katanga industries and other facilities for servicing the mines and the mining community. Through the years UMHK has not only built a copper empire in Katanga that contributed to an autonomous development of the region but has also become the most powerful company operating in Zaire, producing the largest single source of government revenue and three-quarters of its foreign exchange.

When Zaire became independent on June 30, 1960, Union Minière encouraged Moise Tshombe, then president of Katanga Province, to secede, so that Prime Minister Patrice Lumumba would not nationalize the company and its subsidiaries. Nationalization would have resulted in a massive departure of European cadres and in government interference in day-to-day management of the company. The financial assistance given to Katanga leaders by UMHK also played an important role in the establishment of the Katanga gendarmerie and the recruitment of foreign mercenaries who fought to defend Katanga secession against Baluba rebels and UN troops. Budgetary deficits experienced by the central government between 1960 and 1963 were also in part due to the fact that UMHK stopped releasing foreign exchange earnings and paying taxes to the Kinshasa government (see Gérard-Libois 1963 for details).

One year after President Mobutu Sese Seko took power, relations between the Zairian government and UMHK deteriorated. The subjects of contention were new tax measures imposed by the central government on the copper company, the marketing policies of copper, and the application of the Bakajika law (OL 66/363 of June 7, 1966) to mining concessions. But it was the failure to reach agreement on the establishment of the UMHK head office in Zaire by the end of 1966 that triggered the actual government takeover of the operations of UMHK in Zaire. The various claims and counterclaims between the government and UMHK were partially settled on February 15, 1967, when an agreement was reached between the Zairian authorities and the Belgian company Société Générale de Minérais (SGM), a subsidiary of SGB and marketing agent of UMHK. The agreement stipulated that the management of the mines and metallurgical installations in Shaba would be entrusted to SGM under the general control and supervision of the new company Société Générale Congolaise des Mines (GECOMIN). All mineral production would be marketed through SGM's sales organization and GECOMIN would be paid the selling price that SGM obtained in the market less all marketing costs and expenses. SGM would receive a commission of 4.5 percent of the value of all sales made (Radmann 1978). Thus, although UMHK's assets were taken over by the government of Zaire, the company still controlled copper production and marketing in the country. This control was reinfroced by the 1969 agreement under which the government extended SGM's marketing and management control for 25 years and increased UMHK's share of GECOMIN's production value to 6 percent as compensation and fee. In April 1974, an agreement between SGM and Zaire changed the 1969 compensation agreement from 6 percent of annual sales through 1982 to a flat sum of $100 million (IBRD 1975a, 2:24).

Such a picture reveals to some degree the nature of open-ended interest by the core societies, Belgium in particular, in this corner of the periphery. One needs at the onset as well a sense of how central Zaire is to the collective needs of the world system. Indeed, since the colonial period the economic structure established by the Belgians in Zaire was centrally designed to establish in Zairian industries extracting minerals needed by Belgian industries first and then by other countries of the Western bloc. This economic structure, combined with the nature of the aims of the colonial regime, helped Zaire perform its role as producer and exporter of raw materials. Zaire has successfully served the needs of the West in primary commodities for several decades, producing 7 percent of the noncommunist world's copper supply (see Table 7.1), 60 percent (now in the late 1970s down to about 40 percent) of its cobalt, 39 percent of the world's industrial diamonds, 20 per-

TABLE 7.1

Noncommunist World Mine Production of Copper
(percent of total production)

	1950	1955	1960	1965	1970	1972
United States	36.1	32.2	27.1	29.5	30.2	26.5
Canada	10.5	10.8	11.0	11.1	12.8	12.6
Total developed countries	55.9	54.9	49.4	51.4	54.9	52.5
Zambia	13.0	13.1	15.9	16.8	13.2	12.8
Chile	15.8	15.8	14.7	14.1	13.3	12.8
Zaire	7.7	8.6	8.3	7.0	7.3	7.8
Peru	1.3	1.6	5.1	4.3	4.1	4.1
Total developing countries	44.1	45.1	50.6	48.6	45.1	47.5

Source: International Bank for Reconstruction and Development, "Zaire —Appraisal of GECAMINES Expansion Project," 2 vols. (Washington, D.C., December 26, 1975), annex 3.2.

cent of its germanium, and much else (IMF 1968). Of these, copper and cobalt are the most important in terms of quantity and value. Because Zaire is the major producer of cobalt, the government of Zaire and UMHK, today Générale de Carrières et des Mines du Zaire (GECAMINES), have taken the position of leadership in the market and periodically, as during 1978 and 1979, have fixed cobalt prices. Table 7.2 shows Zaire's predominance in world cobalt production in 1978.

TABLE 7.2

World Cobalt Mine Production, 1978
(estimated percent of total world production)

	Percent
Zaire	35.3
Zambia	7.4
Canada	5.9
Australia	11.2
New Caledonia	13.5
Central Economy countries	11.8

Source: U.S., Department of the Interior, Mineral Commodity Summaries, annual (Washington, D.C., 1979).

TABLE 7.3

Noncommunist World Refined Copper Consumption
(percent of total production)

	1950	1955	1960	1965	1970	1972
United States	49.5	42.0	31.9	36.6	31.9	32.7
Canada	3.7	3.9	3.8	4.1	3.9	3.6
Western Europe	38.5	45.1	50.2	43.0	42.6	40.2
Japan	2.3	3.2	7.9	8.5	14.1	15.4
Total developed countries	96.0	96.3	95.3	94.9	95.4	94.2
Total developing countries	4.0	3.7	4.7	5.1	4.6	5.8

Source: International Bank for Reconstruction and Development,
"Zaire—Appraisal of GECAMINES Expansion Project," 2 vols. (Washington,
D.C., December 26, 1975), annex 3.2.

Although Zaire and other developing countries produce almost 50 percent of the noncommunist world's copper, the United States, Canada, Japan,
and Western Europe consume around 95 percent of this production, particularly in their electrical and equipment industries. Consumption of cobalt in
the noncommunist world is also skewed. Figures for 1972 showed the following major users: United States (44.5 percent), Japan (16 percent), United
Kingdom (12.5 percent), and West Germany (10.5 percent). It is unlikely
that poor countries have made significant inroads in this market since then.

In short, during the colonial period, mineral production for export was
the financially predominant economic activity in Zaire. Part of the mining
surplus was transferred to and absorbed by an industrial sector located in
Western countries, especially in members of the Organization of Economic
Cooperation and Development (OECD). The rest of the surplus did not contribute to balanced economic growth in other sectors of Zaire's economy. It
was instead used for the enlargement of the local mining industry and the payment of taxes to the colonial state, which reinvested them in the administrative and economic framework necessary for the continuation of mineral production and exporting. Some of this tax revenue was also used as profit and
transferred to Europe in various forms.

When President Mobutu rose to power in 1965, the economic and investment policies based on dependence on mineral production and exporting were
readopted and reinforced. The nature of the regime that came to power in
1965 not only made possible this continuation and reinforcement of dependence
on the mining sector but also made it necessary. In order to understand fully
the above statement, an analysis of the politics of copper production and export in Zaire since 1965 becomes essential.

THE POLITICS OF COPPER PRODUCTION
AND EXPORT IN ZAIRE SINCE 1965

In order to strengthen the state apparatus and attract foreign capital, President Mobutu undertook a series of administrative and constitutional reforms resulting in the establishment of a personal patrimonial regime in which high-level bureaucrats played a major role in policy making and implementation. (See Chapter 3.) The main feature of the political relationships of the regime was clientage. As such, it necessitated the distribution of considerable sums of money to its internal clients in order to maintain their loyalty. The economy, which had stagnated since 1960, could not provide enough resources to be used for the necessary level of political payoffs.

One of the main tasks Mobutu found when he came to power was to establish the base for the expansion of the financial resources of the regime. Advised by International Monetary Fund (IMF) and International Bank for Reconstruction and Development (IBRD) experts, the government of Zaire opted for the expansion of the modern sector, especially the copper industry and related infrastructure. Such a policy oriented at expanding copper production and export was not new. Economically, Zaire has always been heavily dependent on copper, both for foreign exchange earnings and for financing of government expenditures. However, this dependency on copper became stronger during President Mobutu's regime following the adoption of the 1967 IMF stabilization program, which introduced a monetary reform tightly linked to taxation of international trade and the slow recovery of agriculture (IMF 1968).

In order to restore budgetary control and balance-of-payments equilibrium and to reestablish the profitability of the export sector so as to initiate new investment programs, the government of Zaire accepted IMF proposals and introduced in June 1967 a stabilization program. It first required a devaluation of the Congolese franc. Fiscal policies included in the program and introduced in 1968 involved a series of radical measures designed to raise taxation. The new tax system was intended to compensate for the loss of receipts following the abolition of the dual exchange rate introduced by the IMF in 1963 and also to obviate the need for recourse to Central Bank credit to finance budgetary deficit. In the 1967 stabilization program, the rates of export duties on copper, cobalt, and diamonds were raised substantially, and the duties on agricultural products and all other exports were virtually doubled (IMF 1968).

Instead of serving as an incentive to the diversification of Zaire's mineral and agricultural production and export, the new tax system was used as an instrument for the expansion of the mining industry, especially the copper industry. The government of Zaire, advised by IMF-IBRD experts, concluded that an increase in copper production and export would be the fastest and most reliable way of increasing foreign exchange earnings and of raising government revenues. Hence the economic and investment policies adopted by the government were based on the copper industry.

This sector was considered as the basis for the expansion of the financial resources on which depended other development efforts. Policy making was oriented to solving the problem of this sector as a matter of urgency. All investments pertaining to copper were placed on the priority list, not only direct investments in the sector but also those made in related infrastructure, such as energy and transport for export. Policy makers at both the IMF-IBRD and the government levels felt that investments in copper mining and connected infrastructure had been particularly sluggish in the immediate post-independence period and that Zaire should try to regain its earlier share in the international mining markets. The increased priority given to copper production and export not only suited the Mobutu regime's need for financial resources to be used for political purposes and for the establishment of an economic base for the leadership in power but it was also compatible with the regime's claim for "economic independence" and the role of Zaire as supplier of copper and cobalt on international markets.

The increase in the country's copper and cobalt production capacity was pursued by a two-pronged approach, involving both the expansion of the state-owned GECAMINES and the attraction of foreign private investors to set up new mining companies in unexploited areas.

As said earlier, the priority given by the government of Zaire to copper production and export was justified by the objectives and targets of President Mobutu's regime and the role of Zaire as supplier of primary commodities. Development projects undertaken by the Zairian regime in order to reach its ambitious economic program required, by government figures, domestic investments of $3 billion for the 1971-75 period, which necessitated a gross domestic capital formation of about $2.8 billion for the same period (Government of Zaire 1971). On the basis of available foreign financing and the outlook for demand and supply of copper, which in turn was related to projections of industrial growth in developed and oil-exporting countries, the government was encouraged to undertake a multipart mineral expansion program designed to increase copper and cobalt production and export in the manner sketched in Table 7.4.

Also encouraging were the unusually high real copper prices on the London Metal Exchange (LME) in the period 1965-70. IBRD and IMF experts projected enormous prospective government financial resources from copper. Adopting the medium price projection contained in Table 7.5, it was forecast that, for the medium term, copper would account for 70 percent of export earnings and that, although the short-term outlook was not bright, at the long run copper exports would bring 90 percent of gross foreign exchange earnings by 1980 (IBRD 1975b).

Thus the government of Zaire was encouraged to invest in the copper sector and related infrastructure in order to expand mineral exports and increase government revenues. Chapter 1 demonstrated how quickly these assumptions and dreams were shattered by international market forces. Mining expansion affected more than government finances however; it shaped the development of a tertiary economy, designed the fundamental nature of the modern urban sector as a whole, and encouraged the pauperization of the rural areas. The surplus value and wealth accruing from mineral exports not only accumulated in the mining sector and related infrastructure but also

TABLE 7.4

Copper Production Projections, 1970–90, as Seen in 1974
(thousands of tons)

	GECAMINES	SODIMIZA	SMTF	Total
1970	387	—	—	387
1971	407	—	—	407
1972	425	12	—	437
1973	472	25	—	497
1974	466	25	—	491
1975	470	50	—	520
1976	480	50	—	530
1977	590	70	80	640
1978	550	90	110	740
1979	580	110	125	815
1980	580	110	125	815
1985	650	n.a.	n.a.	1,185

n.a. = not available

Source: International Bank for Reconstruction and Development, "The Economy of Zaire," Report no. 821-ZR, vol. 2 (Washington, D.C., July 23, 1975), p. 44.

TABLE 7.5

Copper Price Projections, 1970–90, as Seen in 1974
(LME U.S. cents per pound)

	Low	Medium	High
1972	—	48	—
1973	—	81	—
1974	85	93	95
1970–74 average	66	67	67
1975	65	68	100
1976	75	82	110
1977	80	100	125
1978	85	108	140
1979	90	116	155
1980	95	124	170
1985	130	200	250
1990	200	245	295

Source: International Bank for Reconstruction and Development, "The Economy of Zaire," Report no. 821-ZR, vol. 2 (Washington, D.C., July 23, 1975), p. 46.

created a bureaucratic and economic elite desirous of modern goods and services. This attracted import-substitution industries with high import content in the manufacturing sector, which also contributed to unbalanced growth and loss of value through unequal exchanges.

In order to understand how national and multilateral emphasis on copper produced this series of complex forces that prevent balanced growth and contribute to the underdevelopment of Zaire's human resources, one has to deal with the whole pattern of national and international investments that created the disharmony.

THE MODERN SECTOR: NATIONAL
AND INTERNATIONAL INVESTMENTS
AND UNBALANCED GROWTH IN ZAIRE

Reginald Green and Ann Seidman (1969) showed that, because of paucity of capital and lack of domestic savings and managerial capabilities, developing countries have to depend on foreign capital for investments. This dependence upon foreign investments and aid results in the determination of national economic policy and even the limitation of domestic investment resources by foreign public and private interests. The consequences of this situation are that investments are made in the more profitable sectors, such as mineral-extracting industries and import-substituting assembly. In the long run, such investments do not create linkages with the rest of the economy, which in turn might create multiplier effects. Linkages are external and the multiplier effects created help foreign investors rather than the host country. The case of the modern sector in Zaire, especially the copper sector, has illustrated for many years this situation of foreign and national investments contributing to unbalanced growth.

Economic and investment policies adopted by Mobutu's regime since 1965 have been directed at a rapid growth of the modern sector, especially mining, transport infrastructure for export, manufacturing, and related activities. From 1970 to 1976, Zaire invested about 31 percent of its GDP but it achieved a growth rate of only 2.8 percent in that period. An unknown but very large percentage of investments during the 1970-76 period went to this modern sector; in constant prices, the value added in mining was "2.7 times that of monetized agriculture in 1970-1972, and 2.9 times in 1974-1976" (IBRD 1977, p. 32). The ratio has probably continued to climb. Specific modern sectors were highly favored.

The continuing expansion of the mining industry and the development of the manufacturing sector as a consequence of new investments established under the 1969 Investment Code resulted in heavy investments in energy estimated at 10 percent of total investments for the 1969-75 period (IBRD 1975d). Investments were based on the collaboration between the Zairian regime and foreign investors, which, as other chapters show, had its ups and downs. But major priorities and objectives of state and foreign capital remained relatively constant. The government sought expansion of mineral production and export so that it could extract tax revenues to be used for political purposes and "development" projects. Foreign investors' objectives were to secure a source of raw materials and to take advantage of the extensive mineral resources by investing not only in mining but also in import-substitution industries that could absorb the surplus produced by both the modern and agricultural sectors.

Government priorities were mainly achieved with investments in the GECAMINES expansion program and the Inga-Shaba power transmission line, while foreign investors' objectives were reflected through investments in the Société Minière de Tenke Fungurume (SMTF), the Société de Développement Industriel et des Mines du Zaire (SODIMIZA), and through various investments in the manufacturing sector (auto assembly plants, flour mills, cement plants, textile mills, and so on).

The two-part GECAMINES expansion program designed to increase production and export of copper and cobalt was begun in 1970. The first five-year expansion program (1970-74) provided for an increase in copper production of 100,000 metric tons to 460,000 metric tons. Investments for this first project were put at $260 million and financed mostly from internationally generated funds and loans of about $21 million from the U.S. Export-Import Bank (EXIMBANK) and the European Investment Bank. The government of Zaire, on its part, granted GECAMINES preferential tax treatment under the 1969 Investment Code to help it finance the expansion program from its own resources. This preferential treatment provided for the exemption until 1974 from all taxes on production of copper exceeding 360,000 tons and of cobalt exceeding 11,000 tons a year, and from miscellaneous duties and taxes related to the importation of equipment goods for the expansion plan (IBRD 1975b, 1975c).

The second five-year expansion program (1975-79) was designed for the opening of two open-pit mines in the Kolwezi area and for the construction and expansion of treatment plants and infrastructure facilities. Copper and cobalt production was expected to increase by 120,000 tons and 4,000 tons, respectively, raising annual total capacity to 580,000 tons of copper and 20,000 tons of cobalt. Investments for the second expansion program were estimated at about $200 million, of which $100 million was a loan from Libya, while the other $100 million was obtained from the IMF. Events overtook phase two.

The overall cost of GECAMINES' expansion program, including working capital and interest charges accruing during construction, was estimated at $440 million, of which 68 percent would be in foreign exchange (IBRD 1975c).

In order to increase copper and cobalt production, the government also signed two important mining conventions with Japanese and Anglo-U.S. interests. The first convention established SODIMIZA in April 1969. A consortium of the Nippon Mining Company and seven Japanese firms owned 85 percent of the share capital, while the government of Zaire took 15 percent with the option of buying up to 50 percent of the share capital. The first phase of the company's investment program consisted of the development of the Musoshi mines located southeast of Lubumbashi along the Zambian border. This phase was estimated to cost $80 million and produce 50,000 tons of copper annually. The new mining company benefited from the special fiscal system, marketing rights, and processing obligations under the 1969 Investment Code. SODIMIZA was to pay no export tax until 1978 and a full rate not until 1993. Both production and tax forecasts were to be altered by events. The company's management consisted almost entirely of Japanese expatriates, and more than 20 percent of its workers were Japanese (IBRD 1975a).

Another important joint venture between the government and foreign investors designed to increase copper and cobalt production was SMTF. (The collapse of world copper prices and two invasions of Shaba have placed actual implementation of SMTF in limbo; but its origins are highly illuminating.) President Mobutu's effort to end the monopoly held by privileged Belgian companies over Zairian mineral resources started with the adoption of new mining laws in 1966 and was followed by the nationalization of UMHK in 1967. This process of replacement of Belgian companies by new multinational companies that promised to collaborate with the Zairian regime and help it to acquire its "economic independence" continued with the takeover of GECAMINES concessions, giving them to new private and joint companies that could exploit them.

It was in this context of replacement of Belgian companies and the expansion of mineral production that the SMTF convention was signed on September 19, 1970, between the government of Zaire and Maurice Tempelsman and Robert Anderson. The two latter represented the following: AMOCO Mine Company, a subsidiary of Standard Oil Company of Indiana; Charter Consolidated, Limited, registered in London but owned by the Anglo-American Corporation of South Africa; Mitsui and Company; the French Bureau de Recherches Géologiques et Minières, which sold part of its shareholding to Omnium Mines (owned by the French-Dutch conglomerate Compagnie Financière de Paris et de Pays-Bas, which in turn is managed by the Anglo-American Corporation); and Leon Tempelsman & Son, Inc.

When one examines SMTF contracts and analyzes the corporate background of participants in the company, one can see that the personal relationship between President Mobutu of Zaire and U.S. businessman Maurice Tempelsman, along with the previous financial backing of U.S., British, and Japanese international banks that directly or indirectly owned businesses in Zaire or have loaned money to the Zairian government, helped the Anglo-U.S. consortium to strike the SMTF deal (Katwala 1979, especially chap. 4).

SMTF involved an investment of about $100 million, which was by far the largest private foreign investment in the copper sector since 1965. The company was given concession rights in the Tenke-Fungurume area, north of the GECAMINES concession. Ore reserves found in the area were said to average 6.2 percent copper and 0.4 percent cobalt. The investment was financed through Eurocurrency loans, most of which were owed to British banks led by Morgan Grenfell and U.S. international banks led by the Chase Manhattan Bank and guaranteed by EXIMBANK. Production start-up depended on the building of the Inga-Shaba power line. SMTF reports (1974) on risk management and control prepared by the company consultants suggest that SMTF investors influenced the government decision to build the $350 million power transmission line.

While foreign multinational corporations and banks were investing in the copper industry, the government of Zaire was pressured to assume the burden of putting considerable sums of money into infrastructure that facilitated copper production and export, such as energy and a modern transportation system. With regard to investments in energy, while investments in Inga I were designed to attract power-intensive industries in the Kinshasa-Bas-Zaire area, those in Inga II and especially in the Inga-Shaba power transmission line were intended to supply cheap energy to the copper industry in Shaba. Most of the financing of the line was secured through international tenders and loans. Citibank of New York led the syndicate that extended the $250 million loan for the Inga-Shaba power line. The loan agreements indicate that Citibank's decision to participate in the financing was based on what it considered were bright prospects of copper revenues for Zaire. It was, in sum, for the promotion of copper production and expansion of its banking activities in Zaire that Citibank extended its part of the loan.

With respect to a modern transport system, government investments were not aimed at facilitating the creation and maintenance of an internal market for locally produced goods, but instead were designed to link the areas where major mineral resources are produced with the seaports. Expenditures in the transport sector have been made in the expansion and replacement of rolling stock in order to increase the railway companies' mineral transport capacity, the expansion of the deep-water seaport at Matadi, that of the principal river port of Kinshasa, and the expansion of the river port of Ilebo, which is the transfer point between the KDL rail system and the Kasai River link with Kinshasa. As such, transport infrastructure modernization was in part linked to the country's role as supplier of raw materials to the developed world. It was also linked to the need for contact with the West and that of the regime in power in Zaire to increase exports and imports.

Public and private investments in the copper sector and related activities contributed to the development of an enclave economy that absorbed the lion's share of national and international resources and that expanded far more rapidly than the rest of the country's economic sectors. The mineral sector not only contained the country's economic power and resources but it also determined Zaire's overall economic performance. The expansion of this enclave economy was reflected in the changes in the GDP after 1969. The main components of the GDP were mining, energy, manufacturing processing, imported agricultural and other inputs, and services. As Table 7.6 illustrates, between 1970 and 1973 mining and metal processing grew by 5.2 percent, energy by 6.1 percent, manufacturing by 6.4 percent, and services by 7.4 percent. During the same period, agriculture grew by only 2.4 percent (IBRD 1977).

Table 7.6 not only suggests that value flowed toward the modern sectors of the economy, leaving the poor sectors poor, but it also shows that the emphasis on the mining industry and related infrastructure reinforced the colonial pattern of unequal exchange by operating economic sectors at greatly different

TABLE 7.6

Zaire: Changes in GDP, 1970–75

	Percentage Distribution			Yearly Growth Basis		
	1970	1973	1975	1970–73	1974	1975
Agriculture	17.6	16.3	15.8	2.4	2.8	-1.0
Mining and metal processing	23.5	23.6	23.4	5.2	3.1	1.0
Manufacturing	8.6	9.0	9.0	6.4	8.0	-1.9
Energy	1.0	1.0	0.9	6.1	-12.5	9.9
Construction	5.0	5.0	6.2	4.9	21.4	7.1
Transport	8.4	7.9	8.2	2.7	9.7	-0.4
Government services	13.2	12.9	13.8	4.0	5.1	6.9
Other services	22.7	24.3	22.7	7.4	9.3	-10.8

Source: International Bank for Reconstruction and Development, "Economic Conditions and Prospects of Zaire" (Washington, D.C., April 13, 1977), p. 2.

stages of modernity in the same society. The overall result of the priority given to the mining sector has been and remains a disarticulated economy whose sectors do not complement each other as equals. As Jean-Philippe Peemans (1975) put it, despite the apparent growth since 1965, the Zairian economy clearly exhibits the features of a disjointed, dependent economy whose surplus is produced through a highly extroverted structure.

The direct and indirect consequences and repercussions of Zaire's dependence on large-scale production and export of copper are clear. The effects for Zaire are not only its budgetary and balance-of-payments deficits and its sizable national debt but also, and more important, the perpetual underdevelopment of Zaire's human resources.

REFERENCES

Amin, Samir. 1976. Unequal Development. New York: Monthly Review.

Gérard-Libois, Jules. 1963. Sécession au Katanga. Brussels-Kinshasa: CRISP-INEP.

Government of Zaire. 1971. Politique, perspectives et moyens du développement, Kinshasa (July).

Gran, Guy. 1976. "Policy Making and Historical Process: Zaire's Permanent Development Crisis." Paper presented at the African Studies Association 1976 Annual Meeting, November 3-6.

Green, Reginald, and Ann Seidman. 1969. Unity or Poverty? The Economics of Panafricanism. Baltimore: Penguin.

International Bank for Reconstruction and Development. 1977. "Economic Conditions and Prospects of Zaire." Washington, D.C., April 13.

_____. 1975a. "The Economy of Zaire." Report no. 821-ZR. 4 vols. Washington, D.C., July 23.

_____. 1975b. "GECAMINES Expansion Program." Washington, D.C.

_____. 1975c. "Zaire—Appraisal of GECAMINES Expansion Project." 2 vols. Washington, D.C., December 26.

_____. 1975d. "Zaire—étude sectorielle d'eléctricité." 2 vols. Washington, D.C., March 18.

International Monetary Fund. 1976. "Zaire—Use of Fund Resources—Stand-by Arrangement." EBS/76/129. March 13.

_____. 1975. "Zaire—Recent Economic Developments." SM/75/225. August 26.

_____. 1968. "The Democratic Republic of Congo—Background Material for 1968 Article XIV Consultation." 2 vols. October 15.

Katwala, Ghifem. 1979. "Bureaucracy, Dependency and Underdevelopment in Zaire." Ph.D. dissertation, University of California, Berkeley.

Lacroix, Jean-Louis. 1967. Industrialization au Congo. Paris: Mouton.

Leclercq, Hughes. 1969. "Evolution des finances publiques de 1966 à 1969." Cahiers économiques et sociaux 7, nos. 2-3:147-95.

Mahieu, M. A. 1925. "L'exploitation du cuivre par les indigènes au Katanga." Congo 11, no. 1:107-29.

Mulumba, Lukoji. "Investir au Zaire." Zaire-Afrique, no. 103, pp. 141-52.

_____. 1973. Industrie minière et développement au Zaire. Lubumbashi: IMPAZA.

Peemans, Jean-Philippe. 1975. "The Social and Economic Development of Zaire since Independence: An Historical Outline." African Affairs 74, no. 295:148-79.

Radmann, Wolf. 1978. "The Nationalization of Zaire's Copper: From Union Minière to GECAMINES." Africa Today 25, no. 4:25-47.

Schumacher, E. F. 1973. Small Is Beautiful. New York: Harper & Row.

Société Minière de Tenke Fungurume. 1974. "Report on Risk Management and Control (SMTF Zaire Copper Project) to the Third Party Lenders." October.

_____. 1970. "Convention." September 19.

U.S., Department of Health, Education and Welfare. 1975. Syncrisis: The Dynamics of Health. An Analytical Series on the Interactions of Health and Socioeconomic Development. Zaire, vol. 14. Washington, D.C.

U.S., Department of the Interior. 1979. Mineral Commodity Summaries. Annual. January.

8

EDUCATION IN ZAIRE:
INSTRUMENT OF UNDERDEVELOPMENT

Galen Hull

INTRODUCTION: EDUCATION
EQUALS DEVELOPMENT?

With the end of World War II and the subsequent demise of the colonial era, the revolution of rising expectations in the developing world unleashed an unprecedented demand for education. It was widely believed that education would provide the key to solving the pressing problems of development. Education was seen by youth as the certain vehicle for social mobility and personal achievement. Students of the developing world and national leaders alike subscribed to the notion that educational development would fuel the engine of national development.

However, by the end of the 1960s, this abiding faith in education began to give way to serious doubts. School enrollment doubled from 1950 to 1965 throughout the world, bringing with it a host of problems. There were shortages of everything from teachers to classrooms to textbooks. The quality of education suffered, particularly in the developing countries. During this period the national education budgets of many countries grew more than twice as fast as the gross national product. Many African countries devoted as much as 20 to 25 percent of their budgets to education, and some as much as 30 percent. It became clear that, instead of providing the stimulus for development that had been expected, education was actually drawing resources away from other areas of development.

In Africa the mood of public officials and educators toward the role of education in development was reflected in the conferences called to map out strategies for educational programs. In 1961 the first such meeting was held in Addis Ababa and was attended by representatives of the newly independent states. Here the consensus was on quantity, on the need to increase educational facilities and student enrollment in order to bridge the gap with the advanced countries. Little attention was paid to curriculum and quality of education. A second major conference was convened in Nairobi in 1968; already the mood had changed from optimism to pessimism. While there had been an increase in most of the quantitative measures identified at Addis Ababa, it was becoming clear that the advances were not sufficient to meet critical development needs. Delegates turned their attention to issues of education for rural development, the high rates of attrition in enrollment, curriculum content, and the rising costs of education.

The 1970s have only served to confirm the incipient pessimism of the late 1960s. One speaks of a world education crisis not just in the developing world, but in the industrial world as well. While non-Western countries share many of the problems in education with those in the West, they are less capable of coping with the crisis because of their limited resources. By the time of the third major Africa-wide conference in 1976 in Lagos, it was painfully evident that educational institutions and policies had failed to meet the basic needs of African societies. Admittedly, some cosmetic changes had been made in curriculum content to include fewer references in history texts to "our ancestors, the Gauls," for example, and more attention to the teaching of indigenous languages. But in other respects the educational system actually served to reinforce the gap between social classes and between urban and rural dwellers. Western-oriented educational programs helped stimulate migration from rural areas to the cities but did little to improve rural life. Nor did education address such social problems as urban poverty, unemployment, and political discontent attendant upon rapid urbanization.

In the early 1960s, scholars began to turn their attention to education as a variable in the process of national integration. The prevailing developmentalist school of thought saw the main causes of underdevelopment as being accidents of history and geography that made some countries start out late on the path to economic growth and modernization. The newly independent countries were seen as suffering from constraints that could be overcome by supplying the missing "outputs," such as better management skills, education, and capital. It was assumed that assistance from the advanced countries could help provide these missing outputs and that the model for development should be that of the industrial Western nations. Educational systems in the former colonies would be the mirror image of those in the metropole, with some modifications along the lines of the U.S. system, and would serve as the engine of national development by producing cadres of educated and trained elites. In this view, education was considered the principal instrument of development.

The opposing view of education, and development in general, gained currency in the late 1960s and early 1970s and has come to be known as the underdevelopment school. According to this theory, the conditions of underdevelopment in the former colonies are the logical result of exploitation by the capitalist metropole. It sees the effects of economic domination of these countries by the advanced economies as being extremely unfavorable for true economic development. It also considers the bourgeois political and administrative structure inherited from the colonial powers as a detriment to development, serving to ensure continued dependency. The world economic system by its very nature relegates the underdeveloped countries to the bottom of the order. Participation in the world system—and its attendant forms of aid and trade—serves to reinforce conditions of underdevelopment and inhibits real autocentric growth.

Implications of underdevelopment theory for the role of education in development follow from this basic framework. Education becomes an instrument of underdevelopment rather than development. The educational system functions to transform rural dwellers into city dwellers, uprooting them from their culture, making them appendages of machines, and creating an army of urban unemployed. The result is that students are not taught how to make a living, speak their own language, think in terms of their own culture, or even produce those things for which they have need in order to subsist. Education in the capitalist economy serves to create a permanent reserve of workers, uprooted from their rural origins, who are available as docile servants of machines and the bureaucracy. At the same time, education is intended to inculcate those values that help to sustain the capitalist order.

This writer subscribes to the basic premises of the underdevelopment school, recognizing that this approach also has its limitations in explaining the failure of developing nations to achieve development. Certainly the experience of the past decade has called into question the assumptions of the development theorists. There is little indication that education has functioned as the motor of national development. On the contrary, it is clear that in most instances education has become an instrument of underdevelopment.

This position has been well articulated in the recent work of Benoît Verhaegen, a Belgian scholar who has worked in Zaire over the past two decades. Verhaegen (1978) argues that the education equals development equation, as an ideology, serves two main functions. One, it affirms the necessity of following the Western model of development. The progress of a society is measured in terms of the literacy rate, the number of textbooks, the degree of urbanization, and the knowledge of international languages. Second, it masks the basic objectives of underdevelopment—the rules of the capitalist game—that dictate that most of the fruits of development be reserved for a privileged few, the strongest. The capitalist economic system is founded on the profit motive, not upon human welfare. The strongest are able to maintain an economic system that increases the gap between rich and poor. Education is used as one key to maintain privileged social status.

Verhaegen (1978) finds the basic weakness of the developmentalists to be their tendency to isolate the system of education from its global social context. He sees the origin of the gap between inputs and outputs not so much in the lack of productivity in the internal system, but in the fundamental contradiction in the capitalist system between the objective and limited needs of economic production and the practically unlimited subjective needs produced by capitalist education. The educational crisis in Africa allows a clear understanding of these contradictions. Initially, education was seen as the principal means of achieving social mobility. The diploma provided a ticket to success for the individual. Individual aspirations tended to be equated, on the national level, with economic development. In terms of objective economic conditions, however, the lack of capital and the dependence upon external markets limited the possibilities of advancing a national economic bourgeoisie.

Eventually, it became clear that the educational system was contradictory to these individual interests as the value of the diploma decreased and the growth of the economy stagnated.

Verhaegen notes that 1972 marked the watershed in the evaluation of the role of education in development. In that year a number of publications appeared that probed the nature and origin of the crisis in education. The year before, Ivan Illich published his celebrated pamphlet A Society without Schools and Paulo Freire his Practical Education and Freedom. Both were radical critiques of the prevailing model of education. Henceforth, the ideas of new pedagogy, continuing education or adult education, rural education, and free schools became subjects of debate and experimentation. The radical critique of the prevailing educational system as represented in the writings of Illich and Freire called for the "de-schooling" of society and a "pedagogy for the oppressed."

The ruling bureaucratic classes of the developing countries took note of the new critical vogue in education, going so far as to attempt to incorporate the new vocabulary into speeches and development plans. They concluded that the traditional system of education inherited from the colonial powers was inappropriate and called for education to be directly linked to the productive function. They spoke of replacing the present system of education with one designed to meet the practical needs of the nation. They recognized that their own political survival would depend on reducing the pool of educated but parasitic unemployed youth who populated the urban areas. Still, all the efforts to reform the educational system that did not take into account the social and economic structure inherited from the West were destined to failure. The only feasible policy that would protect the interests of the ruling classes was the limitation of school enrollment (proposed by development experts) by a selection process that would preserve the present economic order.

These are the basic issues that are the subject of this chapter on education in Zaire. In many respects, as will be seen in other chapters, Zaire represents a model of underdevelopment. The objective of this chapter is to explain how the educational system operates as an instrument of underdevelopment despite the seemingly progressive process of nationalization and its stated aim of making education more relevant to the nation's development needs. Zaire is typical of other African nations in that "radical" changes have been introduced in the educational system without bringing about the salutary effects hoped for. It is the political and economic structure of the regime that has ensured a negative role of education in the development process.

THE EDUCATION SECTOR IN ZAIRE

At the time of independence in the Congo in 1960, the educational system was one of the most complex and unbalanced on the African continent (George 1966). The Belgian colonial administration left a legacy of a massive system of primary schools that produced few graduates. Total primary school enrollment stood at 1,644,000 in 1960, of which 1,460,000 were in subsidized independent schools and 180,000 were in nonsubsidized schools. The postprimary schools had a total of 22,780 Congolese. At the true secondary level in all programs (general, teacher training, and technical), there were 28,951, representing less than 2 percent of the total primary school enrollment. On the basis of the high level of primary enrollment—fully 70 percent of the estimated population of primary school age—the Congo boasted one of the highest literacy rates on the continent.

This was something of an idle boast, however, as the Congo also had one of the highest dropout rates in Africa at all grade levels. Many primary pupils were overage. More than 70 percent of the primary schools provided only the first two grades. An estimate of the enrollments of Roman Catholic and Protestant subsidized schools at independence indicated that fully 43 percent of the pupils were in the first grade and 64 percent in the first two grades. The enrollment rate varied greatly from one region to another, a fact that was to have important policy implications later on. The majority of teachers were nationals who had no teaching qualifications at all.

The system was relatively complex, characterized by two major features: a division of schools between those for Congolese and non-Congolese and between government (or official) and nongovernment schools. In spite of the increasing role of the government in education in the 1950s, the great majority of pupils were attending schools operated by religious organizations (George 1966). More than 75 percent of these were in Roman Catholic schools and 19 percent in Protestant schools. Most Roman Catholic schools were government subsidized, reflecting the rather symbiotic relationship between the church and the colonial administration. Only a few Protestant-run schools were government aided.

At the time of independence a clear distinction was maintained at the primary and secondary levels between schools for Congolese and those for Europeans, even though reforms introduced in 1954 modified the system slightly to provide higher standards for African students. New government primary schools began offering a six-year program of a higher standard with a Belgian curriculum adapted to African conditions. The French language was taught in the first year in addition to indigenous languages. A variety of postprimary schools were established for practical training and apprenticeships.

There were two major types of secondary-level schools. The first category included schools offering short courses of three to four years and the second consisted of institutions known as "secondary" schools. Those in the first category trained clerks, primary schoolteachers, medical personnel, and agricultural workers. From 1948 onward, another system of secondary schools was developed, offering a six- or seven-year program of a more academic nature for Africans. They were staffed almost entirely by Belgian expatriates. Some secondary schools offered a general education program intended as college preparatory, while others were oriented toward vocations. Reforms introduced in 1958 were designed to upgrade all secondary schools to Belgian type and quality. But, by 1960, there was virtually no formal training in vocations other than agriculture; such training took place only in the workplace. Secondary education for girls had only begun. In 1960 fewer than 1,000 were enrolled and none had graduated. But then only a couple of hundred African students altogether had graduated from secondary school.

What emerges from this profile of the primary and secondary educational system at independence is a picture of extreme imbalance between the type of education offered to sons and daughters of European residents and that extended to the masses of Africans. For Africans, the system tried to provide a minimal level of literacy and to some extent training in basic vocational skills. Secondary education for Africans was designed primarily to provide lower level administrators and clerks.

Postsecondary education in the country at the time of independence was offered at two newly established universities, the Catholic University of Lovanium near Kinshasa and the Official University at Elizabethville (Lubumbashi). Lovanium was touted for its impressive physical plant, which included an atomic reactor. Both universities were intended as mirror images of their respective mother institutions in Belgium. Although they both admitted African students from the outset, their enrollment was predominantly European at independence. In 1963 a third university was founded under Protestant auspices in Stanleyville (Kisangani). Among the African population at independence the country counted fewer than 20 university graduates.

As in other newly independent African countries, the end of the colonial era in the Congo brought heightened aspirations and the determination to make national institutions more responsive to development needs. Particularly since the advent of the Mobutu regime in 1965, there has been a great deal of rhetoric on the necessity of bringing the educational system into the service of the nation, expanding the opportunities for education to the masses, and making the substance of education more relevant to practical needs. But, as with other institutions of development, the education sector has been a disappointment.

A World Bank education sector memorandum for Zaire recently laid bare the failure of the system to meet development needs (IBRD 1977). The memorandum chronicles both the results and the problems encountered in the attempt to harness education to development objectives. Despite the attempt of the Zairian government to gain control over the educational system, as late as 1973 (the last year for which consistent data were available) fully 85 percent of primary school and over 60 percent of secondary enrollments were in schools controlled by religious organizations. As part of its overall program of nationalization of Zairian institutions, the government turned its attention first to the system of higher education, officially bringing it under state control in 1971. It followed suit by nationalizing the primary and secondary systems in 1974. The World Bank memorandum concluded, however, that: "The unplanned and uncoordinated growth of the educational sector both before and after independence has not effectively contributed to the development of the human resources required to exploit Zaire's development potential" (p. 1).

Although the educational system had expanded quantitatively in many respects during the period of independence, many of the same problems inherited from the colonial era were still visible in the mid-1970s. Primary school enrollment had grown to 3.3 million, of which a third were overage. Secondary enrollment more than doubled during the period from 1966 to 1972, amounting to over 300,000; still it was only 10 percent of the relevant age group. University enrollment showed the most dramatic increase, from only a handful of nationals at independence to 17,000, or 1 percent of the relevant age group. The World Bank was not optimistic. In spite of these indicators of growth, the country still suffered from a lack of trained and experienced manpower, and it would "probably take at least a generation before the formal education sector of Zaire contributes effectively to development" (IBRD 1977, p. 2).

The outline of the principal problems in the education sector submitted in the memorandum provides an almost classic model of the technocratic form of development analysis. Seven points were addressed. Despite the rhetoric of reform, few significant changes have been made since this 1976 analysis.

Organization and Management

In addition to the practical problem of administering an educational system in a country as vast as Zaire, there remains severe problems of ineffective administrative organization and lack of qualified administrative cadres. The highly centralized nature of the system carries with it the inability to respond to regional needs. Despite numerous studies and recommendations by various agencies such as the World Bank, there appears to have been little improvement in the relationship between central and regional authorities. Indeed, capable regional staff are being underutilized and their responsibilities duplicated by functionaries of the Department of Education in Kinshasa. The effect is an appalling lack of support services to schools in terms of transportation, staff, and equipment. Because the sums officially budgeted for maintenance and equipment seem fairly adequate, it must be assumed that central financial control means that some of the allocated funds are finding their way into the pockets of departmental officials in Kinshasa.

Structure of Education

One of the basic problems of the system is that few graduates of the six-year secondary school program, particularly those who complete the teacher training course, actually become teachers. They prefer to enter the university and receive a scholarship rather than to teach school in the rural areas, where salaries are no more than university scholarships. The result is a glut of students enrolled in literary courses at the university level, for whom the market is increasingly limited. This in turn contributes to the problem of the educated unemployed, especially in urban areas.

Teachers

The World Bank memorandum identifies the shortage of teachers as "the most serious single problem facing the GOZ in education" (p. 3). Because teachers' salaries remain low, they often acquire other part-time jobs, particularly in the cities. Only one-fifth of the country's primary teachers in 1973 had had teacher training, scarcely an improvement over the situation at independence. Pupils admitted to primary teacher training courses are often those who have failed to gain admission to secondary school. At the secondary level, one-third of the teachers are still expatriate. Even though they are paid higher salaries than their Zairian counterparts, there remains a high rate of attrition among expatriates. Only a third of the Zairian teachers are qualified for their posts.

Curricula

The bias in favor of literary courses continues despite the government's stated intention to shift the balance toward science and technical subjects. Teachers in the latter fields continue to be in short supply. Instruction at each level of education still tends toward preparation for the next highest level rather than for practical vocations. Because 70 percent of all primary pupils and over half of secondary pupils do not continue their education, the system is not meeting their individual needs in terms of job preparation or the country's development needs.

Equity

As during the colonial era, there remains a significant imbalance of educational benefits and enrollment among the regions. Some regions, such as Kinshasa and Kasai Oriental, are still favored in terms of facilities and faculty as well as chances for admission. Female students continue to be greatly underrepresented, as are children from poorer families because of requirements that parents contribute to school maintenance costs. At the secondary level this contribution is quite substantial, amounting to an average of 7 percent of per capita income.

Finance

This issue is directly related to the matter of financial management. Budgetary constraints continue to have a serious negative impact on educational planning. The policy of granting rather generous scholarships to university students regardless of their individual ability to pay constitutes a severe drain on the government's financial resources. This is in contrast to the primary and secondary systems where parents are required to pay school fees.

Internal Efficiency and External Productivity

Poor quality of teachers remains the chief cause of internal inefficiency. Dropout rates remain high at all levels. The critical question of external productivity is difficult to measure in the absence of any quantified manpower data. Surveys such as those conducted by UNESCO indicated that much more emphasis needs to be placed on teacher training, commercial and paramedical training at the secondary and university levels, and agricultural training at all levels. Managerial, industrial, and technical training is needed at all levels. Even in the face of the critical manpower needs that have been identified such as for nurses, the government has failed to employ a sufficient number of graduates, ostensibly because of budgetary constraints.

The World Bank was not alone in noting these symptoms of educational underdevelopment. Indeed, by the early 1970s, the formal system of education in Zaire had become so irrelevant to the country's needs that officials began to talk of the necessity for a revolution in education, not just a reform. The president himself showed an awareness of the magnitude of the problem in his public speeches. In 1973 Mobutu called for a total reexamination of the school's monopoly on education, advocating a "de-schooled" society and echoing the radical thoughts of Ivan Illich.

The practical response of public authorities to the crisis of education in Zaire has not been unlike that in other developing countries. There has been a natural tendency for the state to assume greater control over national institutions, especially education, which is considered still to be the key to future development. The momentous decision to create a national university in 1971 was taken amid a program of cultural nationalism that came to be known as "le recours à l'autenticité" (return to authenticity). The program's most visible feature was the draconian decision to change not only the name of the country itself (from Congo-Kinshasa to Zaire), but the names of public institutions and those of individual citizens. In January 1972, the president announced the official changing of his own name to Mobutu Sese Seko Kuku Ngendu wa Zabanga. All Zaire nationals were henceforth required to discard their European given names in favor of authentic traditional names. All foreign monuments that graced the nation's capital were retired to the national museum. All the journals and newspapers of the country were given authentic Zairian names. Government ministries were to be known as commissariats and ministers as commissaires. In the diplomatic realm, the government announced its decision to recognize the People's Republic of China, North Korea, and East Germany in accordance with the remarkable foreign policy principle of "neither left nor right, nor middle of the road."

In 1974, an educational reform commission was established, following upon the sweeping nationalization of higher education in 1971. Among the basic educational goals elaborated were:

1. To achieve universal basic education of six years by 1980;
2. To increase the professional emphasis of secondary and higher education so that they provide the nation with trained personnel necessary for development;

3. To act so that the school is no longer the sole means of advancement in society;

4. To establish government control over the entire education system, including schools run by religious authorities, replacing religious instruction with political and civic education; and

5. To introduce a year of obligatory national service before entrance to the university.

Of these principles, the only one that has been implemented to any substantial extent is that concerning government control of church schools. Catholic and Protestant school directors were replaced by government appointees. But many religious schools continued to function as before, as the government had neither the funds nor the personnel to enforce its decision. By 1976, the government began to reconsider the policy and to encourage religious authorities to resume control of schools it had taken over.

The other policy objectives have fared even less well. The goal of universal basic education in 1980 will not be met. There remains a very high percentage of overaged children in primary schools and the distribution is still heavily skewed in favor of boys. At the secondary level, the desired emphasis on professional training has been impeded by the lack of teachers in those subjects and the absence of manpower data necessary to determine the country's professional needs. Some attention has been given to developing nonformal education programs in the outreach division of the university. In 1972 the Centre Inter-disciplinaire pour le Développement et l'Education Permanente (CIDEP) was established to "serve the masses" through programs of adult education. The obligatory national service program has proved difficult to enforce and highly unpopular with students.

THE ROLE OF INTERNATIONAL ASSISTANCE

The core reality of the involvement of both private and public international agencies in the education sector in Zaire is that their activities have taken place in the absence of any comprehensive education plan. This has meant that the most well-meaning projects are doomed to failure or at best to a very marginal impact on the educational system. As in other sectors of the body politic, increased participation of international agencies has entailed the government's giving up a measure of administrative and financial autonomy. The result is yet another indicator of the regime's inability to manage its own affairs in the interest of national development. Studies and reports of the various international agencies are replete with instances of the failure of the government to respond to even minimal standards of administrative and financial organization necessary for the implementation of projects. The agencies, for their part, continue to assume that the education sector can be revived through the repetition of sound development principles and the inculcation of solid management practices. What is not recognized is that fundamental political change is necessary to bring about the desired effects.

Over the past decade, the World Bank has made major efforts to assist in the development of education and training in Zaire. A World Bank education mission visited Zaire in August 1969 and again in April 1970 with UNESCO staff participation. A UNESCO project preparation mission assisted the Zairian government in preparing an education project proposal for submission in October 1970. The first education project was finally approved and signed in December 1971.

This first project (IBRD 1971) was originally to cost a total of $11.8 million and included an International Development Association (IDA) (the soft loan window in the World Bank) credit of $6.5 million. It was intended to help meet manpower needs by improving and expanding facilities for teacher training and technical education in the major cities. In addition, technical assistance was provided for studies aimed at improving the organization and management of the Department of National Education. The project met with a multiplicity of problems in its implementation and fell two and a half years behind. When it was recosted in 1975, an overrun of nearly $20 million was anticipated due to many factors both in Zaire and abroad. By that time the government was already experiencing serious financial difficulties and was unable to meet the additional costs. Various elements of the project therefore were deleted. Even in its reduced dimensions, the project cost $7 million more than the original total project estimate.

In 1972 an educational planning unit financed by UNDP was established to conduct a manpower study. But the study was hampered by the Department of Education's inability to implement plans and monitor its own progress. By the end of the 1970s, there was still no comprehensive manpower plan, and the unplanned growth of the education sector still failed to meet development needs.

A second World Bank project was mounted in 1976, as a result of a 1973 joint FAO/World Bank study of the rural education sector and a preparation mission in 1974 assisted by UNESCO and WHO (IBRD 1976). The government requested a wide-ranging investment program for rural teacher training and health and agricultural education estimated to cost over $130 million. Even before the bank group's appraisal, however, the government chose to eliminate the health education component because of limited funds and capacity for implementation.

The second project, approved by the World Bank in April 1976, was not signed until December 1976 because the government was unable to agree on terms with the architectural consultants originally proposed. The total project cost was estimated at $48.5 million—greatly reduced from the original request—of which an IDA credit of $21 million was approved. Emphasis was to be placed on meeting the need for rural primary schoolteachers and agricultural technicians. The project included the construction and equipping of five rural primary teacher training colleges in five of the country's eight regions, as well as the rehabilitation and extension of six agricultural technical training institutes and one higher institute of agricultural studies. The project package included technical assistance, management studies, and evaluation. Because the project proposal fell far short of the dimensions envisaged in the 1973 FAO/World Bank study, a third World Bank project is now being contemplated.

Bank consultants cautioned that in view of the difficulties encountered in existing projects, any future projects should only be undertaken when there was clear sign of improvement (IBRD 1977). It remains to be seen just how that improvement is measured and what level of improvement will be acceptable to the World Bank.

In addition to these specific projects, agencies of the United Nations were engaged in two major education sector studies. One was the FAO/World Bank study of 1973, which resulted in a detailed report on the rural sector published in 1974. In November 1975, UNESCO conducted a second study, a comprehensive sector survey, which was published in April 1976. The UNESCO report set out projections for primary and secondary school enrollment to 1990 and the financial implications for increases at all levels. Among other conclusions the report suggested that the growth of secondary enrollment be slowed from 10 to 5 percent and that unit costs at the university level be substantially reduced. The report was based on very scanty manpower data, a key missing ingredient in all education sector studies. Because of the policy implication of reducing secondary enrollment rates and cutting back on university scholarships, the government was slow to respond to the UNESCO report or to act upon it.

One of the few signs the Zairian government has shown of actually attempting to make education relevant to development needs was the creation of the nonformal education center CIDEP in December 1972, shortly after the nationalization of the system of higher education. Following a meeting of U. S. Agency for International Development (AID) consultants, the rector of the National University, and CIDEP's director in April 1974, AID began to formulate a project proposal to help CIDEP by training Zairians in program design and management.

The AID project paper was submitted in June 1977 and carried an estimated total cost of $2.4 million for three years, of which AID was to contribute $863,000 and the Zairian government the remainder (AID 1977). The project envisaged assistance to the poor majority through out-of-school education programs in literacy and agricultural projects with an educational component. It was further intended to help bridge the "social and institutional gap between university faculty, staff, and students and the Zairian masses who lack the skills and means to escape poverty" (AID 1977, p. 4). The project was considered a deliberate effort to enable the university to develop "relevant institutional behavior" in response to national development needs.

The AID/CIDEP project, originally anticipated to run from October 1977 through September 1980, is in some ways consistent with the U. S. congressional mandate to assist poor majorities. It properly identifies the problems of the formal education system, and the university in particular, and approaches them in the context of development goals. Nonetheless, in the absence of an overall assessment of the nation's education and human resources and their relation to national development, this project, like other discrete approaches to development, is likely to be imprisoned and warped by the larger system.

Other foreign assistance has also played a role. Capital expenditures by the Department of National Education vary drastically from year to year. By far the largest portion of capital expenditures on education has been financed by foreign aid. The modest contribution of the Zairian government has in fact declined proportionately in recent years.

Because of the poor record of implementing education programs, there is relatively little foreign public sector investment in the sector. The European Development Fund (EDF) financed an architectural school in Kinshasa in 1975 and the planning of a new teacher training institute. Construction of an institute of electrical engineering in Kinshasa is also being financed by EDF. A number of integrated rural development projects financed by Western countries include training components.

The Belgian government continues to provide the largest share of foreign assistance to recurrent expenditures in the education sector; its aid has consisted mainly of salaries for Belgian teachers and administrators, scholarships to Zairian students, and direct subsidies to the university. Much smaller contributions are being made by the UN Development Program and the French government, followed by West Germany, Canada, the United States, and the Netherlands. They are concentrated mainly on the teacher training and technical institutes. The Ford Foundation has given assistance to the Kisangani campus of the National University for the Center for Education Research. The Rockefeller Foundation maintains a program of support focused primarily on the social science faculty at the Lubumbashi campus, providing U.S. professors, scholarships for Zairian graduate students, and some operating costs. The Rockefeller presence in Lubumbashi reached its peak in the mid-1970s and has since been cut back.

NATIONALIZATION OF HIGHER EDUCATION

The creation of the National University in August 1971 was an event that was the culmination of a process begun several years before (Hull 1974a). Until that time the three universities in Zaire had functioned as separate institutions, two of them private and one official. The effect of the decree creating one university system known as Université Nationale du Zaire (UNAZA) was to bring higher education under government control. The new National University was to be composed of the 3 campuses and the 21 technical and teacher-training institutes under the management of a rector appointed by the president of the republic. The governing body of UNAZA, the Conseil d'Administration, consisted of 13 members all appointed by the president. An important feature of university governance was its control by the Department of Education. The minister of education was named president of the governing board and given the power of veto over its decisions.

As in other African countries, the university in Zaire was among the last institutions to be Africanized and be subjected to the power of the state. The almost sacred notion of institutional autonomy propounded by the foreign founders of the universities in Zaire allowed them to escape the radical changes imposed on other political, social, and economic institutions. For years after political independence the university remained an enclave of foreign culture, administered by Belgians and Americans, with mainly expatriate teaching staff. Curricula and research reflected the traditional format of the metropolitan universities. The system of collegiality, according to which each faculty retained a high degree of autonomy, was based on the principle of academic freedom, the corollary of institutional autonomy.

What emerged from the nationalization decree was the model of a national university that challenged the basic premises of the traditional Western model. The principal instrument of nationalization was the state and its political arm, the Mouvement Populaire de la Révolution (MPR), founded by Mobutu in 1967. The party's doctrine of nationalism was codified in its Manifeste de la N'Sele, which stated as one of its fundamental principles "the exaltation of the values of the country in the intellectual and cultural domain." Among the objectives of the Manifeste in pursuit of this principle was "the rationalization of education" in order to furnish the nation with the cadres necessary for development. In practical terms this principle was to be translated into the centralization and politicization of the system of education.

The impetus for the nationalization decree was provided by student unrest. Following a student demonstration at Lovanium and the intervention of government troops, which resulted in the killing of dozens of students in 1969, the state assumed greater control over the appointment of administrative and academic personnel. By 1971, all three university rectors were nationals appointed by the president. Student protests at the Protestant university (Université Libre du Congo) in Kisangani in December 1970 and again at Lovanium in June 1971 led to the creation of a commission for the reform of higher education (Hull 1976). The commission consisted of 15 members, all but 6 of whom were members of the party's Bureau Politique. Any reform of the educational system was therefore bound to bear the stamp of the MPR.

Then a congress of national professors was convened in July 1971 to legitimize the decisions of the commission. The report of the congress endorsed all of the major themes of the reform. The system of higher education would be centralized under the authority of a single governing body. The various faculties would be regrouped and consolidated in order to avoid the duplication of functions and expenditures. The technical institutes and teacher training colleges were to be fully integrated into the university system, with the notion of expanding access to the university "beyond the children of the bourgeoisie." The report also focused on the cultural context of education, on combating the foreign influence in the formation of the nation's youth. It underscored the importance of civic education and the inculcation of indigenous African values, which could only be imparted by Zairian nationals. This would necessarily entail accelerating the Africanization of teaching cadres.

Finally, the congress pronounced itself on the role of students in the university, emphasizing their responsibilities rather than their rights. The principle of civic responsibility and discipline could be best served by incorporating student activities into the party through its youth organization, the Jeunesse du Mouvement Populaire de la Révolution (JMPR). It was proposed that every student be obliged to serve one year of national service before being admitted to the university and to sign a document declaring loyalty to the MPR. National professors themselves would be obliged to participate in party activities. Those in the social sciences would be required to submit course outlines to academic authorities in order to "put an end to all indoctrination on the order of ideology other than that of authentic nationalism."

The nationalization of the system of higher education in Zaire thus became a logical and predictable outgrowth of the nation's political development. In its basic features, the process in Zaire has not differed greatly from that in other African countries. As Nzongola Ntalaja (1978) has pointed out, the African university has become the ideological apparatus of the state, reflecting in its functions all the characteristics of the postcolonial state. The basic role of the university within the political system is to elaborate and transmit the dominant ideology, the ideology of the ruling class. The university mirrors the contradictions of the society around it. In postcolonial Africa, "it is afflicted by all the ills to be found within the state system, which include normlessness, nepotism, and authoritarianism" (Nzongola 1978, p. 8). The university in Zaire must therefore be seen in the larger political and social context rather than the narrow confines of the institution itself.

Consider the overall political environment. At the end of the 1960s, it appeared on the surface that most of the factors for development in Zaire were present. Central political power had been established under Mobutu. The state had rid itself of its UN tutelage and had its own administrative infrastructure. After the economic reforms of 1967, the elite enjoyed a period of relative prosperity that was fueled by unprecedented levels of foreign investment. Zaire also maintained a favorable image in the realm of international relations among moderates and radicals alike. In the period leading up to the reform of higher education, the three universities experienced rapid growth. From 1966 to 1976, student enrollment grew from 2,000 to over 20,000. The number of doctoral candidates grew from only 10 to 400 during the same period. By 1978 there were 12,000 Zairian university graduates compared with the handful at independence. In some faculties within the university, such as the social sciences and education, the teaching staff was largely Africanized.

By the mid-1970s, however, the basic weaknesses in the political and administrative structure of Zaire had become abundantly evident. Graft and corruption were pervasive at all levels of administration, from the very top on down (see Chapter 5). The centralization of administrative authority in Kinshasa strained the capacity of the system to function and alienated regional constituencies. Regional favoritism and nepotism operated under the guise of correcting the imbalance created during the colonial era. Specifically, there was overrepresentation of decision makers from the president's home region and a corresponding discrimination against those from traditionally advanced regions, such as Kasai and Bas-Zaire. The country came to be dominated by a bureaucratic elite that owed its power and influence to the party.

The National University did not escape any of these tendencies. The university became the repository of self-interest of a bureaucratic and academic elite who regularly couched their public utterances in appropriately revolutionary-sounding phrases while lining their pockets from public coffers. The day-to-day administration of the various campuses and institutes became a matter of parceling out political favors and confusing public interest with private gain. University administrators, and some national faculty members, were among the chief beneficiaries of the president's program of expropriation of commercial property unleashed in 1973. They were derided sotto voce by students and townspeople as acquéreurs—those who accumulated wealth through political favoritism.

Meanwhile, recurrent and capital expenditures on the university system suffered gross discrepancies even though campus administrators found sufficient funds in the budget for elaborate social events that featured student cheerleaders known as groups choc d'animation. There was, at the same time, scarcely enough money on hand frequently to provide a subsistence diet for the student cafeteria. Operating funds for the various faculties were chronically inadequate, although university administrators managed to find money for maintenance of their often sumptuous university-provided homes. Programs of physical expansion of the campuses and institutes slowed to a halt as foreign sources of capital dried up. Even though the government devoted as much as one-third of its total budget to education, of which one-quarter went to higher education, it was so woefully mismanged that basic needs went unmet. In the administration of UNAZA, the MPR slogan "se servir, non; servir, qui" (serve self, no; serve, yes) became a parody of itself.

James Coleman (1977), former director of the Rockefeller program in Zaire, has described a climate of "permissive authoritarianism" in many Third World universities. While this has been generally true of UNAZA, there have been a number of instances of overt physical intimidation and academic coercion by MPR operatives that belie a not-so-permissive authoritarianism. Students who have questioned the authority of the JMPR or have been less than enthusiastic participants in its campus activities have been subject to harassment and physical beatings. There has been at least one celebrated case in which an outstanding student in the social science faculty was forced to change the subject of his senior thesis because it was judged to be too politically sensitive. The government has devised ways of limiting the freedom of expression of national professors by restricting their participation in international conferences and study abroad, in some instances prohibiting travel outside Zaire altogether. As Coleman points out, however, the most common pattern of political pressure on the national professor is a combination of "cooptation and rewards mixed with the threat of withdrawal of resources and status."

Politicization of UNAZA has meant an increasingly limited role of the expatriate teaching staff and especially administrators. The few remaining expatriate deans of faculty have escaped the system of political punishment and rewards dispensed to nationals by the MPR. Because most campus activities take place within the context of the MPR, and because expatriates are excluded from party membership, their participation in university life is limited to basic functions of teaching and research. The subjects of research reflect a high degree of self-censorship. Publications overtly critical of the regime are prudently deferred until the end of contract. Expatriate staff whose salaries are paid by their own government or private foundations enjoy a certain immunity from the vicissitudes of university administration, whereas those on direct hire by the government are subject to some of the same incumbrances (severe housing shortage, delayed salary payments, and so on) as are national staff.

The social operations of the university also reveal contradictions in Zairian society. Nzongola (1978) has argued that the university functions "primarily in the interest of one of the privileged groups in society, the professional intellectual" (p. 11). Despite their relatively privileged position in society, university teachers are dissatisfied with their salaries. Such salaries are lower than those of top-level civil servants and administrative staff in state and private enterprises. Teachers are justifiably displeased with the considerably higher salaries of expatriate staff with comparable qualifications. They are frustrated by their inability to make a positive contribution to social and political change, but generally unwilling to challenge the existing order. In Zaire, even within the ranks of national professors, there is a marked contrast in social status and life-style between those who successfully pursue business interests in addition to their teaching obligations and those who live off their salaries alone. Not a few professors, especially at the Kinshasa campus, have managed to enrich themselves as acquéreurs and through consulting ventures. Some have been launched into political prominence from their university positions.

The former dean of the faculty of social science, Crawford Young, has written of the social mobility functions of the faculty (1977). For the student, admission to the university still opens up the prospect of a privileged career. In principle, admissions quotas to the various faculties are set by the central administration in Kinshasa. In practice, there is immense pressure at the campus level to admit students above the official quotas. Thus admissions procedures are subject to considerable petty corruption by admissions officials. In 1974, for example, first-year enrollment for the social science faculty was set by Kinshasa at 300, but 1,600 managed to gain entrance to the faculty by various means.

Regional quotas, which also reflect ethnic distribution, are a source of conflict within the faculty. Although the quota system is intended to ensure an equitable distribution of students, it is inefficient and works to alienate both those for whom it is designed to help and those it discriminates against. One of the regions favored by the system is Equateur, the president's home region. The high level of unpopularity of the regime subjects students from that region to much animosity on the part of other students. As Young points out, however, the regional imbalance has actually been maintained in the proportion of recent graduates in the faculty from traditionally advanced regions, such as Shaba and Kasai.

Perhaps the most critical factor conditioning student life in recent years is the decline in the relative value of the university diploma. As student enrollment has increased rapidly, so has the rate of unemployment and under-employment among university graduates. This is explained in large part by the disparity between the disciplines chosen by students, on the one hand, and the market demand for professional and technical skills, on the other. The department of international relations, for example, graduated 89 students in 1975, far more than the Foreign Ministry needed in diplomatic service. Nor did the graduates have the kind of management skills that would attract the multinationals operating in the private sector. The creation of the department a few years previously was more a matter of prestige than serious consideration of development needs. The department remained grossly deficient in even the most basic texts and library materials. Its location on the Lubumbashi campus was far removed from the center of diplomatic and commercial activitiy in Kinshasa. In sum, the department served neither the development needs of the nation nor the career goals of its graduates, many of whom joined the ranks of the unemployed or settled for work in unrelated fields.

The issue of student recruitment and the social function of the university is likely to receive increased attention in the near future. Already voices are being raised in favor of the traditional elitist role of the university. Philip Foster (1978) contends that universities "are, and inescapably must be 'elitist' and elite-producing institutions" (p. 8). He maintains that universities "are not the guardians of social equity in any society" nor can they hardly be expected "to rectify those social and ethnic imbalances that spring from historical patterns of development of selective processes that begin well below the level of tertiary education" (pp. 11-12).

In such a social and political environment, university research has contributed little to public policy in most areas of human development. Verhaegen (1978), among those most intimately involved in research in Zaire over the past two decades, states flatly that "there is no research for development in Zaire" (pp. 175 ff.). As late as 1978, he noted that there was no research in such key sectors as agronomy, demography, medicine, or ecology. Within state and parastatal institutions, research has become purely formal and bureaucratized. When valid research efforts have been made the results usually have been ignored by public authorities. Those centers of research that do exist—such as the National Institute for Agricultural Research (INERA), the Institut de Recherches Economiques et Sociale (IRES), and Verhaegen's own Centre de Recherches Interdisciplinaires pour le Développement du l'Education (CRIDE)—operate without clear directives and with little relevance to policy making. Those Zairians who do manage to do substantial research are directly dependent upon foreign organizations and researchers.

This is not to say that Zairian scholars have not made impressive individual efforts in scientific research, particularly in the social sciences. There is already a significant body of work accomplished by several hundred Zairians in such fields as history, linguistics, and sociology, as well as political and administrative science. Typically, though, the research is achieved on a strictly individual basis with little or no financial assistance and scant impact on public policy. A sizable number of Zairian scholars live outside the country and are therefore freer to publish research findings critical of the regime without jeopardizing their immediate career aspirations.

The real functions of research in Zaire have little to do with development, according to Verhaegen (1978). (It must, of course, be assumed that Verhaegen does not mean to include his own considerable body of publications in this generalization.) He distinguishes three functions of research: In the first instance, it serves a symbolic function: ideological legitimation of the political and economic system. It contributes toward acceptance of the persistence of a capitalist economic system dominated by foreign interests. The considerable sums expended by the government and by international agencies on studies and development research are investments in the established economic order. The second function is a social one: the selection or creation of a bourgeoisie du diplôme. The acquisition of a university degree is a ticket into the ruling bureaucratic class. This mandarin class in turn has no interest in the development of a critical spirit of research that can undermine its dominant social position. The third function is what Verhaegen calls "science in the service of technological imperialism." By this is meant the transfer of technology—whether of goods, services, or theoretical models—which ensures continued dependence on foreign economies.

Foster (1978) even questions whether the university ought to be expected to contribute directly to development. He believes that universities are essentially what they ought to be: simply agencies for teaching and research. If, in the course of their activities, they should make a short-term contribution to economic development, social equity, and political stability, so much the better. Foster contends that most African universities have performed the teaching function admirably, but that the research function has been much less in evidence. While he calls for the depoliticization of the university, Foster submits that a constructive relationship can develop between government and university to the mutual advantage of both in the area of fundamental and applied research.

In summary, even a brief review of development issues within UNAZA, one element of the education system, reveals a record of failure to respond to real development needs and a corresponding negative contribution to maintaining dependence on the international economic order. The program of nationalization of the system of higher education provided the semblance of national development without attacking the root causes of underdevelopment.

PROSPECTS FOR EDUCATIONAL DEVELOPMENT IN ZAIRE

Despite an abundance of rhetoric by public authorities affirming the principle of self-reliance and cultural authenticity, and the necessity of making education relevant to development needs, there is little evidence that the educational system is meeting those expectations. The nonformal adult education program affords the one example of a small step in the right direction. But, as with other discrete attempts to reform the system, that program suffers from the absence of an overall manpower development plan and administrative weaknesses.

There remain intimations of real educational development, albeit outside the realm of government planning. One of these is the Mudiwamba experiment described in the dissertation research of David Ewert (1977). It concerns a community development program in the Kwilu area of Bandundu region, under the auspices of the Programme Agricole Protestante. Ewert shows how elements of the Paulo Freire model of conscientization took root among the villagers of Mudiwamba. He documents the application of Freire's philosophy of education but not the adaptation of the Freire methodology. The objective of the Mudiwamba experiment was to initiate a community process "through which people become more competent to deal with local problems, using non-formal education as a tool of social change" (Ewert 1977, p. 234). It took place entirely outside the government's formal institutions of educational and community development.

The people of Mudiwamba established village development committees, held regular meetings to discuss community problems, and established adult education courses. The organizing principle was to use local problems as the agenda for action and to develop a method of solving those problems through community action. Ewert reports that the experiment was successful in implementing certain of the Freire philosophical principles: The villagers became more aware of their own social structure and learned some techniques for increasing agricultural productivity. But while the people of Mudiwamba showed an awareness of "structural oppression," there were few mechanisms available within the political process to bring change. The only attempts at structural change involved isolated acts of resistance on the local level to the more blatant elements of that oppression. Efforts were limited to dealing with smaller problems in the community, such as generating capital, improving agriculture, and learning how to read and write.

The conclusion reached by Ewert is that there was "no evidence of structural change in this Zairian community as a result of the experimental program employing the principles of Freire's philosophy" (1977, p. 282). Thus the principles of the philosophy may well form the basis of an effective educational strategy "even in the absence of political action to change exploitive social structures." The Mudiwamba experiment grew out of a community-level process with the tacit approval of local government officials, but outside the framework of existing policy. Therefore it is unlikely that this educational approach will spread beyond the area included in the Programme Agricole Protestante. Like many other grass-roots experiments in Zaire, it will likely be stifled by the inertia of the state rather than embraced as a model for development. The future does not look promising. It will take far more basic change in the larger development system before education can play a major positive role in improving the human welfare of the majority.

REFERENCES

Coleman, James S. 1977. "The Academic Freedom and Responsibilities of Foreign Scholars in African Universities." Quarterly Journal of Africanist Opinion 7, no. 2 (Spring): 14–32.

Ewert, David M. 1977. "Freire's Concept of Critical Consciousness and Social Structure in Rural Zaire." Ph.D. dissertation, University of Wisconsin.

Foster, Philip. 1978. "The Political Functions of African Universities." Paper presented at the Conference on Higher Education and Political Development in Africa, Bellagio, Italy, August 16–21.

Freire, Paulo. 1970. Pedagogy of the Oppressed. New York: Herder & Herder.

George, Betty. 1966. Educational Developments in the Congo. Washington, D.C.: U.S. Government Printing Office.

Hull, Galen S. 1976. "L'Université et état: L'UNAZA-Kisangani." Cahiers du CEDAF, nos. 1/2: 1–113.

_____. 1974. "Nationalization of the University in the Republic of Zaire." Ph.D. dissertation, Northwestern University.

_____. 1974. "Nationalisation de l'Université en République du Zaire." Cahiers zairois d'études politiques et sociales, no. 3 (October), pp. 171–87.

International Bank for Reconstruction and Development. 1977. Zaire: Education Sector Memorandum. Consultative Group for Zaire Memorandum ZA 77-5, May (dated December 31, 1976).

_____. 1976. "Appraisal of a Second Education Project in Zaire." Report no. 864-ZR and P-1715-ZR. March.

_____. 1971. "Appraisal of an Education Project: Republic of Zaire." Report no. PE-35a and P-991. November.

Nzongola, Ntalaja. 1978. "African University Teachers and Political Change." Paper presented at the Conference on Higher Education and Political Development in Africa, Bellagio, Italy, August 12–21.

United Nations Education, Science and Cultural Organization. 1976. Zaire: Education Sector Survey Report. Paris, April.

U.S., Agency for International Development. 1977. Zaire: CIDEP Staff Development. Project Paper no. 660-0.

Van den Berghe, Pierre L. 1973. Power and Privilege at an African University. London: Routledge & Kegan Paul.

Verhaegen, Benoît. 1978. L'enseignement universitaire au Zaire: De Lovanium a l'UNAZA 1958-1978. Brussels: Centre d'Etude et de Documentation Africaine.

Yesufu, T. M., ed. 1973. Creating the African University: Emerging Issues of the 1970's. Ibadan: Oxford University Press.

Young, Crawford. 1977. "La faculté des sciences sociales a l'UNAZA: Réflexions autour d'un mandat." Etudes zairoises 1, no. 2 (April-June): 154-80.

PART III

ZAIRE: RURAL WORLDS AT THE SYSTEM'S PERIPHERY

9

BLOCKAGE POINTS IN ZAIRE:
THE FLOW OF BUDGETS, BUREAUCRATS, AND BEER

Michael G. Schatzberg

> En effet, concentrés, dans leur majorité, dans la Capital du pays,
> ces citoyens malhonnêtes ont transformé Kinshasa en un véritable
> centre d'exploitation de tout l'intérieur.
> Les trois quarts de la masse monétaire du pays sont concentrés
> à Kinshasa; l'essence, les produits alimentaires, pharmaceutiques
> et autres importés de l'étranger, demeurent à Kinshasa, alors que
> les devises pout leur importation proviennent, en quasi totalité, de
> la sueur des populations industrielles et agricoles de l'intérieur du
> pays.
>
> Mobutu Sese Soko,
Speech before the Second Ordinary
Congress of the MPR (1977)

> Kinshasa nous a promis, mais on attend.
> Zairian administrative service chief

> Les crédits sont à Mbandaka, mais on n'a rien recu.
> Zairian administrative service chief

INTRODUCTION

The question of how rural development might best be achieved has occupied both scholars and statesmen for a considerable time. In recent years,

An earlier version of this chapter was presented at the Conference on
the Role of Small Urban Centers in Rural Development in Africa, Madison,
Wisconsin, November 9-11, 1978. I thank the Fulbright-Hays Doctoral Dissertation Program and the African Studies Program at the University of Wisconsin-Madison for generous financial support. Kenneth Heard, Aidan South-
all, and Crawford Young were kind enough to comment on earlier drafts.
Responsibility for the facts and interpretations presented is wholly my own.

some theoreticians have turned their attention to the role that small urban centers could play in overall strategies of national development. These small towns are often perceived as "missing links" in the chain between the primate cities and the rural areas. For example, E. A. J. Johnson (1970) has argued that small, market-based urban centers are not sufficiently developed in poor countries, and that building up these places would constitute a viable development strategy. Similarly, over the years, R. J. Harrison Church (1969, 1977) has urged the decentralization of industry to small cities. One result of this would be the creation of jobs in more remote areas and, as a result, the absorption of the rural-urban flow. Narelle Townsend (1976) has cogently expressed many of these concerns in her work on hintertowns. In her view, these hintertowns "will constitute a network of 'central places' to support and promote development in the rural areas. Their objectives would be primarily to raise the income level of the active population to ensure a self-sufficient food production for the inhabitants" (pp. 184-85). Secondarily, their functions would be to increase the production of crops for export and reduce rural migration and rural underdevelopment. They would, in effect, form a bridge between the overburdened cities and the ignored agricultural populations. In sum, the hintertowns would promote "a more equitable balance between rural and urban living" as well as a focus for "a spatial and economic strategy for the decentralization of industry and its accompanying infrastructure, integrating the rural areas into national development schemes" (Townsend 1976, pp. 190-91).

Most of these theoretical hopes for the role of the small urban center in African rural development are undergirded by several assumptions: that African leaders and government officials do wish to develop the agricultural areas of their countries; that the presence of small urban centers in the hinterland contributes to the development process; and that it therefore makes sense to build up these small towns because through them resources will filter down to the countryside and alleviate the plight of the farmers. So much for the theory, what of the practice?

In November 1977, President Mobutu Sese Seko offered the delegates at the opening session of the Second Ordinary Congress of the Mouvement Populaire de la Révolution (MPR) a remarkably candid dissection of the problems currently besetting Zairian society. As the citation in the epigraph indicates, three-fourths of Zaire's money supply is concentrated in the capital, and imported gasoline, foodstuffs, and pharmaceutical products rarely find their way to the rural areas, which provide the wealth to purchase them. This problem—the failure of resources to trickle down to the countryside— is also reflected in the statements by the two administrative service chiefs. "Kinshasa has promised us, but we are waiting" and "The funds are in Mbandaka, but we have received nothing" are the frequently heard refrains of administrative personnel in the farthest reaches of the country.

In this chapter it shall be argued that small urban centers, at least in Zaire, may be viewed as blockage points that inhibit the flow of resources from the capital to the countryside and that they therefore constitute an essentially negative element in the developmental equation (Schatzberg 1978). To elaborate on this hypothesis, primary attention will be paid to the relationships of the town of Lisala, comparing its regional capital, Mbandaka, and its hinterland. Lisala is an administrative town in northwestern Zaire with a population of about 27,000 people. It is the site of subregion, zone, and collectivity levels of administration and is headquarters of Mongala subregion (Schatzberg 1979, chap. 1). More specifically, the flow of budgetary resources and salaries, the distribution of administrative personnel, and the commercial distribution of beer throughout Equateur region will be examined. In addition, brief observations will be offered on why Lisala and other small urban centers in Zaire act as blockage points rather than conduits by focusing on the phenomenon of politico-commercial interaction and by analyzing the widely used administrative term interior.

BUDGETS AND SALARIES

The Zairian budget system is complex, and it is necessary to provide a brief outline of how, at least in theory, things work if the following analysis is to make sense. Since 1970 the budgetary process has been decentralized at the regional and subregional administrative levels. Both regions and subregions therefore receive their budgetary allocations directly from Kinshasa. Budgetary ceilings are established in Kinshasa between January and April of each year. These are fixed and, during May, instructions are sent from the Budget Control Service in Kinshasa to all of the budget officers in the regions and subregions. When these ceilings arrive, the regional and subregional budget officers pass them along to the administrative service chiefs at their respective echelons. The service chiefs then prepare their own previsions and estimates for the coming year, usually during June. Each budget officer then corrects the individual estimates to see that they conform to the national instructions and prepares a document that centralizes the estimates for the entire region or subregion. In July, the budget officers journey to Kinshasa to submit budgetary previsions for their administrative officials in the Finance Ministry, an interdepartmental budgetary commission elaborates a budget for the entire nation, and, in September, submits it for approval to the National Legislative Council, which, before December, must vote the budget into law (Schatzberg 1975a, no. 5, p. 3).

While this description seems nice and neat, things rarely happen just this way, and the actual elaboration of the budget often belies the officially accepted prescriptions. There is, first of all, some question as to exactly how effective the decentralization to the subregions has been, for the regional commissioners have resisted the flow of funds away from their control. Quite obviously, they wish to oversee as many of the resources as they can at the regional level. It was therefore with little glee and much covert resistance that they greeted the decentralization measures in 1970. Since that time, there has been much correspondence that criticizes the regional commissioners for failing to do this. In 1972, for instance, their superiors warned them that they would have to conform to the law in these matters and cease blocking funds slated for the subregions (Administrative Correspondence, August 11, 1972; January 21, 1971; January 20, 1973). The result of this opposition has been that some monies destined for the subregions have failed to reach them.

The supposed decentralization has another dimension as well. In theory, the regional and subregional commissioners must further decentralize the funds received from Kinshasa to the benefit of their administrative service chiefs (Administrative Correspondence, January 21, 1971; January 20, 1973). Once again, though, there has been a great reluctance to do this, and repeated warnings to the commissioners have not had substantial salutary effect. Consequently, although the service chiefs are responsible for preparing yearly budgetary documents and previsions, there is every chance that they may never see the funds that the officials in the central government have approved for their use. It would be understating the case to say that this has a negative impact on the delivery of services to the hinterland.

As a case in point, let us examine the fate of funds destined for the Department of Political Affairs. These monies arrive in Lisala, having come directly from the capital. They fall under the control of the subregional commissioner—their principal manager—who is responsible for delegating some of them to the five zones that compose his subregion. When asked how much money he delegates to each zone to cover monthly operating costs, he replied that it was generally around Z 150 to Z 200 (at the time of research, Z 1 = U.S. $2) (Schatzberg 1975a, no. 45, p. 4; Administrative Correspondence, June 17, 1975).

But the situation is rarely this regularized. One experienced territorial commissioner said, "It varies enormously. In general, it was around Z 60 a month for the Zone of Lisala when I was there. Before the visit of the President, however, we were given Z 800. Sometimes there are no funds for two or three months" (Schatzberg 1975a, no. 37, p. 8). Similarly, the current zone commissioner of the zone of Lisala affirmed that he received Z 150 in cash each month for the operating costs of the zone administration. But when pressed, he admitted that in all the time he had been at Lisala (15 months), this had happened but once (Schatzberg 1975a, no. 43, p. 4). Naturally this situation and the concomitant lack of funds can pose serious problems. One assistant zone commissioner noted, "There are sometimes urgent problems. We haven't got the money and that makes the work drag. We can't rent a truck for job-related questions" (Schatzberg 1975a, no. 36, p. 7). Most territorial officials are acutely aware that funds do not trickle down to the zone authorities.

A large part of this problem is the direct result of the way the funds are managed by the subregional commissioner. To a certain extent, he does have the latitude to rob Peter to pay Paul—to take funds destined for one service and allocate them to another. Similarly, he is supposed to see that the zone commissioners receive their monthly subventions, but this does not always happen because of sloppy management. The subregional commissioner is technically required to get the approval of his budget officer before he spends the money. This official has been largely responsible for elaborating the subregional budget and knows where, and for what, the money is to be spent, but he is rarely consulted. The subregional commissioner dispenses the funds as he sees fit, regardless of what the budget might dictate. Lisala's budget officer noted with a shrug that "he undertakes expenses without speaking to me about them. I wash my hands of it. He's an authority" (Schatzberg 1975a, no. 5, p. 6). In effect, the commissioner himself observed, according to the well-consecrated Zairian formula, that "there is only a single chief. It is I who manage the funds" (Schatzberg 1975a, no. 45, p. 4). There is thus some tension between the budget officer and the subregional commissioner. Not only does the budget officer usually fail to get the commissioner to respect the budgetary previsions and delegate funds to the zones composing the subregion but he is equally unable to see that he delegates funds to the administrative service chiefs present in Mongala subregion. This problem is by no means restricted to Lisala (Administrative Correspondence, January 21, 1971; January 23, 1973), and the difficulty probably stems from the fact that commissioners have far more power than budget officers. These latter officials are, at best, councillors to those in power. For the most part, they are simply ignored.

In spite of these difficulties some money does eventually reach the subregional administrative service chiefs. What happens to it at that point? In February 1975, the author was permitted to attend a meeting chaired by Mongala's budget officer. Present as well were the service chiefs for the nine administrative departments that depend on the funds delegated from Kinshasa to the subregional commissioner. At this gathering the budget officer made it clear that this year (1975), for the first time, they were going to be required to divide their own funds among the five zones that make up the subregion. It seems that there had never been a requirement that this happen, so the money was usually spent at the subregion and rarely filtered down to the zones. Of course, there had been complaints and it was in response to these that the service chiefs were required to divide formally the funds at their disposal among the outlying zones (Schatzberg 1975b, p. 34). Interestingly, however, by July 1975, only three of the nine services had complied with this directive.

Tables 9.1 and 9.2 provide the figures for agriculture and sports. It is immediately apparent that there is a marked tendency for funds not to leave the subregional headquarters. Thus, in the case of agriculture, some 57 percent of the funds were absorbed by the subregion in Lisala. Naturally, this caused numerous complaints on the part of the agronomists in the outlying zones. When asked to comment on his role in the budgetary process, one of them remarked that "the subregional agronomist is the manager of the funds. I always make suggestions but there is nothing. There is no follow-up. Nothing at all" (Schatzberg 1975a, no. 20, p. 5). Of course, this official felt that he was not receiving his fair share of the agricultural revenues.

The case of the sports department is quite similar. Here, 76 percent of the funds were destined to be spent either at the subregion or in the zone of Lisala—to all intents and purposes, the same thing, as money for the zone almost never flows to the more distant centers. Moreover, it can probably

TABLE 9.1

Official Distribution of Agricultural Budget, Mongala Subregion, 1975
(in zaires; Z 1 = U.S. $2)

Expense	Subregion	Lisala	Bumba	Bongandanga	Businga	Mobayi-Mbongo	Total
Travel	2,416	300	300	200	200	200	3,616
Repair and maintenance	1,770	434	434	434	134	434	3,640
Office supplies	950	120	120	120	120	120	1,550
Durable material	1,200	230	230	230	230	230	2,350
Total	6,336	1,084	1,084	984	684	984	11,156
Percent	56.79	9.71	9.71	8.82	6.13	8.82	99.98

Source: Administrative Correspondence, June 17, 1975.

TABLE 9.2

Official Distribution of Sports Budget, Mongala Subregion, 1975
(in zaires; Z 1 = U.S. $2)

Expense	Subregion	Lisala	Bumba	Bongandanga	Businga	Mobayi-Mbongo	Total
Inspection	743	0	0	0	0	0	743
Vehicle indemnity	81	0	0	0	0	0	81
Local orders and transportation costs	290	70	50	25	35	30	500
Repair and maintenance	2,050	250	300	300	300	300	3,500
Durable material	1,360	40	40	150	60	150	1,800
Local seminars	500	0	0	0	0	0	500
National championship	1,240	200	200	30	100	30	1,800
Total	6,264	560	590	505	495	510	8,924
Percent	70.19	6.27	6.61	5.65	5.54	5.71	99.97

Source: Administrative Correspondence, February 18, 1975.

be assumed that such inequities were even more striking for those departments that did not formally delegate at all and that an even greater percentage of the total funds never left Lisala, the subregional headquarters. People in the outlying areas therefore were not receiving a proportionate share of the available funds. Table 9.3 presents the percentage of the total population in each of the subregion's five zones. From these tables it seems clear, for example, that although Bumba has one-third of the subregion's people, it received only about 10 percent of the funds destined for agriculture and 8 percent of those devoted to sports.

Thus far, primarily the decentralization of funds from the subregion to the hinterland has been discussed. It would be a mistake, however, to assume that all of the administrative services present in Lisala receive their operating expenses through the intermediary of the subregional commissioner. Indeed, most of them do not, and the budgetary arrangements for these other services vary widely. Some receive funds directly from Kinshasa; others directly from the regional capital in Mbandaka; and still others obtain parts of their funds from Kinshasa, the region, and the subregion. Whatever the source, the prevalent pattern usually holds: The officials who control the coffers at each administrative level are reluctant to loosen the purse strings so that money might flow down to the farthest reaches of the country.

In 1972, for example, the state commissioner for public works decided that he would devote part of his budget to rebuild some of the hospitals that had fallen into disrepair. He divided the funds for Equateur region in the following way: Z 6,750 for the regional capital, Z 3,120 for the headquarters of the four subregions, and Z 10,625 for the 17 zone centers in the rest of the region (Administrative Correspondence, May 25, 1972). Thus, although only about 5 percent of the region's population (134,000) live in Mbandaka, the capital was to receive 33 percent of the hospital funds. It is thus fairly easy to see where the regime's priorities lie.

TABLE 9.3

Population, Mongala Subregion, by Administrative Zone, 1974

Zone	Population	Percent of Subregion's Population
Lisala	142,690	17.90
Bumba	268,545	33.69
Bongandanga	100,800	12.64
Businga	149,819	18.79
Mobayi-Mbongo	135,176	16.95
Total	797,030	99.97

Source: Administrative Correspondence, November 15, 1974.

The postal service is yet another example of the problems of getting money beyond the major cities. The financial arrangements within this department are highly centralized, even by Zairian standards; not a single cent can go into the regions without the written approval of the state commissioner. The problems engendered by this kind of centralization are easy to spot. In March 1975, there was a ten-day period when no mail reached Mbandaka from Kinshasa. According to one postal inspector, this occurred because post office vehicles had broken down and were unable to deliver mail from the airport to the central post office. Funds to have them fixed were requested from the state commissioner, but for some reason or other, the proper papers were never signed (Schatzberg 1975b, p. 58). Similar episodes were also common in Lisala. The head of the local post office noted that his truck needed new brakes before it could be put back on the road. He had wired his superiors in Mbandaka for authorization to spend this money, but he anticipated that it would take at least a month before the approval was forthcoming (Schatzberg 1975a, no. 1, p. 5; 1975b, p. 19).

Other agencies in Lisala that depend on the regional capital suffer the same financial fate. One magistrate put it this way: "Office supplies are bought for us in Mbandaka. We do not manage any funds here. . . . For example, we don't have any paper here. Do you realize, a service like this one without any paper? It just isn't possible." An administrator in Lisala complained, "Everything comes from Mbandaka, even pens. We can't buy a pen without authorization. . . . They send us nothing." Many of the service chiefs have to request special financial approval to inspect their administrative entities. These funds, too, are extremely difficult to obtain. An education official noted that he often had to leave on inspection tours without funds because the state commissioner was personally responsible for signing the financial authorizations (Schatzberg 1975a, no. 22, p. 4, no. 8, p. 7; no. 48, p. 4).

The lesson to be drawn from all this is that budgetary revenues do not trickle down into the Zairian hinterland.

The same arguments could be made for the flow of salaries from the capital, through the regional centers, to the subregional centers, and down into the countryside. Indeed, this is a national problem that has reached serious proportions. In 1970, only 19,500 of the 26,000 permanent civil servants on active service were paid: in 1971, 13,200; in 1972, 16,000. The situation was so acute that the civil service minister had to ask his colleagues in Kinshasa and the regional commissioners to correct the problem (Administrative Correspondence, May 2, 1973). Much of the fault lies with the officials in the various informatiques in Kinshasa who are responsible for programming the computers that draw up civil service pay lists. These computer guardians require numerous "considerations" before the name of a bureaucrat appears on the official salary roles. Even if these demands are met, there are almost always lengthy delays, especially for those who work in the remote areas of the country and cannot afford to go to the capital (Gould 1977a, pp. 13-14). The human dimensions of this imbroglio are tragic and should not be overlooked. One lower-level clerk in Lisala said: "In 1973

I was not paid for seven months. I am still not paid. I owe friends; I write I.O.U.s. How can I manage to live well?" (Schatzberg 1975a, no. 26, p. 4). An administrative service chief who had been in Lisala for about four months had still not received his salary and felt justified in appropriating some of the funds destined for his service so that he and his family might live from day to day (Schatzberg 1975b, p. 70).

Some money does filter down after making its way through the maze of inefficient computers in Kinshasa. Often, though, it does not arrive on time in the outlying areas and this also causes numerous problems for administrative personnel. In theory, state employees in Mongala subregion are supposed to be paid on the twentieth of each month. But one accountant said that in five years payment had never occurred on time. In the ten months this author spent in Lisala, payment of salaries was usually seven, and often as many as fifteen, days late. Because there are few branch banks, when funds arrived in Lisala the state accountants from the four outlying zones would have to make their way to the subregional headquarters to pick up the wages for the workers in their zones. During the rainy season, when many roads are washed out, this causes enormous difficulty, resulting in even more extended delays before the bureaucrats in the other four zones receive their money (Schatzberg 1975b, pp. 50-51).

The administrative files are packed with correspondence complaining about the failure of the funds to arrive on time, or, even if they do, to cover the legitimate claims of those waiting to be paid. In 1969 an Equateur Region inspection team noted that in Ubangi only 13 of 241 chiefs had been paid; in Mongala, 64 of 295; and in Tshuapa, 101 of 198. For the three subregions, only 178 out of 734 had been paid, roughly 25 percent (Administrative Correspondence, October 30, 1969; February 4, 1969; June 10, 1969; January 25, 1973; May 4, 1973; March 11, 1975; February 3, 1972). In March 1975 this problem still existed in Mongala. The subregional commissioner's justification to his superior illustrates some of the difficulties thus far observed:

> The delay in payment of the locality chiefs in my jurisdiction is not a result of my management. My predecessor, because of the lack of funds projected, had used the available monies for the upkeep of the residence of the President of the Republic, the repair of the houses of several functionaries, and the organization of cheerleading seminars in preparation for the official visit accomplished by the President of the Republic during the month of April 1974. [Administrative Correspondence, March 3, 1975]

The failure of subregional officials to rectify these budgetary and salary irregularities a full 11 months after the visit of the president bespeaks a possible lack of zeal and a definite lack of funds. In the interim, the locality chiefs were not receiving their salaries regularly and were undoubtedly seeking other, and probably far less legal, means to make ends meet (Schatzberg 1979, chap. 4).

One conclusion that should emerge from the foregoing analysis of salary flows is that, in general, the closer a bureaucrat stands to the source of the funds, the better his chance of getting paid. As was the case for ordinary budgetary revenues, salaries seem to meet some resistance on their way down the pipeline. They may appear quite irregularly, often after a long delay, and occasionally not at all.

BUREAUCRATS

In some ways the distribution of civil servants throughout the Republic of Zaire parallels the flow of financial resources, for bureaucratic assignments in the hinterland and the flow of salaries are obviously related. Moreover, attention to the distribution of civil servants in Zaire may give a clue as to some of the regime's priorities. Personnel should be considered as much of a developmental resource as money, and the dominance of the state sector in the management of the Zairian economy indicates fairly clearly that those who work for the state have been chosen as leaders on Zaire's long march toward economic development.

Tables 9.4 and 9.5 furnish a breakdown of the permanent civil service for both ministries in the capital and field administration in the regions. In 1974 there were some 10,000 bureaucrats in the capital and another 12,000 in the regions. It must be emphasized that these data significantly understate the total number of bureaucrats in Zaire, as they deal only with those who are known as sous-statut (permanent). The vast majority of those who work for the state fall under another category, sous-contrat, and are not technically career civil servants, but merely work for the state on a short-term, job-related, ad hoc basis. Over the years, they have in fact acquired a degree of permanency, but they can, in theory, be let go when there is no longer a need for the services they provide. Unfortunately, it proved impossible to secure similar data for the distribution, or even the number, of these nonpermanent workers. Best estimates, however, indicate that there may be as many as 150,000 of them scattered throughout Zaire (Vieux 1974, p. 46).

Table 9.4 need not detain us, as the thrust of this chapter is on the distribution of bureaucrats in the regions. Suffice it to say that of the 23,120 permanent bureaucrats on active service in 1974, some 10,831, or 46.84 percent, were stationed in the various administrative departments in the capital. Table 9.5 notes the distribution of the remaining 12,289 (53.15 percent) agents throughout the regions of Zaire. Kinshasa and Kasai Oriental excepted, the distribution is a moderately equal one. The seeming underrepresentation of Kinshasa must take into account the fact that the national ministries, departments, and services are located there. The very definite overrepresentation of Kasai Oriental, on the other hand, can most probably be ascribed to the tenure of Citizen Emungania as minister of the civil service between October 1967 and August 1968 when he systematically engaged in an ethnically oriented hiring policy. Many of the 6,500 clerks hired during his tenure in office were natives of Kasai Oriental and subsequently stationed there (Schatzberg 1975a, no. 3, p. 1).

Table 9.6 combines the totals of Tables 9.4 and 9.5 and gives an overall picture of the distribution of permanent civil servants in Zaire. The di-

TABLE 9.4

Distribution of Permanent Civil Servants in Kinshasa, by Department and Administrative Grade, 1974

Department	Administrative Grade												
	DG	D	CHD	CHB	ATB1	ATB2	AB1	AB2	AA1	AA2	H	Div.	Total
Finances	1	7	38	90	0	28	36	280	259	183	90	1	1,013
Civil service	1	1	6	23	0	0	13	49	58	54	210	0	415
Political affairs	0	4	14	47	1	21	8	61	49	69	14	0	289
Justice	2	4	5	14	1	38	42	491	313	317	116	57	1,400
Magistrates	642	0	0	0	0	0	0	0	0	0	0	1	643
Foreign affairs/Kinshasa	3	5	30	41	13	52	21	71	36	68	21	1	362
Abroad	3	5	45	22	17	27	12	28	14	17	4	0	194
Foreign commerce	1	3	8	15	0	3	1	9	8	15	6	0	69
Defense	0	0	0	5	0	0	5	18	32	74	7	0	141
Social affairs	1	3	9	28	0	8	10	35	67	54	99	127	441
Education	1	2	66	55	31	147	191	311	345	177	19	103	1,448
Health	1	3	13	68	37	28	110	159	349	196	108	15	1,087
Orientation	1	3	15	91	0	4	4	39	58	55	48	1	319
Culture	2	2	10	23	0	2	3	18	38	25	12	0	134
Sports	1	2	8	8	0	4	5	10	18	25	5	2	88
Veterans	1	2	2	12	0	2	0	6	8	12	5	0	50
Labor	1	3	14	40	0	30	12	76	37	46	12	0	271
Agriculture	1	2	12	32	15	16	28	51	58	89	41	3	348
National economy	0	5	12	48	0	31	6	31	31	24	10	0	198
Mines	0	1	7	28	0	15	13	36	35	26	35	1	197
Transportation	1	4	19	59	0	18	70	236	128	125	111	1	772
Public works	1	4	12	42	0	22	12	55	259	104	224	4	739
Energy	1	2	9	7	0	5	2	7	8	11	15	0	67
Land	0	0	1	5	0	7	11	57	20	34	11	0	146
Total	665	67	355	803	115	508	615	2,134	2,228	1,800	1,223	318	10,831
Percent	6.13	0.61	3.27	7.41	1.06	4.69	5.67	19.70	20.57	16.61	11.29	2.93	99.94

Note: The abbreviations used for the administrative grades are as follows: DG, directeur-général; D, directeur; CHD, chef de division; CHB, chef de bureau; ATB1, attaché de bureau 1è classe; AA1, agent auxiliaire 1è classe; AA2, agent auxiliaire 2è classe; H, huissier; Div., diverse.

Source: Commission Permanente de l'Administration Publique, October 24, 1974.

171

TABLE 9.5

Distribution of Permanent Civil Servants in the Regions, by Administrative Grade, 1974

Region	Administrative Grade												
	DG	D	CHD	CHB	ATB1	ATB2	AB1	AB2	AA1	AA2	H	Div.	Total
Kinshasa	0	0	9	33	0	17	24	90	193	102	21	5	494
Bas-Zaire	0	2	14	92	14	40	103	181	423	98	20	25	1,012
Bandundu	0	1	17	67	12	18	53	134	403	398	56	18	1,177
Equateur	0	1	15	81	20	37	98	251	286	348	19	26	1,182
Haut-Zaire	1	0	19	105	23	42	202	423	469	231	58	108	1,681
Kivu	0	1	13	77	23	34	114	254	485	203	47	46	1,297
Shaba	2	2	19	95	32	47	71	221	82	572	76	27	1,246
Kasai Occidental	0	1	14	61	17	38	61	101	412	402	100	57	1,264
Kasai Oriental	0	1	23	66	21	39	107	184	321	1,141	946	72	2,921
Unknown	0	0	1	0	0	2	1	1	3	6	1	0	15
Total	3	9	144	677	162	314	834	1,840	3,077	3,501	1,344	384	12,289
Percent	0.02	0.07	1.17	5.50	1.31	2.55	6.78	14.97	25.03	28.48	10.93	3.12	99.93

Note: The abbreviations used for the administrative grades are as follows: DG, directeur-général; D, direc-teur; CHD, chef de division; CHB, chef de bureau; ATB1, attaché de bureau 1è classe; AA1, agent auxiliaire 1è clas-se; AA2, agent auxiliaire 2è classe; H, huissier; Div., diverse.

Source: Commission Permanente de l'Administration Publique, October 24, 1974.

TABLE 9.6

Distribution of Permanent Civil Servants in Kinshasa and the Regions,
by Administrative Grade, 1974

Administrative Grade	Kinshasa Ministries		Regions		Total	
	Number	Percent	Number	Percent	Number	Percent
DG	665	6.13	3	0.02	668	2.88
D	67	0.61	9	0.07	76	0.32
CHD	355	3.27	144	1.17	499	2.15
CHB	803	7.41	677	5.50	1,480	6.40
ATB1	115	1.06	162	1.31	277	1.19
ATB2	508	4.69	314	2.55	822	3.55
AB1	615	5.67	834	6.78	1,449	6.26
AB2	2,134	19.70	1,840	14.97	3,974	17.18
AA1	2,228	20.57	3,077	25.03	5,305	22.94
AA2	1,800	16.61	3,501	28.48	5,301	22.92
H	1,223	11.29	1,344	10.93	2,567	11.10
Div.	318	2.93	384	3.12	702	3.03
Total	10,831	99.94	12,289	99.93	23,120	99.92

Note: The abbreviations used for the administrative grades are as follows: DG, directeur-général; D, directeur; CHD, chef de division; CHB, chef de bureau; ATB1, attaché de bureau 1è classe; AA1, agent auxiliaire 1è classe; AA2, agent auxiliaire 2è classe; H, huissier; Div., diverse.

Source: Commission Permanente de l'Administration Publique, October 24, 1974.

recteur-généraux, directeurs, chefs de division, and chefs de bureau are the highest ranks and are commonly referred to as positions of command. There are a total of 2,723 civil servants in these four grades. Of these 2,723 agents, 1,890 (69.40 percent) are located in Kinshasa ministries, while only 833 (30.59 percent) are assigned to posts in the regions. The regions would thus appear to be underrepresented as far as the distribution of these high-ranking, and highly paid, bureaucrats are concerned. Similarly, examination of the last three categories or grades, agents auxiliaires de première classe, agents auxiliaires de deuxième class, and the lowly huissiers, shows that, in this case, the regions appear to be slightly overrepresented vis-à-vis the capital. Of the total of 13,173 bureaucrats within these three grades, 5,251 (39.86 percent) are stationed in national ministries, while 7,922 (60.13 percent) work in the regions.

This pattern of either relative under- or overrepresentation of high- and low-ranking bureaucrats is important for a number of reasons. First, the fact that high-level civil servants are scarcer in the regions than in Kinshasa means that new development policies are less likely to bubble up from the bottom than be imposed from the top. This is certainly no surprise, but it might be argued that development plans and schemes would have more impact and a greater chance of successful implementation if they came from the regions themselves rather than from Kinshasa. In addition, the overrepresentation of lower-level bureaucrats in the hinterland means that many of those assigned to monitor or initiate developmental actions may not feel that they have sufficient authority to do so effectively. What might be called an "implementation mentality" is rife throughout the lower levels of the administrative structure, and field administrators will often pass problems along to the next highest level rather than actively and creatively try to solve them on their own (Schatzberg 1979, chap. 5).

The third consequence results from the fact that, in general, those in the regions are lower paid than those in the capital. Many studies of small urban centers have shown that administratively based towns often seem to depend on the salaries of the local bureaucrats to motor the local commercial and economic systems (Hinderik and Sterkenburg 1975; Steck 1972; Boutillier 1969; Auger 1973). This was certainly the case in Lisala, and merchants would often refer to the date critique, which occurred some two weeks after payday when the bureaucrats had no money left to spend and the next payment was still some two to four weeks away. During this period the merchants suffered almost as much as the functionaries.

The failure of high-ranking bureaucrats to filter down (or, more correctly, be assigned) to the regions closely parallels the distribution of bureaucrats within Mongala subregion. The same pattern is not only prevalent regarding administrative rank (that is, the high-ranking tend to be assigned to the subregion rather than the zones) but also in terms of absolute numbers, as Table 9.7 bears witness.

Table 9.7 shows quite clearly that almost one-half of the state bureaucrats in Mongala work in Lisala. This has several important consequences that deserve mention. In the first place, many services are represented at the subregion but not in the zones. This heavily influences the delivery of administrative and social services to the vast majority of the population of the subregion who live outside Lisala. In the remoter zones where the representatives of a particular service are not present, it means that the daily supervision of such tasks is left to the already overburdened representatives of the territorial administration, the commissioners. With their heavy political and administrative responsibilities, these officials often do not have the time to monitor fields like social affairs, justice, or veterans affairs. In addition, the exceedingly poor state of the local roads means that the officials in charge of these services who reside in Lisala are often unable to get out and supervise their administrative responsibilities in the zones. The already described difficulties that many officials have in getting funds for inspection tours also contribute to this problem.

Two examples should suffice: Because magistrates of the public prosecutor's office can rarely leave Lisala, there are often abuses in the local ju-

TABLE 9.7

Distribution of Bureaucrats for Selected Administrative Services, Mongala Subregion, 1974

Service	Zone					
	Lisala[a]	Bumba	Bongandanga	Businga	Mobayi-Mbongo	Total
Sports	12	6	0	1	1	20
Administrative transportation	90	13	8	11	0	122
Economic affairs	1	1	0	1	0	3
Telecommunications	15	0	3	2	1	21
Social affairs	18	20	4	1	0	43
National orientation	3	0	0	0	0	3
Budget control	4	0	0	0	0	4
Land (cadastre)	6	0	0	0	0	6
Housing office	1	0	0	0	0	1
Accounting	7	0	1	0	0	8
Post office	16	0	4	0	0	20
Tax office	5	0	0	0	0	5
Public prosecutor's office	10	0	0	0	0	10
State security	1	0	0	0	0	1
Health	83	77	36	47	49	292
Veterans' affairs	1	0	0	0	0	1
Political affairs[b]	79	23	18	21	24	165
Total	352	140	74	84	75	725[c]
Percent	48.55	19.31	10.20	11.58	10.34	99.98

[a]Includes both the subregion and the zone.
[b]Includes territorial commissioners and Jeunesse du Mouvement Populaire de la Révolution personnel, as well as administrative workers.

[c]Includes both permanent (sous–statut) and nonpermanent (sous–contrat) civil servants. Data were not found for the following services: veterinary, agriculture, public works, tribunal, prisons, national education, labor, and almost all parastatals. The figures presented here are therefore underestimates of the real total, probably imprecise, and should be treated only as estimates.

Source: Archives, Mongala Subregion, Political Affairs Department, Lisala, bureaucratic rosters, 1974.

175

dicial system, as the collectivity courts tend to be dominated by the chiefs; because the lone veterans affairs official can seldom leave Lisala, there is no one to make sure that the veterans who reside in the remote areas receive their monthly stipends. In general, these funds are disbursed by the zone accountants and collectivity chiefs, who are wont to appropriate them for their own purposes (Schatzberg 1979, chap. 4; Schatzberg 1975b, p. 100).

In the educational sphere, this problem can be particularly acute. Lisala is a local learning center of some importance. There are ten primary and an equal number of secondary schools with a combined total of about 10,000 pupils. This represents approximately 35 percent of the town's total population (Schatzberg 1979, chaps. 1, 3). Nonetheless, it is extremely difficult to obtain teachers in this town, and serious staff shortages are normal. At the start of the 1973 school year, six of the local secondary schools had to begin classes without the necessary manpower. Of a total of 81 teachers actually needed, only 51 (63 percent) responded to their assignments and appeared in Lisala (Administrative Correspondence, September 8, 1973). When asked to explain this chronic problem, one education official noted that young teachers "do not find the means to live here [Lisala]. They leave because no one takes care of them. They are not well paid; they are not housed; there is no transportation [to get to school]. There is the question of salaries which do not arrive." In sum, they prefer to remain in the large cities where both amenities and salaries are likely to be far more regular (Schatzberg 1975a, no. 37, p. 3; no. 17, p. 3).

If the shortage of educational personnel in Lisala is acute, then it is catastrophic in the smaller centers like Businga, Mobayi-Mbongo, and Bongandanga. The high school principal in Bongandanga, for instance, had to make do with no books, no desks, and no chairs, and when he complained about the problem he was told "débrouillez-vous." There has never been a full complement of teachers in his school. In 1974-75 the ministry in Kinshasa assigned 11, but only 2 actually appeared. The situation was so tragic that the zone commissioner detached one of his college-educated assistants to give courses part time. The subregional commissioner was aware of this tragedy, but soon found that the funds promised to ameliorate conditions in this school were centralized in Mbandaka and could not be pried loose (Schatzberg 1975b, pp. 49-50; Administrative Correspondence, June 18, 1975).

The distribution of public health personnel is also a problem in Mongala. The director of Lisala's only hospital had established a network of 18 rural dispensaries whose primary function was to deliver health care to the surrounding rural population; 8 of these were closed because of the lack of personnel. Thus the village farmers suffer because qualified personnel are not present in more remote areas (Schatzberg 1975a).

BEER

A brief section on beer is included here in the hope that it might prove illuminating to examine the distribution of a commercial and nonadministrative resource to see if it conforms to the pattern already observed for both

TABLE 9.8

Bralima Brewery Beer Sales in Equateur Region and Regional Population,
by Subregion, 1974
(in .72-liter bottles)

Subregion	Population	Percent	Beer Sales	Percent
Mbandaka (capital)	134,852	5.00	16,550,400	56.99
Equateur	372,690	13.83	5,057,184	17.41
Tshuapa	503,572	18.69	1,537,420	5.29
Ubangi	860,664	31.94	2,550,324	8.78
Mongala	812,680*	30.16	3,041,860	10.47
Zongo	9,503	0.35	6,000	0.02
Outside regions (Kiri, Bandundu)	—	—	302,136	1.04
Total	2,693,961	99.37	29,039,324	100.00

*Note the discrepancy between this figure and the one cited in Table
9.3. It is undoubtedly due to the use of different sources and underscores
the difficulty in arriving at any reasonably accurate population estimates in
Zaire. All such figures must be treated as approximations and not as precise data amenable to sophisticated statistical manipulation.

Source: Recalculated from figures provided by Bralima brewery,
Mbandaka; and Archives, Equateur Region, Economic Affairs Department,
"Synthèse des activités socio-économiques," June 16, 1975, Mbandaka.

budgets and bureaucrats. As shall be seen, in some respects it does and in
others it does not. Table 9.8 provides a breakdown of the beer sales and
population of Equateur region, by subregion.

It is obvious that the percentage of the population living in the various
subregions does not correspond to the percentage of beer sales in each area.
The regional capital, Mbandaka, has only 5 percent of the region's total population, but it nevertheless consumes close to 57 percent of the local bottled
beer. In part, of course, this can be attributed to the fact that the brewery
itself is located in Mbandaka and that therefore the local bar owners are not
dependent upon the whims and inefficiencies of the state-owned river transportation agency. It is also in part explained by the high concentration of administrators and civil servants in the capital who form a fairly regularly paid
clientele. (The official price of beer is high and is certainly not within easy
reach of the vast majority of the agricultural population.) It can also be seen
that merchants in Equateur subregion buy approximately the amount of beer
that one would be led to expect on the basis of its population alone, holding
all other factors constant. On the other hand, traders in the Ubangi, Mongala, and Tshuapa subregions do not purchase the expected amounts of beer
that their people demand (Schatzberg 1979, chap. 5).

At first glance, then, it would appear that the distributive pattern of beer in Equateur region is roughly congruent with the pattern of resource flow for administrative personnel and budgetary funds: a tendency for the higher administrative levels to absorb the lion's share of whatever there is to be had. But Tables 9.9, 9.10, 9.11, and 9.12 furnish a closer look at the distributive pattern within each subregion, and need some explanation.

Tables 9.9 and 9.10 present a picture of the distribution of beer sales from the Mbandaka brewery within the Tshuapa and Ubangi subregions. These two subregions are far removed from Mbandaka and its brewery in terms of both absolute distance and ease of transportation. In Tshuapa, Boende (the subregional headquarters) absorbs most beer sold in the subregion.

TABLE 9.9

Bralima Brewery Beer Sales in Tshuapa Subregion, 1974
(in bottles)

Zone	Total Sales	Percent of Regional Sales	Percent of Subregional Sales
Boende (chef-lieu)	1,265,676	4.35	82.32
Ikela	0	0.00	0.00
Djolu	0	0.00	0.00
Befale	5,724	0.01	0.37
Bokungu	16,692	0.05	1.08
Monkoto	249,328	0.85	16.21
Total	1,537,420	5.26	99.98

Source: Recalculated from figures provided by Bralima brewery, Mbandaka.

While it is impossible to be certain why this is the case, it may be speculated that it has to do with the fact that it is linked to Mbandaka by river, and that the presence of many bureaucrats provides a market that can be exploited. That very little beer consumed in this subregion seems to filter beyond Boende tends to confirm the basic hypothesis that resources do not trickle down into the hinterland.

Ubangi subregion is quite similar in this respect. Gemena, the subregional center, absorbs some three-fourths of the beer sold in the subregion. The only other even moderately important center of beer consumption in this part of the country is Libenge, and this town is located along the Ubangi River and is thus directly linked to Mbandaka. Here, too, the more remote towns

of Budjala, Bosobolo, and Kungu do not receive any beer directly from Mbandaka (although some probably does arrive via independent traders). Thus, as
far as the distribution of a commercial resource is concerned, the towns in
the remote and inaccessible parts of the subregion find themselves at a dis-
advantage.

But Tables 9.11 and 9.12, representing the distribution of beer sales
in the Equateur and Mongala subregions, provide data that do not support the

TABLE 9.10

Bralima Brewery Beer Sales in Ubangi Subregion, 1974
(in bottles)

Zone	Total Sales	Percent of Regional Sales	Percent of Subregional Sales
Gemena (chef-lieu)	1,967,460	6.77	77.14
Budjala	48,000	0.16	1.88
Kungu	0	0.00	0.00
Libenge	534,864	1.84	20.97
Bosobolo	0	0.00	0.00
Total	2,550,324	8.77	99.99

Source: Recalculated from figures provided by Bralima brewery,
Mbandaka.

TABLE 9.11

Bralima Brewery Beer Sales in Equateur Subregion, 1974
(in bottles)

Zone	Total Sales	Percent of Regional Sales	Percent of Subregional Sales
Basankusu (chef-lieu)	533,196	1.83	10.54
Bomongo	345,696	1.19	6.83
Ingende	699,344	2.40	13.82
Bolomba	766,360	2.63	15.15
Bikoro	2,712,588	9.34	53.63
Total	5,057,184	17.39	99.97

Source: Recalculated from figures provided by Bralima brewery,
Mbandaka.

TABLE 9.12

Bralima Brewery Beer Sales in Mongala Subregion, 1974
(in bottles)

Zone	Total Sales	Percent of Regional Sales	Percent of Subregional Sales
Lisala (chef-lieu)	323,688	1.11	10.64
Bumba	1,159,212	3.99	38.10
Bongandanga	294,000	1.01	9.66
Businga	1,258,960	4.33	41.38
Mobayi-Mbongo	0	0.00	0.00
Zongo*	6,000	0.02	0.19
Total	3,041,860	10.46	99.97

*Zongo is an autonomous subregion and is placed here for convenience only.

Source: Recalculated from figures provided by Bralima brewery, Mbandaka.

basic hypothesis. In Equateur subregion, for example, contrary to expectations, Basankusu, the main administrative center, does not account for anywhere near the lion's share of the beer sales. Instead, there is a fairly equal distribution of beer sales among Basankusu, Bomongo, Ingende, and Bolomba, while about 50 percent of the total is accounted for by the zone center of Bikoro. The difference between the distributive pattern here and the one prevalent in Tshuapa and Ubangi is explicable largely in terms of proximity and transportation. Equateur subregion is the closest of the four to Mbandaka and its headquarters (Basankusu) and other zone centers are connected to the regional capital by either road (Bikoro) or river. The merchants thus deal directly with the brewery in the capital. They do not have to pass through a chain of distributors, most of whom choose to locate in the subregional centers, as is the case in Ubangi and Tshuapa.

The distributive pattern in Mongala subregion does not conform to the hypothesis either. In this case, however, transportation rather than proximity is the key factor. Lisala, Bumba, and Businga are linked to Mbandaka by river. Lisala's administrative preeminence is therefore not apparent in examining the data on the distribution of beer sales in this subregion. The commercial markets in Bumba and Businga are at least as important as the one in Lisala and, in the case of Bumba, probably more so. As far as the two very remote centers are concerned (Bongandanga and Mobayi-Mbongo), little or no beer reaches these areas. These towns have no direct transportation links with Mbandaka and merchants there have to go to either Businga, in the case of Mobayi-Mbongo, or Lisala, in the case of Bongandanga. By the time they reach these places, the beer has already evaporated.

That the data on two of the four subregions in Equateur region do not support the hypothesis perhaps suggests a partial solution to the trickle-down problem. The figures presented in Tables 9.9 to 9.12 indicate that where road and river transportation are available and link far-flung centers with the regional capital, commercial distribution of resources is not dependent on, and does not seem to follow, the administrative hierarchy. Where transportation facilities are lacking, on the other hand, the commercial patterns closely reproduce the administrative ones because merchants desire to locate in towns where there is a bureaucratic clientele.

The lesson to be drawn from this is that, although many of the small urban centers in this part of Zaire are administratively based, commercial markets do exist—and probably can be created—without a significant administrative presence. The beer sales statistics for small centers such as Businga, Bumba, Libenge, and Monkoto and the zone centers in Equateur subregion all support this assertion. To dissolve the administrative blockage points, therefore, it will probably be necessary to develop further regional and subregional transportation networks. This is far from an original conclusion, but the banality of the observation does not make the strategy less imperative.

THE "INTERIOR" AND THE BOURGEOISIE

Thus far, it has been argued that administrative centers, rather than facilitating the flow of resources to the rural areas, are likely to impede it. Why should this be the case? To answer this question, both the way field administrators perceive the more remote parts of their nation and the way in which they deal with whatever funds or resources do happen to come their way are analyzed. Both elements are essential to understanding why resources do not trickle down in Zaire.

The term intérieur, or interior, is often heard in Zaire. It is used by people in everyday settings, and is an integral part of Zairian political discourse occurring in newspapers, bureaucratic documents, and conversations among administrators in the field. It is a symbol that categorizes perceptions about space in Zaire and, because it is a categorization, "it is also a political tool, establishing status and power hierarchies" (Edelman 1977, p. 62).

In general, there are two connotations attributed to the word interior. One, the less widely used, is spatially absolute; the other, and more commonly used, is relative. The absolute connotation was best expressed by a bureaucrat who noted interior "comes from a language which is not exact. It [the interior] is situated in relation to Kinshasa. Everything which is not at Kinshasa is in the interior; because at Kinshasa you can leave the country for the exterior" (Schatzberg 1975a, no. 22, p. 2). More widespread, however, is the relative use of the expression. One administrative service chief in Lisala put it this way:

> When you are in Kinshasa, the interior means [those places] out-
> side of the capital—the regions including their headquarters. When
> you are at the regional headquarters, it means the subregions and
> zones. When you are at the subregional headquarters, it means
> the zones and the collectivities. One is never in the interior.
> [Schatzberg 1975a, no. 16, p. 2]

More specifically, though, interior has a relative meaning that reflects the
administrative hierarchy of the country. One of Lisala's magistrates mentioned that

> it is a question of the places where one finds institutions that are
> administratively inferior to me. Lisala is a subregion. A zone
> comes after a subregion. At Lisala we consider the zones as in-
> ferior and, therefore, in the interior. If I was at the zone, the
> collectivities would be administratively inferior in relation to the
> zone, and thus would be the interior and so on. We go on tour in
> the interior. It is relative. It depends on the authority who is
> speaking. The judicial institutions at Bumba, for example, are
> inferior to the Parquet at Lisala. It is therefore the interior.
> [Schatzberg 1975a, no. 23, p. 2]

Explicit in this view is the idea of inferiority, of administrative subordination. Implicit in this perception is the belief that those administrative
units and locations that are bureaucratically subordinate, the interior, are
somehow not as important and far less valuable.

There is almost always a negative connotation accompanying the term
interior. When asked, one service chief replied that the interior was composed of all those people who did not live in either Kinshasa or the other large
urban centers; another bureaucrat dismissed the interior, quite simply and
pejoratively, as "la brousse, quoi" (Schatzberg 1975a, no. 13, p. 2; no. 11,
p. 3). More often than not, the use of interior establishes a definite symbolic
representation of the social hierarchy. A territorial commissioner expressed
this hierarchical dimension as follows: "The people who are accustomed to
the life in the city are afraid to come to the interior. There is ease in travel
in the city. There are good houses, pleasures. The interior equals people
who live far from the city. . . . The people of the subregional headquarters
have marked themselves off a bit from the people in the zones" (Schatzberg
1975a, no. 37, p. 4).

There is thus the very real implication that people in the interior are
somehow different from, and perhaps inferior to, those who live in the urban
centers. Because the idea of the interior is quite relative, the notion of social
hierarchy implicit in the term stretches all the way from the capital in Kinshasa to the smallest village in the hinterland.* Indeed, one collectivity offi-

---

*David Gould (1977b) has noted the same phenomenon, but has cast his
analysis in terms of dependency theory and speaks of the peripheralization
process.

cial said: "Here we are in the urban center. The interior is those who live
in the villages themselves" (Schatzberg 1975a, no. 54, p. 2).

The connotations of interior have been emphasized because they are far
more important than a mere linguistic sidelight on administrative jargon and
perceptions. Policy debates and decisions are partially structured by these
connotations, and it is thus crucial to be familiar with them. In earlier parts
of this chapter it has been noted that administrative resources—notably budgetary funds and bureaucratic personnel—do not reach the outlying parts of
the country. Or, when they do, it is usually too little and too late to have a
positive developmental impact on the lives of the village farmers. A factor
contributing to this failure is the view of the rural areas that the term interior
conveys. Although never stated explicitly as such, it might be tentatively argued that the perception of the interior as subordinate helps to create a climate in which it does not seem quite so important for funds to reach the lowest levels of the administrative hierarchy. A case in point is the attempt of
Zairian authorities to use the funds generated by the tax on beer consumption
for rural development projects. In 1973 policy makers in the capital decided
to use these revenues to develop the rural areas, and the territorial commissioners at each level were requested to submit a list of priority development
projects. At first, these projects were rejected because they almost invari-
ably suggested the further development of subregional centers. National officials elicited a second set of projects, and this time some emphasis was
placed on the collectivities in the rural areas. Nevertheless, most of the proposed projects called for such "developmentally oriented" schemes as building the chief a new house, repairing administrative rest houses, and electri-
fying the collectivity offices (Schatzberg 1979, chap. 5).

While some symbols (administrative subordination, lack of importance,
relative backwardness) evoked by the term interior contribute in a small way
to the failure of resources to reach the countryside, there is another reason
that is probably even more important. Put directly, endemic corruption
characterizes all levels of Zairian polity and society (Gould 1977a; Young
1978). President Mobutu's brand of patrimonial pork-barrel politics has in-
cubated and nurtured a rapacious policito-commercial bourgeoisie. Public
office and access to public funds are used at all levels of the administrative
system to create new opportunities for capital accumulation and commercial
aggrandizement. The situation has become so serious that it can no longer
be considered functional, as many political scientists did until fairly recently
(Mpinga 1973). Indeed, in his November 1977 speech before the opening session of the MPR Congress, Mobutu spoke openly and critically of the "impôt
invisible," an invisible tax, a required consideration, which is necessary before even the most ordinary sorts of administrative services will be per-
formed (Mobutu 1977, p. 12). But it must now be asked whether President
Mobutu's condemnation of these corrupt practices is sincere. Local-level
corruption is openly modeled on the behavior of the president and his entourage. Most Zairians are aware that Mobutu's personal profits while in office
have been enormous. Furthermore, in May 1976, he told a mass rally in
Kinshasa that while it was not good to steal too openly, it was permitted to
"yiba na mayele," or steal shrewdly (Gould 1977b, p. 359).

The regime's toleration, and indeed encouragement, of the misappropriation of public funds has had a direct and dramatic impact on the frequency with which resources reach the remote areas of the countryside. In 1970, for example, it was discovered that one reason the zone commissioners never had enough money to operate their administrations was because the subventions sent from the capital never reached them. The subregional commissioners blocked these funds at their level and used them to fuel their personal commercial enterprises. Although this practice was officially castigated, the president decided that if there were any unspent budgetary funds at the end of the year, the commissioners would be permitted to use them for their own private purposes. This decision was conveyed to the commissioners at a meeting with the state commissioner for political affairs in Kinshasa. This decision was both tangible "compensation" and a gesture to "encourage" the subregional commissioners in their tasks. Imagination is not required to realize that under such circumstances the budgetary remains would indeed be record setting (Administrative Correspondence, May 25, 1970).

Although state officials are not permitted to engage in commerce of any kind, this law has been openly flouted throughout the Mobutu regime. In 1975, for example, it was discovered that a shipment of gasoline destined for the zone of Bongandanga had been waylaid by the local zone commissioner. In theory, the gasoline was supposed to have been used to keep the vehicles of the Public Works Department on the road, but the commissioner intervened and sold it to a private plantation at an enormous personal profit. The local head of the Public Works Department complained to his superiors, and the commissioner's indiscretion cost him a two-month suspension without pay. This "punishment" did not even have the force of a mild slap on the wrist, as the commissioner had cleared much more than twice his monthly salary with this illegal sale. Significantly, no one asked him to return his ill-gotten gain. Such events were common coin throughout Equateur region and go a long way toward explaining why the various administrative services in the remote parts of the country never seemed to have enough gasoline to get around (Administrative Correspondence, February 4, 1975; July 8, 1975).

Those who have access to funds of any kind are most reluctant to let them slip through their fingers. Most notorious in this respect are the financial officers of the subregions and zones. At Mongala headquarters in Lisala, for example, three officials must sign forms before funds may leave the coffer. The budget officer, the chief accountant (ordonnateur-délégué), and the subregional accountant all have to affix their signatures before, say, a merchant can be paid for the delivery of his goods to the state. In Lisala, many traders confirmed that they had to grease all three palms before the funds could be pried loose from the cashbox. One merchant estimated that if he were owed Z 800 by the state, it would take a total of Z 100 in bribes to these three officials before the funds would appear in his hand (Schatzberg 1975b, pp. 106, 108).

In some ways, the beer situation is quite similar. In areas that suffer from recurring or quasi-constant beer shortages due to the vagaries of the distributive system, beer is a scarce resource, and those with positions of power and authority immediately purchase the few bottles that do appear. If, as often happens, some of the state bureaucrats and commissioners themselves own bars, it is reasonable to assume that their establishments will be more likely to have beer than the bars of ordinary traders. In Bongandanga, a town not well serviced by the brewery in Mbandaka, when a shipment of beer arrives it is immediately purchased and then either consumed or resold at an exorbitant profit by relatively wealthy state employees (Schatzberg 1975b, pp. 46–47). In Lisala, the two bars owned by state accountants were good bets to have a supply of beer in reserve whenever there was a widespread shortage and other bars were forced to close (Schatzberg 1979, chap. 5).

Thus, when resources do arrive in the small, up-country towns, more often than not they will somehow be appropriated by those members of the local politico-commercial bourgeoisie and used for their own ends. Although for the sake of illustrating a pattern civil servants have been considered a resource and it has been argued that the lack of trained bureaucrats—particularly health and educational personnel—is a drawback for the rural areas, this line of reasoning presupposes that the administrators in question are both dedicated and honest. Unfortunately, it is no longer possible to maintain that the majority of Zairian functionaries are either. There are exceptions; some officials in the hinterland are doing their best and are struggling to keep their services going against almost impossible odds. But there are far too many gluttonous members of the politico-commercial bourgeoisie intent on appropriating whatever resources do trickle down into the Zairian countryside, and this is the key reason why resources are blocked at the level of the small urban centers where these officials are most likely to be found.

FINAL THOUGHTS

The argument throughout this chapter has been that resources in Zaire do not filter down into the rural areas. Most wealth that flows down from the capital in Kinshasa never reaches its intended destinations. Instead, the resource flows are interrupted at various points along the way and only rarely reach the farmers in the villages. The blockage points that impede the flow of resources correspond to the cities and small urban centers, which are dominated—politically and economically—by members of a politico-commercial bourgeoisie. The members of this social class are adept at absorbing funds and other resources and at putting them to their own selfish uses. The data presented on the allocation of budgetary funds and on the distribution of bureaucrats in the hinterland tend to support this blockage point hypothesis.

The data on the commercialization of beer, on the other hand, support it only in some cases. It was seen that where small towns are linked directly with the source of the beer supply in Mbandaka, they are not dependent on the whims of suppliers and depositors in other commercial centers. In these cases, the flow of beer to the hinterland does not resemble the flow of budgets and bureaucrats and is probably far more equitable. The key in establishing such direct links to the source of supply is probably the river and road transportation systems. Where these can be, or are already, developed, it may be possible to avoid having beer pass through larger urban centers (blockage points) on its way to the consumers. But where these systems are nonexistent, beer must pass through the urban and small urban bottlenecks and usually fails to reach consumers in the hinterland.

The lesson for development planners ought to be reasonably clear: Avoid the blockage points and channel resources directly into the rural areas. This, alas, is more easily said than done. The small urban centers in Zaire are dominated by members of a politico-commercial bourgeoisie who have a personal stake in seeing that resources do not trickle down into the villages. As long as resources are directed through these urban-based administrative structures, there is little hope that they will reach their rural destinations. Indeed, to the extent that it might prove possible, I would argue that Zairian administration should be divorced from participation in further developmental initiatives. The data on beer commercialization have at least suggested that where free, or moderately free, markets can be created in the rural and semiurban areas, there is a chance that some resources will eventually find their way into the poor parts of the country. But this is a suggestion and a hope—not a solution.

Finally, this study has shown that, at least in Zaire, the assumptions that have guided theoreticians are simply not supported by the realities of the situation. In Zaire one can no longer assume that government officials and political leaders genuinely wish to develop their country. In situations of scarcity, they probably perceive that funds committed to development schemes in the rural areas cannot be applied to the proliferation of their own commercial enterprises. It is a zero-sum situation and, thus far, the politico-commercial bourgeoisie has played the game to its own advantage. Moreover, because the small urban centers function as blockage points, it is difficult to see what positive role they currently play in stimulating development in the rural areas. Last, it simply may not be a viable strategy to build up small urban centers. If the blockage points were to become larger and more bureaucratized, even fewer resources would filter down to the village population. The plight of the farmers remains acute and solutions must be found. But given the administrative base of most Zairian towns, it seems highly unlikely that small urban centers will have much to contribute to the amelioration of life in the rural areas.*

REFERENCES

Administrative Correspondence. Zaire, Archives, Mongala Subregion, Political Affairs Department, Lisala.

---

*For lack of space, the other, and equally important, side of the coin has not been considered: that Zairian small urban centers are also points of extraction. Resources, both human and financial, are siphoned from the rural areas (see Schatzberg [1978, pp. 4-6; 1979, chap. 4]).

Auger, Alain. 1973. Kinkala: Etude d'un centre urbain secondaire au Congo-Brazzaville. Paris: ORSTOM.

Boutillier, Jean-Louis. 1969. "La ville de Bouna: De l'époque pré-coloniale à aujourd'hui." Cahiers ORSTOM (Sciences Humaines) 6:3-20.

Edelman, Murray. 1977. Political Language: Words That Succeed and Policies That Fail. New York: Academic Press.

Gould, David J. 1977a. "Disorganization Theory and Underdevelopment Administration: Local 'Organization' in the Framework of Zairian National 'Development.'" Paper presented at the African Studies Association, Houston, November 2-5.

_____. 1977b. "Local Administration in Zaire and Underdevelopment." Journal of Modern African Studies 15:349-78.

Harrison Church, R. J. 1977. "The Case for the Development of Medium Size Towns in West Africa." West Africa, nos. 3130, 3131, pp. 1341-43, 1419-21.

_____. 1969. "Some Problems of Regional Economic Development in West Africa." Economic Geography 45:53-62.

Hinderik, J., and J. Sterkenburg. 1975. Anatomy of an African Town: A Socio-Economic Study of Cape Coast, Ghana. Utrecht: Department of Geography of Developing Countries, Geographical Institute, State University of Utrecht.

Johnson, E. A. J. 1970. The Organization of Space in Developing Countries. Cambridge, Mass.: Harvard University Press.

Mobutu Sese Soko. 1977. Speech before the Second Ordinary Congress of the MPR.

Mpinga-Kasenda. 1973. L'administration publique du Zaire: L'impact du milieu socio-politique sur sa structure et fonctionnement. Paris: Pedone.

Schatzberg, Michael G. 1979. Politics and Class in Zaire: Bureaucracy, Business, and Beer in Lisala. New York: Africana Publishing.

_____. 1978. "Islands of Privilege: Small Cities in Africa and the Dynamics of Class Formation." Paper presented at the Conference on the Small City and Regional Community, Stevens Point, Wis., March 30-31, 1978.

_____. 1975a. Unpublished interviews.

_____. 1975b. Unpublished field log.

Steck, B. 1972. "Mokolo dans ses relations avec le milieu rural environnant." Cahiers ORSTOM (Sciences Humaines) 9:287-308.

Townsend, Narelle R. 1976. "Hintertown Strategy for Regional Development in Tropical Africa." Pan-African Journal 9:181-94.

Vieux, Serge A. 1974. L'administration zairoise. Paris: Berger-Levrault.

Young, Crawford. 1978. "Zaire: The Unending Crisis." Foreign Affairs 57:169-85.

10

COLONIAL PEASANTIZATION
AND CONTEMPORARY UNDERDEVELOPMENT:
A VIEW FROM A KIVU VILLAGE

Elinor Sosne

INTRODUCTION

> Kinshasa enriches itself too much, and unfortunately at the ex-
> pense of our provinces. We must, in my opinion, sacrifice lux-
> ury to utility, and consider the country no longer as the extension
> of Kinshasa, but as a whole composed of eight provinces (accord-
> ing the importance it deserves even to the smallest village), plus
> the capital. [A. Tudiesche, in Farcy 1971a, p. 62]

> When I get married, I want to have ten children, five boys and
> five girls. One boy will be an agricultural officer; another a
> schoolteacher; a third an administrator; a fourth a veterinary of-
> ficer, and the fifth a priest. One girl will marry an agricultural
> officer; one a schoolteacher; another an administrator; the fourth
> a veterinary officer. The fifth girl will be a nun. [A young
> Ngweshe woman, July 7, 1971]

> A peasant class: that means a class that draws its resources and
> its economic independence from the free work of its own land; a

The research for this paper was carried out under the auspices of the
Institut pour la Recherche Scientifique en Afrique Centrale and with a grant
from the Foreign Area Fellowship Program. Invaluable aid of various sorts
was also provided by the Musée Royal de l'Afrique Centrale at Tervuren,
Belgium. All material without specific attribution in the text derives from
the author's field notebooks. The overview of peasantization, presented in
the first section, summarizes the conclusions reached from the reading of
the primary sources. It is hoped that a more complete account will be published elsewhere. Finally, the author thanks Doris Hendrickson, B. Jewsiewicki, Richard Sigwalt, and Crawford Young for their comments on an
earlier draft. The author, of course, remains responsible for the final product.

stable class, attached to the soil and to the family, hard-working, prolific, satisfied. [Governor General Ryckmans, Congo belge 1935, p. 12]

Seemingly unrelated, these quotations contain three important themes: peasantization, peripheralization, and the emergence of local classes. Together, the processes that these themes describe have profoundly influenced the 300,000 Zairians who live in the traditional Shi kingdom of Ngweshe, the core of Walungu zone. In colonial times, part of Kabare Territory, Walungu was given territorial status, first in 1961, then definitively in 1966, by dividing the older administrative unit into two. Thus the discussion of Belgian policies and their impact largely holds for Kabare zone too and generally parallels the "development of underdevelopment" in other parts of Kivu region that were organized into sovereign indigenous kingdoms before 1900 and subjected to intensive European agricultural settlement after World War I.

Two of the three interrelated themes, peripheralization and local class formation, owe much to Immanuel Wallerstein's "world-systems" approach. Wallerstein's model focuses on two overlapping dichotomies, one spatial or geographical (economic core versus periphery) and the other class (bourgeoisie versus proletariat) (1976). Lying on the periphery of the capitalist world system, Zaire contains, as the first quotation suggests, its own spatial dichotomy characterized by unequal exchange between Kinshasa and the outlying areas of the country. Kivu region, where the author spent two years in the early 1970s, is one of these internal peripheries.

Again like the larger world system, Zaire has its own class distinctions. As a condition for maintaining its privileged position, an upper stratum (a national bourgeoisie) has begun to operate through a co-opted intermediate stratum, which collectively exploits the masses below (compare Wallerstein 1976, p. 351). In Ngweshe today this intermediate stratum, or local elite, is composed of those who have been dubbed "bureaucratic capitalists" (Schatzberg 1977, p. 220), including both the local representatives of the central government, admired by the young woman quoted above, and the political authorities within the indigenous state hierarchy; those who may be called "ecclesiastical elites," including priests, nuns, church officials, and laymen (such as teachers) who work closely with them; and a small group of local traders, speculators, and African plantation owners, themselves often drawn from the first two categories. Controlling, respectively, the kingdom patrimony (land and cattle), local parish funds and land, and the new resources petty capitalism and graft have generated, these people stand well apart from a local peasantry.

The last theme is the emergence of this peasantry through a process sometimes called "peasantization" (Saul and Woods 1971, p. 108). In Bushi (the country of the Shi), a policy of peasantization was consciously formulated and actively pursued by Belgian Congo authorities, who hoped thereby to create a stable peasantry tied to the land but forced to participate in a wider economic system involving nonpeasants (compare Saul and Woods 1971, p. 105). Most effective in drawing the Shi into the capitalist world system, this policy failed to raise local living standards to even the modest level that Governor General Ryckmans, quoted above, optimistically foresaw. Simultaneously, by differentiating a peasantry from an emerging local bourgeoisie and by ensuring its bare survival during colonial times, peasantization drastically reduced the possibility of peasant development in a postcolonial state.

The first section of this chapter examines the policy justifying the forced peasantization of the Shi, a policy shaped by the requirements of a European plantation economy. The underdevelopment of Kivu and the emergence of a bureaucratized local elite were its concomitants. In the second and longer section, by describing three overlapping fields of action—the political field of the Ngweshe kingdom and the modern nation-state, the economic field of plantation and marketplace, and the religious field of the Catholic church—the ongoing "divergence between the life-styles of the 'haves' and the 'have nots'" and the "ensuing 'convergence'" of elite interests (Williams 1974, p. 112) is explored. In doing so, it is hoped that the reader will get a sense of what it means to be a peasant living today in a peripheral periphery—a Shi village in Kivu.

PEASANTS, PLANTERS, AND LOCAL ELITES

The Shi are mixed agriculturalists and pastoralists inhabiting a high plateau (1,600 to 2,200 meters) suitable for cultivating grain crops, beans, and bananas; steeply sloping hilltops and low-lying marshes provide natural pasture. With pleasant year-round temperatures (16° to 20.5° C) (Hecq et al. 1963, p. 19) and normally ample rainfall (1,445 millimeters per year) (Kevers 1956, p. 3; Royaume de Belgique 1957, pp. 8-9), the area was ideal for European settlement. The dense and rapidly growing African population, viewed as a natural labor reserve, made European settlement eminently practical.

Obliged to mobilize Shi labor initially for provisioning administrative and military outposts and later for work on plantations, the administration turned to the chiefs and the traditional government they controlled. Cattle and land, the two most valued local resources, were the foundations on which local kingdoms had been built. Although no one, other than kings, queen mothers, and a very few chiefs, had large standing herds, every man who hoped to achieve full adult status had to have access to cattle. Without a cow, no man could take a wife, and without a wife and a son to perpetuate his position, a man remained a legal minor. Vital to social reproduction, cattle circulated through a complex system of contracts, which cross-cut a similar set of contracts based on the allocation of land.

Unlike in most African agricultural societies, in Bushi a man did not have rights to land controlled by his kin. Apart perhaps from those members of the royal Mwoca clan, who were closely related to the king, descent groups were not landholding units. Only a man's eldest son, who succeeded to his father's position when the father died, was normally ensured of access to land. All remaining sons could get land only by approaching a landholder and negotiating a contract with him. The grantor in this contract became the grantee's "master" or "ruler," while the grantee became his new master's "subject." The new subject, in turn, assigned fields to his wife or wives, who were his "subjects" and the primary producers of agricultural goods. Like the grantee, the master, too, was a subject, owing allegiance either directly to one of the six Shi kings (Kabare, Ngweshe, NaKaziba, NaNinja, NaLuhwinja, and NaBurhinyi) or, if he were less well placed, to a village headman or a large area authority. Again, unlike in other parts of Africa, contractual rights to land were not secure, as, theoretically, all land consignors could confiscate and reallocate plots held by any subject who did not provide the customary tribute and labor.

This roughly hierarchical structure, forged contractually, was ideally suited for indirect rule. After World War I, with the founding of several coffee plantations near Bukavu, indirect rule led to increased forced labor recruitment mediated by chiefs. Shi forced laborers cleared and planted the new agricultural concessions, built the road to Uvira (by which plantation produce could be transported to Lake Tanganyika and by lake to Kigoma, the railhead of the Central Line to Dar es Salaam), and constructed the buildings necessary to house the nascent administration. For these Shi, forced work soon became just another form of tribute owed to their chiefs, albeit one they often tried to escape (Province du Kiva, 7th Séance 1928, p. 2).

Through plantations and forced work the administration sought, from the mid-1920s, to create a second Kenya—with one difference: Where the Kenya highlands were divided into islands of native reserves in a sea of European planters, Bushi was to contain "reserves" of European settlement in a sea of peasant labor (Province du Kiva, 11th Séance 1927, pp. 7-9). One reason for the chartering in 1928 of the Comité Nationale du Kivu (CNKi), a typical concessionary company, was to further this goal. Recruited by CNKi and encouraged by the success of the earlier pioneers, aspiring planters rushed to Kivu in the last years of the decade. By 1930 the outlines of a colonial economic system that was to prevail until, and even beyond, independence has been traced.

The policy of peasantization evolved gradually. By 1937, Flemish peasants provided administrators and planters with a model that they hoped would meet local needs. Like their Belgian counterparts, the Shi were to remain subsistence farmers, drawing the essentials of their livelihood from the land and supplementing their resources, as necessary, through work for larger farmers (read, "European planters") (Province du Kivu, 1937, pp. 42-43) and the sale of surplus crops (to Bukavu and the mines to the west and southwest) (Province du Kivu, 1934, pp. 36-44). Although modified slightly in the 1940s and 1950s, this was the model that was to prevail.

Ensuring both a continued supply of plantation labor (at virtually no pay) and an uninterrupted flow of food to the mines and the city required the improvement of land that was already overpopulated (all the more so because so much of it had been appropriated for European plantations), denuded of forests, and badly eroded. The increased use of forced labor—the only means to both ends—resulted in a decade (1933-43) of intensive overexploitation of Bushi, its lands, and its people. Forced labor grew the food that was sold to mining agents at prices substantially below prevailing market rates (Province du Kivu, 1932, pp. 64, 67; 1939, p. 78; District du Kiva 1944, p. 14). Because arable land was scarce, swamps were drained and, like steep slopes formerly in pasture, planted in food crops with forced labor. Other pastures were reforested, once again with forced labor (Territoire de Kabare 1935, p. 15; Province du Kivu, 1934, pp. 137–39; District du Kivu 1943, p. 20).

The combination of uncoordinated agricultural schemes (many for so-called educational purposes), the replacement of the staple sorghum by less nutritive manioc, the forced sale of Shi milk (to provide the growing European population with fresh milk, butter, and cheese), and the even greater push for production during World War II (Province du Kivu, p. 1934, p. 47; 1938, p. 91; 1940, pp. 11–13; 1943, pp. 4–5; 1944, pp. 8–10; District du Kivu 1940, p. 11; "Rap. d'Inspection" 1940, pp. 42–45; 1942, p. 7; 1944, p. 18) all had dramatic results, though not those intended. By 1943, the vital balances of people to cropland and cattle to pasture had shifted, plunging the region into a disasterous famine that even the administration could not ignore (Territoire de Kabare 1943b; 1946, p. 1; Province du Kivu, 1943, p. 67). The importation of massive amounts of food, sold locally at cost, together with still closer supervision of imposed cropping, largely limited death from starvation to the very old and the very young (District du Kivu 1943, p. 19).

Such aid was merely palliative. Even before the war was over, the administration admitted that something had to be done to reestablish the fragile equilibrium its policies had disturbed. It first turned to intensifying its soil improvement campaign (Province du Kivu, 1945, p. 157; District du Kivu 1944, p. 6) and then to imposing a regime of "voluntary" peasant settlements both of a formal paysannat model, under the auspices of the Anti-Erosion Mission and the National Institute for the Study of Agronomy in the Congo, and of a less formal sort, directed by the provincial agricultural and veterinary services (District du Kivu 1944, pp. 30–32). The application of this "scientific" program for peasant development required yet additional labor to protect the land from soil erosion (by building terraces and runoff ditches and by planting windbreaks), to improve it (by planting nitrogenous fallow crops, enclosing pasture, and composting), and to reforest it.

The capstone of peasantization was the introduction in the mid-1950s of cash cropping of tea and coffee on lands to which peasants were to hold secure title (Territoire de Kabare 1954, p. 45). Meant to create new peasant resources and to tie peasants to the land once and for all, it did not fulfill its promise. Before tenancy could be secured through the registration of land in customary tenure (TFC), local chiefs were required to sign release forms duly noting that traditional dues had been paid. By refusing to do so, chiefs were able to prevent many of their subjects from acquiring the average size plots (25 ares each) and to appropriate large holdings for themselves. Until the 1960s, a very few chiefs held most TFC land on which they established new or extended old commercial plantations. Thus the ultimate measure for promoting peasantization encouraged the growth of a small African planter class.

Throughout the colonial period, European planters held the key to forced peasantization. Their primary concern was a steady supply of local labor at a wage rate that would ensure the profitability of their farms despite fluctuations in world market prices. This the colony provided (for example, Province du Kivu, 1937, p. 43) but little more (compare Jewsiewicki n.d.). Refusing to invest the funds in the infrastructure—roads, ports, storage facilities, and services (such as electricity and water)—needed to make Kivu coffee competitive, the colony left Bukavu and its Shi hinterland largely isolated from the Congo exchange network as well as from the rest of the world. For want of capital investment, peripheralization was ensured.

Perhaps the people who profited most from peasantization, plantation development, and an inadequate infrastructure were the traditional Shi authorities, especially those at the upper kingdom levels, and their allies, the mission-educated elite. While the latter took advantage of new employment opportunities created by colonialism, the former profited by mediating between, on the one hand, their subjects and the administration and, on the other, their subjects and the planters. As intermediaries between peasants and planters, chiefs were the primary recruiters of native labor until the mid-1950s (Territoire de Kabare 1952, p. 59). For their role in labor recruitment, chiefs received gifts and cash bonuses from the planters (Territoire de Kabare 1931), as well as all or part of their subjects' wages (Territoire de Kabare 1926; 1930, pp. 1-2; District du Kivu 1949, p. 4; Province du Kivu 1954, p. 4). As intermediaries between their subjects and the administration, chiefs supervised all forced work, collected all taxes, helped take human and animal censuses, and, most important to the administration, interpreted and enforced all administrative orders. Those chiefs who refused to perform their new bureaucratic roles were simply replaced. Upper-level kingdom officials were rewarded for their service with a portion of the tax revenues (for example, Province du Kivu, 8th Séance, 1928; 1934, p. 118). All chiefs, upper and lower, continued to exact traditional dues and corvées even after 1952 when the administration replaced them by a new repurchasing tax (rachat de corvée) (District du Kivu 1949, p. 8; Territoire de Kabare 1952, pp. 55-56).

In addition to bureaucratized traditional authorities, the colonial administration needed faithful, literate auxiliary personnel. With few official (secular) schools in the territory, literacy was controlled by the Catholic church. The first Catholic missions were established in southern Ngweshe (Nyangezi) in 1906 and in western Ngweshe (Burhale) in 1921, each soon setting up central and outlying primary schools. From among the educated children of catechists and other early converts were drawn the new clerks, court recorders, and agricultural and veterinary instructors, as well as schoolteachers, plantation foremen, and the African clergy.

Chiefs as well as administrators required literate assistants. Both chiefs and the new literati benefited from an alliance that enabled the former to maintain positions their lack of literacy threatened and rewarded the latter in traditional ways—with large land grants and many cattle. As older chiefs died or were removed from office for dereliction of duty, members of the new educated class were often appointed to replace them; for example, an exmember of the Force Publique and head of the Ngweshe police force was named chief of the most densely populated traditional area in the kingdom; a former catechist and primary schoolteacher received another large kingdom area; an educated plantation foreman got several villages.

By 1960 the local political hierarchy, composed of descendants of earlier chiefs and reinforced by increasing numbers of the educated, retained a firm hold over peasants' lives. Its bureaucratized officials had become low-level functionaries, such as tax collectors and overseers of forced agricultural work. With the king and the territorial administrator above and their subjects below, these chiefs spent much more time conveying orders from the top down than communicating wishes from the bottom up. Deprived in theory of their tributary prerogatives, upper-level chiefs were compensated from above in new ways that ensured their loyalty to the king, not to their subjects. Denied a share of the salaries and repurchasing taxes distributed to the chiefs at the top, only the headmen at the bottom of the hierarchy suffered. Still, the basic outline of the old system endured, leaving the poor more powerless politically than before.

Colonial economic changes altered peasant lives more fundamentally. by 1960 the Shi peasant lived on a plot of land too small to meet his family's basic needs, worked on a plantation, and participated in a welter of badly coordinated and highly unpopular agricultural and veterinary schemes. Daily, he had to juggle the demands of local authorities for tribute and corvées, requests by planters for labor, and work imposed by the administration via chiefs and African auxiliary personnel. Wages remained low as did administratively set prices received for foodstuffs. Together with his fellow villagers, he was a member of a large peasant labor pool surrounding islands of Europeans settled on one-tenth of the best land (Territoire de Kabare 1957, p. 44). Some of his cropland had been planted in tea and coffee, which he did not drink and could not sell. His pastures and swamps had been put into crops. Additional pasture had been turned into forest. With land and cattle scarce, he was more at the mercy of local chiefs than ever before.

Under these circumstances, it is no wonder that the Shi eagerly awaited independence. Independence became synonymous with a new economic millennium without forced labor, taxes, or tribute and with abundant food. Some people, in fact, stopped cultivating, believing that providence and the state would see to their needs (Chayeka 1969, p. 8). Others, wiser, continued their labors. All, provident and improvident alike, were trapped by the deteriorating economic situation that accompanied the series of uprisings that swept the new nation in 1960-61, 1964, and 1967 (compare Verhaegen n.d.; Masson 1970). Inadequate food supplies now had to support not only Shi peasants but also thousands of Rwandan refugees, as well as tens of thousands of Bukaviens who fled to the countryside. Roads deteriorated, marshes were no longer drained, the pace of soil erosion accelerated, and famine and protein malnutrition ensued (Ndatabaye 1970). The village the author entered in 1971 was struggling to recover from both its colonial period experiences and those of the turbulent 1960s. What follows is a discussion of the situation as the author knew it at the end of 1972.

THE WIDENING GAP: A VIEW FROM A VILLAGE

Resulting in the peripheralization of Bushi, the peasantization of its people, and the alliance of bureaucratized traditional chiefs with the mission-educated elite, colonial period programs established the framework for the continued exploitation of the peasant after 1960. Today the local exploitative system is just a smaller version of the postcolonial Zaire system at large. Through it, government officials, kingdom authorities, entrepreneurs, schoolteachers, and even the clergy pursue their interests at the peasants' expense. How the elite continue to exploit the peasant masses and, in doing so, widen the existing gap, will be described from the viewpoint of a peasant in the village the author studied.

Each Ngweshe village stands at the intersection of three fields of action—the political (composed of nation, kingdom, and village), the economic (defined by production, market, and plantation), and the religious (circumscribed within the Catholic diocese and parish). Although overlapping and interrelated, these fields can be analytically distinguished and their action individually assessed.

With some 300,000 inhabitants to Kaziba's 20,000, Ngweshe is by far the larger of the two previously sovereign Shi states composing Walungu zone (formerly Walungu Territory). Because its capital is also the zone headquarters, political action in Ngweshe often takes precedence over or even coincides with the politics of the zone. As in the past, king and queen mother rule the kingdom, conveying orders to 15 large area chiefs ("notables"). Nine former area chiefs, demoted by the colonial administration to the status of "subnotable," are now subject to their own area chiefs. Beneath these authorities, village headmen govern the peasants at the bottom, either directly or through still lower-level landholders. All men who remain in the countryside must find a place in this system.

The village studied (population 700) is one of 373 such units. Its headman, a distant member of the royal family, is immediately subordinate to a subnotable living an hour's walk to the west, who, in Shi terms, is his "father" (actually his father's father's father's older brother's son's son). This subnotable, himself the "son" of the king (in fact, the son's son's son's son's son of the present king's great-great-great-great-grandfather), has been subject administratively (since 1962) to a chief still further west, who governs the large kingdom area known as Irongo; Irongo belongs to the queen mother. Thus the village is defined politically as the easternmost local unit of Irongo area. Its inhabitants are either the headman's immediate subjects or the subjects of his subjects. All directives move downward along this chain of command, and tax and tribute move upward.

Any understanding of how this field affects peasants' lives must begin at the top with the territorial administrator (TA), today known as the zone commissioner. Relatively ineffectual in 1972, the TA acted more like Kinshasa's ambassador to Ngweshe than the executor of national policy at the local level. The TA's marginal position in Walungu may be traced to the local application of the policy of indirect rule, which reinforced indigenous political hierarchies at the territorial administration's expense.

Recognizing that without strong administrators territories might cease to be effective organizational units, the colonial administration sought to revitablize them through a 1957 royal order (Arrêté Royal of January 22), implemented only after the decree of May 10, 1957, that reorganized local African communities. Through the decree and the order, the latter creating territorial councils, the administration hoped to strengthen the administrative apparatus of African communities (Province du Kivu, 1955, p. 2) and to give territories a firm foundation for future democratic action (Congo belge 1958, pp. 28-29). Independence intervened after the Ngweshe kingdom government had been reorganized according to the new decree but before the territorial councils had become fully functional.

At independence, as today, national decision makers had three options: to allow local governments to operate largely on their own; to enhance the prestige, authority, and resources of the TA and shore up the shaky territorial councils; or to replace both territorial and local African governments by something new and different. Lacking funds and personnel, the government could neither completely reorganize nor successfully reinforce Kabare Territory, which, in 1960, contained four Shi kingdoms, including Ngweshe. Instead, it conceded local control by dividing the territory into two and by appointing Ngweshe's king as Walungu's TA (from late 1967 to 1970).

The king's departure for Kinshasa, where he was seated in the national assembly in 1970, did nothing to reestablish the autonomy of the territorial administration. How firmly Ngweshe rulers, operating under a kingdom slogan of "order leads to progress," have remained in control throughout the 1960s is suggested by the following events. In 1961, during the time euphemistically referred to as "the troubles," Walungu Territory (effectively Ngweshe kingdom) was the only one in South Kivu district to collect tax monies and make regular deposits in its central bank account (Province du Kivu 1961). And in 1964 the regent of Ngweshe responded rapidly to the call of the central government by mobilizing 20,000 warriors to repulse rebels invading from the south (Samba 1970, p. 125).

The organization that makes such action possible, although formally modeled on the 1957 decree and its successor, a 1969 legal ordinance, is a variant of the immediate precolonial pattern. As noted, the hierarchy of traditional officials has been retained. It has been fortified by a series of councils, in structure and function nearly equivalent to those that existed in 1900. In 1958, the old inner or restricted council of the king's favorites became a seven-member "permanent college," which was transformed in 1971 into a four-member cabinet (composed of the queen mother, two area notables, and a village headman who had once been a foreman on a European plantation). The old council of chiefs has become the kingdom council, including, in 1972, 17 ex officio members (the king, his mother, and 15 of the area chiefs and subnotables) and 58 "elected" members chosen largely from among the remaining chiefs, subnotables, and village headmen (Arrêté Ministeriel 1025 June 9, 1970). (Their terms of office should have expired in 1975 and a new and larger council "elected" to adjust the number of councillors to the expected population increase.) Below the council of chiefs, but not recognized by either the decree or the ordinance, stand 15 local councils presided over by the area chiefs and composed of leading subnotables, village headmen, and larger landholders. Subnotables convene subarea councils, and village headmen preside over village councils attended by all adult men.

This organization both enriches the members of the king's cabinet and their close associates and empowers them to act on their own behalf. Their power derives from the control they exercise over policy formulation and implementation. Once decided on a course of action, cabinet members pursue it ruthlessly through the hierarchy of kingdom, area, and village councils, which have become little more than instruments of peasant oppression. Although judicial decisions can still be appealed through the councils in the opposite direction, only rarely do popular demands now move upward. Originally organized as deliberative bodies, the kingdom council and its three subcommittees—Interior Affairs (in charge of inheritance and succession, land, and cattle), Social Affairs (dealing with economy and finance, public works and corvées, education, public health, and agricultural and veterinary works), and Justice—today automatically approve all cabinet requests.

Profit comes from salaries, land, and graft. If, in 1972, the cabinet members each received monthly stipends of only Z 40 to Z 50 (100 makuta equaling Z 1, which then was equivalent to U.S. $2) these sums still represented earnings more than ten times those of the average peasant. Added to their salaries were the benefits derived from the sale of cash crops grown on the enormous tracts of TFC land they had personally appropriated, land held in addition to the more extensive areas they still administer traditionally. In 1970 the king and the cabinet together had 400 hectares of TFC land, while seven other individuals (among them the former regent and an area chief) held another 427 (Collectivité local de Ngweshe 1970a).

Finally, until 1972 cabinet members controlled the employment of more than 200 patronage workers (2 accountants, 2 clerks, 5 secretaries, 55 police, 84 road workers, 14 census officials, 7 carpenters, a number of sawyers, 2 masons, 3 surveyors, 10 janitors, 8 water workers, and 9 TFC councillors). As of 1972, neither these workers nor the village headmen required to preserve the "order" necessary for "progress" (and who had been placed on the payroll only in 1970) had been paid for from two to four years. Where was all the money going? It is not known for sure, but one district official complained of "the enormous sums of money taken from the kingdom treasury to maintain the cabinet personnel" (District du Kivu 1972). (A similar situation in Lisala is described by Michael Schatzberg [1977].)

Despite attempts to control the Ngweshe hierarchy, most notably by trying vainly to suppress the cabinet, the Zaire state had been unable by 1972 to overcome the legacy of the colonial past. Attempts to co-opt local authorities had also failed. From 1972 to 1974, when the king sat on the central party's Political Bureau in Kinshasa, the Ngweshe government, under his mother's direction, continued to act as it saw fit. A national program of governmental recentralization (compare Gould 1977), which included the changing of all local titles—king to burgomaster, notable to ward head (chef de quartier), village headman to precinct leader (sous-chef de quartier)—did not alter the chiefs' relationship to their subjects or to the state.

Incorporating everyone into the Mouvement Populaire de la Révolution (MPR) only further legitimized the old positions by making the burgomaster head of the kingdom MRP, the war chiefs heads of the area party cells, and the precinct leaders heads of village-level cells. Wearing party buttons, carrying party cards, and singing the national anthem (whose French lyrics few understood) at the opening of all council meetings, everyone rallied publicly to the party cause (Territoire de Walungu 1972). Only in private was displeasure expressed at the forced levying, retroactively to 1971, of party dues. At Z 1.20 for a man and his wife in 1971 and in 1972, the inhabitants of Walungu could be expected to turn in more than Z 1 million. Anyone who refused to pay risked going to jail.

Local people clearly understand the system and have learned to work within it. Depending for their very livelihood on the hierarchy of kingdom officials, peasants express their discontent through symbolic defiance and passive resistance rather than through open rebellion. When told to attend council meetings or to participate in collective forced labor (for example, repairing or building schools, maintaining wells), peasants often stay at home. When ordered to enclose common pasture, cut down banana plantations, or build new, conpact villages of mud and wattle houses, they may agree to do the work but put it off until neighboring villages have undertaken similar projects. When chiefs demand payment of tribute (irhulo) or tokens of subjection (nshigo), both illegal, peasants oblige but refer to their payments as burhabale, freely proffered aid.

From 1960 until 1972, when the registration of land held in customary tenure was abolished over the king's protests (Ndatabaye 1970), peasants rushed to register small family plots and thereby secure their tenancy. Although a number of chiefs still tried to stop them, and others put obstacles in their paths, most chiefs, recognizing the immediate profit to be made from the cash payment of customary dues, signed the necessary release forms. For example, the headman of the village studied collected Z 22 in customary tribute from the local veterinary officer, a newcomer to the village, who then registered 11.79 hectares of land (Collectivité locale de Ngweshe 1970b). Most of it was former common pasture, but several hectares had long been cultivated by village residents.

Once a peasant obtains land and thereby places himself within the political system, he pursues one of two goals—finding a wife if he is not yet married or providing for his family if he is. As he strives to realize his goal, he must earn the money to pay taxes and party dues (and thus remain out of prison) and procure basic subsistence needs, such as food, food supplements his wife cannot grow, tools, household utensils, and clothing.

The average peasant also hopes to acquire certain "luxuries," such as a kerosene lamp and the kerosene to keep it lit, new (as opposed to used) clothing, a few pieces of costume jewelry, perfume and body oil, and, almost extravagantly by local standards, a wristwatch or clock and a transistor radio. These items may be obtained through participation in the local economic field by negotiating a cattle contract, working the land, trading in local and/or distant markets, laboring for wages on a local plantation, and sometimes cash cropping. In pursuing these ends, the peasant constantly comes up against his chief, local bureaucrats working for the regional government, traders, and plantation owners or managers, all of whom exploit him.

In order to marry, a man must find a cow, since bridewealth is not payable in cash. Of preference (because cattle contracts involve continuing obligations to one's cattle partner), he will buy one at a market for, in 1972, from Z 75 to Z 100. Most men do not have this kind of money and are forced instead to arrange a cattle contract. In the past, a man might get a cow from a local chief in return for settling on the chief's land. Today, with land and cattle scarce, a peasant must turn more often to his kin, affines, and friends. From whomever procured, a cow does not come cheaply. A substantial counterprestation—several goats or sheep, a bull, an old or barren cow, or cash —must always be paid, as well as every third calf. When called upon, the recipient of the cow must also work for its donor, and when the cow and her progeny die, he must remit a quarter as tribute to mark the end of the relationship and express his hopes of renewing it.*

The result of many cattle contracts negotiated individually is a network of ties that link village residents both to each other and to individuals living within a 10-kilometer radius. This network cuts across the political field defined by the allocation of land.

Cattle may be important in Bushi, but the land is still more basic. A peasant's dependence on the land ties him to his village, keeps him firmly subjected to his chief, and obliges him to pay illegal tribute. The peasant family today lives in one or more beehive-shaped, thatched huts, shaded by its bananas and surrounded by its fields. Family plots are subdivided into small parcels, some of them planted in beans intermixed with sorghum or corn and others in sweet potatoes or manioc. To supplement wet season (late September to mid-April) crops grown on village land, beans are sown, in June, in marshes still drained by forced labor, which the headman must provide. About one year in three, early or heavy rains flood these swamp fields before the October harvest. When flooding occurs, a family must tide itself over by foraging for wild food, harvesting immature root crops, or consuming stored beans until the first of the village-grown beans ripens in late December.

In addition to the crops people normally plant, each able-bodied, adult, taxpaying man is still required, by the 1969 ordinance, written in language virtually identical to the 1933 and 1957 decrees, to grow "educational" crops

---

*Like land contracts, cattle contracts, with their high counterprestations and continuing obligations to return calves to the donor, were outlawed in 1972 (Territoire de Walungu 1972). According to that decision, once a cow calved twice, one calf was to be given to the donor and then the relationship was to be terminated. When the author left the village at the end of 1972, however, both cattle and land contracts were still being negotiated and those in noncompliance with them prosecuted in court. It is not known whether the new law has been systematically applied and, if so, what its effects have been on local social and political relationships.

and food for the cities and the mines. Varieties and amounts are fixed yearly by the regional commissioner on the recommendation of his subordinates. This work, together with health measures (such as clearing paths and bush surrounding houses, building latrines, and proper disposal of trash), labor in the swamps, reforestation, and pasture improvement, is supervised by a local agricultural officer employed by the regional agricultural service.

Because his territory is vast, the agricultural officer can spend only two days a year in each village. In his visits to the village studied, he inspected farms and homesteads, "arrested" noncompliers with the law, and got drunk on peasants' beer. People "arrested" paid "fines" of from K 50 to Z 1 and several bottles of beer ("Primus" or banana), for which no receipts were given and which the officer put in his pocket (or drank). Some people do the work the law still demands of them. Most do not, preferring to take their chances that the official will be too short of time (or too drunk) to inspect their work or, if he does, that they can escape punishment by means of a bribe equal in value to a week's labor on a local plantation. For these reasons, although virtually unchanged since colonial times, the program of forced labor no longer looms so large.

While the agricultural officer enriches himself at the peasants' expense as he oversees field and homestead work, the veterinary officer, responsible for only a slightly smaller territory, exploits the peasants in the guise of enforcing animal husbandry rules. The veterinary officer under whose jurisdiction the village lies is the man whom villagers rightly accuse of having stolen their land. Just as he got his land by buying off the village headman, he also bought his way into the veterinary service; with only two years of primary education, he was hardly qualified. (The local agricultural officer, in contrast, finished the requisite four-year secondary course.) Officially, the veterinary officer keeps the village livestock census (actually kept in the sample village by the headman) and sees that animals are inoculated, when vaccine is available (as it usually is not). Otherwise, he is most conspicuous in the two local markets where he supervises trade in cattle, inspects meat, and collects market "taxes," which he shares with the market sweeper. Legally, in the countryside, no market taxes are due.

The two local markets—one meeting on Sundays and Thursdays, a 15-minute walk to the east; the other on Saturdays and Wednesdays, a 75-minute walk to the west—define another aspect of the economic field. Forming part of a circuit of markets, in existence before 1900, they were moved in colonial times to fixed sites along major roads, were adjusted from a five- to a seven-day week, and were then, as they are now, subjected to administrative regulation (Territoire de Kabare 1950, 1959). They were originally relocated and controlled in order to eliminate porterage and to ensure a steady flow of food to the mines and the city. Mineworkers and Bukaviens still get their food at the expense of Shi women, who continue to haul on their backs loads of up to 50 kilograms of manioc, beans, or sweet potatoes from market to market on successive days.

In the marketplace one finds these women porters as well as other women who hawk their surplus crops; teenage girls who walk five hours to

Bukavu to buy salt, sugar, hulled rice, or soap to resell; boys who sell cigarettes and matches; and other part-time vendors, such as meat sellers and,
at tax time, unemployed men who take livestock to the low-lying forests in-
land and return with forest products (such as peanuts) to sell. To supplement
its resources, almost every family brews banana beer (from one to three
times a month), which it sells at home or in a market stall at a profit of
K 30 to K 50 each brewing.

The selection of items locally available is completed by the commerce
of full-time itinerant traders (such as cloth and clothing peddlers) and a very
few wealthy entrepreneurs (like the wife of an Ngweshe cabinet member) who
own or rent trucks used to transport bottled beer and other commodities from
Bukavu to the countryside and food to the city on the trip back. Some traders
also truck in goods from as far away as Bujumbura and Uganda. When roads
are impassable, the products these vehicles normally haul become scarce.
Other shortages result from the continued practice of fixing market prices
by administrative ordinance. When prices are set too low to justify trade in
an item, even staples like palm oil, salt, and manioc disappear.

Another way to earn cash is by working on a local tea, quinine, or coffee plantation. Plantation labor (and attempts to escape from it), so important in colonial times, plays a much less dominant role today. Since 1956
the number of plantation jobs has drastically declined, while the population
has risen.* (Among the reasons for this decline are the conversion of coffee
plantations to tea and quinine, the latter requiring little upkeep; the closing
of a number of plantations since 1960; and the fact that once a plantation has
been cleared and planted, much less labor is needed to maintain it.)

In 1972 only 20 men, one-fifth of those in the village, worked on plantations with any regularity. For the most part, these 20 villagers worked
within 5 kilometers of their homes, a distance set in colonial times by the
fact that wages and supplementary obligations were reduced for planters whose
workers lived nearby (Territoire de Kabare 1943a, p. 22; Bulletin administratif du Congo belge 1938, pp. 621-23; 1952, pp. 1065-67; 1953, pp. 1673-
79, 1994-96; 1954, pp. 469, 565; 1955, pp. 896-97, 903-16). Plantations
within this range from the sample village included three owned by Pharmakina
(a German multinational), two owned by a Belgian concern, and one owned by
two Italian brothers. With the Zairianization decree of 1973, Pharmakina,
the largest holder of local plantations, remained untouched. Presumably
the other local plantations were taken over by new Zairian owners.†

In 1972 the official wage rate for unskilled labor varied from K 20 to
K 25 for an eight-hour working day. Plantation laborers working six-hour

---

*Throughout the 1950s, approximately 30,000 plantation positions were
filled in Kabare Territory (Territoire de Kabara 1957, p. 19). In the late
1960s, only 20,000 agricultural positions were available in the entire province (Farcy 1971b, p. 39).

† The next largest owners of plantations in Kabare Territory were the
companies of Irhabata and Gombo, both acquired by CELZA, which reportedly
(Gould 1977, p. 377) belongs to Mobutu.

days earned even less, most reporting wages of Z 2 to Z 3 a month. Family allocations, required by law for one's wife and children, were provided for only two children, if paid at all; a man with three or more children legally inscribed in his identity book was simply not hired. No distinction in pay was made for years of service, the most senior worker being paid the same as the most recently hired. Even so, plantation jobs remain in high demand, as they offer the only local source of regular income. Teenage girls, too, work on plantations. They are paid on a piecework basis for harvesting tea and removing bark from cut quinine trees. In 1972, even an especially able tea picker could make no more than K 10 a day. With her pay as capital, a girl will usually enter the part-time market trade.

Industrial crops provide a final means of earning cash. As noted, tea and coffee were introduced in the mid-1950s, even though the administration admitted then that it did not have sufficient factory capacity to process the projected harvests (Territoire de Kabare 1959, p. 4). Processing capacity was still inadequate at independence when these peasant plantations were just beginning to bear. Nevertheless, peasants were forbidden to uproot tea bushes and coffee trees and replace them with food. During the author's stay, it was also impossible for peasants to market coffee legally, and, as a result, the wives of the 38 villagers with coffee trees (most with from 20 to 30, a few with as many as 200 to 300) clandestinely traded with merchants in Rwanda, a six- to seven-hour walk away.

Peasant tea planters could not do this because green tea must reach a processing plant no more than four hours after being picked. Additional factories were never built; no transport was provided, and tools and fertilizer remained expensive and difficult to obtain. Most of the tea plots were therefore allowed to go wild. In 1970 the European Common Market launched a "development" project to reclaim those plots grouped in larger blocs and close to a road. The project, Relance du Théiculture au Kivu, called for renovating the two government tea factories, supplying peasants with tools and fertilizer, and hiring foreign experts to teach peasants how to care for tea (Commission Agricole du Kivu 1970, 1971). No effective program was ever proposed to explain the goals of the project to the peasant producers, perhaps because the experts brought in were technicians rather than community developers. For example, one expert, who had previously worked in India, spoke no language local people understood, insisted that the natives "had tails," and complained that the peasants refused to follow his orders. He was quickly disillusioned with the program, and so were they.

Tea reclamation did not catch on, at least not among the peasants it professedly meant to help. Besides the lack of communication between program planners and peasant producers, tea growing did not pay. Two European planters estimated the potential monthly income from the average 25-are plot at Z 1 to Z 2. These estimates confirmed the calculations of the one villager who enrolled in the program. Given the low returns even success would bring, and considering the amount of labor needed to tame wild tea, the administration's abysmal record of alternately encouraging and forbidding cash cropping, and the fact that comparable sums could more easily and surely be earned by brewing beer three times in one month, it is hardly surprising that most peasants who owned plots of tea preferred to sell them to local speculators for the sum of Z 1 each. Several of these speculators, many of them chiefs, were already fairly large planters; others were on their way to becoming small plantation owners.

Faced with the continued exploitation of peasants by chiefs, representatives of regional services, plantation owners, traders, and speculators, the Catholic church has tried, if not to stop exploitation, then at least to make it easier to bear. Controlling social services and salvation, the church is dedicated to uplifting lives as well as saving souls. Without the resources needed to operate effectively at the local level, the church, too, has fallen back upon the chiefs, with the unfortunate result that peasants now perceive its programs as elitist.

Facing west politically and lying economically between the mines and forests of Maniema and the city of Bukavu, the village faces east in matters that are now called religious (dini) toward the Catholic mission in Ciherano. Ciherano parish, created in 1960 out of the older parish of Burhale (founded in 1921), encompasses three large kingdom political divisions—its namesake, Ciherano area; Lurhala area, still farther east; and Irongo, where the village lies. Today 30 to 40 percent of all Shi are baptized Catholics, while many of those who are not consider themselves Catholics without the benefit of baptism. Catholic and non-Catholic alike, the Shi are avid churchgoers; on Sunday mornings the church overflows. Despite an ongoing policy of Africanization, there are just not enough priests, let alone African priests, to staff all the parishes. In 1972 Ciherano's three priests were all Europeans.

People's perceptions of the church begin with their feelings toward the clergy. Perceiving African and European priests differently, peasants feel fully comfortable with neither. Partly their unease derives from the distance an enormous pastoral load puts between priest and parishioner. Priests spend virtually all their time hearing thousands of confessions each week, baptizing hundreds of babies and catechumens, saying mass, performing marriages, administering last rites, and burying the dead. They have little time left for cultivating warm human relationships with individual Christian peasants. With scale has come cold calculation. A diocese policy forbidding priests to drive the sick to local hospitals (ostensibly because of inadequate insurance coverage) does little to endear the clergy to their peasant parishioners, particularly those clergy, like the European priests of Ciherano, who strictly adhere to them. And a European priest's image only further suffers when he marries two couples in a double ceremony and confuses their names!

The European clergy, of course, are outsiders, while the African priests may be from the people (most coming from commoner, not royal, families) but, unfortunately, may not remain of them. Many European priests patronize Africans. They demand respect and impose rules (such as tranquillity at mealtimes) that accentuate their social distance from their flocks. To approach a European priest or enter his home or office takes courage few villagers can muster. In comparison, African clergy at other parishes are easier to approach. Even at mealtimes, their doors remain open, but very few peasants go in. Formidable furnishings, a complete set of tableware, indoor plumbing, meat on platters, and beer in mugs—all indications of opulence—make peasants feel supremely ill at ease. Priests, or so villagers say to each other, are privileged indeed, much closer to elites than to peasants.

The identification of elitism with the church likewise carries over into the realm of church-operated services, most notably medical care, schooling, and community development. Two dispensaries in the parish serve a population of some 45,000; the one nearest the village is run by African nuns. Although the sisters charge modest fees and claim never to refuse treatment to indigents, peasants visit them reluctantly for fear of being turned away. Here, again, a perceived social barrier places distance between peasants and the church. In doing so, it lends support to the notion that modern medicine is for the privileged, while indigenous medicine is for the peasants.

In the area of education, peasant perceptions are more nearly correct. Most local government-subsidized schooling is administered by the diocese. Even including the very few subsidized Protestant and secular schools and the unsubsidized and substandard "parents schools," founded and run by the kingdom and supported financially by the local population, the number of classrooms comes nowhere near to meeting the region's needs.* Of the villagers born between 1930 and 1950, only half the men had any schooling (normally one to three years); none of the women did. In 1972, 61 percent of the school-aged boys in the village, but less than 8 percent of the girls, were attending or had attended school. Catholic primary school principals, therefore, have very real power—they determine who will enter school and who will not. By admitting the children of their friends and of the already privileged, they perpetuate the local status quo.

Even the diocese program for local development has become an elite endeavor sustaining the status quo and has thereby aroused peasant suspicions of all development projects. Like most everything else the church does, the program is well intentioned but grossly understaffed and underfunded. Overseen by a European priest in Bukavu and staffed by students and graduates of the Social Institute for Rural Development, formerly the Catholic-run African Social Institute but now part of the Zaire university system, the plan concentrates far too much on "development from above" and much too little on "development from below" (compare Pitt 1976). In doing so, it allies the elites of the parish with the clergy and opposes both to the peasants; it has therefore been ineffective in cultivating grass-roots support.

---

*No data was found on classroom space in Ciherano parish. However, in 1972 in neighboring Burhale parish, which is at least as large, there were 2,800 students (most of them boys) in the 81 regular primary classrooms in the central and branch schools. In addition, two religious orders had places for 826 girls in 22 classrooms. Elsewhere in Ngweshe, schooling for girls is unusual. Interestingly, in some sense, the church considers the parents schools as its own. The fiftieth anniversary brochure, celebrating parish achievements, lists eight of them in Burhale (Paroisse de Burhale 1971, p. 12).

The master plan outlines two successive stages for local campaigns—
the mobilization of popular support and then popular action (Farcy 1971a).
Mobilizing support requires, first, convincing every individual of his Christian responsibility for self-improvement and community development. Through
sermons preached in church and through the indoctrination of schoolchildren,
members of Catholic adult and youth groups, and catechumens, the clergy
hopes to reach those people, especially the responsible leaders of the Christian community, who are open to development and who will make the idea
their own.

The action phase begins with the recruitment of a team, composed of
semiprofessional developers and students in field placements, that will define the objectives of the local campaign and set them in motion. Once organized, the team approaches the parish council, or in its absence sets up a
parish development committee, to assist it in devising a campaign slogan and
in formulating a plan of action. Village subcommittees are then formed to
take the slogan and the plan directly to the people.

In Ciherano, the campaign's key word is <u>progress</u>, which the local orga-
nizer (a graduate of the African Social Institute) explained as meaning: "What
the Church teaches for the progress of the world's peoples who aspire to improve their lot and the importance of progress in the avoidance of war and
disorder, and in the establishment of social justice and of unity in charity."
Progress, is, of course, the goal acclaimed in the Ngweshe kingdom slogan,
"Order leads to progress," and using it in this development campaign has
been greeted most approvingly by kingdom officials. Implemented in the name
of progress, the most significant effect of this local plan for action has been
the perfect marriage of clergy, schoolteachers, entrepreneurs, and chiefs.

Serving as the chairman of the Ciherano Central Development Committee is a well-meaning and progressive, Catholic area subnotable. The other
central committee members are the directors of three nearby primary
schools (two Catholic, one Protestant), three Catholic teachers, the African
nun who directs the local dispensary, the parish head priest, two area chiefs,
another subnotable, two catechists, a plantation foreman, and a trader (who
is also a village headman). The five subcommittees, presided over by five
local chiefs, are similarly constituted. It is little wonder, then, that the one
tangible achievement of this campaign—the organization, in 1971, of a consumer's cooperative, located at the mission and funded by shares offered for
sale to the local population (but bought up mostly by committee members)—
is commonly believed by peasants to be a profit-making venture to enrich
local elites at the peasants' expense.

Thus, from the peasants' perspective, the church serves peasant interests little better than the chiefs and the other elites whom peasants encounter
as they pursue their economic ends. Effectively independent of the kingdom
hierarchy, the church can, and sometimes does (especially at meetings of
the full kingdom council), oppose the local political bureaucracy. But by
choosing to work with and through it in such key matters as development,
the church dissipates its power and fails to realize its limited potential. As
a result, the three fields—political, economic, and religious—and the actors

who dominate them are merged in the mind of the peasant, who perceives them all as working together to undermine his best interests.

CONCLUSION

The roots of the present opposition of a small but locally powerful elite to a large peasant mass have been traced to the colonial policy of peasantization (developed to reconcile the conflicting demands of European planters for labor and the mines and city for food), together with the bureaucratization of the Ngweshe political hierarchy, reinforced by incorporating increasing numbers of the educated. Occupying social statuses as varied as chief, regional service representative, trader, African planter, schoolteacher, and clergyman, and operating in all three interrelated fields, the elite of Ngweshe still derive from two basic social categories—those who had a stake in local government before the imposition of colonial rule and those who gained a foothold after having received an education in Catholic schools.

Whichever their claim, the elites continue to use positions within or privileged access to the local kingdom government for self-enrichment at the peasants' expense. And even those, such as the clergy, who may not be seeking purely personal gain have been forced or, at least, feel constrained to operate within the strictures laid down by Ngweshe officialdom. As long as this situation persists and successfully promotes local law and order, peasant progress will be blocked as the gap between peasants and elites widens.

REFERENCES

Bulletin administratif du Congo belge.

Bulletin officiel du Congo belge.

Chayeka, E. H. J. 1969. "Les Coopératives." Bukavu: Report of the Institut Social Africain, Bukavu.

Collectivité Locale de Ngweshe. 1970a. "Rapport annuel TFC." Gabriel Kasongo, December 23. Ngweshe Archives.

_____. 1970b. "Rapport annuel des Titres fonciers coutumiers au groupement de Mwimbi-Irongo." Patrice Ruenda, December 28. Ngweshe Archives.

Commission Agricole du Kivu. 1970. "Projet 211.004.31—Relance Théiculture au Kivu. Procès-Verbal de la deuxième réunion de la commission tenue le 2 decembre 1970 à l'hotel de ville sous la Présidence de M. le Commissaire Provincial et Gouverneur de Province A.I."

_____. 1971. "Procès-Verbal de la 4e Réunion de la Commission Agricole du Kivu, Sections Nord et Sud, Tenue à Bukavu, le 14 juin 1971 sous la Présidence de Mr. B. Kufundu, Directeur Provincial de l'Agriculture et Président de la Commission Agricole du Kivu."

Congo Belge. 1958. "Conseil de gouvernement 1958: Discours du Gouverneur General H. Cornelis."

_____. 1935. "Discours du Gouverneur General Ryckmans à l'ouverture du Conseil du Gouvernement."

District du Kivu. 1972. Letter 3072/503/F.21 from the vice-president sous regional du MPR, Omankoy Yuhi-Kasongho, to the provincial governor. Bukavu: Interior Affairs Archives.

_____. 1949. "Note sur le rachat du tribut." t'Kint de Roodenbeke, September 28. Uvira District Archives.

_____. 1943. "Situation vivrière du Territoire du Kabare. Exécution des travaux imposés. Du 5 nov. au 27 nov. 1943." F. Aurez. Kabare Zone Archives.

_____. 1941. 1944. "Rapports annuels AIMO" (Affaires Indigènes et de la Main-d'oeuvre). Madison: University of Wisconsin, Zaire Colonial Documents.

_____. 1940. 1942. 1944. "Rapports d'Inspection du Territoire de Kabare." Uvira District Archives.

Farcy, R. P. Henri. 1971a. "Essai de manuel pour la mise en état de développement des paroisses." Mimeographed. Bukavu.

_____. 1971b. "Mémorandum sur la Region du Kivu et le Diocèse de Bukavu." Mimeographed. Bukavu.

Gould, David. 1977. "Local Administration in Zaire and Underdevelopment." Journal of Modern African Studies 15, no. 3:349-78.

Hecq, J., A. Lefebvre, E. Vercruysse, and A. van Wambeke. 1963. Agriculture et structures économiques d'une société traditionnelle au Kivu (Congo). Série scientifique 103. Publications of l'Institut National pour l'Etude Agronomique du Congo with the l'Institut Belge pour l'Encouragement de la Recherche Scientifique Outre-Mer.

Jewsiewicki, Bogumil. 1974. "Une conception d'histoire économique et sociale du Zaire moderne." Likundoli, E.H.Z. 2, no. 2:205-20.

_____. n.d. "Le colonat agricole européen au Congo belge, 1910-1960: Problèmes politiques." Manuscript.

Kevers, G. 1956. "Contribution à l'étude du Kivu. Monographe de la Region de Walungu en Territoire de Kabare." Bulletin agricole du Congo belge 47, no. 5:1243-62.

Masson, Paul. 1970. Dix ans de malheurs (Kivu 1957-1967). Vols. 1 and 2. Brussels: Max Arnold.

Ndatabaye, Mwami Ngweshe-Weza III. 1970. "Mémorandum a la Commission Provinciale de la Province du Kivu de Passage à Walungu le 12 sept. 1970. Obj: Problèmes généraux dans le Territoire de Walungu." Bukavu: Interior Affairs Archives.

Paroisse de Burhale. 1971. 50 Ans . . . 1921-1971. Bukavu.

Pitt, David C. 1976. Development from Below: Anthropologists and Development Situations. The Hague and Paris: Mouton.

Province du Kivu. 1961. Letter 209/61 from Omarhi, Adrien, president of the provincial government to the Commissaire de District, June 27. Uvira District Archives.

_____. 1954. "Avis et considérations du Gouverneur de Province sur le rapport d'enquête de l'AT." Babilon, January 10.

_____. 1927-29, 1932-59 (before 1934, Province Orientale; 1934-48, Province de Costermansville). "Comptes rendus des Conseils des Provinces du Congo belge." Documents from: Bibliothèque Africaine, Brussels; Archives Africaines, Brussels; Archives Générales du Royaume, Brussels. Microfilm from the Centre d'Etude et de Documentation Africaine.

Royaume de Belgique. 1957. Ministère des Colonies. Aperçu sur l'economie agricole de la Province du Kivu. Publication of the Direction de l'Agriculture, des Forêts et de l'Elevage.

Samba, Guillaume. 1970. "Les institutions traditionnelles politiques du 'Bugweshe' dans la conjoncture politique des années 1959-1967." Mémoire de licence. Louvanium.

Saul, John S., and Roger Woods. 1971. "African Peasantries." In Peasants and Peasant Societies, edited by Teodor Shanin, pp. 103-14. Baltimore: Penguin.

Schatzberg, Michael. 1977. "Bureaucracy, Business, Beer: The Political Dynamics of Class Formation in Lisala, Zaire." Ph.D. dissertation, University of Wisconsin-Madison.

Territoire de Kabare. 1959. 1960. "Procès-Verbaux du Conseil de Territoire."

_____. 1950. Letter 35/O/AE/C from the territorial administrator, Ver-
meersch, to the district commissioner, October 30. Uvira District
Archives.

_____. 1946. "Note sur les causes actuelles directes et locales des disettes."
Eeckhout, January 26. Bukavu: Agricultural Service Archives.

_____. 1943a. "Rapport d'inspection plantations Région Walungu-Nya-Ngezi."
May 15. Kabare Zone Archives.

_____. 1943b. Letter 4292 Agri/Viv from the territorial administrator, G.
Schmit, to the provincial governor. Uvira District Archives.

_____. 1930. 1931. 1935. 1952. 1954. 1957 (until 1935, Territoire de
l'Unya-Bongo). "Rapports Annuels AIMO." Uvira District Archives.

_____. 1926. "Rapports semestriels sur l'administration générale du terri-
toire." Uvira District Archives.

Territoire de Walungu. 1972. "Résolutions prises par la Reunion tenue à
Walungu en date du 14/4/72 à laquelle participaient tous les Chefs de
poste, chefs des services administratifs et les chefs coutumiers de
deux Collectivités locales de Ngweshe et Kaziba." Milo Iliang Abande,
April 15. Bukavu: Interior Affairs Archives.

Verhaegen, Benoît. n.d. Rébellions au Congo. Brussels: Centre de Recherche et d'Information Socio-Politiques.

Wallerstein, Immanuel. 1976. "A World-System Perspective on the Social
Sciences." British Journal of Sociology 27, no. 3:343-52.

Williams, Gavin. 1974. "Political Consciousness among the Ibadan Poor."
In Sociology and Development, edited by Emmanuel de Kadt and Gavin
Williams, pp. 109-39. London: Tavistock.

OTRAG Concession

National Capital
Regional/Provincial Capital
Sub-Regional/District Seat
Zone/Territorial Seat
Village

11

"THE RANSOM OF ILL-STARRED ZAIRE": PLUNDER, POLITICS, AND POVERTY IN THE OTRAG CONCESSION

Allen F. Roberts

INTRODUCTION

First presented in 1732, Voltaire's <u>Zaire</u>, from which the title of this chapter is drawn (Act II, Scene II, Line 494), is considered his most famous tragedy (Blum 1972, p. 38). In the eighteenth century, when it was written, the Central African republic, now of the same name, was best known to Europeans as a blank space on their maps. There is, however, a certain irony in the coincidence, as those familiar with the play* and with the republic's

---

*The plot of the play is as follows: Zaire has been the slave of the Saracen sovereign of Jerusalem since early infancy; she knows nothing of her heritage or identity and has joyously accepted her destiny of bondage, especially since learning of her master's love for her. In a plot portions of which were influenced by or borrowed from Racine, Corneille, and Shakespeare, Zaire's brother brings her ransom; but the Saracen will not part with the girl. Zaire learns of her background from her brother and is torn between her love for the master who has enslaved her and her desire to be true to her heritage. Her allegiance vacillates between the two, and the pride of the Saracen is wounded when he mistakenly assumes Zaire's brother to be a secret lover. He slays Zaire in a rage, only to commit suicide when he learns of his error. Master and slave perish, then, while those who would have separated the two for their own profit must forever suffer their loss.

Anthropological research in Zaire from December 1973 to December 1977, upon which this chapter is based, was financed by the National Institute of Mental Health (Grant in Aid No. 1-F01-MH-55251-01-CUAN), by the Committee on African Studies and the Edson Keith Fund of the University of Chicago, and by the Society of the Sigma Xi. A first draft of this study was read by Galen Hull, Pauline Stone, and Crawford Young, some of whose thoughtful comments have been integrated into the text. While I thank all these agencies and individuals for their generosity, I alone am responsible for the content of the present writing. This chapter is dedicated to a Zairian friend, K.K.,

recent history will recognize, and as the tale of the OTRAG concession illustrates all too well.

> The Zairian patrimony should belong to the Zairians, who should
> be done with all these foreign implantations sucking the blood of
> our people. [P. 26]

On March 26, 1976, a contract was signed between the government of Citizen-President Mobutu Sese Seko of the Republic of Zaire and a German-based firm called Orbital Transport und Raketen A.G., better known by its acronym, OTRAG. Those few Western journalists who have lent the matter their attention have noted the unusual nature of this contract. Meant to provide a site suitable for the launching into orbit of "any sort of satellite for any country requesting it" (Lutz Kayser, chairman of OTRAG, cited in Thiam 1978, p. 35), OTRAG is granted virtual sovereignty over a tract of land in northeastern Shaba region about the size of the U.S. state of Montana. As reporter Tad Szulc (1978) has noted, "the only similar situation in the world currently exists in the 1903 Panama Canal Treaty" (p. 80).

The terms outlining the jouissance intégrale—the full or complete possession, enjoyment, and use—of the concession are indeed remarkable. OTRAG "has the right to possess and use the territory without restriction for the purpose of launching missiles into the atmosphere and into space . . . and to take all measures which, in the opinion of OTRAG, are related directly, indirectly or otherwise" (Article 1, Section 2; my emphasis)* "provided that these do not threaten the security of the country" (Art. 2, Sec. 1). This might read "the rest of the country," as, given the wording of Art. 1, Sec. 2 ("or otherwise"), all responsibility for the lands of the concession itself appears to have been abdicated. The German company thus has the power to divest of their homelands the several hundred thousand inhabitants of the area.† Leaving aside the controversial questions of OTRAG's political purposes and the ultimate impact of Mobutu's 1979 efforts to revoke elements of the agreement, consider, above all, the iniquitous nature of Mobutu's prerogatives and priorities concerning rural regions.

Both Mobutu and OTRAG have treated the concession area as a simple piece of real estate. Such imperialistic insensitivity seems oddly incongrous

---

*The contract has been published in its entirety in Afrique-Asie (Bourderie 1977, pp. 28-30); these passages are reproduced from there. While great controversy has surrounded the purposes, means, and most other aspects of OTRAG, the contract itself appears authentic; a copy was allegedly stolen from the Zairian Embassy at Bonn, and was perhaps leaked to Afrique-Asie by the East Germans (Wilson and Legum 1978).

†The city of Kalemie and lesser towns, Catholic schools and missions, industrial fishing concerns, the substantial tin mines at Manono and the potential mineral deposits near Moba, cattle ranches, and a large portion of the new U.S.-financed North-Shaba Maize Project are all within this territory.

---

a truly dedicated public servant who made our stay so enjoyable, and whose example will always inspire me.

and atavistic* from one who has made such statements as his quote cited earlier here, or who has called so stridently for a "recourse to authenticity." Yet, when the history of Zaire, and in particular its rural sectors, is considered more closely, it becomes clear that Zaire is indeed "ill-starred," that historical authenticity is a woeful tale of its repeated rape and bondage. Zaire's rural citizens of every generation for a century or more have paid a heavy ransom, and still have yet to win their freedom. Here, then, is a more detailed view of the political and economic history of the area ceded to OTRAG.

ETHNOGRAPHIC SKETCH OF THE
SOUTHERN LAKE TANGANYIKA REGION

There are two major ethnic divisions within the area ceded to OTRAG, the Luba and Lubaized peoples in the western and southern parts and the BaTabwa (with whom we are most familiar) in the eastern, where OTRAG headquarters is located. Most of these people follow matrilineal descent and share many social structural features with the other societies of the "Matrilineal Belt" of Central Africa. They are small-scale farmers, and those living along Lake Tanganyika are ardent fishermen as well. There are indications that intraregional precolonial trade was significant, especially along the shores of the lake. The well-developed exploitation of local resources (especially iron and salt), BaTabwa state, was prohibited by the colonial power, so that people be obliged to purchase European goods and thus to enter the greater colonial and world economies (while assisting local colonialist merchants). (Compare Vellut [1977]. The early politics and trade of this region are discussed in A. F. Roberts [n.d.].)

While to the west and south of the concession area there existed organized, precolonial "kingdoms of the savanna" (Vansina 1970), within its bounds there was no such political cohesion. Rather, there were small chiefdoms led by men of select lineages of the various clans, each autonomous; there were no other corporate groups as that term is usually defined, and leadership and dependence were structured only in the loosest manner. As a Tabwa writer has noted, "In the Marungu, each individual . . . is independent" (Kaoze 1910, p. 418). (Such matters are discussed much more fully in Nagant [1976] and in A. F. Roberts [1979].) Such independence of spirit has rendered impossible more recent attempts to establish farming or other sorts of locally run cooperatives in the area. People are distrustful of anyone who would presume to impose his will on others, although each individual aspires to have his own opinion be heard and followed. The result, when united action is sought, is usually constant, jocular haggling.

---

*Atavism is defined as "the reappearance of a characteristic in an organism after several generations of absence, caused by a recessive gene or complementary genes . . . also loosely called 'reversion,' 'throwback'" (American Heritage Dictionary 1969, p. 82). To press the metaphor, we would stress that Mobutu has inherited the trait from the Belgian colonizers, but would add that, sadly enough, several generations have not transpired between its manifestations.

POLITICAL HISTORY

This section is in some ways a complement to Vellut's fine study "Rural Poverty in Western Shaba" (1977). Throughout the last 150 years or so, the area under discussion has suffered the incursions of one set after another of marauders or more permanent overlords, the legitimacy of whose claims to power the local populace may have rejected, but has been powerless to oppose. The arrival of Lunda chief KaZEMBE in the late eighteenth century and early Bemba warring drove many from their settlements in the Movwe marshes southeast of Lake Mweru, and later Bemba and Ngoni raiding further stimulated the exodus northward into the Marungu Massif. Later still, strife in the Zambian portion of the land called LiTabwa, owing to Tabwa chief NsAMA's increasing participation in long-distance trade and his conflict with the notorious coastal slaver-trader Tippu-Tip, impelled others of NsAMA's own Zimba, or "Leopard," clan to flee northward. At about the same time, Nyamwezi ivory hunters and traders from central Tanzania and "Arab" or "Swahili" slaver-traders from Zanzibar and the coast began exploiting the area, often with highly disruptive results. By the time the first European settlers reached the area in the early 1880s, the general political situation was one of siege, of rapidly shifting alliances among local chiefs, coastal slaver-traders, gun-bearing Ruga-Ruga mercenaries from Tanzania, and soon the Europeans themselves. Each faction strove at all costs to obtain whatever material or other benefits there might be available. (Useful sources for the study of the history of this period include I. Cunnison [1969], A. D. Roberts [1967, 1973], Tippu-Tip [1974], and M. Wright and P. Lary [1971].)

The local rural farmers were the great victims in such an arena. Because they were forced to live in palisaded villages, they could not tend their fields properly. The various war parties pillaged the fields to sustain themselves, or fired them as a tactic of siege. Famine resulted. The rinderpest epizootic of the 1890s decimated the game, locusts ate their crops, and epidemics of smallpox and viral infection further plagued the population. When, in the 1890s, missionary and Free State officials were able to establish peace in the area, local people were especially receptive to their efforts (this in comparison with other regions of Zaire that had not been so afflicted). The Europeans quickly exploited the disaffection of the populace for those who had so mistreated them in the past.

The true designs of the Europeans soon became apparent. For some years the Free State agents of Leopold II reigned only nominally; the real power, both political and economic, was that wielded by the White Fathers established along Lake Tanganyika. Early on, these latter maintained a de facto "Christian Kingdom" with the mission at Mpala as its capitol; justice and even capital punishment were dispensed from there by a lay auxiliary, a standing army was maintained under its own flag, a currency was issued, and a state religion imposed.* Later, these overt powers were curbed by a colonial regime anxious to leave no doubt in the minds of rival imperialists (the English and the Germans, but especially the former) as to who really

---

*This is the subject of a separate article by A. F. Roberts, now in preparation.

ruled the Congo. Even so, the priests maintained a certain distance from the
colonial government for many years. Some of their number remained quite
high-handed through the first decades of this century. Recalcitrant traditional
chiefs were deposed and replaced with men more amenable to mission policy,
local-level politics were joined and manipulated through a network of catechists placed in rural chapelles-écoles, and those individuals who would resist their will were summarily turned over to the forced-labor corvées of
the Free State authorities.

The priests' overall goal was to destroy and replace that which they
deemed pagan, and thus unproductive, with that which would lead the local
people to modernity and participation in the evolution of their region. Many
of the schools and other organized activities they instituted have had lasting,
positive effect.* At the same time, something has remained of the disattach-
ment from the rest of the Congo as implied by the pursuit of the "Christian
Kingdom" along Lake Tanganyika. Nowadays, local resentment of their obvious exploitation by certain Zairian officials is informed by a feeling of regional (within the bounds of the "Kingdom") chauvinism. In turn, it is likely
that this is interpreted as superciliousness, and is resented by government
officials.

As a contemporary writer noted, after some years of colonial occupation, lakeside people became nostalgic for the "old days" when, as all was
in flux, the advantages might shift to the favor of any faction (Schmitz 1912,
p. 571). It was obvious, especially in the Leopold years, that the "politics
of plunder" (a phrase employed by V. Naipal [1974, p. 12] in the context of
modern Argentina), pursued so ardently by all factions prior to 1885, were
still in march, but with the difference that the occupying forces maintained
a strict monopoly over the most significant benefits to be so gained. (Whatever clandestine resistance to European rule that transpired over the years
was greatly hampered by the same "independence" of local individuals, as
mentioned above.)

In the 1930s, a major reorganization of indigenous social and political
institutions was effected, in part in response to British and French programs
of indirect rule; in part to streamline and otherwise decrease everyday contacts between rural Congolese and overly taxed territorial administrators,
always astonishingly few in number;† in part to agree better with a Belgian
monarchist cosmology. Extensive studies were undertaken by colonial agents

---

*Monsignor Roelens, stationed at the Baudouinville/Moba mission for
over 50 years, was a significant figure in both Congolese and Belgian politics.
In his many writings, he manifested great disdain for the intellect of those
Congolese within his pastoral domain. A perusal of his notions of the inherent "depravity" of the members of his congregation living "in the tyranny of
the Demon" (1946, pp. 30, 32) leaves no doubt as to the price paid by the
BaTabwa for their entrance to enlightened modernity.

†One of the most useful, critical appraisals of the legislation, personnel,
and problems of this era remains an unfortunately obscure document prepared
under the auspices of the Archives of the Belgian Congo (1958); see also E.
Bustin (1975).

to determine and to "reconstruct" the grandes chefferies—the paramountcies of the past—which, it was felt, must have existed prior to the disruptive wars with the slavers. A feudal model was imposed, and feudal vocabulary employed. The empires of several paramounts were "reconstituted"; within these, the grand chef has his fief, and vassal subchiefs then had their own dependent domains, for which they owed homage and tribute to their suzerain. Such terms and the principles behind them were inappropriate to local history and social structure.

Those persons not of the suzerain's lineage or clan who did not profit from such an hierarchical system greatly resented its imposition, and still do.* Within the greater context of colonial occupation, there was felt (at least by the outsiders) to be a secondary occupation, this by the chiefs appointed and supported by the Belgians. Here was yet another example to rural farmers of the "politics of plunder" of which they had so long been the victims. As Vellut has noted, such "chiefs gave colonial rule its African mask" (1977, p. 307).

With independence in 1960, many felt that a new order would be possible and forthcoming. As early as 1959, Tabwa factions had supported the formation of Moise Tshombe's CONAKAT party, and they continued to do so even during the most critical moments of the next several years (Gérard-Libois 1966, pp. 25, 70). Several of the most prominent members of the secessionist Katangan government (for example, Joseph Kiwele, first minister of education) were lakeside people, who had long benefited from the education provided by Catholic schools and seminaries. While there was generalized support for a separation from the central government of Leopoldville among the BaTabwa and others in the central and southern portions of the concession area, the BaLuba to the west opposed CONAKAT and soon formed governments of their own at Manono and later at Albertville/Kalemie (Willame 1964, p. 116). Intense fighting in the early 1960s occurred throughout much of the concession area between the forces of the state of Katanga, Sendwe's North Katanga, and the Leopoldville regime.[†] In 1964, the region was again embattled, by Simba (or false) "Mulelist" troops who drew recruits from disaffected local youth.[‡] Albertville/Kalemie was again occupied and the scene of fierce fighting; hundreds perished, and tens of thousands fled to rural refuges, putting a severe drain on resources there.

Because it was important on the local level, it was hoped that the 1930s feudal hierarchy of chiefs might be altered with the advent of independence.

---

*The rigidity with which these models were conceived, imposed, and have been maintained may be unusual in the greater Zairian context; the consequence—a long-standing and often bloody conflict between two major clans, one with, the other without, substantial government-supported local-level political power—will be the subject of future writing.

[†]At one point in 1962, the mobilized Katangan troops of the notorious mercenary Jean Schramme used Kansimba—now the precise location of OTRAG headquarters—as a base of operations to the north and west (Kabembe 1962).

[‡]Informants compare the attitudes and activities of the Simba with those of present-day Jeunesse du Mouvement Populaire de la Révolution (JMPR) party members.

After 30-some years of close control of the system's imposition, this was not to be a revolution, but only a rebellion. Those who felt their identity with the land to be such that they and not the imposed chiefs had a legitimate claim to power wanted the same benefits as the imposed system had for so long conferred upon their enemies. Several years of low-level strife followed, masked by national events and culminating in 1964 with the mass assassination, perpetrated by the established chiefs, of the firebrand leaders of the underground. The order of the 1930s was thus reconfirmed, and it stands yet today.* With the first rumors of imminent invasion by the Katangan gendarmes late in 1976, the same conflict erupted once again. An alleged plot was discovered by government agents in which both Zairian officials and the same established chiefs were to be murdered, this to facilitate the "liberation" of Katanga by a force from Angola that would invade Shaba region via Moba. (Several of those implicated were still in prison at Kinshasa in late 1977. Neither in the Shaba I nor II invasions did any direct war activity occur in Moba zone.)

Given this history, there is some justification for the claims of local people that the Zairian government has chosen to ignore them in a punitive fashion. It is said that when Mobutu was approached by a delegation asking for greater development of Moba zone, his refusal was to the effect that the area is rebellious and unprofitable.† People inhabiting the concession have found their ethnic origin to be a stigma in competition for jobs, and some have changed their names and identities to those more marketable. Given the manner in which some administrative personnel and JMPR party members ruthlessly pursue their own profits,‡ it is felt that the central government of General Mobutu is yet another in the long series of occupying forces; that the politics of plunder are still very much in effect; and that only the name of the ultimate suzerain has changed, to an "authentic" one. That the OTRAG concession should consist almost entirely of their lands is an even more sinister affirmation that their fears are well founded.**

---

*The most influential of the imposed chiefs is an acquéreur whose extensive cattle ranches are adjacent to those taken over by Mobutu himself; he was a deputé in the Katangan government, is a member of the Order of the Leopard, and, in 1977, ran for elective office.

†When the author heard this story in 1976, it had already been passed along many branchs of the grapevine; the original incident probably occurred in 1975. A fruitful area for future research would be the transmission of stories from or about Kinshasa to remote rural settings, the images people have of Mobutu and his advisers, and the factors from local history that effect this perception.

‡Contrast Mobutu's statement on this, le mal zairois or Zairian affliction (as cited in Young [1978]), with recent reporting that "the President, according to diplomats and businessmen, rakes off 10 percent on most international business deals" (Darnton 1979).

**Aside from the nature of the contract, very little has reached the press concerning OTRAG's relation to politics internal to Zaire. That OTRAG lent

Germane to this discussion is a consideration of the government input to rural regions, such as that along Lake Tanganyika. In other words, what benefits do local people derive from their government?* One immediately thinks of health care delivery, education, and the maintenance of order. These will be considered briefly.

As of 1977, rural dispensaries had ceased operation along the lake because of a lack of Western medicines and the repeated failure of zonal health authorities to pay nurses' salaries. There is, then, no health care whatsoever provided by the government from the outskirts of Kalemie to the Zambian border, except at Moba. (The dispensaries at Tembwe, Mpala, and elsewhere, long maintained by the colonial government, were still open in 1974.) The hospital in Moba lacked a medical doctor from 1975 to late 1977 (when the author left the country).† By 1976 Western medicines were either lacking or woefully scarce throughout southern Zaire, this the calamitous result of Mobutu's having nationalized and centralized (at Kinshasa) the pharmaceutical distribution industry.‡ Little, if any, was available at Moba hospital. Late in 1976, for instance, the total medical allotment for Moba zone from Kinshasa for one month consisted of 1,000 Nivaquin malaria-suppressant tablets (100 milligrams) and the same number of aspirin; this was to suffice not only for the hospital but for outlying dispensaries as well.

A common occurrence is for shipments from Kinshasa to be pillaged en route, only the wooden cases, empty or filled with rocks, arriving at Moba. Most medicines available in the lake region are now imported, legally or (perhaps more frequently) illegally, from Tanzania or Burundi. Because of the risks involved in smuggling, prices for essential drugs have become staggering. For example, in late 1977 a single 500-milligram tablet to combat schistosomiasis cost Z 2.50 (then about U.S. $2.80) on the black market —the only source from which any were available. Treatment requires from 14 to 20 tablets for an adult.

Mobutu support during the Shaba II war, flying "medical and other aid," was indeed rash, as Wilson and Legum suggest (1978, p. 2), the more so in that the Katangan secession of 1960 was espoused by most living within its concession, many of whom still hold the memory dear.

*Michael Schatzberg (1977, chap. 4) considers this same issue in the vicinity of Lisala in Equateur region. His findings make it clear that the situation along Lake Tanganyika is similar to that in other areas of Zaire.

† The doctor was discontent to remain in such a backwater, and spent much of his time moonlighting at the European-run cattle ranches in the Marungu Massif. Reliable sources hold that when he left Moba he took with him most of the instruments and bedclothes of the hospital, which he sold elsewhere. See C. D. Roberts (1979) on these and related issues.

‡ As an adjunct of this policy, the voluntary agency Caritas was no longer allowed to supply medicines to local White Fathers for distribution or sale at nominal fees.

There are schools only in the vicinities of Kalemie, Mpala, and Moba along the lakeshore; there are none from Moba to the Zambian border.* The Catholic mission at Mpala, since 1971 only visited several times a year by European missionaries from Moba, was once a center of education. Many adults there can read, although there is no printed matter available to tax this skill. Schools are still run in the mission buildings, but the teachers have few books or supplies they do not purchase themselves, and they are only infrequently paid. One dedicated teacher continued to work, although not paid for two full years. His name was on the payroll at Kinshasa, but someone between there and Mpala was drawing his salary. Thus the teachers generally are greatly disillusioned, their loyalty to their calling severely strained.

Public order is maintained by a small force of the Zairian army at Moba; by policemen employed by traditional administrators of the collectivités, or paramountcies, and the localités, or chiefdoms, subordinate to the latter; or by members of the JMPR. The authorities of Moba zone rarely if ever visit outlying villages. Mpala, the largest village between Kalemie and Moba, is located on a road from Moba and is easily accessible by boat from there; it received only three official visits between 1975 and late 1977—two general inspections by the zonal commissioner and a homicide investigation.†

Localité policemen generally concern themselves with cases brought before the chief for adjudication, and assist the localité clerk in collecting taxes and in issuing paid permits and documents. Their salaries are fixed by law, while localité judges and clerks receive a set percentage of each fine exacted. As one candid insider remarked, "Our payment follows the amount collected; if there are no judgments, well, there is no salary for us."

The local MPR party cell is led by a dirigeant, who commands a fluctuating force of voluntary JMPR members. At his Bureau Politique, he can settle small affairs such as fighting in bars or the making or selling of illegally distilled liquor (rutuku) when brought to his attention by JMPR members. At Mpala, the dirigeant is an entrepreneur and bar owner who sells rutuku in

---

*Rural primary schools, which once radiated outward from these centers and were to be found in most large villages, have been closed in the last few years; it is possible that in once again taking control of local education mission authorities may reopen some of these.

†In this case, the army officer came by road and felt pressed to return to Moba the same day; he summarily arrested all suspects and others involved in the case, including septuagenarian Chief Mpala and all his hamlet headmen (for having allowed the crime to transpire). All spent more than two months in prison at Kalemie awaiting a hearing; theoretically, only the higher court at Lubumbashi is competent to judge murder cases, but this one was settled out of court, the judicial authorities receiving Z 150 (then U.S. $300) and six goats from the accused murderers. The others, including the chief, were then released without further ado.

his own establishment. He thus has free bouncers and can curb the competition at will. More important cases for litigation are forwarded to the civil courts or to his superiors at Moba, should they involve subversion. Being a lifelong member of the community he serves, he is loathe to do this, sharing as he does the general fear of, and antipathy for, the representatives of the Kinshasa government, and knowing that such an action would visit a certain and considerable escalation of physical punishment and fines upon the offender. Instead, he usually contents himself with containing and controlling the course of many local conflicts, often enough to his own personal profit.*

Mobutu himself has admonished his subordinates, this at a public meeting, that "if you steal, do not steal too much at a time. You may be arrested. Steal cleverly, little by little (yiba na mayele)" (cited in Gould 1978, p. 18). The key word here is mayele (yiba, meaning "to steal," and na, meaning "with" or "and"). It may be given the glosses "craftiness," "wile," or "sly intelligence." As it is used in KiSwahili by those living along Lake Tanganyika, an individual bragging will employ the word to describe his having outwitted an adversary. But if applied to the actions of a third party, it carries a nuance of sorcery, implying that the person has faculties beyond those of ordinary folk. To outwit is one thing, to be outwitted quite another.† Bureaucratic corruption, then, joins the ranks of acts within the category of sorcery. Mobutu and his followers, in stealing cleverly, little by little, are fit successors to earlier "sordid buccaneers" of the colonial era, "greedy without audacity, and cruel without courage," without "an atom of foresight or of serious intention in the whole batch of them," and "[un]aware [that] these things are wanted for the work of the world" (Conrad n.d., pp. 98-99).

As in other documented cases of politico-military occupation, there are many collaborators from among the oppressed. (See E. Mumbanza [1975] for a discussion of African roles in assisting the implementation of colonialism in the Congo.) The "rip-and-run" ethic of the mid-nineteenth century

---

*The quality of public order achieved by party representatives in rural settings is exemplified by the actions of the same dirigeant. On one occasion, in 1977, when fishermen committed to another buyer refused to sell him their catch (that he, as middleman, take it for resale to Kalemia), he had them arrested by the JMPR on the pretense that they were selling fish at a price too high, and thus ruining the market. The preservation of low local prices for fish has been a matter of great concern for area businessmen (many of whom are employed by the government); buyers from Kasai or other protein-starved regions are willing to pay fishermen higher prices than they are; such individuals are denied passes and buying permits to visit the area.

†It is probable that the term carries the same connotations in Lingala—the language of the Zairian armed forces and of General Mobutu—as it does in KiSwahili, the lingua franca of Shaba region and the language from which many elements of Lingala are drawn. The Dictionnaire Classique Lingala gives "intelligence, spirit or thoughtfulness, ruse or artifice" as translations (p. 46).

made all very aware of the advantages of political gamesmanship. Through the years, those who cooperated most heartily with the priests and administrators received very tangible benefits. Those who sometimes don JMPR uniforms and who are sent or spontaneously go on missions do as well.

There is another side to this same issue. David Gould has discussed the tolerance of upper-echelon government agents for corruption by their inferiors (following their own example but at a lesser scale): that this is the structure of the government, as loyalty is but a function of continuing economic self-interest (1978, pp. 91-92). In a rural setting, even in the most remote villages seldom if every visited by appointed officials, there is always the possibility of entry into the lowest ranks of the party government. By the occasional assumption of a JMPR role, a marginal character may share in the plunder and gain immediate power not otherwise available to him through such traditional channels as kinship and affinity, which he can then utilize in local-level political matters in which he may be involved.* In this way, violence directed toward the government by alienated individuals becomes counterproductive to them; instead, it is dissipated in local situations of no relevance to national politics.

As has been demonstrated in many other studies, where traditional political authority, as the strong arm of the greater religion and cosmology, is systematically discredited, as has been the case here, for the sake of "progress" as defined from without, unless other religious or national ideology is espoused in its place, a general alienation and lack of social accountability must result.† At the local level, this is reflected in an increase of sorcery accusations. (The articles by Richards, Willis, and others in M. Marwick's [1970] collection on witchcraft and sorcery are informative in this regard.)

Whereas in the past, ceremonies and religious societies provided for the release of tension and the working out of solutions through collective consideration and action, most of these forms of mutual recognition and redress of social ills are no longer available. But as local people say, "Sorcery and theft are of one path, and deceit is their brother." They are manifestations of the utter disregard of the rights and sanctity of self of one's fellows. Nowadays, umilitant—a Swahili rendering of the French, the state of being a "mili-

---

*Small merchants, itinerant diviners, smugglers, and those otherwise considered "without strength"—that is, the proper temperament—for sustained farming frequently become JMPR members. Such individuals, in a U.S. context, would be called hustlers.

†Attempts by the government to present "the MPR . . . as a church, and its Founder a Messiah" (Engulu 1974) have not been successful in the lakeside area. One of the Kinshasa government's greatest shortcomings is its assumption (evident in many policies and in the attitude of many administrators) that rural citizens are unsophisticated rustics. Instead, even in remote villages many are assiduous listeners to Swahili broadcasts from Tanzania, West Germany, South Africa, and elsewhere, and are otherwise remarkably well-informed and astute political critics.

tant" supporter of Mobutu (and thus of being among those sharing in the plunder through party membership)—joins ulozi (sorcery) as a great and equal evil. It may contribute to one's downfall and death should the injustices perpetrated sufficiently imbalance the social order. People laugh and feel vengeful delight when a government agent or collaborator meets his demise or dies in their midst (if he has taken advantage of them in the past). The old system has its hidden strengths. A good chief is deemed one who intervenes and protects his people from harassment by party or government authorities.* When such people become afflicted, this is attributed to the general, undefined power of the chief, and to his successful maintenance of relations with the ancestral and earth spirits. It is said that at "real independence" (Uhuru wa Kweli),† JMPR militants and those like them will be forced to flee into the bush, to live there by themselves, outside of community, like animals or sorcerers.

As a final indication of the feeling of local people concerning their relationship with Mobutu's government, it may be noted that when someone has been arrested and is taken to the zone offices at Moba, it is usually possible for his kinsmen to pay either a fine, or a "fine" (see second note on page 221 as an example), or both to obtain his freedom. The Swahili verb to describe this action is kukombolea (to ransom someone). The etymology of this word is very revealing. Kukomba means "to scrape out, hollow out, clean out," as one does "the nutty part of a young cocount." Kukomboa means "ransom, redeem, deliver," but also to "make hollow, convex, hence make crooked, warp, put out of shape . . . and so, figuratively, cause difficulty to" (Johnson 1971, p. 218). In other words, it is recognized through the verb's nuances that paying a ransom divests the donor not only of his wealth but of something internal, something of his shape, essence, or dignity.‡

ECONOMIC HISTORY

The economic pursuits of people living within the concession, in both precolonial and more modern times, are for the most part centered about agriculture (although fishing in Lake Tanganyika has become of great significance as well). The most frequently mentioned crops in earliest written descriptions

---

*In Norman Miller's terms, a state of "mutual hostility" exists, with a "revival" of traditional principles applied to these modern circumstances (1968, p. 186).

† The elections of the fall of 1977 raised what proved to be ill-founded hopes for Mobutu's ouster.

‡ The Swahili expression for "to pay a bribe" in use in Shaba is similarly graphic: kukata midomo means, literally, "to cut off the lips." "To seal the lips" would be a possible gloss, but the gesture accompanying the phrase—a flick of the index across the mouth, like the snick of a dagger—makes the connotation obvious.

of the area are finger millet, sorghum, and maize. (See, among others, J. Thomson [1968, 2:30]; Livingstone in H. Waller [n.d., p. 300]; and C. Trapnell [1953, p. 63].) But manioc, which has become the much-favored staple, was already a principal food source in the region in the last half of the nineteenth century (Storms 1884, p. 12). The early European settlers—agents of Leopold II's International African Association (AIA) and the White Fathers—introduced others for their own diet—potatoes, wheat, beans, onions, and various garden vegetables among them. These grow particularly well in the high plateaus of the area (Chambon and Alofs 1958, p. 31). The priests distributed gratis the seed of such European crops, and in the early years apparently purchased "all" the produce to stimulate the local economy (DeGeorgi 1923, p. 500).

The first AIA outpost in the region was founded in 1883 at Mpala, where the Lufuko River, emptying into Lake Tanganyika, has formed a wide delta. This has long been a site favored by farming people,* and is capable of supporting a relatively large population. The White Fathers were ceded the AIA post in 1885, and two years later obliged the local chief to relinquish his rights to half the delta lands as his tribute to them for that year (Joubert, October 14, 1887). The mission soon became known as "the granary of Tanganyika" (White Fathers, Diaire Mpala, January 16, 1896), and supplied many of the other missions and European installations in the greater lake region, both from its own gardens and from produce obtained through trade with local people.† Small steamships and schooners arrived at and departed from Mpala several times a week to load there such produce, coffee,‡ and limestone quarried nearby (White Fathers, Diaire Mpala, August 18, 1901).

With the advent of World War I, the White Fathers began growing surplus crops and purchasing others for the war effort; local people were coerced into increasing their farms and providing other services. In 1915, 58 metric tons of manioc flour, 26 of potatoes, 6 of wheat, and 2 of onions were obtained at Mpala (White Fathers, Diaire Mpala, November 8, 1915); and at one point, 53 metric tons of food were sent from the Baudouinville mission to support Congolese troops (White Fathers, Diaire Baudouinville, January 14, 1915). While no data are available concerning production by African residents for their own consumption or trade with persons other than the missionaries, this nevertheless gives an indication of significant agricultural activity in the region at a point still early in the colonial era.

---

*Bored stones, or kwes, found at Mpala and elsewhere through the Marungu Massif are indicative of late Stone Age cultures, and were perhaps used as weights for digging sticks or other agricultural tools, as they are or have been used by Kalahari Bushmen. See F. Cabu (n.d.) and R. Doize (1938).

†In 1895, for instance, 1.6 metric tons of potatoes and the same amount of wheat were exported from Mpala (White Fathers, Diaire Mpala, February 16, 1895).

‡Almost 2 metric tons of coffee were produced in 1899 (White Fathers, Diaire Mpala, January 15, 1900); local people still grow some coffee for their own use, but there is no attempt at cash cropping.

The White Fathers continued to stimulate agricultural organization and expansion in the concession area. Methods were taught at their various schools, and a special class for 30 in practical agriculture was established at Mpala. In 1923, it was estimated that local people around that mission were growing some 100 metric tons each of wheat, potatoes, and onions (De-Georgi 1923). (B. Jewsiewicki [1977] provides a valuable, wider context for this discussion with his recent article on the integration of African farmers into the capitalist market for food crops during the interwar years.)

According to the writers of a long summary of agricultural progress and prospects in the area, "the principal objective in Tanganyika [District] of the Service of Agriculture [has been] the preservation of the capital constituted by the cultivable lands" (Chambon and Alofs 1958, p. 29). Although much of the land is not suited for farming (one estimate is that only 10 percent of lands are arable [White Fathers 1956, p. 348]) and reportedly only about one-half of 1 percent of lands within Tanganyika district was being cultivated by Africans in 1955 (53,000 hectares of some 83,300 square kilometers [White Fathers 1956]), those lands that are productive are especially so. These include deltas, such as that at Mpala, alluvial valleys, such as at Kala near Moba, or less rich lands in the plateaus where grain and pulse crops thrive nevertheless. The Agricultural Service saw as its primary mission in the district the dissemination of information and minor policework. For the most part, the land and the farmers could take care of themselves, with the assistance of the White Fathers.

This, then (and we are speaking particularly of the old territory, now the zone of Moba), was an agricultural region of significance and great potential. Foodstuffs were exported toward the industrialized portions of Katanga (compare Jewsiewicki 1977, p. 322), but, significantly, relatively few men left to work at the mines.* There was some drift over the borders toward German and English centers, but this was most often for political reasons as well as for economic ones. It is likely that a combination of factors made it more interesting to people to remain in the area to farm; important among these was the resistance of the White Fathers to any attempts at emigration from their mission centers.† When recruiters did come from the Bourse du

---

*Most migration from the rural portions of this area has been to local towns such as Moba, Manono, or Kongolo or to the city of Kalemie; at the same time, few from other areas have come to settle in these towns (or such was the situation in the 1950s). Some of the better-educated people have gone on to Lubumbashi or to Bujumbura as well (White Fathers 1956).

†The White Fathers, especially in the years around the turn of the century, felt threatened by the possibility of an exodus from their missions, and took severe measures to ensure that it not occur. "Deserters," when apprehended by mission personnel, were flogged and placed in chains to do forced labor at the mission (White Fathers, Diarie Baudouinville, September 4, 1900); April 25, 1902). In the colonial years, travel by Congolese was only by official pass, as it has become once again under Mobutu's regime.

Travail at Elizabethville, few men were willing to accept their offers, and the priests actively expressed their regrets concerning those who did (White Fathers, Diaire Baudouinville, March 10, 1913). When the missionaries themselves were requested to assist in the recruitment, their retort was that the colonial government had designated Baudouinville and much of the surrounding territory as an agricultural preserve, from which recruitment was prohibited (White Fathers, Diairie Baudouinville, June 17, 1913). While it is not clear to what degree this was official—no legislation or decree is cited in the diary—later the arrangement seems to have been formalized, certain areas being closed to recruitment and others open only with expressed administrative approval (White Fathers 1956, p. 510). This is the more striking, given the complexity of administrative efforts to keep other regions of the province open to labor recruiting (see Vellut 1977, p. 305 and passim).

In 1955, 1,514 metric tons of beans, 540 of wheat,[*] 309 of sorghum, 302 of onions, and 236 of potatoes were produced for export from the territory of Baudouinville/Moba (White Fathers 1956). A few figures for maize and manioc exportation (in metric tons) are also available for the same territory and zone:[†]

	1948	1949	1950
Maize	15,516	12,312	12,222
Manioc	39,610	32,960	31,454

Most of the manioc was and is destined for use at Albertville/Kalemie, while the maize is transported much further by railway to the mining cities to the southwest.[‡] BaTabwa do not make bukali polenta from corn flour, but only from manioc; to the southwest, a mixture of both or only maize is favored. Also, corn may be preserved for longer periods than can manioc. It is interesting, then, to compare the above with more recent figures (in metric tons), again for Moba zone (from Division Régionale de l'Agriculture 1976):

	1973	1974	1975
Maize	4,904	5,950	7,817
Manioc	73,584	92,521	64,974

---

[*]Crawford Young (personal communication) has suggested, correctly, that this situation, so unusual for the Congo, was a reflection as well of Monsignor Roelens' substantial political influence. In this and other subtle ways, the "Christian Kingdom" along Lake Tanganyika persisted throughout the colonial period, lending the area a special nature.

[†]From Service Agricole (1951, pp. 19, 21). Consistent annual agricultural statistics were not obtained by this author.

[‡]The railway linking Lake Tanganyika with the mining centers to the south was completed in 1915 to export copper and import food to the mining towns. The Germans had completed the line from Dar es Salaam to Kigoma on the lake the year previous. See Marissaux (n.d.) and Jewsiewicki (1977).

Clearly, something has gone radically awry in maize production in the area, while manioc has increased dramatically (although the three years show significant fluctuation).*

Everyone in the concession area, except those inhabiting regions of highest altitude, grows manioc (<u>Manihot ultissima</u>) for his own consumption, both as <u>bukali</u> polenta (made from the tuberous roots) and as a vegetable (from the fresh leaves); root scrapings and spoiled supplies are fermented and the product distilled to make <u>rutuku</u> liquor. Maize is only grown to be eaten fresh on the cob, to be mixed with millet in making <u>kibuku</u> beer, or to be exported as a cash crop. It grows best on the plateaus and least well in the poor, sandy, often eroded soils of the lakeshore. Manioc grows everywhere,† and especially well in sand (Jones 1959). Manioc is a "famine crop," survinving locust swarms, bushfires, and most climatic aberrations. It requires very little care, and even seems to produce poorer root crops with fertilizer than without (Jones 1959). These features are not shared by maize.

The areas where maize grows best, then, are the plateaus of the Maseba and Marungu Massifs (again referring primarily to Moba zone, most immediately effected by OTRAG occupation).‡ The gently sloping or flat, grassy plateau tops contrast with the steep, "savage peaks and precipices, alternating with deep gloomy ravines and glens," as one early European visitor described their flanks (Thomson 1968, 2:32). Travel across the plateau tops is relatively simple, either by foot or by wheeled vehicle; getting there is quite another problem. The cash cropping of maize depends upon an infrastructure of roads by which merchants can approach the production areas to begin crop export, or upon a regular schedule for transport barges visiting such critical points as Mpala, Moba, and Zongwe, to which sacks of maize can be carried on the backs of porters and held in depots (as was done in the past). During the colonial years, roads established in the 1930s were kept up by a combination of paid and requisitioned laborers, and shipping was consistent. Since independence, this is no longer the case.**

Informants spoke of having lived, as had their parents, in the maize-producing areas, but of having left there or of having had to cease growing

---

*The dramatic drop in manioc production between 1974 and 1975 can be correlated with the great scarcity of fuel and the resultant drop in transport facility and with the restrictions placed on travel by the government.

†Manioc does not grow above 1,800 meters (Chambon and Alofs 1958, p. 38).

‡For information on maize growing and related matters in the northwestern portion of Tanganyika subregion, see A. Saulniers and S. Saulniers (1975) and R. Shoemaker et al. (1976).

**Because well-maintained roads also allow the soldiers or administrative personnel of the zone to visit, people are not so eager to keep the roads open even though this would facilitate crop export. <u>Salongo</u> work parties observed responded to the call to work on roads, but filled potholes with grass covered lightly with dirt. Urban details cut grass along the roads, but demurred in the face of tasks for which they considered they should be paid.

maize for export when the roads became impracticable through lack of maintenance, merchants could no longer obtain truck parts or fuel, and/or regular shipping stopped. They complained bitterly of having grown crops that then rotted after harvest, unsold. It is also said that those Zairian merchants who do have trucks in working order do not visit villages along those roads still open; they prefer to trade in dried fish rather than in cereal crops, as the profits are greater, surer, and more immediate. Many local people openly applauded the reversal of the 1973 nationalization of small, expatriot businesses, hoping that the return of the "Europeans" would bring a resumption of grain trading and an influx of consumer goods long absent from the market.* Many say they would return to cash-crop farming were it again made feasible.†

With the deterioration of smaller roads, maize cannot be exported as it once was, but neither can local farmers participate in the money economy to the extent to which they became familiar in colonial times. Where, then, in 1956, the most significant population movement within the concession area was from places of lesser to those of greater agricultural potential (but still within the interior plateaus) (White Fathers 1956, p. 510), there is now a steady drainage of all these areas, either toward Moba (where there are stores and other amenities) and towns beyond or to the lakeshore (Commissaire de Zone de Moba 1976, p. 13). Tiny hamlets can now be found at every crook and bend of the shoreline affording enough space for a house; fields are cut high into the slopes rising abruptly from water's edge. These are often so vertiginous that a standing joke exists as to the quickest manner by which both crops and farmer may return to his home after a day's toil or for an impromptu visit. Established villages such as Mpala have increased in population at a rate that angers chiefs superior in the colonial/independent hierarchy who are obliged to remain at their chefs-lieux in the interior.

The lakeside soils are especially poor: often sandy or clayey, very shallow, subject to erosion, and often interrupted by rocky or lateritic outcroppings (Chambon and Alofs 1958, p. 22). Manioc grows well there, maize

---

*The example of one Goan merchant at Moba is typical. Prior to the nationalization, he had run a small "conglomerate," with a truck seeking produce in the interior, a small iron-bottomed boat fishing off Moba, and several stores up the coast toward Zambia where retail goods were sold and dried fish and other produce purchased. Between late 1973 and 1977, when he recovered his business, five different Zairian acquéreurs possessed his various operations, each successively replaced for political or other arcane reasons. When he learned of regaining his business, he wondered what remained.

†The grain depot at Moba port stands in silent testimony to the troubles of the region, and to the difficulties revival will present. Most of the corrugated roofing has long since been "employed elsewhere," parts of the walls have been demolished or are overgrown with underbrush, and its use now is an occasional one, by those awaiting the infrequent visit of boats from Kalemie.

does not. Manioc roots will hold the soil of steep slopes during rains, the shallow ones of maize cannot.

People move to the shore to participate in fishing, both for their own protein needs and to obtain entry into the money economy. Even should they be able to grow maize for export, time might be better spent catching and drying fish. Shipping on Lake Tanganyika to such points as Mpala is now limited to that of small-time, local merchants who, when gasoline is available, travel to and from Kalemie and Moba with their outboard-powered craft.* These entrepreneurs are more interested in carrying dried fish, small livestock, or passengers than they are bulky sacks of manioc or maize, which bring them relatively little profit. While the farmer will often accompany his own produce to Kalemie, the boat owners themselves visit villages all along the shore to purchase dried fish; as middlemen, they transport these to Kalemie, making an immediate, substantial profit.† Most of the maize reaching the government's attention, then, must pass through Moba port.

The radical drop in maize production, then, is a function of the disappearance of a transport infrastructure. It is also correlated with population shifts, which have other, wide-ranging politico-economic ramifications.

We are left with the question: If this area was once so vitally linked to the rest of Katanga, and was of such significance agriculturally that it was placed off limits to industrial recruitment, why has it been allowed to deterioate since independence? Are the products once exported to the urban centers no longer required? The answer to the last is, of course, negative; great amounts of maize and even onions and other vegetables now, of necessity, are imported from countries to the south of Zaire, some of the latter being brought into Lubumbashi from South Africa. An immense maize-growing project is to be undertaken on either side of the Lukuga River in the Kongolo-Nyunzu region, this with substantial financial and other support from the U.S. Agency for International Development, its immediate goal "to achieve self-sufficiency in maize production within the shortest possible time frame" (Shoemaker et al. 1976, p. 64).

Some of the political issues discussed above, and others of wider import must be (re)considered. The organizers of the North-Shaba Maize Proj-

---

*In the mid-1970s, Moba was still visited on a somewhat regular basis by the small, iron-bottomed diesel boats of Greek merchants from Kalemie and by the larger ships of the railroad company. As of early 1979, however, ship and rail traffic was so severely restricted because of fuel shortages that the largest ports were only being visited once or twice monthly, and the smaller ones like Moba perhaps not at all; and rail schedules were halved.

†One entrepreneur purchased seven dried fish for 10 makuta in a village south of Moba; he then sent his wife with a portion of these by train from Kalemie to Likasi, where a single fish was being sold for more than 100 makuta at the market. Because of this profit margin, such transporters are heavily taxed and "taxed" (that is, officially and unofficially) by Zairian customs, coast guard, veterinary, and other officials from whom they must obtain permits and other papers.

ect feel their plans to be feasible, for, "in contrast to attitudes in the recent past, there now appears to be an awareness by national leaders at very high levels that <u>the quick-fix mechanized approach does not represent a viable alternative</u>" to the local-level development they propose (Shoemaker et al. 1976, p. 64; my emphasis). The word "mechanized" might have been deleted from this understatement, for what is most at issue is a lack of "foresight or of serious intention," as Joseph Conrad wrote, "so wanted for the work of the world " (n.d., pp. 98-99). This in turn is a direct corollary of bureaucratic corruption.

In general, the industrial segment of Mobutu's Zaire progressed admirably in the early 1970s, while copper prices were still high; to be more accurate, the industrial segment in or closely related to Kinshasa did so (see Young 1978, pp. 170-71). In a land where "everything is for sale, everything is bought" (a lament by Mobutu cited in Young 1978, p. 172), from great concessions to small audiences, the attention of those in a position to take advantage most readily of an influx of financial support or of funds generated by the state itself would be most profitably focused upon those means of production able to offer the most immediate and significant returns.

Industry and small-scale agriculture are not comparable in this regard. While industry may depend upon its consumers, who must have sufficient assets to eat properly and still have a surplus (see Jewsiewicki n.d.), the chain of agricultural production and exchange beginning with the rural farmer and ending with large capital is a far longer and more complex one—and one that cannot be exploited so readily, at least for such great and quick profit, as can industry. A farmer can be (and in Zaire is) forced to pay personal taxes and further amounts on produce-export permits, travel permits, canoe permits, and the like, the proceeds from which can be embezzled; but this is the penny-ante fare of backwater administrators and agents. Industry will pay millions for the most intangible advantage. For those insecure about their continuation in a position to extort, it is better that they take as much as possible as quickly as possible (a point made by Gould [1978]). Industry in Zaire, then, is not like a flower on a healthy plant, but rather is parasitic, from which only a select few can draw sustenance (compare Jewsiewicki n.d., introduction).*

Compared with the Goodyear plants, the oil refineries, and other similar projects given glossy press coverage within Zaire, the equally vaunted maize-production drive of the mid-1970s seems laughable at best. The policy of the Agricultural Service in colonial times for Tanganyika district has been continued since independence; there is no extension service, only taxation.†

---

*It is significant to note that Mobutu has assigned to GECAMINES, the great mining conglomerate, the tasks of local road maintenance, supervision of Sendwe Hospital, and maize production. The citizen-president, whose own wealth from copper profits is immeasurable (see Young 1978), is willing to share the gravy if GECAMINES is willing to share the goose.

†Rural agents have as a primary task the enforcement of laws concerning required food production; they also collect taxes for charcoal making, oil-

We were told in June 1976 by an agricultural agent from Moba that, indeed, the zone would be participating in the maize-production drive, but not for a while, as he would have to wait until the new type of corn he had received from his superiors could be planted, grown, and harvested and then distributed as seed. He had received less than a half-dozen ears; such was the extent of local implementation, this in a region once celebrated for its agricultural output.*

Ultimately, then, that an area with such agricultural potential should be placed in peril by presidential accords with a German-based rocket company makes little difference (except to those living within its bounds); a "quick-fix . . . approach" is inapplicable to agricultural problems, and so attention is more profitably directed elsewhere. If a substantial profit may be drawn at the expense of people already defined as rebellious and troublesome, so much the better.

REFERENCES

Archives du Congo Belge. 1958. Section Documentation. Documents pour servir à la connaissance des populations du Congo Belge: Aperçu historique (1886-1993) de l'étude des populations autochtones . . . suivi di l'inventaire des études historiques, ethnographiques et linguistiques conservées aux Archives du Congo Belge. Leopoldville.

Blum, C. 1972. Notice . . . et notes explicatives: "Zaire" de Voltaire. Paris.

Bourderie, J. 1977. "Mobutu vend un dixième du Zaire pour des fusées allemandes." Afrique-Asie 141 (August 8): 26-30.

Bustin, E. 1975. Lunda under Belgian Rule: The Politics of Ethnicity. Cambridge, Mass.: Harvard University Press.

Cabu, F. n.d. "Monographie sur les kwés." Reprint from Katanga Illustre.

Chambon, R., and M. Alofs. 1958. Le district agricole du Tanganika. Brussels: La Direction de l'Agriculture, des Forêts et de l'Elevage.

Cohen, B. 1977. "Rocket Range in Zaire—Who Does It Threaten?" New African Development 2, no. 10:977.

---

palm cutting, and the like. At Mpala, the agent was afraid to perform such tasks, as he felt himself to be the repeated victim of sorcery by those he would control.

*As of September 1977, nothing further had been heard of this program at Mpala.

Colitt, L. 1978. "A Case of Imagination." Financial Times, July 7.

Commissaire de Zone de Moba. 1976. "Rapport annuel de l'année 1975; Section A: Politique Zairoise; Titre I: Population Zairoise."

Conrad, J. n.d. Heart of Darkness. 1st ed. 1910. New York.

Cunnison, I. 1969. "Kazembe and the Arabs." In The Zambesian Past: Studies in Central African History, edited by E. Stokes and R. Brown. Manchester.

Darnton, J. 1979. "Zaire Could Be Very Rich but Now It Faces Ruin." New York Times, February 11.

DeGeorgi, M. 1923. "Voyage agricole au District du Tanganika-Moero." Bulletin agricole du Congo Belge 14, no. 4:469-534.

Dictionnaire classique Lingala, Dictionnaire Lingala-Francais, Francais-Lingala. n.d. Kinshasa.

Division Régionale de l'Agriculture (Région du Shaba). 1976. "Rapport annuel de l'année 1975, Sous-Région du Tanganika."

Doize, R. 1938. Les boules de pierre perforées des collections de Préhistoire du Musée du Congo Belge. Annales du Musée Royal du Congo Belge, vol. 1, pt. 3.

Engulu, B. 1974. "Speech of the State Commissioner for Political Affairs and for Coordination of Party Activities, to Regional Education Authorities, at N'sele (Kinshasa)." Taifa (Lubumbashi), December 6.

Gérard-Libois, J. 1966. Katanga Secession. Madison: University of Wisconsin Press.

Gould, D. 1978. "Underdevelopment Administration: Systemic Corruption in the Public Bureaucracy of Mobutu's Zaire." Paper presented at the Rockefeller Foundation Conference, Bellagio, Italy, August 7-11.

Jewsiewicki, B. n.d. "Moderniser l'agriculture itinerante en Afrique Noire: quelques enseignements tirés de l'histoire rurale du Zaire (ex Congo-Belge)." Paper distributed by the Université de Sherbrooke, Sherbrooke, Quebec, Canada.

_____. 1977. "Unequal Development: Capitalism and the Katanga Economy, 1919-1940." In The Roots of Rural Poverty in Central and Southern Africa, edited by R. Palmer and N. Parsons. Berkeley: University of California Press.

Johnson, F. 1971. A Standard Swahili-English Dictionary. London.

Jones, W. 1959. Manioc in Africa. Stanford, Calif.: Stanford University Press.

Joubert, L.-L. 1884-1927. "Diaire." Incomplete photocopy at the Musée National du Zaire at Lubumbashi.

Kabembe, L. 1962. "Rapport des activités en étude concernant la bonne marche vers la pacification." Dispatch from Baudouinville (Etat du Katanga), October 15.

Kaoze, S. 1910. "La psychologie des Bantu." In A. Vermeersch, "Les sentiments superieurs chez les Congolais." Revue congolaise 1:406-37.

Lamb, D. 1978. "From Deep in Africa, West Germans Take Aim on Space." Washington Post, August 22.

Marissaux, A. n.d. Albertville: Note historique. Brussels.

Marwick, M., ed. 1970. Witchcraft and Sorcery. New York: Penguin.

Miller, N. 1968. "The Political Survival of Traditional Leadership." Journal of Modern African Studies 6, no. 2:183-201.

Mumbanza, E. 1975. "L'Afrique à la fin du XIXe siecle et la colonisation européenne." Zaire-Afrique 97 (August/September): 425-33.

Nagant, G. 1976. "Famille, histoire, religion chez les Tumbwe du Zaire." 3 vols. Ph.D. dissertation, Ecole Pratique des Hautes Etudes, Paris.

Naipal, V. 1974. "Argentina: The Brothels behind the Graveyard." New York Review of Books 21, no. 14, September 19.

Palmer, R., and N. Parsons, eds. 1977. The Roots of Rural Poverty in Central and Southern Africa. Berkeley: University of California Press.

Roberts, A. D. 1973. A History of the Bemba: Political Growth and Change in Northeastern Zambia before 1900. London.

_____. 1967. "The History of Abdullah ibn Suliman." African Social Research 4:241-70.

Roberts, A. F. n.d. "Enclave of Order, Seat of Dissent: The Establishment of a 'Christian Kingdom' in Central Africa." In preparation.

_____. 1979. "Heroic Beasts, Beastly Heroes: Principles of Cosmology and Chiefship among the BaTabwa of Zaire." Ph.D. dissertation, University of Chicago.

Roberts, C. D. 1979. "Mungu na Mitishamba: Illness and Medicine among the BaTabwa of Zaire." Ph.D. dissertation, University of Chicago.

Roelens, V. 1946. "Les rayons et les ombres de l'Apostolat au Haut-Congo." Grands Lacs 61 (4-6/82-84):22-40.

Saulniers, A., and S. Saulniers. 1975. "Rural Development Project for the Tanganyika Sub-Region: Interim Feasibility/Design Report." USAID/afr-C-N43, IQC-WO#3 CRED.

Schatzberg, M. 1977. "Bureaucracy, Business, Beer: The Political Dynamics of Class Formation in Lisala, Zaire." Ph.D. dissertation, University of Wisconsin.

Schmitz, R. 1912. Les Baholoholo. Brussels.

Service Agricole du Congo Belge. 1951. "Rapport annuel de l'année 1950, District du Tanganika."

Shoemaker, R., et al. 1976. "North Shaba Maize Production." Unclassified project paper. USAID no. 660-11-199-059.

Storms, E. c. 1884. "Voyage à Oudjidji." Manuscript. Fonds Storms, Archives du Musée Royal de l'Afrique Centrale.

Szulc, T. 1978. "Germany Rearms." Penthouse, March, pp. 76-78, 80, 82.

Thiam, M. 1978. "L'OTRAG, un 'Cap Kennedy' africain." Africa 102 (June/July): 33-37.

Thomson, J. 1968. To the Central African Lakes and Back. 2 vols. 1st ed. 1881. London.

Tippu-Tip. 1974. Maisha va Hamed bin Muhammed el Murjebi, yaani Tippu Tip. Swahili text with translation by W. H. Whiteley. Nairobi.

Trapnell, C. 1953. The Soils, Vegetation and Agriculture of N. E. Rhodesia. Lusaka: Government Printer.

Vansina, J. 1970. Kingdoms of the Savanna. Madison: University of Wisconsin Press.

Vellut, J.-L. 1977. "Rural Poverty in Western Shaba, c. 1890-1930." In The Roots of Rural Poverty in Central and Southern Africa, edited by R. Palmer and N. Parsons, pp. 294-316. Berkeley: University of California Press.

Waller, H., ed. n.d. The Last Journals of David Livingstone in Central Africa, from 1865 to His Death. 1st ed. 1875. Detroit.

White Fathers (Missionnaires d'Afrique, Pères Blancs). 1956. Enquête socio-religieuse dans les missions des Pères Blancs, Afrique Sub-Saharienne. Rome.

_____. 1892-1947. Diaire de la Mission de Baudouinville. Manuscript. Archives of the Bishopric of Kalemie-Moba.

_____. 1889-1935. Diaire de la Mission de Mpala. Manuscript. Archives of the Bishopric of Kalemie-Moba.

Willame, J.-C. 1964. Les provinces du Congo: Structure et fonctionnement. Vol. 1. "Kwilu, Luluabourg, Nord-Katanga, Ubangi." Leopoldville: IRES.

Wilson, A., and C. Legum. 1978. "'Dr. Strangelove' and the Big Rocket Hoax." The Observer, February 5.

Wright, M., and P. Lary. 1971. "Swahili Settlements in Northern Zambia and Malawi." African Historical Studies 4, no. 3:547-73.

Young, C. 1978. "Zaire: The Unending Crisis." Foreign Affairs, Fall, pp. 169-85.

_____. 1971. "Rebellion and the Congo." In Protest and Power in Black Africa, edited by R. Rotberg and A. Mazrui. London: Oxford University Press.

12

THE POLITICS OF PENURY
IN RURAL ZAIRE:
THE VIEW FROM BANDUNDU

René Lemarchand

In the village where I work the people are starving; they are reduced to eating field rats."

A Peace Corps volunteer, Kikwit, 1978

Les quatre plus célèbres chefs français invités au Zaire par le
Président Mobutu, Roger Vergé, Gaston Lenôtre, Paul Bocuse
et Jean Troisgros, avaient mijoté le menu suivant: amuses-
gueules, loup froid farci, mousse de crevettes garnie de caviar
rouge et noir, purée de tomates et de cresson, volaille truffée
"Président Mobutu", accompagnée d'une sauce au porto, quenelles
de crêtes de coqs, champignons de Paris, morilles, purée de
haricots verts, fromages avec du pain aux noix, charlotte aux
framboises. On ne sait pas qui s'est partagé les restes.

Jeune Afrique, March 28, 1979

Rural poverty is not a new phenomenon in Zaire; what is new is the unprecedented scale of pauperization, the depth of the social dislocations it has
engendered, and the mechanisms and attitudes that lie in the background of
this massive affliction.*

*Part of the data presented here was collected in the course of a field
trip to Kikwit and the surrounding areas in the spring of 1978. I have drawn
rather extensively from open-ended interviews with local officials, missionaries and rural dwellers in Kikwit, Kenge, and Lusanga. Supplementary
evidence was gathered in Kinshasa from additional interviews with government officials and from various statistical and documentary sources. My
field research in Bandundu was made possible by a small grant from the
American Philosophical Society. I wish to record my indebtedness to the
Society as well as to members of the Mennonite church in Kikwit for their
kind hospitality.

237

Although agriculture has been repeatedly described by Mobutu since 1973 as the "priority of priorities," the proportion of public expenditures devoted to the agricultural sector tells a very different story. From 1968 to 1976 agriculture received less than 1 percent of total budgetary expenditures; only in 1969, 1971, and 1973 did the share of the agricultural sector exceed this preposterous percentage, with, respectively, 2.1, 1.3, and 1.9 percent of the total annual expenditures allocated during this nine-year period. About 60 percent of Zaire's high mortality rate has been attributed to malnutrition. The average daily per capita caloric intake is 85 percent of the minimum recommended by the World Health Organization, and the protein intake about 50 percent of the minimum requirement. As one report puts it, "This represents a total 'protein gap' for the population of Zaire of more than 200,000 metric tons of protein per year; if present trends continue this will reach 380,000 tons by 1980." Even though the agricultural potential of the country could sustain at least three times its present population, hundreds of millions of dollars worth of maize, rice, wheat, and meat must be imported every year to meet current needs.

Better than statistics, Taine's portrayal of the French peasantry on the eve of the Revolution appropriately conveys the dilemma faced by millions of Zairois in the 1980s: "The people are like a man walking in a pond with water up to his mouth: the slightest dip in the ground, the slightest ripple, makes him lose his footing—he sinks and chokes." Many have already sunk (Lefebvre 1973, p. 7). Given the ridiculously low rate of returns on their crops, made lower still by a rampant inflation, it is hardly surprising that thousands of peasants have taken to the bush, returning to a subsistence-type economy that had taken the Belgians half a century to eliminate. While some survive on hunting and scavenging, others have flocked to the nearest towns in search of employment. Out-of-work laborers and vagrants form a floating mass of rural proletarians who keep moving back and forth from their rural homelands to the cities. Avoiding the "dips in the ground" is becoming more difficult every day.

Anyone traveling through Bandundu (as the author did in the spring of 1978) cannot fail to notice the symptoms of malnutrition and disease: the swollen bellies of kwashiokor-ridden infants in the villages, the human dregs in the maternity wards of rural mission stations, the hostile and hungry looks of the unemployed on the Lever plantations, the weeping and lamentations of women huddling over the body of a dead child at Lusanga (formerly Leverville). Hunger is indeed the great enemy of the rural masses—as it was during the Great Fear of 1789 in rural France. But unlike what happened in France, where fear was primarily experienced by the authorities and the bourgeois, prompting citizens to arm in self-defense against starving peasants, in Zaire fear is essentially a peasant reaction. Fear of retribution is the principal "tranquillizer" of the rural sectors.

Exploitation is the key to an understanding of the appalling conditions prevailing in the countryside: the enormous disparities of income and wealth between the rural masses and the political class (including landlord-politicians) have created a situation where the former are increasingly denied the bare minimum of material security—what Scott calls "the right to subsistence" (Scott 1975, p. 500). The cash returns on their marketable output are no longer sufficient to meet the peasants' basic needs, and in many cases the cultivation of cash crops leaves them too little time and energy to invest in subsistence farming. Sheer extortion has been substituted for market exchange. Meanwhile, traditional social obligations have ceased to be honored, creating a deep social malaise accompanied by recurrent tensions within the clan and the family.

The surplus* obtained from the sale of agricultural commodities is siphoned into the complex networks of exchange that link the rural elites to civil servants and politicians beyond the national boundaries of Zaire and into the overlapping linkages of multinational corporations, Western business interests, and international development agencies. The appropriation of an ever larger share of the agricultural production by the political class is inseparable from the penetration of the rural sectors by political elites whose strategic positions in the political system and the army enable them to control both the production and marketing of agricultural commodities as well as the sale of consumer commodities to the rural masses. At the elite level self-interested exchange is the rule rather than the exception. The trade-offs that keep the system going cover a broad spectrum of mutual back-scratching and reciprocal benefits. At the village level, however, the terms of exchange are not negotiable. They are enforced through the brutal logic of the Mobutist state: noncompliance inevitably brings forth retribution. The only alternative for the peasants is to take to the bush. A vicious circle develops in which rural stagnation feeds upon coercion, and the likelihood of coercion increases in proportion to the levels of exploitation tolerated by the state.

The mechanics of this "catch-22" situation will be spelled out in greater detail in the following sections. By way of introduction to this dismal state of affairs, let us turn briefly to the so-called Idiofa incidents of February 1978. Although they went largely unnoticed outside Zaire, and received only the scantiest coverage in the Western press,† they throw a dramatic light on the dilemmas faced by the rural populace and help to explain what otherwise may seem like an inexplicable capacity to tolerate the intolerable.

PROTEST AND RETRIBUTION: IDIOFA, 1978

Compared with the orgy of violence that burst upon the rural populations of Bandundu in the wake of the 1964 rebellion, the Idiofa killings may seem

---

*I am aware of the ambiguity inherent in the uncritical use of the term surplus (Dalton 1963, 1969). The term is here meant to refer to the difference between the labor cost of producing cash crops and the final sales price of such crops, in other words to the profits derived from the sale of agricultural commodities.

†One notable exception is Alan Cowell (1978).

like a minor incident; the loss of some 350 lives at the hands of the Forces Armées Zairoises (FAZ) appears almost inconsequential against the tens of thousands of casualties reported during the 1964 insurgency. Regardless of how one may react to the scale of the 1978 massacre, there is little doubt that retribution in this case was totally out of proportion to the threats posed to the provincial authorities.

Although the precise nature of the circumstances that led to the carnage remains unclear, a number of facts seem reasonably well established. Following the murder of a comptable de collectivité—a rural accountant—near Idiofa, in late January, a detachment of the FAZ (some say the Garde Présidentielle) was promptly dispatched to the scene. According to the report of one missionary, a vast mopping up operation of subversive elements was immediately undertaken in the surrounding villages. The prime target of the ratissage was the Idiofa-based Kimbanguist church community, widely suspected of harboring anti-Mobutist sentiments. Shortly before the army sprang into action the Kimbanguists had apparently organized an ingathering of the faithful in a nearby village, a few miles from Idiofa. There the entire Kimbanguist community was wiped out—men, women, and children—in the course of a My-Lai-style operation. Fanning out from the Kinbanguist base toward Idiofa, the FAZ then engaged in a number of search-and-destroy operations. It was in the course of one such operation that several members of Mulele's family, including his mother, were captured. All were buried alive on the spot. In Idiofa 12 leading Kimbanguist personalities were subsequently rounded up and publicly hanged—but not until members of the local U.S. Peace Corps were summoned to watch the macabre spectacle from ringside seats specially reserved for the occasion. According to the estimates of local missionaries, a total of approximately 350 people were killed in the course of the operation.* Of these perhaps half were said to be Kimbanguists.

The Idiofa incidents are cited here because they cast a revealing light on several aspects of the political universe of the rural masses that are relevant to this discussion. For one thing they illustrate a major element of continuity between the colonial and postcolonial situations, that is, the absence of a viable basis for the emergence of organized social protest, a fact that must be explained in large part by the brutality of the repressive apparatus available to the state. Now as before syncretistic religious movements provide the main outlet for the frustrations experienced by the rural masses (Munay 1978); more than ever before, however, the probability of wholesale, indiscriminate repression is a key ingredient of rural stability. As much as their grinding poverty, their sense of utter despair in the face of repeated exactions by the agents of the state is what keeps the Zairian peasantry in a mood of apparent placidity.

The Idiofa killings also cast a particularly lurid light on the nexus of solidarities that ties together the military and the political elites in the capi-

---

*The figure of 2,000 killed advanced by an opposition group in exile, the Comité du Zaire, seems grossly inflated (Cowell 1978).

tal and the provinces. The operation could not have been conducted with such gruesome efficiency without the active complicity of the <u>commissaire de sous-région</u>, the <u>commissaire de zone</u>, and <u>collectivité</u> officials. Whether one can legitimately speak of class interests to designate these various actors and their relationships to the instruments of production is open to debate. Opinions will differ as to the significance of class interests in this context and the utility of the concept for purposes of analysis. What is beyond question is that the conditions that make for rural exploitation are inseparable from the chain of vested interests that runs from the summit to the base of the social pyramid. The links cut across many different institutional spheres. The army, the gendarmerie, the civil service, the secret police, and the local government authorities are all to some extent, and in one form or another, the accomplices as well as the beneficiaries of the corrupt system that perpetuates rural exploitation. The standards of corruption and venality set by top government officials percolates all the way down to the <u>région</u>, <u>sous-région</u>, and <u>collectivités</u>. A perpendicular split separates the privileged few from the rural and urban masses; and, among the former, access to privilege is inseparable from the favoritism, greed, and inefficiency that have helped drive the countryside back into the nineteenth century.

Before turning to a more detailed analysis of the Zairian political economy—a euphemism for what might be described as institutionalized kleptocracy—let us take a closer look at the anatomy of the rural sectors in Bandundu and see whether anything like a common social denominator can be identified among the various categories that enter into the definition of the Zairian peasantry.

PEASANTS, POSTPEASANTS, AND SUBSISTENCE CULTIVATORS

The very uneven penetration of the capitalist mode of production into the countryside, along with the different types of social formations resulting from this situation—including the "back-to-the-bush" movements triggered by the combination of impoverishment and coercion—have produced a remarkably variegated social landscape in which labor-exporting enclaves are found side by side with subsistence agriculture, <u>paysannats</u>, and capitalist farming. Cash-crop farmers, plantation workers, fruit cutters, migrant laborers, hunters, and scavengers are the main components of what is often uncritically referred to as the Zairian peasantry. Their political horizons are as fragmented as the bases of their insertion into the capitalist economy, yet they all are to some extent the victims of capitalist accumulation.

The most striking aspect of rural society in Bandundu is its bifurcation along two separate paths, one leading to the formation of what might be described as a "postpeasant" society (Scott 1978), the other to a regression into a subsistence-type agriculture. The trajectories followed by each sector are radically different, and they both in turn deviate markedly from that of the peasant sector. The latter includes a number of subgroups, including capitalist farmers, small-scale rural producers, paysannats workers, and rural laborers; all are engaged in the production of an agricultural surplus of one kind or another, yet their relationships to the nonpeasant rural and urban sectors differ.

Of a total provincial population of perhaps 3.5 million, an estimated 80 percent are engaged in subsistence agriculture. One might say that approximately three-fourths of what was the peasant population at the time of independence have gone back to the situation of precarious subsistence that characterized most rural Africans at the beginning of the colonial era. For the overwhelming majority of the rural masses, economic survival has little to do with the production of a marketable surplus. Most live from hand to mouth. To avoid chronic starvation, hunting is a necessity; the kinship system provides the basis for a rudimentary division of labor in which men engage in hunting and fishing and children in scavenging, while the growing of food crops remains the responsibility of the wives. Market transactions are intermittent and reduced to their simplest expression—the occasional selling of caterpillars and eels in villages or in the vicinity of the various company stores owned by the Plantations Lever au Zaire (PLZ). What little cash is derived from these transactions is used for the purchase of matches, pails, loincloths, and other basic commodities. For this permanently marginal population there is little hope that starvation can be kept at bay over the long run; nor is there any indication that serious efforts are being made to limit the extent of economic deterioration in the cash-crop and livestock sectors. Thus, the prospect of a further exodus of rural elements into subsistence agriculture is raised.

The form of marginalization observable within the perimeter of the PLZ plantation economy is very different. Here one finds a rural proletariat entirely dependent for its livelihood on the income opportunities offered by one of the largest multinationals operating in Tropical Africa. Postpeasant communities are widely dispersed throughout Bandundu; yet it is primarily in and around Lusanga that postpeasantization finds its most advanced expression. It is here that a capital-intensive and land-extensive oil palm plantation system was first introduced in 1911 under the auspices of the Lever-controlled Huileries du Congo Belge (HLB). The clearest manifestation of postpeasantization lies in the presence of a rural wage-labor force drawn from proletarianized villages, but whose growing economic pauperization stems from the play of economic forces that are entirely beyond the control of the village or the region.

Resistance to the kinds of productive arrangements that led to the process of postpeasantization has been a major feature of the history of plantation societies. Bandundu is no exception. It was apparently beyond Lever's comprehension that the use of native chiefs for the recruitment of workers might engender recalcitrance and anger on the part of both chiefs and subjects. Passive resistance to exploitation was seen as a sign of laziness. As Lever himself noted in 1913 (Wilson 1968, p. 176):

The fact is, the native has few wants, a little salt and a little cloth are his indispensables. After this, beads, brass rods and other

luxuries. Chief Womba of Leverville can be taken as an example.
Twelve months ago he and his people were poor and few in number, and were keen to bring fruit. After twelve months or less
of bringing fruit he is rich and lazy, has 10 wives, and his village
is about 4 times the size it was, but he gathers little or no fruit.
. . . The Palm tree is in these parts the Banking account of the
native and he no more thinks of going to the Bank for fruit for
money when his wants and ambitions are supplied than a civilized
man would. His bank is always open when he wants to draw on it.

The foregoing portrayal of the "lazy native" throws considerable light on the
rationale behind the use of force during the colonial epoch. "Laziness" at
this point quickly turned into anger and violence. By 1931 the effects of the
Depression—leading to an unprecedented drop in the price of palm kernels
(from Fr 1.80 a kilo in 1927 to Fr 0.25 in 1930 [Sikitele Gize a Sumbula
1976]) and palm oil—together with a growing reliance on forced labor, especially among the Pende populations, culminated in a major rural rebellion.
What became known as the Pende Revolt exhibited the same combination of
peasant violence and localism analyzed by Scott in other contexts (Scott 1979).
It was as much an expression of rural anger against the chiefs and the administration as it was a desperate attempt to counteract the enormous social dislocations engendered by the massive displacement of thousands of villagers
from their traditional milieus. To the threats posed to their subsistence and
social solidarities the Pende reacted by a violent reassertion of their traditional social identities.

From the Pende Revolt of 1931 to the Mulelist rebellion of 1964 and the
Idiofa incidents of 1978, the history of rural protest in the Kwango-Kwilu reveals a complex mixture of sociopolitical identifications, in which ethnic,
politico-religious, and class orientations combine in different syntheses. Today it is primarily within the context of the PLZ plantation economy that rural
class differentiation is most apparent. It is at this level that objective class
disparities are most evident between rural workers, on the one hand, and
plant operators and managers, on the other. The greatest source of potential
conflict stems from the migration of large numbers of unemployed plantation
workers into the village communities and various enclaves of capitalist farming. The rapid growth of a disaffected class of unemployed rural proletarians
reflects the growing reticence of rural laborers to continue to work on plantations in return for a salary that has become virtually meaningless in the face
of runaway inflation. The alternative they face is either to move into the subsistence economy or to work as journaliers (ordinary laborers) on capitalist
farms.

In many ways the plantation sector is a microcosm of the wider social
system. Control of productive activities is in the hands of a small managerial class that is wholly dependent on foreign capital for its rewards; the top
rungs of the managerial ladder are occupied by politicians whose loyalty to
the state is repaid by the enormous profits they reap from their positions as
obliged middlemen between expatriate interests and rural laborers. The disparities of income between the petty managerial bourgeoisie and the salaried

workers have increased dramatically over the last few years. The sharp drop in real wages paid to plantation workers is a major factor behind the massive decline of the PLZ labor force since 1971; from a total of roughly 15,000 in 1971, the number of fruit cutters employed in 1978 dropped to 7,175. The existing pattern of income distribution suggests a growing polarization of interests along class lines and serious recruitment problems.

"This problem of labour has grown as an ominous dark cloud" (Wilson 1968, p. 176). Lever's remark, penned in 1913, is even more pertinent in 1978. For one thing labor is increasingly invested in activities that were once the responsibility of the state. Road maintenance is a case in point: no fewer than 1,400 workers were permanently employed in 1958 for the sole purpose of maintaining 3,800 kilometers of roads in and out of Lusanga. The crux of the labor problem, however, lies elsewhere. It lies in the existence of a wage structure that has remained basically unchanged over the last ten years, while the price of basic consumer commodities has increased at least tenfold during the same period. This is especially the case for the coupeurs de fruit sous-contrat, the salaried fruit cutters, who form the bulk of the PLZ labor force, and to some extent for the coupeurs agricoles, who operate as independent producers and sell palm fruit collected on privately owned palmeries to the PLZ.

The basic monthly salary paid to a coupeur de fruit sous-contrat was Z 10 in 1971 and Z 11.5 in 1978.* Family allowances entitle him to 109 makuta per child and per month. A salary increase of 2 percent per annum is the rule, as well as a bonus (prime de rendement) of 5 makuta for each load, or régime, delivered above the normally expected output. (Each régime consists of a load of 18 kilos of palm fruit: the average output expected of a fruit cutter varies between 30 and 40 régimes per day, the correct minimum being left to the appreciation of the chef d'équipe, or capita.) To fully appreciate the significance of these figures, it is important to note the prices fetched by some basic commodities sold at one of the company stores in Kwenge: one box of matches, 12 makuta; a piece of soap, 29 makuta; a pair of shoes, Z 16.71; a pair of trousers, Z 10.96; a plastic bib, Z 3.44; a piece of cotton cloth (4 meters x 3/4 meters), Z 13; one liter of oil, Z 1.80. To put it differently, the price of a box of matches (12 makuta) is equivalent to the amount of labor invested in the collecting and delivery of roughly 45 kilos of palm fruit. It takes one-third of a man's monthly earnings to purchase a plastic bib for his child; a month's wages will just about suffice to buy a pair of cotton trousers. One might also add that these preposterous wages are paid to individuals who perform one of the most dangerous and exhausting jobs one can imagine, climbing up anywhere from 50 to 80 feet above ground to collect fruit bunches and then transporting them to the nearest collecting

---

*The official rate of exchange for Z 1 was $1.60 in May 1978 (there are 100 makuta in one zaire); the unofficial rate, however, was closer to $3.00. Since then Zaire's currency has been devaluated by 50 percent. The current rate of inflation is about 100 percent a year.

station. As the Zairian director of the PLZ told this writer (with the tone of voice of someone lamenting a loss of cattle): "Nous enregistrons parfois des chutes spectaculaires."

The coupeurs agricoles are remunerated according to the volume of palm fruit delivered to the mill. For each load of 60 kilos (one mabaya) they received, in 1978, 94 makuta. Although it is estimated that a diligent cutter will deliver three or four lubaya per day, few are able to reach this level of output. Moreover, a substantial cut on their earnings is generally exacted by the chief authorities who claim rights of ownership over the palmeries. Exploitation here stems from two separate but closely connected sources: from the increasingly unfavorable rate of exchange enforced upon the rural producer through the price and wage policies of monopoly capitalism and from the exactions of économie lignagère, in the form of prestations to the chiefs.

The conditions of extreme penury attendant upon the process of post-peasantization reflect the drastic deterioration in real wages paid to plantation workers. This alone would be enough to explain why they are decidedly worse off now than they were during most of the colonial period. Another contributory factor, however, is that the primes d'engagement and primes de rendement (that is, the bonuses received by workers at the time of employment and, subsequently, on the basis of performance) are no longer practiced. In 1940, for example, a cutter employed by the Compagnie du Kasai would receive Fr 100, a machete, and a blanket as prime d'engagement, along with a carte de fournisseur that entitled him to rebates on certain commodities sold at the company store. One former cutter admitted that prior to 1950 "the bonuses and advantages accorded to the bons coupeurs . . . were considerable" and remembered having received on various occasions for his diligence "ten bags of salt, seven machetes, pieces of cloth, several yards of americani cloth, pots and pans, and small articles." When he was awarded the médaille du mérite, he received "beer, 100 francs [$20.00], and permission to buy gun powder at a reduced price at the store" (Jewsiewicki and Mabeng 1974, p. 209). HLB policies were basically the same. Such bonuses and privileges are unheard of today. Finally, one must also take account of the fact that food scarcities now compel the PLZ to shift part of their labor force to the cultivation of food crops. In the Kwenge station, about 350 workers are employed part-time on the growing of maize, manioc, rice, and potatoes, for which they receive minimal remuneration. The time spent on the growing of food crops entails a net loss of income.

As the foregoing suggests, the distinction between peasants and post-peasants is not always clear. It is not uncommon, for example, for salaried plantation workers to engage in farming and for small independent farmers to double as fruit cutters when the season and the circumstances permit. Similarly, smallholders may divide their time, for which they will be paid a small salary, and work on their own plots. Nonetheless, as social categories plantation workers and subsistence agriculturalists must be distinguished from small and large landowners: here the farm is the basic unit of production; commercial and not subsistence production is the rule; the sale of an agricultural surplus on the market is the dominant form of transaction.

At this point a further distinction is necessary between, on the one hand, those capitalist farmers whose property varies in scale between 100 and 500 hectares and whose profits are heavily dependent on the availability of rural wage labor and, on the other, those small farmers who own between three and ten hectares of land and whose labor force is essentially drawn from their immediate family. These small farmers number approximately 5,000 in Bandundu. Their economic interests are radically at odds with those of the large-scale exploitants agricoles. The latter generally combine the functions of absentee landlords and commerçants, and their rate of profit on the sale of agricultural commodities is inversely proportional to the prices paid to the producers of these commodities.

The small independent farmer has been hardest hit by the rampant inflation. While the cost of basic consumer goods has been skyrocketing, the prices paid to rural producers has remained consistently low. Between field and market, the huge gap between producer and consumer prices becomes evident. In 1978 a 30 kilo bag of peanuts that sold at Z 6 in the villages fetched Z 15 on the Kikwit market and Z 20 in Kinshasa; a 40 kilo bag of manioc was sold at Z 7 in the villages and at Z 15 in Kikwit. A 50 percent margin of benefit on agricultural commodities is a standard practice among commerçants. The ceiling on prices set by the government is virtually never observed. When one considers that government officials are often among those who stand to profit most from the violation of official regulations, the logic of the situation becomes clear.

To ensure a minimum agricultural output, coercion is necessary. Thus many of the features associated with the cultures obligatoires formula practiced during the colonial period have reappeared in a new guise. Beginning in the 1970s a system of cultures imposées was introduced that compels the peasants to devote a minimum acreage to the cultivation of specific crops—for example, manioc, peanuts, rice, millet, beans—according to a calendrier agricole set up by regional authorities after consultation with the moniteurs agricoles. Each farmer with a family must devote at least 25 acres to the cultivation of cultures imposées; for each unmarried man and woman the minimum acreage has been fixed at 15 acres. Noncompliance entails heavy fines. Exempted from this rule are paysannats, which explains the relative success met by this type of farming in Masi-Madimba, Idiofa, and Feshi.

Paysannats were first introduced in Bandundu in 1939/40 in response to policies aiming at the promotion of a class of independent smallholders. Their rights of ownership to the land and their easy access to agricultural extension services and feeder roads were seen at the time as the best guarantees of social stability and rural prosperity. In practice, as some had predicted at the time (Malengrau 1949), the scheme proved a mixed blessing for its presumed beneficiaries. It remains so today, though for different reasons. It would seem that much of the land on the paysannat is controlled by petty officials who do not hesitate to have recourse to wage laborers (journaliers) to till their own plots; or else the plots are "leased" to neighboring peasants who agree to surrender part of the crop in payment of their usufructuary rights.

Consider, for example, the case of the Masi-Madimba paysannat, which involves approximately 1,500 hectares of land distributed among 17,000 cultivators. Coffee is the main crop, with peanuts, maize, and soja grown in smaller quantities. As many as 1,200 journaliers are employed on the paysannat, mainly on coffee plots. Some agricultural extension agents, agronomes de zone, and cooperative officials have been reported to own one or several plots, thus combining the roles of civil servants, landowners, and employers of rural labor—to which might also be added that of commerçant-cum-traffiquant. The Zairian coffee crop has seldom been exported through the official channels of the Office National du Café (ONC) but via trusted intermediaries (including army men) with a view to avoiding fiscal impositions (export taxes and export surcharges).* As a result of such illegal practices it is estimated that the state lost approximately Z 200 million worth of coffee foreign exchange earnings in 1976 (Young 1978, p. 174).

The trend toward proletarianization is even more evident on the large farms, many of which are owned by civil servants turned acquéreurs, following the 1973 decree on zairianization (Gould 1977, 1979). Though some have now been turned over to European managers, thus restoring the status quo ante, the employment of journaliers remains a standard practice. The starvation wages paid to these rural workers are symptomatic of the exploitative practices associated with rural capitalism. The basic pay rate for rural workers in 1978 was 38 makuta a day; in Kikwit the salary earned by a journalier was fixed at 50 makuta. One landowner, more generous than most, claimed that his workers earned as much as Z 18 to Z 20 a month. And a key minister in Kinshasa, owner of 155 hectares of farmland in the sous-région of Bulundu, admitted paying his workers Z 1 a day, which he described as "un trés beau salaire." This does not take into account the fiscal charges and unofficial levies imposed upon salaried workers, which in some cases may amount to as much as 50 percent of their cash earnings.

To return once again to the point made earlier, rural pauperization in Zaire must be seen in the light of the catastrophic decline in the level of real wages paid to rural laborers since independence (see Chapter 1) and the concomitant dramatic increase in the price of consumer commodities. Thus, on the basis of a real wage index of 100 in 1960, the real wages paid in 1978 vary between 15 and 20; for an average price index of 100 in 1960, the corresponding index in 1978 is 6,000.

---

*In February 1976 the Office National du Café was notified by way of an executive order that the role of the office would henceforth be limited to controlling and monitoring the quality of coffee, certifying the grading, and recording the volume of coffee exports—thus removing all marketing functions from the ONC, to the benefit of major producers. The decision, however, merely formalized a state of affairs that had been going on almost since the creation of the ONC in 1972. Few other parastatal bodies have been as notorious for mismanagement, incompetence, and corruption as the ONC.

This brief exploration of the conditions of the rural sectors in Bandundu suggests that, although penury is clearly a ubiquitous calamity, it has engendered different forms of economic marginalization depending on the context in which it operates. The distinction between subsistence, peasant, and post-peasant sectors suggests different patterns of adaptation to the conditions of economic scarcity, as well as different levels of pauperization within the general category of "paupers." Within rural society a measure of internal differentiation has developed—as between small-scale landholders and landless laborers, subsistence cultivators and plantation workers, land-rich and land-poor, and so forth. Rural exploitation is thus often mediated through individuals who are themselves part of the rural society, even where they belong to nonpeasant rural groups. Above and beyond these patterns of internal differentiation, a system of multiple dependencies operates to keep the rural masses in a condition of permanent exploitation and subordination: the traditional notables, local government officials and commissaires du peuple, and commercial interests are the key elements of an informal coalition whose raison d'être is to extract a maximum agricultural surplus from the masses. Besides their common adherence to the imperative of self-enrichment, they all share a firm commitment to the prophylactic virtues of coercion, a disposition nurtured through the legacy of Belgian colonial rule. There is virtually no room for social maneuver in this kind of situation. Against such overwhelming odds, the prospects of a meaningful improvement of rural conditions are virtually nil.

Let us at this point shift our perspective and look at rural-urban interactions from the standpoint of the elite sector. Here special attention will be paid to the capitalist ethos of the state bourgeoisie and its mode of penetration into the rural areas.

ETHICS OF KLEPTOCRACY:
CLASS AND PRIVILEGE

Cynicism is a universal feature of Third World bourgeoisies; few, however, are more cynical than the Zairian bourgeoisie when it comes to profit seeking. "Everything is for sale, everything is bought in our country. And in this traffic, holding any slice of public power constitutes a veritable exchange instrument, convertible into illicit acquisition of money or other goods" (Young 1978, p. 172). In these words in 1977, President Mobutu denounced the roots of what he called "le mal zairois" (the Zairian disease); in a different context the same observation might have been presented as a counsel of wisdom to one of his protégés. A few years earlier, as some will recall, Mobutu did not hesitate to suggest "discreet theft" as one possible route to social success; in view of the standards of ethical behavior set by the presidency one could hardly expect his entourage to endorse a more rigorous code of morality.

The operative norms of the Zairian bourgeoisie are nowhere more clearly spelled out than in Tshitenji-Nzembele's booklet, Devenez Riche Rapidement, a kind of get-rich-quick primer evocative of a curious synthesis of Guizot and Norman Vincent Peale. The key to personal enrichment lies in "liberating the mind of all doubts as to the legitimacy of material wealth." Specifically, the reader is invited to "make the quest for wealth and money an obsession," "take the necessary risks," "utilize other people's money to build his own fortune," "diversify his activities in order to multiply his gains," and "learn how to utilize human resources." Such strategies follow naturally from certain self-evident axioms—"The world belongs to the rich; a man is more of a man when he has more wealth; become rich and the rest will follow naturally." It is equally evident, according to the author, that "the more advanced races have always been obsessed by wealth" (p. 17), just as "God is incontestably a God of abundance" (p. 16). Hence "vous devez aimer l'argent et le poursuivre inlassablement. Aimez l'argent à la folie, adorez-le en pensée et en acte: il finira par venir à vous" (p. 21).

The history of Zaire, we are told, offers numerous examples of batisseurs de fortune—"the Tshombe Kapenda . . . the Tshibalanga . . . the Dokolo, Kisombe, Mwimbi and others"—who amassed considerable wealth through politics: "la politique offre encore bien des possibilités d'enrichissement actuellement, mais la competition y devient de plus en plus serrée" (p. 31). A key source of rapid enrichment is offered through "les grands bouleversements":

> Soyez à l'affût. Les grands bouleversements offrent l'occasion des plus grandes fortunes changements de régime politique, remaniements ministériels, crises monétaires, changements de cours des produits à la Bourse, guerres, etc. Les USA, l'Allemagne ont bâti leur fortune sur les bouleversements de la seconde guerre. Plus près de nous l'accession à l'indépendance a permis l'enrichissement considerable de certains citoyens. Les changements de régime ont offert leur chance à de nouveaux bénéficiaires. Il en va de même à chaque remaniement gouvernemental. [P. 39]

A major precondition, however, is to accept wealth with an open mind: "Désirez-le avec force, faîtes-en un image mentale vive, une vision obsédante, complète et détaillée" (p. 51).

By way of a suggestion the author proposes to promote development through the systematic creation of millionaires:

> Une suggestion: Créons systématiquement des millionaires. Et cela en grand nombre. En adoptant cette suggestion, nous créerons facilement 30 à 40 millionaires authentiques chaques mois, soit environ 400 par an, ou 4,000 en dix ans. Ce serait une belle réalisation pour notre programme de développement national. Pour mémoire signalons que les riches USA enfantent 500 nouveaux millionaires chaque année, soit 5,000 tous les dix ans. [P. 104]

As a developmental formula the systematic creation of "millionaires authentiques" has at least the merit of originality—and bears testimony to the richly diversified professional experience claimed by the author, whose "can-didature en sciences politiques economiques et sociales" led him to serve as a diamond expert with Britmond-De Beers in London, and subsequently as a member of the Zairian delegation to the United Nations.

Were the book to appear in serialized installments in Le Canard En-chaíné, there is little doubt that it would immediately boost up the sales of this excellent satirical French weekly. Seen from another perspective, how-ever, Tshitenji-Nzembele's work is sadly illustrative of the crass material-ism that actuates the thinking and behavior of a great many Zairian civil ser-vants and businessmen. It reflects a kind of primitive capitalist ethic in which there are no holds barred to the categorical imperative of self-enrich-ment. As such it sets the tone for the normative context within which the state bourgeoisie operates.

Access to political office is the indispensable prerequisite for access to wealth—and wealth in turn serves as the key qualification for remaining in of-fice, or for reentering the political arena when, after a temporary disgrace, candidates are once again called upon to serve the interests of the nation as ministers, commissaires politiques, or commissaires du peuple. Elections are a largely desultory exercise; no structural change ever follows a turn-over of political elites. Since the dice are so heavily loaded in favor of the ruling bourgeoisie, the only tangible result of the vote is to confirm the domi-nant position it has acquired in the political system through fraud, corruption, and skulduggery.

The coalescence of economic and political power is by no means unique to the Zairian political scene. A similar phenomenon can be observed in the Ivory Coast, Senegal, Nigeria, or Upper Volta. As a general proposition Michael Cohen's observation that "there are presently [in the Ivory Coast] only two important analytic classes which deserve recognition as politically and economically significant—the rulers and the ruled" (Cohen 1974, p. 194) would seem to apply equally well to Zaire, as would his analysis of the politi-cal origins of social mobility in the Ivory Coast. It is at the level of the re-lationship between rulers and ruled that the ease of Zaire deviates substan-tially from that of the Ivory Coast and other African states. Political office in Zaire is not used as a base for the development of exchange strategies de-signed to meet the needs of a rural clientele, but as an instrument for the appropriation of material benefits that are seldom repaid in any tangible form. There is virtually no redistribution of public resources at the grass roots.*

---

*Note in this connection Gould's characterization of the functions per-formed by the administration: "The Zairian administration serves as an agency of intimidation and petty repression for the overwhelming majority of the population, while at the same time remaining permeable to the ruling class which in this sense is essentially a political-administrative bourgeoisie. It has developed authoritarian structures to take political power away from the local peripheries and centralize it in an autocratic party which has in ef-fect captured the state structure. . . . Self-enrichment, private accumulation,

Exemption from fiscal obligations and undue harassment is about as much as anyone can expect at that level in the way of benefits.*

The circular relationship between economic wealth and political power is made clear by the returns of the 1977 legislative elections. As shown by the figures in Table 12.1, a very large percentage of elected officials at the national level (that is, commissaires du peuple and commissaires politiques, the former serving as legislators and the latter as members of the Political Bureau) is drawn from the private and parastatal sectors. Of the 18 elected members of the Political Bureau, 90 percent belong to the industrial, commercial, and agrobusiness sectors; similarly, the vast majority of commissaires du peuple elected in 1977 are industrialists, managers, stockholders, traders, and businessmen. Among those elected in Bandundu, at least one-third are cattle ranchers (éleveurs), traders (commerçants), or businessmen (hommes d'affaires), and one-fourth are identified as industrialists, stockholders, and managers of private or state-controlled enterprises. Many hold jobs in different sectors of the economy, for example, as planter and commerçant, cattle rancher and administrateur de société, and so forth.

Few, however, can claim as many strategic positions as Matanda Wa Tenu, from Kalinda (Kwilu), who in addition to serving as administrator of the Société de Credit aux Classes Moyennes et à l'Industrie and of the Société de Cinema National is also engaged in a number of lucrative activities involv-

---

consumption of luxury good, favors to potentially useful allies or friends, repression of challengers, and self-perpetuation are the rule of the day" (Gould 1977, p. 8).

*Exempting one's friends and allies from fiscal impositions is a key strategy used by local officials to create networks of support for themselves. Given the multiplicity and sheer arbitrariness of taxes levied in urban centers, hardly anyone is immune from such pressures. Consider, for example, the items subsumed under the title "Canevas de quelques taxes à percevoir," a memorandum issued by the autorités de zone urbaine of Kikwit:

> taxe sur consommation de pains (1 mkt our 2 mkt par pain suivant poids), taxe sur contribution personelle, taxe exploitation magasin, taxe ouverture magasin, taxe voirie magasin, taxe ouverture kiosque, taxe restaurant, taxe exploiation hôtel, taxe chambre hôtel par nuit (10%), taxe sur production usine, taxe état civil, taxe voirie immeuble etage (100z un immeuble), taxe sur dépôt bois, taxe exploitation station essence, taxe sur spectacle, taxe sur divertissement public, taxe ouverture casinos forfait), taxe exploitation casinos (10% sur recettes), taxe voirie industrielle, taxe voirie exploitation garage, taxe qado [sic], taxe sur boisson alcoolisée, taxe sur production boisson sucrée., taxe occupation terrain, taxe sur entretien et gestion marches publics, taxe sur TV en couleurs, taxe sur TV en noir et blanc, taxe sur radio meuble, taxe sur radio portative.

TABLE 12.1

Socioeconomic Background Characteristics of Commissaires du Peuple and Commissaires Politiques Elected in 1977

| | Commissaires du Peuple | | | | Commissaires Politiques | | | |
| | Bandundu | | Zaire | | Elected | | Appointed | |
	Number	Percent	Number	Percent	Number	Percent	Number	Percent
Industrialists, stockholders, administrators, or holders of managerial positions in public and private economic sectors	9	26	44	34.9	13	65	4	33
Businessmen (commerçants)	9	26	17	13.5	1	5	—	—
Planters, cattle ranchers	5	11	11	8.7	4	20	—	—
Sous-contrat civil servants and employees	6	17	25	19.8	—	—	—	—
Holders of managerial positions in noneconomic sectors	6	17	29	23.0	2	10	8	66
Total	35	100	126	100	20	100	12	100

Note: These figures are based on a limited sample, reflecting the data available for roughly 40 percent of the commissaires du peuple at the national level and 57 percent at the provincial level (Bandundu); for the commissaires politiques the figures reflect the data available for roughly 90 and 80 percent of elected and appointed commissaires, respectively. Moreover, the above tabulation is based on the type of position held and not on individual officeholders; thus, several of the positions listed may, in fact, be held by the same individual.

Source: Daniel Van Der Steen, "Elections et réformes politiques au Zaire en 1977: Analayse de la composition des organes politiques," Cahiers du CEDAF, no. 2/3 (1978), pp. 34, 74.

252

ing the transport and retail of consumer commodities and palm oil. It is interesting that this highly successful businessman-politician served as chef de cabinet to the minister of planning and industry in 1963 and, subsequently, as first vice-president of the Mouvement Populaire de la Révolution (MPR) and commissaire urbain in Kinshasa. Yet in one respect the case of Matanda Wa Tenu is typical of most officials elected in 1977; the vast majority already exercised political functions of one kind or another before or since Mobutu's seizure of power in 1965 (Van Der Steen 1978, p. 31). Only 16 percent of the commissaires du peuple and 12 percent of the elected commissaires politiques have never held political office prior to 1977. The circulation of elites effected through the ballot box is therefore tantamount to a reentry of the political class into the political arena via its control of the economy, thus confirming a pattern that, despite the retrocession measures of 1975, remains the most salient characteristic of the Mobutist state.

Wealth is the key resource through which candidates to electoral office are able to buy the vote of the rural electorate and thus secure a political base for themselves in the countryside; in many cases, however, the accumulation of wealth at the top is made possible through the systematic exploitation of the rural sectors by members of the state bourgeoisie. The rural masses are, in effect, subsidizing their own exploitation.

Control of the agrarian sectors by members of the political class requires access to capital resources, and these, in turn, can be obtained only through proper connections. These operate at different levels and form a continuous chain of complicities from the local communities to the capital city. At the local level, ethnic, regional, or clan solidarities play an important role in facilitating the acquisition of land for a relatively small price; local notables—chiefs, elders, or clan heads—are generally willing to bargain away their proprietary rights in return for assurances of individual favors and material benefits. Noncompliance is just as likely to bring forth severe penalties. The next step is to secure appropriate marketing and transport facilities. Here the cooperation of the commercial bourgeoisie is indispensable. It is at the level of provincial urban centers that such cooperation is most actively sought out. The collecting, storing, and transport of agricultural commodities in most instances is the responsibility of a provincial class of commerçants whose economic and political interests are inseparable from those of the landowning political class. Many of these traders are themselves landowners. Just as these services are evidently of critical importance for the maintenance of a viable commercial circuit from the bush to the capital city, it is equally imperative for these intermediaries to cultivate their political connections in the capital city. Import licenses, credit facilities, and tax breaks of one kind or another can best be secured through the political clout of friends and business associates in Kinshasa. A third type of network is that which links various members of the political class at the center. In a sense, the second network can operate only once the third has already been established. For it is at the center that lateral trade-offs among politicians and civil servants can yield the highest dividends in terms of access to import licenses, credit facilities, and tax evasion. It is at this level, too, that the instruments of coercion can be most readily mobilized should the occasion arise.

For a concrete illustration of what is involved here, let us turn briefly to the story told by Mafema (a citizen) in the course of an interview in 1978. Mafema is currently minister of public works and the owner of 155 hectares of land near Fatundu, his village of origin in Bandundu province. He also has a farm near Kinshasa on which he raises 300 pigs. The Fatundu farm includes 105 hectares of manioc and 50 hectares of groundnuts, plus enough pasture to sustain 40 head of cattle. According to Mafema, "It all began with one truck, an initial investment of Z 2,000 on the land, and 45 women." Today he has a labor force of 150 or 200 men, whose salary is fixed at Z 1 a day, two tractors, a truck, and a barge. Some of the female laborers employed by Mafema have since retooled themselves as seamstresses. Equipped with five sewing machines, they make garments for schoolchildren—"dans le cadre d'une entreprise d'habillement pour écoles." He is also a senior partner in the Société de Commercialisation Agro-Industrielle (SOCOMAGRI), which controls hundreds of hectares of palm plantations in the Fatundu and Mbumba areas. But the SOCOMAGRI is also the vehicle through which imported manufactured products are commercialized among the rural communities and the main purchasing agent of agricultural produce in the Bulundu sous-région. As a société de commercialization the SOCOMAGRI controls both the sale of consumer commodities and the purchase of agricultural produce.

In building up his rural fiefdom, Mafema took full advantage of his privileged access to the lineage and clan organization of Fatundu, but he also had ample opportunities to expand his network of personal connections far beyond his rural homeland. As Commissaire d'Etat aux Affaires Foncières shortly after independence, then as Délégué Général for the Chanic and the Onatra, he gained strategic entrées into several public and parastatal sectors directly involved in the rural economy, including river transport and real estate transactions. Furthermore, through his close personal friendship with Takizala, once a leading politician of the Mobutu regime and a central figure of Bandundu politics, he could count on the full support of the provincial authorities when the time came to expand and diversify the activities of the SOCOMAGRI. Meanwhile, contacts already had been established with the three personalities who, together with Mafema, were to become partners in the SOCOMAGRI: Lihau, an old-time politician who served as commissioner of justice in the College of Commissioners in 1960; Balanda, a conseiller of the Cour de Justice; and a leading commerçant named Muladika. By then, the Mafema enterprise was securely anchored to a vast network of political connections that spread from the village communities of Fatundu to the very center of the political system.

The case of Mafema is by no means unique. Countless examples could be cited of politicians and civil servants whose stake in the survival of the Mobutist state stems from their vested economic interests. As prime participants in, and organizers of, the exploitative system built around the countless frauds and speculation that accompany the extraction and marketing of food-

stuffs, they bear a major share of the responsibility for the catastrophic decline of the rural economy. Yet fraud and speculation are not the exclusive
privilege of a handful of top civil servants; they lubricate the wheels of the
administrative machinery at almost every level, from collectivités and sous-
régions to ministries and parastatal bodies at the center. Only in the rarest
of instances have regional authorities denounced the symptoms of the "mal
Zairois."

A notable exception to the rule occurred in February 1978, when, in order to prepare the ground for the stabilization program contemplated by the
Zairian government to meet the conditions of an IMF loan, all regional commissioners were invited to hold regional meetings designed to lay bare the
roots of the rural malaise. The minutes of one such meeting, held in the
Kivu, are revelatory of the kinds of corrupt practices through which resources
are siphoned from the rural areas and sold to local consumers at exorbitant
prices (when they are not diverted through illegal channels for sale outside
the country). To quote:

> The commissioners stated that fraud and unfair commercial prac-
> tices also have a very debilitating effect on the economy of the re-
> gion. They remarked that planes loaded with merchandise destined
> for particular points in Kivu often arrive at their destinations with-
> out cargo, the goods having been ripped-off at intermediate stops.
> Likewise, they indicated, price-gouging has become a way of life
> in Kivu, with prices on agricultural goods often tripling between
> field and market place. The Commissioner from Bukavu attributed
> this condition to foolishness on the part of the Kivu consumers and
> anti-revolutionary greed on the part of the market women. . . .
>
> The commissioners complained of lack of credit facilities for the
> farmers. They also noted that some government agencies had
> failed to respond to the needs of farmers and fishermen of the re-
> gion. . . .
>
> The Commission found that at least a third of the debts owed to
> the State and its parastatal enterprises remains unpaid. Likewise,
> taxes and other duties are often evaded by individual companies in
> Kivu. The Commission noted with consternation that many of the
> debtors and tax evaders are protected by special government
> agents and high cadres de l'Etat. . . .
>
> The Commission for agriculture noted a general decline in re-
> gional agricultural output over the past several years; it cited a
> shortage of food products on the market due to an inadequate trans-
> portation system and the transfer of land from food production to
> the production of quinine and bananas.

It is equally pertinent to note the nature of the remedies suggested by the
Commission for Financial Questions:

> The Commission proposed that all cadres de l'Etat at whatever
> level they are situated, be punished for offering protection to all

the disloyal debtors who owe money to the State and its parastatal
organisms. The Commission further suggested that the principle
of separation of interests between government activities and private business be applied. . . .

Turning its attention to custom's fraud, the Commission . . .
proposed that all efforts be made to flood the markets in Zaire with
consumer goods which are currently the object of fraud and contraband. It also suggested that prices on the market place be set according to cost of production. As for traffickers in contraband the
Commission asked that their names be published, and that the appropriate government services be given adequate equipment to arrest their passage across the border.

Cleaning the Augean stables of the Mobutist state can hardly be accomplished through the application of aseptic measures that would at the same
time threaten the very survival of the state. What little legitimacy the state
can claim for itself is rooted in the opportunities for self-enrichment offered
through political office; hence any attempt to operate a "separation of interests between government activities and private business" is bound to undermine the basis of the partnership on which the state apparatus rests.

Nor is it conceivable, under the present circumstances, that appropriate
fiscal and investment policies will be initiated for the purpose of improving
the conditions of the rural sectors. Such policies are simply not compatible
with the class interests of the state and commercial bourgeoisies. Generating
enough tax income to invest in the development of a rural infrastructure would
require the implementation of drastic reform that would run directly counter
to the vested interests of the ruling bourgeoisie. For it is not just from the
confiscation of an agricultural surplus from the peasantry that civil servants,
army men, and commerçants derive the bulk of their profits but also from
the confiscation of huge tax revenues from the state. One can push the argument a step further and suggest that further reductions of agricultural output
will inevitably work to the advantage of the ruling class. To put it succinctly,
the smaller the output, the higher the demand, and hence the higher the rate
of profit on the sale of agricultural commodities. Perhaps the richest opportunities for windfall profits arise from the purchase of foodstuffs from foreign
suppliers. Overinvoicing, kickbacks, and illicit gains on foreign exchange
transactions are never so tempting and lucrative than when involving millions
of dollars worth of imported commodities. The constellation of forces and
vested interests that conspire in not allowing agriculture to get off the ground
are the same that operate to keep the peasant masses in a state of permanent
economic stagnation.

CONCLUSION

Since class power in Zaire is so deeply embedded in kleptocratic market transactions conducted under the aegis of the state, there is no reason to

expect that the state will allocate a larger share of benefits, opportunities, and income to the rural masses. Any attempt on the part of the state to shift the distribution of income away from its clients would undermine the foundation of the existing class forces on which it must rely for its own political survival.

Thus far we have deliberately emphasized the disjunction between the political class and the rural masses. Although this duality helps illuminate some crucial aspects of rural poverty, the processes of internal differentiation at work in the rural and urban sectors suggest a more complex picture. We already had occasion to note the general nature of the forces around which the rural society tends to fragment. We must now turn to the opposite end of the political spectrum. On what basis can one differentiate among different subgroups within the political class? How much closer does this bring us to an understanding of rural poverty?

As a point of entry into these questions, it is essential to underscore the fundamental role played by the structures of distribution—as distinct from the means of production—in the overall process of class formation. Cohen's observation is very much in point: "To discern the structure of exploitation one may suggest that a much greater concentration is needed on the particular relationship held to the means of distribution and exchange rather than to the means of production" (Cohen 1972, p. 241). In Zaire as in much of Africa, the means of production (including, in many instances, land resources) are generally in foreign hands. What remains directly under the control of the political class are the distributive networks through which cash crops are transported, sold, or smuggled out of the country; through which cloth, shoes, cigarettes, tractors, trucks, cars, and spare parts are imported and allocated; through which credit facilities are extended or withheld; salaries paid or illegally appropriated; taxes and customs duties collected or canceled. At this level, a major line of cleavage can be discerned between those privileged few who take full advantage of their access to the "external estate" (Cohen 1972, p. 246)—that is, foreign corporations, international development agencies, aid programs, expatriate enterprises, and so forth—to extract vast benefits from their transactions with foreign donors, buyers, and distributors and those less privileged elements who operate largely within the context of domestic networks.

What separates the top mandarinate from the "middle-ranking state bourgeoisie" is that the former's rewards and privileges are intimately tied up to the "external estate." Not only are their benefits largely conditioned by their voluntary subservience to foreign interests, but for this very reason they appear to act as the obedient trustees of such interests within the domestic arena. Their "market capacity"—to use Giddens' phrase, meaning "all the relevant attributes which they may bring to the bargaining encounter" (Giddens 1972, p. 103)—is essentially a function of their strategic political connections at the center of the political system. It is this privileged access to power that, in effect, is being exchanged for material benefits.

To be sure, this rough distinction between the foreign-induced mandarinate and the middle-ranking domestic bourgeoisie leaves ample room for al-

ternative classifications, as between, for example, the presidential clique
(made up of Mobutu's kinsmen and relatives), the ruling brotherhood (consisting of another layer of trusted kinsmen and representatives of key ethnic
clusters), and the prospective bourgeoisie (whose weight in the political system depends on their technocratic skills and the influence they gained in the
course of their early [pre-1965] political career) (Rymenam 1977). A more
important qualification concerns the nature of the external estate. Far from
constituting a monolithic entity, it includes a variety of economic and political
configurations whose weight is being felt at different levels. It would be
preposterous to assign the same political significance to, say, the International
Monetary Fund (IMF), the World Bank, Lever Brothers, and Tempelsman.
Quite aside from the fact that they pursue policies that are far from being consistent with the class interests of the foreign-induced bourgeoisie, they do
not possess the same leverage vis-à-vis these class interests. As members
of the political class bargain for ever larger shares of external resources,
they go about this task with radically different degrees of flexibility vis-à-vis
their foreign interlocutors. The IMF's Blumenthal is unquestionably a much
tougher customer than Tempelsman.

Clearly, the structure of privilege in Zaire is no less diversified than
the external matrix of dependency within which it continues to flourish. If we
are to view officeholders "as being in the position of a holding company delegated by foreign interests to run the show on their behalf" (Cohen 1972, p.
240), it is equally important to examine the exact nature of the holding relationship and to recognize that for some the show is rapidly coming to an end.
But this does not detract from the fundamental fact that the state has been,
and continues to be, the central element in the structuring of class power
and that even in the absence of external resources the distributive pattern of
capitalist accumulation would remain basically unchanged. What might change
are the terms on which benefits are handed out and the social or ethnic identity of the recipients. Out of the class forces that have operated over the last
two decades has emerged an indigenous bourgeoisie deeply enmeshed in the
web of exploitative market relationships that runs from the top to the bottom
of the social pyramid. To dislodge it from its positions acquises, and hope
that social policies inspired by a sense of equity will follow, will require far
more than the financial housecleaning operation currently undertaken under
the auspices of the IMF.

Even in the best of circumstances, assuming that the reformist efforts
displayed by the IMF do, in fact, succeed in eliminating the worst forms of
corruption and currency offenses in certain key ministries and banks, this
kind of assault on class privilege will not ipso facto eliminate the root causes
of rural poverty. The class structure of Zaire has already crystallized to the
point where the political system enjoys enough autonomy to ensure the survival
of its own class interests. A concerted attack on rural poverty would presup-
pose not only a major alteration of existing patterns of resource distribution
but a radical transformation of class alliances at home and abroad as well.
The equity problem, in other words, lies at the heart of the rural crisis, and
no equity-oriented policies are likely to succeed short of a major social revo-

lution. This fundamental minimal condition is what the "external estate" refuses to accept and acknowledge.

REFERENCES

Cohen, Michael. 1974. Urban Policy and Political Conflict in Africa. Chicago: University of Chicago Press.

Cohen, Robin. 1972. "Class in Africa: Analytical Problems and Perspectives." Socialist Register 1972 (London): 231-56.

Cowell, Alan. 1978. "Zaire: Stabilité sur fond de violence." Voix d'Afrique, no. 59 (May).

Dalton, George. 1963. "Economic Surplus, Once Again." American Anthropologist 65: 389-94.

_____. 1960. "A Note of Clarification on Economic Surplus." American Anthropologist 62: 483-90.

Giddens, Anthony. 1973. The Class Structure of Advanced Societies. New York: Harper & Row.

Gould, David. 1977. "Local Administration in Zaire and Underdevelopment." Journal of Modern African Studies 15, no. 3:1-31.

Jewsiewicki, Bogumil, and Mabeng. 1974. "Les coupeurs de fruit de palme du Kwango-Kwilu." Lindukoli, ser. B, nos. 1 and 2:199-220.

Lebebvre, Georges. 1973. The Great Fear of 1789. Translated by Joan White. New York: Pantheon.

Malengrau, Georges. 1949. Vers un paysannat indinène. Brussels: IRC.

Munayi, Muntu-Monji. 1978. "Le prosélytisme des sectes parmi les acculturés du Kwilu-Kwango et du Kasai (1941-1960)." Zaire Afrique, no. 123, pp. 135-54.

Rymenam, Jean. 1977. "Comment le régime Mobutu a sappé ses propres fondements." Le Monde Diplomatique, May.

Scott, James. 1979. "Revolution in the Revolution: Peasants and Commissars." Theory and Society 7, nos. 1 and 2:97-134.

_____. 1978. "Some Notes on Post-Peasant Societies." Peasant Studies 7, no. 3:147-54.

_____. 1975. "Exploitation in Rural Class Relations: A Victim's Perspective." Comparative Politics 7, no. 4 (July): 489–532.

Sikitele, Gize a Sumbula. 1976. "Les causes principales de la révolte Pende en 1931." Zaire Afrique, no. 109, pp. 1–34.

Van Der Steen. 1978. "Elections et reformes politiques au Zaire en 1977." Cahiers du CEDAF, vol. 2/3.

Wilson, Charles. 1968. The History of Unilever. Vol. 1. New York: Praeger.

Young, Crawford. 1978. "Zaire: The Unending Crisis." Foreign Affairs 57:169–85.

PART IV
INTERNATIONAL LINKAGES: STABILIZATION AND CONFLICT

13

ZAIRE IN THE WORLD SYSTEM:
IN SEARCH OF SOVEREIGNTY

Galen Hull

INTRODUCTION

Umba di Lutete, state commissioner of foreign affairs and international cooperation, proudly remarked in an address on Zaire's foreign policy in October 1978 that his country was "open to the world" (1978). The constitution of Zaire, he noted, "may be the only one in the world which provides that, if required by the Continent's higher interests, the country may cede a portion of its national sovereignty." Zaire has not had occasion to invoke this provision of its constitution in the interest of continental solidarity. Ironically, however, the history of the country since independence records numerous episodes and relationships that have impinged on Zaire's national sovereignty. Recently, in particular, the government of Zaire has been obliged to cede a portion of its sovereignty to international lending agencies and has been reoccupied by foreign troops. In sum, Zaire is on the verge of becoming the first former African colony to revert to de facto control by foreign powers.

This recolonization process can be clearly seen in all realms of policy: economic, foreign, and military. In June 1978, for example, international financial brokers met in Brussels and decided to grant the International Monetary Fund (IMF) authority to take over effective control of the Zairian economy (for a fuller discussion of the role of the World Bank, see Chapter 14). On November 29, 1978, the IMF's representative, in his capacity as principal director of the Central Bank of Zaire, issued a document forbidding all credit and exchange facilities to President Mobutu's uncle, Litho Moboti (Africa Confidential 1979). A few weeks later the ban was extended to no less than 50 leading Zairian companies, many of them owned by Mobutu's closest friends and political allies. Meanwhile, nearly a year after the second "invasion" of Shaba province by rebel troops, the government of Zaire still relied upon Moroccan and Senegalese paratroopers to maintain law and order in the region. These are but the most salient examples of the Mobutu regime's inability to perform the most basic functions of a modern nation-state.

This chapter examines both the roots of Zaire's dependence upon foreign powers in the conduct of its foreign policy and the interests of those powers in Zaire. In the international division of labor, Zaire belongs to the periphery. Its abundance of mineral resources and its strategic location in the heart of Africa have ensured Zaire the abiding interest of the advanced capitalist countries of the center. During the colonial era the entire administrative and economic infrastructure of the country was in the hands of the Belgians. A national bourgeoisie was practically nonexistent, the result of an extremely regressive colonial policy. After independence the country remained dominated by multinational corporations that retained potent economic and political weapons with which to pursue their interests. A small indigenous elite began to emerge whose interests were tied to the dominant foreign interests. Under the Mobutu regime this elite has become entrenched and has dictated the nature and direction of foreign policy, as previous chapters have detailed.

During the period from 1960 to 1965, Zaire's external relations were largely determined by Western powers operating within the United Nations framework. The country was deprived of any sustained national political leadership, its sovereignty undermined repeatedly by internal rebellion and external domination. Since the coup d'etat that brought Mobutu to power in 1965, foreign policy has served two important functions in the exercise of political and economic power. In the first instance, an official policy of nationalism has emphasized economic independence (more spoils for the local elite) and cultural authenticity. The ideology of nationalism, now officially enshrined as "Mobutism," has been used to rally the masses to the spirit of Patrice Lumumba in support of his successor, the Supreme Guide. The second function, closely related to the first, is political: the perpetuation of the political and bureaucratic elite in power. Military, financial, and political aid from the Western powers serves primarily to hold this elite in place. In turn, the nation's foreign policy is oriented fundamentally toward maintaining favorable conditions for foreign investors in Zaire and serving the political and strategic interests of Western powers.

Whenever these two functions have come into conflict, the ideology of economic independence has given way to more pragmatic considerations, those that are necessary for the maintenance of the established order. A pattern developed that showed a correlation between domestic tranquillity and bold initiatives in foreign policy (Kabwit 1976). The much-touted program of nationalization was followed by retrenchment, of denationalization. The struggle for national sovereignty is therefore compromised in the interest of maintaining the bureaucratic and political elite in power.

NATIONALIZATION AND DENATIONALIZATION

At the time of independence in 1960, Western interests in Zaire were predominantly Belgian. One company, Société Générale de Belgique, controlled directly or indirectly 70 percent of the economy (Weissman 1974, p. 23 ff.). Its influence in the mining industry was virtually absolute and was concentrated in copper, cobalt, diamonds, and uranium in Katanga (Shaba) and Kasai. It controlled Union Minière du Haut-Katanga, which held exclusive mining rights over most of Katanga until 1990. The mining industry produced 22 percent of the country's GNP and 60 percent of its exports, of which three-fourths came from Katanga. Société Générale collaborated closely with the Belgian government, which provided administrative and military support.

France, West Germany, and Italy were the leading consumers of copper and other minerals from Zaire. In addition to their direct economic interests in Zaire, the French were equally concerned with maintaining their traditional sphere of influence in their former colonies in West Africa as they maneuvered to challenge the Belgians in Zaire. Stephen Weissman (1974) distinguishes several motives for U.S. policy in Zaire, of which the most important was maintaining access to mineral resources. Zaire then produced 9 percent of the Western world's copper, 50 percent of its cobalt, and 69 percent of its industrial diamonds. Direct U.S. investment in Zaire was marginal, totaling less than $20 million. Most U.S. business interests were indirect, traceable through European companies or governments doing business in southern Africa. Another group of businesses were those who anticipated future investments and were thus sympathetic to African nationalist interests. Finally, there were U.S. trading interests, which were especially marginal. Weissman attributes U.S. policy formation in Zaire during the early period of independence to an attitude of anticommunism rather than economic interests.

Shortly after his assumption of power, Mobutu sought to consolidate the economic power of the state and create a larger revenue base by nationalizing the mining industry. The first step was the Bakajika law of June 1966, according to which all foreign-based companies whose main activities were in Zaire were required to establish their head office there by the end of the year (Radmann 1978, pp. 35-36). The law also provided that the state should have all mining rights granted before independence and made no mention of compensation. Union Minière objected to the transfer of its head office to Zaire. In negotiations with the Zairian government it offered counterproposals. At stake was the very nationality of the company and decisions that would entail changing its articles of association with the unanimous consent of shareholders. Union Minière offered a compromise solution that Mobutu seemed prepared to accept as late as November 1966. However, by the end of that year negotiations had broken down and Mobutu decided to nationalize the mining industry.

On December 31, 1966, the Zairian government officially announced its decision to expropriate Union Minière and to transfer its assets to a new company to be known as Société Générale Congolaise de Minerais (GECOMIN). The announcement bore the semblance of a declaration of economic independence, the assertion of sovereignty by the Zairian government over the nation's natural resources. Mobutu forbade all contacts with Union Minière in Brussels (Radmann 1978, p. 37). The new company was to be 55 percent owned by the state, and 30 percent of the shares were to be offered to the public. Eventually, GECOMIN was to become a fully state-owned company.

The appearance of nationalization gave way in time to the reality of denationalization for a number of reasons (Comité Zaire 1978a, pp. 107-9).

Union Minière still held several trump cards. Although a Zairian decree halting all copper exports was issued at the end of 1966, Union Minière had enough stockpiles abroad that it could continue deliveries for at least five months. Fully 70 percent of the country's earnings in hard currency were derived from the export of copper. Without these earnings, other industries that depended upon foreign exchange were seriously affected. The country was soon close to bankruptcy. Furthermore, GECOMIN depended almost entirely upon foreign personnel for its operations and would be hard put to find new personnel or new markets for its copper. Finally, other foreign interests were unlikely to risk investment in Zaire for fear of nationalization.

GECOMIN was therefore obliged to enter into negotiations with the Société Générale des Minérais (SGM), an affiliate of Société Générale de Belgique, which was entrusted with the sales of all products of Union Minière. The two companies reached an agreement in early 1967 that provided for the marketing of GECOMIN products and technical assistance necessary for continued operations. In exchange for these services, SGM was to receive a commission of 4.5 percent of the total value of GECOMIN production; the salaries of the foreign technicians were also to be paid by GECOMIN.

In September 1969, the capitulation of the Zairian government was complete when it agreed on terms of compensation (Comité Zaire 1978a). The agreement provided for an extension of 25 years of the technical assistance arrangement begun in 1967. For the first 15 years SGM was to receive 6 percent of the total value of GECOMIN's production, a sum that would represent 100 percent of the profits if the price of copper remained the same. Zaire also dropped its claim of 7.5 billion Belgian francs in payment for shipments in transit and renounced its control over Union Minière's operations beyond its borders. In 1974, GECAMINES (the new name acquired during Zairianization, Générale de Carrières et des Mines du Zaire) entered into a joint venture with SGM for the marketing of mining products. As long as copper prices remained high, GECAMINES prospered. But with the decline in prices beginning in 1974, the company's fortunes fell sharply, and the Zairian economy began a downward spiral from which it has yet to recover. Union Minière, meanwhile, was able to diversify its interests and to expand its operations around the globe.

As with other programs of nationalization undertaken in Zaire, the most visible effect in the mining industry has been the Africanization of management personnel, which was completed in 1974 (Radmann 1978, p. 44). But, in 1978, GECAMINES still relied heavily upon expatriates as technical personnel, a fact that became the cause célèbre of the Franco-Belgian intervention during the Shaba II "invasion" in Kolwezi.

The process of denationalization outlined here attests to the oligarchic nature of political power. Decisions by the Zairian government were intended to protect the interests of a small group of bureaucratic elite who personally profited by the Africanization measures. Their interests were compatible with those of foreign capital, which continued to maintain effective control over the Zairian economy. The predominance of Belgian interests gave way in time to other international investors, notably U.S., Japanese, French, and

Italian. The nation's sovereignty remained compromised as the Zairian economy retained its extroverted orientation toward the international capitalist order.

The nationalization-denationalization syndrome was not the only economic process diminishing Zaire's sovereignty. The momentous decision to devalue the national currency in 1967, core of the IMF-enforced stabilization program, was mainly intended to restore confidence to foreign investors. While it managed to accomplish this aim, the effect on the population was not positive. Real wages in both the private and public sectors continued to decline. The Mobutu regime embarked upon a program of prestige projects as the price of copper on the world market rose. An extremely favorable investment code enticed foreign investors on an unprecedented scale.

Meanwhile, the Mobutu regime sought to extend the program of nationalization to other sectors—the system of education in 1971 and 1974 and the domestic economy in 1973. The president publicly denied that foreign assets were being seized, and reiterated the principle of an open-door policy for foreign investors. All Zaire wanted, he maintained, was an equitable share of the profits. With the spectacular failure of the 1973 measures and the subsequent retrenchment, even the pretense of nationalization has been dropped. The prospect of economic independence has simply receded ever further into the web of debt, inflation, and reliance upon international financiers (see Chapter 1).

ZAIRIAN POLITICAL FOREIGN POLICY IN THE 1970s: THE MASK OF NEUTRALITY

The official principle guiding Zairian foreign policy as defined in the 1969 Manifeste de la N'Sele is positive neutralism. It is a principle that has been elaborated and embellished in a variety of slogans. In 1971 a broad policy of recours à l'autenticité was enunciated that emphasized a genuine African orientation of Zairian nationalism in all aspects of public policy. In December 1972 President Mobutu delivered a speech in which he described the policy in terms intended to be understood by the masses: "According to the doctrine laid down by the M. P.R., we are neither rightist, leftist, nor even centrist. We have opted to follow a path which is ours exclusively: genuine Zairian nationalism" (quoted in Umba di Lutete 1978, p. 9). In terms of foreign policy, this implied a course of action modeled neither on the West nor the East. Zaire would not "import ideologies which mean absolutely nothing to the great majority of its people, since they do not understand them." Rather, Zaire would "draw from these ideologies as the need arises, in accordance with its interests and value system, without having to decide on principle that it should remain at mid-point between two ideologies" (quoted in Umba di Lutete 1978, p. 9).

Indeed, during the early 1970s, when the Zairian economy was experiencing relative prosperity and domestic discontent was subdued, Mobutu managed to create the impression that he was embarked on a course of nonalignment in foreign policy. He enjoyed a period of success as a mediator in conflicts between neighboring African states. He was called upon by General Idi Amin shortly after the coup that brought Amin to power in Uganda in 1971 to resolve the conflict with Tanzania, which harbored the ousted president, Milton Obote. Again, in 1973, Mobutu was asked to conciliate conflict between Burundi and Rwanda arising from the flow of refugees out of Burundi. Together, Zaire and Tanzania were able to help stabilize the situation; for a favorable and more detailed account of Zaire's foreign policy in this period, see Jeannick Odier (1975).

Meanwhile, Mobutu fashioned himself as an ardent foe of neocolonialism and racism. In speeches to the Organization of African Unity, the conference of nonaligned countries, and the United Nations, he lashed out at the neocolonialist powers and condemned the racist oppression of white minority regimes in southern Africa. When Zambia decided to close its border with Rhodesia in 1973, Mobutu declared his solemn support, saying that whoever attacked Zambia was also menacing Zaire. He could also claim to be in the forefront of the struggle against Portuguese colonialism because of Zaire's long-standing support for one of the Angolan nationalist liberation groups, Holden Roberto's Frente Nacional de Libertação de Angola (FNLA).

While Mobutu continued to make periodic visits to Western capitals to shore up bilateral relations and encourage private investment in Zaire, he made a number of moves intended to demonstrate an independent stance in international relations (Kabwit 1976, pp. 4-8). In 1972 he announced that Zaire was withdrawing from the Organization Commune Africaine et Malagache (OCAM), the Francophone economic community it had belonged to since 1965. He charged that OCAM was being manipulated by the French. This caused momentary strain in relations with France, but the two countries were soon back on more cordial terms than ever before.

The most dramatic development during this period was the overture toward the socialist world. In 1972 Mobutu visited Romania and explored the possibilities of technical assistance from that country. Then, in January 1973, he made a pilgrimage to Peking, which resulted in formal diplomatic relations between Zaire and the People's Republic of China and the signing of an economic agreement. Heretofore, the Mobutu regime had denounced China for its support of revolutionary movements in Zaire and its subversive role throughout the Third World. Zaire had maintained very warm relations with Nationalist China; the Taiwanese were assisting in a variety of projects ranging from rice production to the construction of the presidential domain at N'Sele. Upon his return from Peking, however, Mobutu unceremoniously expelled the Nationalist Chinese to make room for his new-found friends from the People's Republic.

A second visit to Peking at the end of 1974 solidified the new relationship, a tie that served a number of purposes. It helped to dampen the criticism by the relatively small progressive element of Zairian intellectuals of overreliance upon neocolonialist powers. It also brought assurances from Peking that there would be no further support for Marxist groups resisting the Mobutu regime. The Chinese promised enthusiastic assistance for Zairian agricultural projects and certain forms of military aid. The army's elite 15,000-man Kamanyola division that was sent to protect the Shaba region during the rebel "invasions" was fully equipped by the Chinese. Although Chinese aid to Zaire has remained relatively small, it nevertheless symbolizes a shift in China's African policy toward containment of alleged Soviet advances and away from support for progressive revolutionary regimes.

The style, if not the substance, of the Mobutu regime changed markedly following the visits to China (Kabwit 1976, pp. 6-10). Mobutu was clearly swayed by the accomplishments of the socialist revolution in China and the effectiveness of the Maoist ideology in mobilizing the masses. While carefully denying charges that Zaire was embracing communism, Mobutu embarked upon a "radicalization" of the program of cultural nationalism. Henceforth, Zairian nationals would be forbidden to wear Western-style suits and ties; instead, a Chinese-style suit was installed as the national attire. A program of "voluntary" Saturday morning work projects was designed to emulate the Chinese spirit of self-reliance. The official political doctrine of the Mouvement Populaire de la Révolution (MPR) became known as "Mobutism," a pale imitation of Maoism.

Finally, Mobutu found it expedient to break diplomatic relations with Israel in the wake of the Arab-Israeli war of October 1973. Israel had furnished substantial technical assistance to Zaire, particularly in the formation of elite army units. The Israelis had been a very useful political and ideological ally in Mobutu's struggle to rid the country of dissident elements in the 1960s. Zairian support for the Arab cause in the Middle East conflict was clearly intended to bring the country petrodollars from the oil-rich Arab nations. In 1974 Mobutu made a grand tour of the Arab world, including Saudi Arabia, Kuwait, Egypt, and Abu Dhabi. Heads of state from other Arab countries were invited to visit Kinshasa.

Despite the appearance of neutrality in international relations that these developments provided, Zaire's involvement in the civil war leading to independence in neighboring Angola and its subsequent conflict with the socialist government of that country reveal the extent to which Mobutu remained dependent upon the West. Since the early 1960s, Zaire had lent assistance to Holden Roberto's FNLA liberation movement against Portuguese colonialism in Angola. During the same time Zaire was becoming an important client of U.S. interests in Central Africa. While the United States maintained an official policy of support for Portugal as a NATO ally, it was also quietly taking steps to bring about "self-determination" of the African majority. (For a detailed account of U.S. policy in Zaire and Angola during the 1960s, see Weissman [1978, p. 399 f.].) The United States began to supply covert "financial, non-military aid" through its Central Intelligence Agency (CIA) to Roberto in Zaire.

With the demise of the Portuguese empire in 1974, the stage was set for civil war between the forces of the Popular Movement for the Liberation of Angola (MPLA), led by Agostino Neto and supported by Cuban troops, and Roberto's FNLA, as well as a third group—the National Union for the Total Independence of Angola (UNITA) under Jonas Savimbi. In their covert attempt to assist the FNLA, Mobutu's troops (according to some estimates, over 11,000) suffered a swift defeat at the hands of the MPLA (Africa Contemporary Records 1976-77, pp. B534-35). Zairian troops began pouring into Angola in the last quarter of 1975, but by November the MPLA was installed as the official government of the People's Republic of Angola. The only other foreign troops fighting against the MPLA were South African, making evident to the world the collusion between Zaire and the apartheid regime.

By January 1976 the northern front, manned by Zairian troops, had disintegrated as the MPLA consolidated its control over the region. In the process, the traffic on the vital Benguela railway linking Zaire's copper belt and the Angolan port of Lobito was disrupted, placing an additional burden on the already enfeebled Zairian economy. In his usual opportunistic fashion, Mobutu moved quickly to make amends with the Angolan government. In February 1976 he responded to Neto's appeal for reconciliation by declaring Zaire's neutrality and an end to support for the FNLA. Although the two countries did not establish diplomatic relations, Neto and Mobutu pledged not to interfere in each other's internal affairs nor to use refugees from their conflict for political ends. Nevertheless, relations remained strained. Zaire was accused by Angola of giving covert assistance to the Front for the Liberation of the Cabinda Enclave (FLEC), which sought independence for the tiny oil-producing Angolan enclave between Zaire and the Congo. For its part, the Mobutu regime was still concerned about the continued presence in Angola of "Katangese gendarmes" from Zaire who had fought for the secession of Katanga (now Shaba) province in the early 1960s and subsequently supported the MPLA during the civil war.

Zairian involvement in the Angolan civil war brought an end to the facade of neutrality in foreign policy. South Africa's offer of a $6.7 million credit for the import of South African foodstuffs and Zaire's decision to ship a large portion of mineral products through South Africa in 1976 severely weakened Mobutu's self-styled image as spokesman for African liberation. In fact, imports of South African meat, processed foods, and dairy products had never been discontinued completely since the colonial era and were now reaching preindependence levels. Zaire's dependence upon the apartheid regime became increasingly evident as witnessed by the range of South African canned goods and fresh fruit available in such cities as Kinshasa and Lubumbashi (Africa Contemporary Records 1977), p. B536).

The image of nonalignment was further tarnished during the Angolan fiasco by renewed dependence on Zaire's traditional benefactor, the United States. For the first time since independence a U.S. defense secretary (Donald Rumsfeld) visited Africa, including only Zaire and Kenya. For fiscal year 1976, the U.S. military aid package to Zaire was $19 million and for fiscal year 1977 it was $30.4 million, including antitank weapons, helicopters, and communications equipment, as well as training for the Zairian army. Weissman, in his study of the role of the CIA in Zaire and Angola (1978, p. 405), maintains that, "unlike the Zaire operations of 1964-67, U.S. military aid (during the Angolan conflict) was entirely covert in nature although CIA Director Colby warned that the chances for exposure were considerable."

Weissman shows that by the middle of the fall of 1975 the United States had spent nearly $23 million on covert activities, half of it on arms provided to the FNLA and UNITA, both directly and through replacement of arms supplied by Zaire and Zambia (1978, p. 406).

While it is clear that Zaire was used as a surrogate by the United States to further its own interests in attempting to contain what was perceived as a Soviet-Cuban threat, it may also be argued that the Mobutu regime acted in the interest of its own political survival. Two students of Zairian foreign policy have held to this point of view. Nzongola (1978, pp. 147-48) argues that Zaire's intervention, "far from being a simple execution of American directives . . . was primarily related to [its] struggle for survival, a desire that coincided with the foreign policy objectives of the United States." The Mobutu regime intervened in Angola "to defend its own class interests as well as to discharge its obligations as a junior partner of U.S. imperialism." Ghislain Kabwit (1976, p. 15) observes that by supporting the FNLA "Mobutu wanted to see in Angola a political regime whose leadership not only shared his political philosophy but which also owed its survival as a viable organization to Zairian support."

Thus the Mobutu regime in the early 1970s attempted to define its foreign policy in terms of nonalignment, "neither leftist, rightist, nor centrist." By the end of its disastrous involvement in the Angolan civil war, however, it was again explicitly clear that in reality the regime had not altered its basic dependence upon the United States and European powers that had given birth to it in 1965. If Mobutu was successful in establishing favorable relations with the communist government of the People's Republic of China, it was because the latter was beginning to define its own foreign policy objectives in terms of containment of Soviet hegemony rather than the defense of international proletarian movements. The domestic intent of Zaire's foreign policy remained to hold the privileged bureaucratic elite in place.

THE SHABA CRISES AND THE DECLINE OF SOVEREIGNTY

Whatever question remained as to Zaire's orientation in foreign policy was dispelled by the Mobutu regime's behavior during two successive "invasions" of its southern border in 1977 and 1978 that came to be referred to as Shaba I and Shaba II. The effect of these events was to throw into even sharper relief the regime's dependence upon Western powers and their Third World allies. Just as the conflict in the Congo of the early 1960s brought great power confrontation and division among the African states, the Shaba crises revived prospects for East-West conflict and tended to polarize African nations along ideological lines. One side, composed of the "moderates," claimed "continental solidarity" as its goal. The other consisted of the "radical" states, whose banner was "international proletarianism." The moderates who came to the defense of the Mobutu regime contended that Zaire's sovereignty was threatened by "invasions" by Katangese mercenaries trained and

financed by the Soviet Union and Cuba and supported by the Angolan government. The opposing view held that the conflict was essentially an internal affair of Zaire, a popular uprising against a corrupt regime propped up by
Western capitalism (see Hull 1977, pp. 4-9).

From the outset of the first Shaba "invasion" in March 8, 1977, the
identity of the rebel force was in dispute (see Chapter 4, opposition groups).
AZAP, the official Zairian press agency, charged that it was an "invasion"
by "5,000 Cuban-led Katangese mercenaries from Angola." They were seen
as "foreigners" invading a sovereign state. A somewhat different version
was presented by spokesmen for the rebel group, the Front for the National
Liberation of the Congo (FLNC), which claimed responsibility for the incursion (Afrique Asie, April 13, 1977). FLNC denied that its troops were either
"gendarmes, Katangese, or secessionists." It claimed to be a "revolutionary
and progressive movement" with political and military discipline, working
closely with the Zairian masses to overthrow the Mobutu regime. Regardless of the actual extent of support provided to the rebels by the MPLA government of Angola, the uneasy truce between Zaire and Angola was now broken.

The Angolan government, for its part, was still busy consolidating its
authority more than a year after independence. It continued to be threatened
by rump actions of FNLA and UNITA. The month before the rebels crossed
the Angolan border into southern Zaire, President Neto announced over national radio that Western powers led by the United States were planning a major
military operation against Angola, code name "Operation Cobra" (Hull 1977).
The same day Neto denounced the "intolerable provocations on an almost
daily basis" along Angola's northern and southern borders. He described
Operation Cobra as a plan involving the Zairian army and the U.S. military
in conjunction with troops of FNLA and FLEC. The initial attack was to be
launched against Angola's oil-rich Cabinda province. Judging from this ac-
cusation, it would seem that Angola had grounds for aiding the Katangese
rebels. Shortly after the "invasion," however, the Angolan government presented a statement to the United Nations denying that it had anything to do
with the situation in Shaba. It also denied the presence of any Cuban soldiers
among the insurrectionary forces.

Within days after the "invasion," the government of Zaire had sent out
cries of alarm to its allies and friends. The response was slow, especially
from the United States. The State Department did sponsor an emergency air-
lift of military and medical supplies to Zaire, and the Carter administration
thus became engaged in its first foreign conflict. Even then, Secretary of
State Cyrus Vance sought to minimize the danger involved by stating that there
was no evidence that Cubans were participating in the incursion. Mobutu later
publicly decried the limited support provided by the United States, claiming
that it showed weakness in the face of Soviet-Cuban willpower and strength.
Indeed, considering the extent of U.S. involvement in Zaire over the years,
Mobutu might have expected the United States to be more forthcoming. At the
time, U.S. banks, led by Citibank, were deeply involved in attempts to head
off bankruptcy by the debt-ridden Zairian government. Irving Freidman,
Citibank's senior international adviser, had recently paid a visit to Kinshasa

and worked out an arrangement between Zaire and its creditors to keep Zaire from defaulting on its massive loans (see Chapter 1; also Belliveau 1977, pp. 23-27).

Several factors contributed to the administration's decision to assume a low profile. Not the least of these was the U.S. public mood, which had already resisted involvement in the Angolan civil war. The administration was itself involved in a wide-ranging reevaluation of its African policy. The broad outlines of a new approach were just emerging when the hostilities began. Undersecretary of State Philip Habib, testifying before a congressional committee on March 3, 1977, had hinted at a kind of "Africa for the Africans" principle. Neither the United States nor any other foreign power, he said, should try to impose its ideas and solutions on the African people. In the Congress there was resistance to giving additional aid to a regime that was seen as both dictatorial and corrupt.

The most plausible explanation for the U.S. role was that decision makers in the administration calculated that U.S. objectives could be achieved through cooperation with European allies and moderate African states whose interests were also at stake. This was borne out by the entry of Morocco and France on the side of the Mobutu regime. On March 25 Zaire's foreign minister visited Rabat and briefed King Hassan II on the deteriorating situation in Shaba. Even though no significant fighting had yet been reported, nearly one-third of the province fell into rebel hands by the end of the month. Within two weeks of the meeting in Rabat, the Moroccan government dispatched 250 troops to Kinshasa.

In taking the lead among African states in support of Mobutu, Hassan clearly hoped to enhance his standing as a leader among the moderates. Moroccan troops had been instrumental in the UN operations during the Katangan secession of the early 1960s; some of the veterans of that campaign were among those sent in April 1977 to Shaba. It is most likely that Hassan had received assurances of financial and military aid from various sources before undertaking the Zaire mission. Although the State Department disavowed any advance consultation with Morocco, including any request for permission to use U.S.-made military equipment in Zaire, the Moroccan government had long enjoyed a close relationship with the United States. During the current fiscal year, U.S. military sales credits to Morocco amounted to $30 million. King Hassan could also count on financial support from oil-producing Arab states as well. By far the most significant measure of assurance came from the French government, which agreed to underwrite the mission with logistical aid (Washington Post, April 8, 1977).

The French role was decisive in saving the Mobutu regime. In recent years, France had shown an increasing interest in Zaire. President Giscard d'Estaing had shown a particular fascination for Mobutu, paying him a visit in 1975 and observing the mutual political and cultural interests of the two countries. Although not a member of NATO, France supported the Belgians in urging diplomatic and military sessions in early March to discuss the Zaire situation. Because the United States seemed to be dragging its feet, and the prospect of any intervention under the auspices of the Organization of

African Unity was remote. Giscard stepped into the breach. On March 23 he sent René Journiac, a former colleague of Jacques Foccart, the powerful head of the French Secret Service, to Kinshasa (Le Nouvel Observateur, April 18, 1977). Journiac met twice with Mobutu, who pleaded for French aid, saying that he counted more upon France than on any other nation. There followed a lengthy meeting between Journiac and Undersecretary of State Habib in Paris, which in turn was followed by a meeting between Giscard and Secretary of State Vance on April 2. After a few days of three-way telephone communication between Kinshasa, Paris, and Rabat, Giscard gave the green light for a Shaba mission. Paris claimed to have informed Washington of its decision in advance, but the State Department denied any "coordination" with the French.

On April 10 the Elysée announced that it had placed ten Transall cargo planes and a DC-8 at the disposition of Morocco to facilitate its Zaire operation (Le Monde Hebdomadaire, April 7-13, 1977). It stated that the planes were carrying equipment and Moroccan military materiel but no soldiers. However, Zairian sources attested to the fact that the French planes were transporting Moroccan troops. By the end of May, the Franco-Moroccan mission had turned the tide and the Moroccan government was able to announce that its troops were being withdrawn.

The French scored a propaganda coup during the Shaba mission when the fourth Franco-African summit conference was held in Dakar April 19 and 20. The purpose of the conference was to discuss a proposed joint African defense force designed to "impede foreign intervention" (Le Monde Hebdomadaire, April 21-27, 1977). Many of the participants at the conference, most of them from former French colonies, expressed their gratitude toward France for having demonstrated its support for African "solidarity." Zaire's foreign minister, Nguza Karl-I-Bond, in particular thanked President Giscard for his aid. The final communiqué that emerged from the Dakar conference indicated the desire of the participants to create a formal structure grouping the Francophone heads of state in order to maintain mutual security. Although this idea remained vague and undefined, Giscard promised to step up French contributions to the special African solidarity fund established the previous year.

The Belgian role in the first Shaba crisis was quite restrained, in view of its history as the former colonial power and its continued economic and cultural interests in Zaire. To be sure, the Socialist party government of Prime Minister Leo Tindemans was the first, actually, to send aid to Mobutu in the form of light arms. It lent a degree of moral support by urging the 30,000 Belgian citizens residing in Zaire, including the 3,000 in the disputed mining town of Kolwezi, to remain in the country. At the same time, U.S. nationals were being pulled out of the contested areas. Nevertheless, the Belgians did not take the leading role one might have expected.

The Belgian aloofness may be explained in part by the fact that the program of nationalization unleashed by Mobutu in 1973 greatly affected Belgian interests. This was but another instance in a long history of vexations he had provided the Belgians in the struggle for economic independence. During the early days of the crisis, there were rumors in European circles to the effect that Brussels would not mind terribly if Mobutu fell. Belgium was preparing for national elections at the time of the crisis, and Tindemans was attempting to keep his coalition government in power. His own Socialist party was concerned with not giving the opposition a campaign issue. In ceding the principal role in the save-Mobutu mission to the French, the Belgians were able to complain publicly that France was overly eager to gain a greater share of Zaire's riches.

Less than 14 months after the beginning of the first Shaba crisis, the rebel troops of FLNC, the bête noire of the Mobutu regime, opened up a second offensive. On May 11, 1978, they began occupying key mining and railway towns in Shaba province (see Hull 1978a). The Zaire news agency AZAP initially reported that Zairian troops had beat back a rebel attack on the railway center of Mutchatsha by "Katangese gendarmes" aided by "whites who have been identified as Cubans." It also reported that an attack involving 4,000 rebels was launched on the key mining town of Kolwezi. AZAP alleged that the offensive, code name "Operation Dove," had been conceived "in Havana and perfected in Algiers where the rebels were trained." The Western press picked up the allegation, reporting yet another "invasion" of Zaire by "communist-backed Katangese."

The 9,000 government troops of the highly touted Kamanyola Brigade sent to Shaba province after the first invasion proved ineffective in repulsing rebel advances. Within days it was reported that Kolwezi had fallen to the rebels and that they were advancing toward the strategic airbase at Kamina to the north. It was estimated that some 2,500 Europeans in Kolwezi were being held captive, most of them Belgian technicians employed by the mining companies. Their number included some 400 French nationals as well as Americans and Britons (Hull 1978a).

Thus the stage was set for a familiar unfolding of events. The Mobutu regime, helpless to defend itself, called upon its friends in the West to beat back the Soviet-Cuban communist menace. The setting varied only slightly from that of the year before. This time, however, the consequences were considerably more tragic. Already over 200,000 refugees had fled Shaba province into Angola to escape retribution at the hands of Mobutu's ill-trained and undisciplined troops following the failure of the first "invasion." Shaba II was to claim hundreds of innocent (and not so innocent) victims.

The response from Mobutu's friends this time was much more swift and decisive. The West was becoming increasingly apprehensive about the Soviet-Cuban presence in Africa. Giscard, the leading man in the drama of Shaba I, had just emerged victorious in a life-and-death struggle against the Left in the French elections and was more eager than ever to pursue his version of "la mission civilisatrice." The Carter administration, under the influence of Zbigniew Brzezinski, was now in a less conciliatory mood toward the Soviet-Cuban presence than it had been a year before.

The turn of events in Shaba II hinged on the perceived threat to the lives of the Europeans. There were conflicting and sketchy reports filtering out of Kolwezi as to what exactly had happened. A Zairian exile group in Belgium published an extensive report, "Kolwezi '78," in which it was argued that the first

two or three days of the occupation of Kolwezi by the rebels were characterized by "correct and disciplined" behavior (Comité Zaire 1978b, pp. 4-7).
The report concludes that it was in fact Zairian soldiers who first opened fire
on Europeans and that Zairian army Mirages bombarded the African section
of the city.

Whatever the truth of the matter, the reports of Europeans being killed
triggered immediate response. The Pentagon placed the Eighty-second Air-
borne unit on alert, the first such action taken by the Carter administration.
The following day, May 18, the State Department announced that 77 U.S. nationals, most of them employees of a mining construction firm, had been
evacuated from Kolwezi. The administration also stepped up the delivery of
$17.5 million in "nonlethal" military aid to Zaire, consisting of medical sup-
plies, petroleum, and air transport. The Belgians and French sprang quickly
into action. Waves of Hercules C-130 transports loaded with 1,750 Belgian
soldiers left Brussels for Kamina as French Foreign Legionnaires left Cor-
sica en route to Kolwezi via Kinshasa. Belgian Prime Minister Tindemans
described the Belgian operation as purely humanitarian, intended to save expatriate lives, while imputing less noble motives to the French operation.
Between 600 and 1,000 French legionnaires were dropped on Kolwezi. As
word of the Franco-Belgian intervention arrived in the city, the civilian death
toll mounted, final estimates reaching over 800, of whom as many as 200
were European. Within a few days the Belgian troops, followed by the French,
began their exit from the city, having driven the rebels into the bush (Hull
1978b, p. 18).

Just as in the wake of the first Shaba crisis, a Franco-African conference was held in Paris beginning one week after the occupation of Kolwezi by
the rebels. Again discussion turned on the urgent need for an inter-African
peace-keeping force. In early June, following a meeting of the Western powers in Paris to determine how best to confront the tenuous situation in Shaba,
a plan was put into effect that was to result in the virtual occupation of Zaire
by foreign troops for an indefinite period of time. French troops were to be
replaced by an inter-African force, initially composed of 1,500 Moroccans
transported by U.S. planes. They were soon joined by troops from Senegal,
the Central African Empire, Togo, Gabon, and Egypt—a total of over 2,500
(see Comité Zaire for a chronology of events [1978b, pp. 13-17]).

The Western-backed plan for the inter-African occupation of Zaire
was met by undisguised indignation on the part of progressive African states.
In a special message to the press on June 8, 1978, President Julius Nyerere
of Tanzania vehemently denounced the plan, accusing Western powers of seeking to recolonize Africa (Washington Post, June 9, 1978). With obvious reference to Zaire, Nyerere declared: "We must reject the principle that external powers have the right to maintain in power African governments which are
universally recognized to be corrupt, or incompetent, or a bunch of murderers,
when their people try to make a change."

Nyerere's cry went unheeded. Nearly a year after the second Shaba crisis, and long after the governments of Zaire and Angola agreed to normalize
relations and restrain their respective rebel groups, the inter-African force

still occupied Shaba province (New York Times, February 4, 1979). The predominantly Moroccan and Senegalese force had taken over the basic functions of law and order. In February 1979 the Belgian government decided to send back 250 paratroopers to Zaire, ostensibly to protect the white communities of Kinshasa and Bukavu, neither of them located in Shaba province (Washington Post, February 7, 1979). The decision was reportedly made because of increasing disorder and violence in the two cities and the presumed threat to European lives. With this action, even the pretense of the inter-African nature of the occupying force had to be dropped.

While Belgian and U.S. actions in the Shaba crises may be understood in terms of traditional interests in Zaire, the French role merits closer attention (Hull 1978b). Why should France have taken such bold and assertive measures in an area outside its traditional sphere of influence? French investments in Zaire are quite limited: $20 million, compared with $60 million for Great Britain, $80 million for West Germany, and over $800 million for Belgium. French government investments consist mainly of short-term loans, a domestic satellite, equipment for the Voice of Zaire, and a few Mirage jets. Private investments are limited to a few factories, bank loans, and a relatively small (6.4 percent interest) participation of two French groups in the mining company, Société Minière de Tenke Fungurume (SMTF), which operates in Shaba.

France imports most of its copper needs from Mexico and Zambia and cobalt from Morocco. Although most of Zaire's copper goes to Europe (mainly Belgium), little of it reaches France and virtually none is imported by the United States. Cobalt, on the other hand, is a critical raw material, even more important then copper, to an understanding of foreign interests in Zaire. While Zaire produces only 6 percent of the world's copper, it accounts for about 35 to 40 percent of the total cobalt production. The United States imports 98 percent of its requirements in cobalt, 70 percent of it either directly or indirectly from Zaire. Cobalt is one of seven critical raw materials in which U.S. industry is vulnerable to imports. Hence the question of French involvement in Zaire in terms of key strategic raw materials hinges on the extent to which French interests are tied to and dominated by the United States and the extent to which the United States is dependent upon Zaire for its mineral needs (Charles Rivers Associates 1977).

In terms of trade, France has also played a rather marginal role in Zaire. In recent years, however, there has been a noticeable increase in both absolute and relative terms (Van Der Steen 1977). By 1976 France had become Zaire's second most important importer after Belgium. Zaire's exports to France as a percentage of the total showed a slight decline from 11 percent in 1968 to 7 percent in 1975.

Officially, French policy in Africa is summed in the slogan "Africa for the Africans." This is interpreted to mean that Africans must be able to settle their differences without the interference of "foreign powers lacking ties with Africa, and who try to introduce ideologies alien to the continent" (Hull 1978b, p. 11). Giscard explained French intervention in the first Shaba crisis in terms of helping Zaire to defend its security against elements coming from the outside. He also invoked the principle of solidarity by which he meant the special relationship of Europe to Africa. During the second crisis, another justification was added: the defense of the lives of French nationals.

Most press accounts of the Shaba crises tended to explain the events in terms of political and ideological considerations as well. Crawford Young (1978) lent his weight to this interpretation. In his discussion of the "unending crisis" in Zaire, Young concluded that "economic calculations played a much lesser role than political motivations in the Shaba crises" (pp. 180-81). He argued that the gestures of support for Zaire from such disparate countries as China, Iran, and Egypt, as well as the moderate Francophone states, were stimulated by their fear of the "evil hand of social imperialism." French motives, Young maintained, were explained in terms of the personal relationship between Giscard and Mobutu and the French desire to prove to moderate African states that they could rely on the protection of Paris.

The Young thesis tends to minimize rather significant economic aspects of international relations. Beyond the facts of the economic domination of France by the United States and the interrelatedness of the two nations' interests in Zaire, there were also important economic relationships with such countries as Saudi Arabia and South Africa in the picture. France relies heavily upon Saudi Arabia for oil imports and on South Africa for a variety of minerals, including uranium. Both of these countries saw it in their national interests to support the Mobutu regime.

CONCLUSION

This chapter has examined the relationship of Zaire in the nation-state system and its search for national sovereignty. In spite of the Mobutu regime's avowed intention to assert its economic independence in the world system, it has not only ceded decision-making authority in financial and economic matters to international agents but has seen decline in its ability to perform basic politico-administrative and military functions of a sovereign state. Zaire under Mobutu has submitted to a process of recolonization, placing itself in virtual tutelage of foreign powers. In effect, there exists in Zaire a symbiotic rapport between these powers and a corrupt and inefficient politico-administrative bourgeoisie, which explains the regime's willingness to allow foreign powers to perform the functions of the state in their own interests rather than the national interest.

Among the events of 1976 to 1978 were the three clearest demonstrations of Mobutu's willingness to surrender ever more sovereignty in order to retain at least some of the political and economic rewards of power.

Economic and Financial Management

In an unprecedented move, the Mobutu regime, in the summer of 1978, submitted to outright control by agents of the International Monetary Fund of the management of its economic and financial affairs (Africa Confidential 1979). Not only has the process of economic nationalization launched in 1973 proved to be an utter failure but Zaire also has succumbed to pressure from its international creditors to face up to its enormous indebtedness. The IMF team's mission in Zaire was to attack the corruption and privilege in high places that have cost the country hundreds of millions of dollars a year. Mobutu understands that the IMF holds the key to Zaire's economic future, that it represents the last hope for recovery. The country's massive aid and credit schemes are entirely dependent upon the government's compliance with IMF guidelines, which are monitored by its agents. Failing this, funds for the proposed stabilization plan will not (in theory) be forthcoming.

The IMF team's primary role in 1978, and very likely beyond, was to oversee credit and foreign exchange procedures that were flagrantly abused in the past. Foreign exchange from exports were to be strictly allotted to certain sectors of the economy. A third of it was to be held by the Central Bank to begin paying off the country's outstanding debts. The rest was to be passed on to commercial banks, which may spend it on priority items, such as food imports, pharmaceuticals, and vital consumer products. Only a tiny fraction was to go for the purchase of petroleum products (Africa Confidential 1979).

The degree to which expatriates were implanted to oversee the operations of the nation's banking and financial institutions represents the most rigorous set of conditions ever imposed on an IMF member (Africa Confidential 1979). In light of mounting internal political unrest and the regime's increasing dependence upon world economic forces, Mobutu has no option but to comply with IMF decisions. In doing so, at least in principle, Mobutu has not hesitated to sacrifice some trusted and loyal members of his political and bureaucratic elite. Even then, he has managed to favor those he considers essential to the maintenance of the established order.

Political and Military Administration

In the aftermath of two successive "invasions" of Shaba province, Zaire has submitted to open-ended occupation by foreign troops. Although the threat of invasion has been withdrawn with the normalization of relations with neighboring Angola, Shaba province is still being patrolled by a 2,500-strong inter-African peace-keeping force (New York Times, February 4, 1979). Zairian soldiers remain undisciplined and unreliable. The occupying force has virtually taken over the normal functions of maintaining law and order. There are reports that Zairian soldiers have been disarmed by Moroccan and Senegalese troops. There is no indication that Mobutu has attempted to reconcile the opposition groups involved in previous "invasions," thus ensuring the necessity for continued dependence on foreign troops for the maintenance of political order.

Both the French and Belgians have undertaken training programs for Zairian military personnel, but without any salutory results. The Zairian army is still rendered ineffective because of corruption among senior officers and chronic food shortages and lack of pay among the ranks. The Belgian decision to send paratroops to Zaire one year after the second Shaba crisis was a clear indication that even the inter-African force was insufficient to protect vital interests of foreign powers. In the absence of reliable security measures, the mining industry has been unable to induce enough foreign experts to return to Kolwezi to ensure mining operations.

The OTRAG Concession

In one instance the Mobutu regime has in fact relinquished all aspects of sovereignty over an area of 150,000 square kilometers in northeastern Shaba province (see Chapter 11). On March 26, 1976, Mobutu signed a contract with a West German-based firm known as OTRAG (Orbital Transport und Raketen A.G.). As Allen Roberts points out in Chapter 11, the terms of the contract are truly remarkable. OTRAG has the right to use the territory without restriction for the ostensible purpose of launching missiles into the atmosphere. The only other such infringement on the rights of a sovereign state is to be found in the 1903 Panama Canal Treaty.

Although OTRAG maintains that the project is strictly commercial and that it has no military implications, a number of progressive African states have expressed their suspicion that it might somehow be related to the defense of South Africa. The West Germans have secretly discussed nuclear cooperation with South Africa in recent years. This raises fears that the OTRAG project is part of a NATO plot, aided by the CIA, to help the West Germans develop a cruise missile that could be used against the progressive countries surrounding South Africa.

No other instance of the Mobutu regime's ceding of Zairian sovereignty has been so blatantly tied to the president's own personal interests. Mobutu was personally given 47 percent of the profits from the aviation subsidiary of OTRAG that transports materiel to the site in Shaba province. There is also reason to believe that Mobutu chose the Shaba site for political and strategic purposes, hoping once again to draw upon the aid of foreign friends to bring stability to a troubled country.

This chapter also has outlined the interests of Western powers and their allies in Zaire that explain their continued willingness to prop up the Mobutu regime. Only Belgium among the traditional friends of Mobutu has shown a degree of reluctance to defend the regime at all costs. Despite congressional questioning of U.S. programs of assistance to Zaire, U.S. policy has remained essentially pro-Mobutu, avowedly for lack of any viable political alternative. Meanwhile, as 1979 begins, France continues to enjoy a special relationship with the Mobutu regime because of its key role in saving the regime on two successive occasions. After all, as Giscard has pointed out himself, it is only fitting and proper for the world's two largest Francophone countries to be on cordial terms. For the Zairian people, it does not matter which elephants are playing in the grass.

REFERENCES

Africa Confidential. 1979. "Zaire: Can the IMF Succeed?" 20, no. 1 (January 3): 1-5.

Africa Contemporary Records: Annual Survey and Documents 1976-77. 1977. Edited by Colin Legum. New York: Africana Publishing.

Belliveau, Nancy. 1977. "Heading off Zaire's Default." Institutional Investor, March, pp. 23-27.

Charles Rivers Associates. 1977. "Implications of the War in Zaire for the Cobalt Market." Paper prepared under contract for the U.S. Department of Interior, June.

Comité Zaire. 1978a. Zaire: Le dossier de la recolonisation. Paris: Editions l'Harmattan.

_____. 1978b. "Kolwezi '78." InfoZaire, no. 5 (July-August).

Hull, Galen. 1978a. "Mobutu Regime Crumbles: West to the Rescue." In These Times 2, no. 29 (June): 7-13.

_____. 1978b. "The French Connection in Africa: Zaire and South Africa." Paper presented at the African Studies Association meeting, Baltimore, November 4.

_____. 1977. "Whose Victory in Shaba?" Africa Report, July-August, pp. 4-9.

Kabwit, Ghislain. 1976. "Zaire's Foreign Policy in the 70's." Paper presented at the African Studies Association meeting, Boston, November 3-6.

Nyerere, Julius. 1978. Press release delivered on June 8 to foreign envoys accredited to Tanzania concerning recent events in Africa, issued by the Embassy of Tanzania in Washington, D.C.

Nzongola, Ntalaja. 1978. "The U.S., Zaire and Angola." In American Foreign Policy in Southern Africa: The Stakes and the Stance, edited by René Lemarchand, pp. 145-70. Washington, D.C.: University Press of America.

Odier, Jeannick. 1975. "La politique étrangère de Mobutu." Revue française d'études politiques africaines 120 (December): 25-41.

Radmann, Wolf. 1978. "The Nationalization of Zaire's Copper: From Union Minière to GECAMINES." Africa Today 25, no. 4 (October–December): 25–47.

Umba di Lutete. 1978. "The Foreign Policy of Zaire." Address of the State Commissioner of Foreign Affairs and International Cooperation, Georgetown University, Center for Strategic Studies, October 9.

Van Der Steen, Daniel. 1977. "Echanges economiques extérieurs du Zaire: Dépendance et développement." Cahiers du CEDAF, no. 4–5.

Weissman, Stephen R. 1978. "The C.I.A. and U.S. Policy in Zaire and Angola." In American Foreign Policy in Southern Africa: The Stakes and the Stance, edited by René Lemarchand, pp. 383–432. Washington, D.C.: University Press of America.

_____. 1974. American Foreign Policy in the Congo 1960–1964. Ithaca, N.Y.: Cornell University Press.

Willame, Jean Claude. 1978. "La second guerre du Shaba." Enquêtes et documents d'histoire africaine, no. 3. Leuven, Belgium. Centre d'Histoire de l'Afrique.

Young, Crawford. 1978. "Zaire: The Unending Crisis." Foreign Affairs 57, no. 1 (Fall): 169–85.

14

THE GROWTH OF INTERNAL AND EXTERNAL OPPOSITION TO THE MOBUTU REGIME

Ghislain Kabwit

On November 24, 1965, Lt. Gen. Joseph Desiré Mobutu, commander of the Armée Nationale Congolaise (ANC), seized power in a bloodless coup d'etat in Leopoldville. He dismissed President Joseph Kasavubu (the father of Congolese independence) and the Kimba government by decree and assumed the presidency for five years. The coup was virtually without incident. Mobutu told the press that his action was not a military coup, but a duty performed to save the country from anarchy and chaos (Mobutu 1966).

His speeches were received with great enthusiasm and relief, as many people were becoming increasingly alarmed by the possibility of further civil war generated by the feud between Moise Tshombe and Kasavubu and their followers. Each of them was trying to become the next president of the Congo. Under the new constitution of 1964, the impending presidential elections were supposed to take place six months after the convening of the new Parliament, that is, in March 1966. Thus the military intervention tended to be viewed by the Congolese masses as a lesser evil (Centre de Recherche et l'Information Socio-Politiques 1967).

It should be pointed out at the outset that the Mobutu regime enjoyed considerable popularity in its early years because it held the promise of peace and stability. The regime also conveyed a deceptive early impression "of solving the material problems which mattered the most to each of the relevant social forces. Everyone seemed to like the idea of having a strong national leader serving as a neutral arbitrator and a reconciler" (Nzongola 1978, pp. 12-13).

However, it did not take long for some to see through the contradictions of the new regime. The sources of opposition to the Mobutu regime since the beginning are to be found in the autocratic and predatory nature of his regime. This chapter proposes to undertake an historical overview of the major forces that manifested this opposition and gave evidence to the decline of the regime's popularity. By the late 1970s, with its loss of legitimacy confirmed and demonstrated, the Mobutu regime has turned more and more to harsh economic measures to control growing internal and external opposition that is challenging its very existence. This in turn encouraged further opposition and restiveness on the part of the population, by no means limited to the Shaba I and II crises. It seems evident that radical change at the top is inevitable.

THE STUDENTS' RECURRING
CONFLICTS WITH THE MOBUTU REGIME

Zairian students had always maintained powerful student organizations prior to Mobutu's seizure of power in 1965. In the aftermath of independence, the well-known Congolese student associations were AGEL (Association Générale des Etudiants de Lovanium) and UGEC (Union Générale des Etudiants Congolais). The latter was the more influential. It was recognized worldwide, for it had active chapters in Belgium, France, West Germany, Canada, and the United States. Despite the creation of a one-party system, the Mouvement Populaire de la Révolution (MPR) and its subsequent youth wing, the Jeunesse du Mouvement Populaire de la Révolution (JMPR), UGEC, maintained from the first its independence and distance vis-à-vis Mobutu and his JMPR.

In 1967 UGEC denounced in strong terms the Mobutu regime for what it saw as a "total lack of personal liberty in the country." It blamed the regime for being under the orders of "the imperialists and neocolonialist forces." Tense relations developed between UGEC and MPR. In January 1968 Lovanium students unexpectedly staged a noisy demonstration against the visit of Hubert Humphrey, then vice-president of the United States, whom they accused of high hypocrisy for having laid flowers in front of the Lumumba Memorial. In the students' eyes, the United States had been implicated in the murder of Patrice Lumumba, and so Humphrey's gesture was considered most inappropriate. Some students were arrested and later released. However, the government ordered the reconstitution of UGEC, which was still seen by the regime as the center of Marxist and Maoist ideas (Comité Zaire 1978, p. 238).

The latent tension between the students and the government suddenly erupted in the open on June 4, 1969. According to published reports, several hundred students, dissatisfied with the insufficient living allowances provided by the state, inflated prices of commodities, and what they considered extravagant expenditures by Mobutu's government, and frustrated by empty promises made by the government to take care of their particular problems, marched from Lovanium University into the center of Kinshasa to demonstrate their grievances. In the ensuing melee, a violent confrontation with a unit of the national army, panicky soldiers opened fire on unarmed students, killing between 40 and 60. The exact toll was not known because to avoid bad publicity the government ordered a secret burial (Klein 1970, p. 10). Other sources have advanced higher casualty figures. A Belgian doctor who treated the wounded counted 112 dead, among them 68 civilians (Chomé 1975, p. 185). A peaceful protest march had turned into a massacre of students.

Meanwhile, the regime closed Lovanium University and banned all student organizations except JMPR. However, student sympathy strikes shut down all the institutions of higher learning in Kinshasa, Lubumbashi, and Kisangani. About 500 students were arrested and others were confined to the campus or shipped to their homes. All the students were subsequently released except 34 ringleaders, who were charged with subversive activities against the security of the state; they were tried and given sentences varying from 2 to 20 years in jail. However, on October 14, 1969, the president pardoned the students and allowed them to return to school. It seemed that Mobutu had reacted too harshly against the students when there was no clear reason to believe that the regime was being threatened. Nevertheless, true to his nature as an autocrat, Mobutu chose not to take any chances (Klein 1970, pp. 10–12).

The government then ordered the restructuring of the university system in order to disperse the students and to tighten control over the central administration of the three existing institutions. In the summer of 1970, the government decreed that Lovanium University (Kinshasa), the State University of the Congo (Lubumbashi), and the Free Congo University (Kisangani) were to be consolidated into one national university with three campuses, later known as Université Nationale du Zaire, or UNAZA (see Chapter 8).

Mobutu's recurring battle with the students erupted again the year following the creation of UNAZA. Lovanium students wanted to commemorate the fourth of June as the unofficial day of martyrdom for freedom against Mobutu's dictatorship and reign of terror. The ceremonies were to take place within the confines of the university. The government reacted with its characteristic harshness. It ordered the university closed and all students sent into the army, supposedly "to learn military discipline." The students were brutally arrested and then taken to paratrooper training camps at Ndjili. Some were reported to have been beaten the whole night. Of 3,007 students registered at UNAZA-Kinshasa (Lovanium), 2,887 were summarily conscripted into the Zairian army, as were a large number of students from UNAZA-Lubumbashi (Chomé 1975, pp. 186–87). Since that incident, the Zairian students have never been at ease with the Mobutu regime. Incidents continue in the early months of 1979.

THE CHURCH-STATE CONFLICT

President Mobutu's running battle with the Catholic church came to a head during the radicalization process launched with great fanfare on January 4, 1975. At its root were the regime's efforts to crush all resistance and to make the power of the president complete. The church's opposition to Mobutu, however, began earlier during the introduction of the doctrine of Zairian "authenticity" in 1971.

In October 1971 President Joseph Desiré Mobutu changed the name of the country from Congo-Kinshasa to Zaire, a misnomer the Portuguese Diogo Cão gave to the mouth of the Congo River, locally known as "Nzadi." The Congo River became the Zaire River. Along the same lines, a new MPR green flag was adopted as a symbol of a new nation. Toward the end of 1971, General Mobutu changed his name to Mobutu Sese Seko. Not long afterward, all Zairians were urged, later required, to abandon their former Christian names and to adopt authentic Zairian ones. The government's move led to a clash with the powerful and influential Catholic church, which attempted to no avail to resist these unwarranted changes. The Catholic church's hierarchy questioned the foundations of the doctrine of authenticity and wanted to know whether a modern nation-state could be run on a traditional village model advocated by the regime's spokesman. The struggle for influence in Zaire ultimately led to the forced exile of Cardinal Joseph Malula, who fled to Rome for his personal safety (Adelman 1975).

In 1975 the simmering conflict suddenly erupted in public. The Mobutu government announced that all mission schools would be put under state control. Those that resisted the edict would simply be closed down. In addition, Mobutu outlawed the teaching of religion in all schools and said that "Mobutism," simply defined as "the teachings, thoughts and actions of Mobutu," would be taught instead. It was not clear to what extent these measures were to be implemented on a nationwide basis, considering the basic reality that virtually the entire elementary and secondary school system was run by the church, overwhelmingly the Catholic church. As expected, the Catholic church adamantly refused to have anything to do with the administration of state schools, although the small Protestant and Kimbanguist sects attempted to cooperate with the government on the new ruling. In an open letter to their missions, the country's 25 Catholic bishops charged the government with the suppression of religion and vowed to continue speaking out on this crucial issue (Africa Report 1975, pp. 2-3). Needless to say, Mobutu could afford to confront the powerful Catholic church only as long as he was politically unchallengeable. But, by 1976, Mobutu's popularity was at a lower and lower ebb. The Catholic bishops used the pulpit and went on the offensive. Decrying the ills plaguing Zaire under Mobutu, Archbishop Eugene Kabanga, in a 1976 pastoral letter to his diocese of Lubumbashi, said: "In the past the colonizers crushed our dignity as human beings and as Africans. Today our situation is much worse, brought about by the behavior of our own brothers" (Miso Gaa 1976, p. 12). It was reported that Mobutu was outraged by this stinging attack but was powerless to silence the archbishop.

Weakened by his disastrous intervention in Angola on behalf of the Frente Nacional de Libertação de Angola and the União Nacional para Independência Total de Angola, and saddled with monumental economic and financial woes, Mobutu finally decided to launch a reconciliation between his government and the church in 1976. An official circular went out to the civil servants, stressing dialogue rather than confrontation. It also stated that "bishops should be consulted as a matter of course." Cardinal Malula, a "villain" forced to flee to Rome for his safety in 1973, returned and was installed in a new residence. Mobutu restored to him the Order of the Leopard, the national honor Mobutu had taken back at the height of their quarrel. Here was yet another example of one of the basic contradictions of the Mobutu regime: the government's tendency to make radical decisions, then quietly backing down when its changes failed to work out (Randall 1976, p. 1).

Not surprisingly, in September 1976, the Mobutu government, after a stormy meeting with the Catholic bishops, was finally forced to return all previous mission schools to their respective churches. It was widely reported by the local press that, between 1975 and 1976, discipline had broken down in schools, academic standards had dropped, some directors were corrupting young girls by forcing them to sleep with them before they could advance in their studies, and some teachers were openly consuming alcoholic beverages on the school premises. However, before the bishops would agree to take back the schools, they made it clear to Mobutu that religion would be taught and that moral excesses and corruption would no longer be tolerated in the school system (Miso Gaa 1975, pp. 4, 7).

Having been muzzled by Mobutu since 1975, when the government announced that it was taking over all church-run schools, the powerful Council of Catholic Bishops went public in the wake of the Shaba II crisis by issuing a public condemnation of the Mobutu regime in August 1978. Decrying what it called "the basic failures of the national institutions to live up to the moral ethics and standards," and thus contributing to "le mal Zairois" (the Zairian sickness), the council called the political authorities to work together with the Zairian people to strive for the larger goal of national reconciliation and recovery (Miso Gaa 1978, pp. 1, 3, 5, 7, 12). After having been on the sidelines for many years, the church had unmistakably joined the growing popular opposition against the corrupt regime of President Mobutu.

EXTERNAL OPPOSITION: EXILE GROUPS IN ACTION

Since coming to power in November 1965, Mobutu has ruled Zaire with an iron fist. Opposition has been swiftly and ruthlessly dealt with. From the outset, his basic power has stemmed from his iron grip over the army, numbering today about 40,000. The totalitarian nature of the regime ultimately impeded the efforts of the internal opposition to mobilize the masses to oppose the creation of a one-man government. Therefore it is no exaggeration to state that the years since the late 1960s have been years of trials and tribulations for the Zairian internal opposition. Many of those who could not join the new order were forced to flee into exile abroad.

By January 1975, President Mobutu, after a ten-year rule, was at the zenith of his political power. Credit must be given to him for having united the country and having held it together. In many political circles, the pre-1965 Congo was synonymous with chaos. To be sure, this involved a tremendous concentration of power in one man symbolized by the presidential father figure.

Over this decade regional separation and political and military opposition were effectively dealt with, and the MPR had become the sole political party. Most of Mobutu's vocal opponents were dead, in jail, or in exile. Other potential sources of opposition or disunity were either crushed or brought within the controlled framework of the MPR. For instance, the rebellious and independent-minded trade unions were tamed and their leaders were incorporated into the MPR and the Political Bureau of the party. Recurring troubles with university students were harshly dealt with by killing some, arresting others, and sending the rest into the army. Both the army and potential political opponents were kept under surveillance by the Centre National de Documentation (CND)—Mobutu's secret police. All organized women's activities and youth came under the umbrella of the MPR. No other political activity was allowed to operate without the blessing of the party. Finally, as just discussed, the Mobutu regime launched a campaign to neutralize the Catholic church as a potential political force in the country.

Nonetheless, this facade of unity and stability under the umbrella of the MPR masked basic structural weaknesses. In the mid-1970s, the seemingly secure political system started showing cracks. The famous case of "le coup d'etat monté et manqué" (alleged attempted coup d'etat) in June 1975 during which the U.S. ambassador, Deane Hinton, was dramatically expelled from Zaire for allegedly directing the coup against Mobutu began to expose the myth of stability to the outside world. It clearly demonstrated that the loyalty of the amry's officers was questionable. It also gave the Zairian external opposition to the Mobutu regime a needed wedge.

Up to this point, the Zairian exile opposition to the Mobutu regime, some elements of which began in the mid- and late 1960s, had had a difficult time against the obstacles just cited. Unable to organize at home, the opposition did find fertile grounds in Western Europe, specifically in Belgium. There, because of historical and colonial ties, it was treated with considerable sympathy over many years.

In the late 1970s, one can define a cluster of political groups in opposition to Mobutu's government, most of them operating from Western Europe, especially from Brussels and Paris. Three major opposition groups have been identified by European political observers (Le Monde, March 30, 1977).

The first group, known as the Rassemblement des Congolais Progressistes (RCP), consisted of the Front for the National Liberation of the Congo (FLNC) and the Mouvement d'Action pour la Resurrection du Congo (MARC). A spokesman of FNLC, which claimed responsibility for the invasion in the Shaba I crisis, said that the FNLC insurgents were neither gendarmes, Katangese, nor secessionists." The FLNC chief has been Nathaniel Mbumba. He was a police officer in Shaba province until 1967 when he was arrested and beaten for having himself intervened in what he thought was an illegal arrest. Having escaped to Angola, he founded the FLNC in 1968. According to its statutes, the FLNC was to be a "revolutionary and progressive movement" with politico-military discipline and integrated with the masses (Afrique-Asie 1977).

MARC is centered in Brussels and publishes a newsletter, Miso Gaa (Open Your Eyes). It was led by Kanyonga Mobateli until 1978, when he was killed during Shaba II in mysterious circumstances. He was found in Brussels with a bullet in the head; Mobutu's secret agents were suspected of foul play. The group is now led by Daniel Monguya Mbenge, who detailed much of Mobutu's corruption in a recent (1977) book.

The second group was made up of the Front Socialiste Africain (FSA) and other smaller groups. The FSA was led by Cléophas Kamitatu and operated from Paris. Kamitatu, a former minister of the interior in the Congo, was imprisoned by Mobutu in June 1966 during the infamous public hangings known as Les Conjurés de Pentecote, was freed in 1967, but was almost rearrested in 1970 when he fled into exile in France. There he published in 1971 a very critical book entitled La grande mystification du Congo-Kinshasa: Les crimes de Mobutu. The FSA was obviously anti-Mobutu and offered to cooperate with the RCP. In early 1977 he published another, comparably critical work. Then, to general public astonishment, Kamitatu announced in July 1977 that he was returning to Zaire to work with Mobutu to improve the economic situation. His departure signified the demise of the FSA as a significant opposition group.

A third major group, called Forces Democratiques pour la Liberation du Congo (FODELICO), is led by Antoine Gizenga, former vice-prime minister in the government of Patrice Lumumba. Following the assassination of Lumumba in 1961, Gizenga installed a government in Stanleyville for a short period of time. He remained in jail from 1961 to 1964 until he was released by Tshombe, and then fled into exile in the Soviet Union. Recently, he has been operating from Geneva. Gizenga has claimed to be affiliated with the Parti de la Révolution Populaire (PRP) led by Laurent Kabila. The PRP has conducted guerrilla warfare in Kivu province in eastern Zaire for over a decade; it has publicly argued that it does not need Gizenga's support. Recently, the latter was reported to be held in jail in Angola allegedly for being a "Western spy."

There are also splinter groups appearing under different banners and slogans, such as Mouvement National Congolais (MNC), led by Paul Roger Mokede; Parti Populaire Africain (PPA), led by Clement Kabinda; and Convention des Democrates Socialistes (CODESO), led by Ali Kalonga, who split from MARC in 1977, accusing MARC of being "less progressist" (Rymenam 1977, pp. 9-10).

In the wake of the Shaba II crisis in mid-1978, the Zairian ex-ambassador to Iran, Mbeka Makoso, resigned. He declared that his main concern now was to coordinate the activities of all these often disparate groups. His newly formed umbrella to help him achieve this goal is Mouvement National pour l'Unité et la Reconciliation (MNUR). Mbeka said that he would formulate an all-encompassing program of opposition to the Mobutu regime in the hope that the various resistance groups will join. It will be only then that "they will be able to form a united front against Mobutu" (To the Point International 1978, p. 29). Reports from Brussels have confirmed the author's original suspicions that the MNUR is unlikely to be successful in bringing groups together to fight their common enemy.

Although many Zairian opposition groups have been receiving material as well as moral support—witness the case of the FLNC, which received a green light from the Neto government in Angola in 1977 and 1978—their basic weakness is that they have not succeeded in forming a united front. Apparently, all they have in common is their conviction that Mobutu and the name "Zaire" must disappear, either willingly or by violent means (To the Point International 1978, p. 29). Various analysts of the Zairian opposition have asserted that, were the West to find a valid spokesman of the united opposition, he could be groomed to take over from Mobutu. But the opposition's internal divisions have allowed Mobutu to ignore his opponents in large measure and to make contemptuous remarks about them such as: "The dogs can bark but the caravan passes."

RECENT GENERALIZED OPPOSITION TO MOBUTU

Since 1976 Mobutu's government has been more and more clearly discredited in the eyes of the Zairian masses. Some Zairians openly say that he has been too long in power and he should willingly consider relinquishing the presidency. This loss of legitimacy has become one of the major factors in any analysis of political and economic change.

This generalized opposition does not seem to be an organized phenomenon, as the autocratic and oppressive nature of the Mobutu regime has not tolerated the growth of any internal organized opposition. Rather, it seems to be a spontaneous phenomenon whose causes can be said to be massive economic failures, deterioration in the social conditions, and predation on the population by the army, the secret police, party cadres, and any official who enjoys a modicum of power. In a recent study, Nzongola (1978) made the following theoretical analysis:

> With a steadily declining standard of living, coupled with an extremely high incidence of malnutrition, a thorough corrupt and ineffective state apparatus, and a growing external debt and dependency, the Zaire Republic has become the model neocolony in Africa today. The neocolonial character and tasks of the state have been made abundantly clear by the alienation of the country's territorial, political, and administrative sovereignty, the U.S.-backed aggression in Angola, and the necessity to rely on imperialist support to preserve an unpopular regime. [P. 12]

Today, despite the injection of massive Western aid, Zaire is disintegrating economically (as Chapter 1 demonstrated). Central to the recent degree of political disaffection has been a frightening pauperization of the masses throughout the country. Inflation was reportedly 100 percent in 1978 and black market dealing was rife. Confidential reports in early 1979 by acquaintances from Zaire say that since the November 1978 devaluation of the currency by 20 percent, one U.S. dollar is being exchanged on the black market for five zaires. The official rate is Z 1 for U.S. 80¢. The end results have been a dramatic erosion of purchasing power of all rural and urban classes. Hoarding and speculation in essential foods on a massive scale are a way of life in Zaire. As Africa Confidential put it: "Up until November 1978, the price of staple food had multiplied by around 12 in seven years. Since then, in many parts of Zaire it has doubled" (January 3, 1979).

Summarizing the economic desperation that has recently gripped Zaire under Mobutu, an old telephone worker bluntly told correspondent John Darton (1978):

We are plunged in despair. Perhaps one-quarter of the people in
Kinshasa are working. Crime is up, students cannot find jobs,
even the cost of medicine is out of reach. It is all Mobutu's fault.

And a 29-year-old teacher, whose monthly salary does not allow him to
make ends meet, cynically said: "We are the sacrifice generation, our children maybe they can turn the country around. But for us, we are the losers.
Zaire is getting more and more like India everyday." Echoing the same argument, a middle-level civil servant in Kinshasa rhetorically asked: "What
place is there for an honest man in Zaire? I'll tell you: none. You can only
operate with bribes and favors. Everyone feeds off each other and one man's
fortune is another's blessing. It's gotten so the average person does not believe in anything anymore" (Lamb 1978).

By 1977, as his legitimacy eroded and his regime became increasingly
contested by a generalized opposition to his autocratic rule, Mobutu was
forced more and more to harsher measures to control the restless populace.
In 1977, following the invasion of Shaba province by Katangese exiles of the
FNLC, Nguza Karl-I-Bond, Zaire's widely respected foreign minister, was
sentenced to death for treason for allegedly withholding vital information about
the Katangese attack from Mobutu (Washington Post, August 14, 1977). However, most diplomats in Kinshasa agreed that Nguza's real crime was to have
been mentioned too prominently as a possible successor to Mobutu (Kaufman
1978).

There were rumors circulating through foreign embassies that he had
died in prison. In the aftermath of the proclamation of amnesty in June 1978
for some political prisoners, Nguza was suddenly released and reappeared in
Kinshasa. In October 1978, he was reportedly allowed to travel to Holland
to seek medical treatment. To the astonishment of the exiled opposition in
Brussels, he said he was returning to Zaire to work with Mobutu. In March
1979 he was restored to his post at the Foreign Ministry. Few of his countrymen have done as well.

In late January 1978, as many as 700 civilians—émigré groups in Brussels advanced a figure of 2,000 civilian victims (Le Soir de Bruxelles 1978b)—
were reportedly killed by a savage government suppression of a putative rebellion in the Kwilu-Idiofa area in Bandundu province, about 500 miles from Kinshasa. There have been reports that a mass murder occurred following the
airing of grievances against the government by local members of the Kimbanguist sect. The repression was finally revealed by U.S. missionaries and
U.S. Peace Corps volunteers who had been in the area and were forced to
watch the public hangings (Ottaway 1978; Kaufman 1978).

Then, in March 1978, 90 persons, including 67 military officers, were
arrested and put on trial in the case known as Le Procès des Terroristes à
Kinshasa for allegedly plotting a coup d'etat against Mobutu. Fourteen persons were sentenced to death. Thirteen military officers were promptly executed at dawn following the verdict, while the others were given long prison
terms of up to 20 years (La Libre Belgique 1978; Le Soir de Bruxelles 1978a).
Then came a massive purge of hundreds of officers and noncommissioned officers from Shaba, Bandundu, and East and West Kasai provinces, mainly

members of the Luba, Bakongo, Kasai, and Lunda groups. A roundup of suspected civilians from these main groups took place in Kinshasa (Ottaway 1978). In publicly announcing the executions of officers on television, Mobutu was clearly attempting to intimidate everyone from joining the growing opposition to his unpopular rule:

> I solemnly declare that from now on, I will be without pity against
> all attempts of that kind. In the past executive mercy has been
> mistaken for weakness. But now whoever tries again to use the
> sword will perish by the sword. [Darnton 1978]

If President Mobutu was trying to silence his critics internally and externally, his efforts manifestly failed. Two months later, the guerrillas of the FNLC attacked and seized Kolwezi on May 8, 1978; Western intervention (see Chapter 13) was all that preserved Mobutu. The swing to greater repression that started in 1977 did not abate. In the wake of the Shaba II crisis, refugees arriving in Zambia from Kolwezi asserted that the Zairian army had killed hundreds of Lunda tribesmen in retaliation for their alleged support of the Katangese exiles. As Young wrote: "Finally, the post-Shaba I and II army 'pacification' campaigns created for the first time in Zairian history a large rural refuge exodus into Angola, which some estimate at more than 200,000" (Young 1978, p. 14). Furthermore, recent reports by the UN High Commission for Refugees, the International Red Cross, and the Protestant churches have openly accused the Zairian government of blatantly violating a general amnesty granted in October 1978 to the citizens of Shaba province who were returning home after having left the war zone. Refugees who have returned to Zaire from neighboring Angola have complained to UN officials that they have been detained, imprisoned, and beaten, clear violations of the letter and spirit of general amnesty (New York Times 1979).

CONCLUDING REMARKS

It seems clear that despite recent talks in the Western capitals of "democratizing" the Zairian regime, it is doubtful that any meaningful reforms can significantly alter the nature of Zaire's one-man government and restore to it the political legitimacy it began with. In the late 1960s, the Mobutu regime did enjoy a degree of popularity among the Zairian masses weary of continuing strife and chaos. Nonetheless, as the dust settled, people began to realize that they were dealing with a military dictatorship. Since 1966, sporadic opposition against Mobutu has continued at home and overseas. To be sure, as the dictatorship tightened political control over the entire nation from 1967 to 1975, it succeeded in stifling dissent by the opponents of the regime by killing many, jailing some, and forcing others into exile. Clearly, the early 1970s were the years that saw Mobutu at the zenith of his power. The sum of political and economic policies was perceived overseas as symbolizing Zairian stability. Mobutu, in Jules Chomé's words, became "Le guide supreme."

The generalized discontent and unrest of the late 1970s, which have manifested themselves since 1976 in spontaneous peasant revolts and illegal strike actions by urban and mine workers, secondary school and university teachers, and state employees, are impressive and symbolic signs of a considerable repudiation of Mobutu and his government. His vulnerability and loss of legitimacy are well established. The main challenge confronting the opposition groups, still divided both at home and overseas, is how to channel this generalized rumbling and opposition into an organized and viable movement that will ultimately destroy the Mobutu regime.

REFERENCES

Adelman, Kenneth L. 1975. "The Church-State Conflict in Zaire: 1969–1974." African Studies Review 18, no. 1 (April): 102–15.

Africa Report. 1975. "The Style of Mobutu: How Authentic?" 20, no. 2 (March–April): 1–3.

African Confidential. 1979. "Zaire: Can the IMF Succeed?" January 3.

Afrique-Asia. 1977. "Mobutu face à la revolte populaire," no. 132 (April 4), pp. 9–12.

Bahri, Mohamed. 1967. "Mobutu repond aux questions de Mohamed Bahri." Jeune Afrique, July, pp. 1–25.

Bustin, Edouard. 1969. "Confrontation in the Congo." Current History 52, no. 37 (March): 168–74.

Centre de Recherche de l'Information Socio-Politiques. 1967. Congo 1965: Political Documents of a Developing Nation. Princeton, N.J.: Princeton University Press.

Chomé, Jules. 1975. L'ascension de Mobutu: Du Sergent Joseph Desiré au Général Sese Seko. Brussels: Editions Complexe.

Comité Zaire. 1978. Zaire: Le dossier de la recolonisation. Paris: Harmattan.

Darton, John. 1978. "Despite Unrest, Mobutu Keeps Tight Lid on Zaire." New York Times, April 24.

Derniere Heure. 1976. "Monseigneur Eugene Kabange, Archevêque de Lubumbashi, souligne les maux dont souffre le pays," May 26–27.

Jeune Afrique. 1967. "Interview: Mobutu on Union-Minière," no. 313 (January 8), pp. 16–19.

Kamitatu, Cléophas. 1977. Zaire, le pouvoir à la portée du peuple. Paris: Harmattan.

_____. 1971. La grande mystification du Congo-Kinshasa: Les crimes de Mobutu. Paris: Maspero.

Kaufman, Michael T. 1978. "Zaire: A Mobutu Fiefdom Where Fortunes Shift Quickly." New York Times, June 3.

Klein, Martin. 1970. "Congo-Kinshasa Simmers." Africa Report 25, no. 1 (January): 10-12.

Lamb, David. 1978. "Corruption, Poverty Belie Zaire Slogans." Los Angeles Times, August 20.

_____. 1977. "The Cult of Mobutu." Washington Post, April 14.

Libre Belgique. 1978. March 18.

Mobutu, Joseph Desiré. 1966. Le President Mobutu vous parle: 24 November 1965-24 November 1966. Leopoldville: Edition Grafica International.

Monguya Mbenge, Daniel. 1977. Histoire secrete du Zaire. Brussells: Editions de l'Espérance.

Miso Gaa (Journal of the Zairian Emigrés in Belgium). 1978. "La déclaration des évêques du Zaire: Apel au redressement de la nation," no. 42 (July-August).

_____. 1976. "Mobutu's Attempt to Blackmail the Zairian Catholic Bishops regarding the Return of Schools to the Churches," no. 26 (October-November).

Monde. "Les groupes d'opposition à Mobutu," March 30.

New York Times. 1979. "Zaire Is Reported to Violate Shaba Refugees' Amnesty," February 5.

Ndovi, Victor. 1978. "The Ghosts That Haunt Mobutu." New African, no. 131 (July), pp. 13-14.

Nkrumah, Kwame. 1967. The Challenge of the Congo. New York: International Publishers.

Nzongola, Ntalaja. 1978. "The Continuing Struggle for National Liberation in Zaire." Paper presented at the Twenty-First Annual Meeting of the African Studies Association, Baltimore, November 1-4.

Ottaway, David B. 1978. "Zaire Tragedy: Cycle of Revolt and Repression." Washington Post, June 4.

Randall, Jonathan C. 1978. "Mobutu: Success through Failure." Washington Post, June 18.

Rymenam, Jean. 1977. "Comment le regime Mobutu à sapé ses propres fondements." Le monde diplomatique, no. 278 (May), pp. 1, 8-11.

Le soir de Bruxelles. 1978a. March 18.

_____. 1978b. "L'armée zairoise exercerait une repression meurtriere en region Bandundu," February 27.

To the Point International. 1978. "Zaire: Ex-Ambassador Coordinating Exile Opposition," July 21.

_____. 1977. "Zaire: Rebel Who's Who," May 9.

Tshombe, Moise. 1967. My Fifteen Months in Government. Plano, Tex.: University of Plano Press.

Washington Post. 1977. "No. 2 Man Is Purged in Zaire," August 14.

Young, Crawford. 1978. "Zaire: The Unending Crisis." Foreign Affairs, Fall, pp. 169-85.

_____. 1967. "Congo-Kinshasa Situation Report." Africa Report 12, no. 7 (October): 12-18.

15

DEVELOPMENT VERSUS THE WORLD SYSTEM: INTERNATIONAL AID ACTIVITIES IN ZAIRE

Guy Gran

A THEORETICAL INTRODUCTION TO CONFLICTING PARADIGMS

As the 1970s draw to a close, it is painfully clear that involvement in the world system has been singularly unrewarding for most of the people of Zaire. Previous chapters have chronicled the varied internal processes that create and perpetuate extreme poverty, malnutrition, and powerlessness. The political dimensions of imprisonment by the world system have been laid bare as has the parasitic nature of international corporate activities. Against this record of human misery, spokesmen of this larger order still claim that through international development assistance the constraints to development can be overcome and the human needs of the poor majority be met. This chapter proposes to explore whether this is so, whether foreign aid is primarily part of the problem or part of the solution for the Zairian people.

Amazingly, after 30 years the field of international development oversight is still in its infancy. Legislators, scholars, and journalists have done very little of substance. The involved agencies, especially the multilateral ones, have willingly conspired with host governments to keep most country, sector, and project papers out of the public domain. Surprisingly, neither the World Bank nor the U.S. Agency for International Development (AID) has internally any critical or creative evaluative channels. The World Bank's postproject evaluation is little more than a paper-pushing exercise; AID does, with rare exception, little more. Indeed, only in the mid-1970s have AID and the World Bank begun to build into project design the capacity to marshal some of the data necessary for a modicum of quantitative evaluation.

This presupposes that there are even any intellectually valid criteria of evaluation now agreed upon and being applied. But no such state of affairs exists. The state of the art of conventional economic criteria, embodied in cost-benefit and rate-of-return analyses, use world prices, ultimately dependent on world wealth and income distribution, to determine profitability in a given location. It quantifies elements of production, treating human beings as labor or costs. It says nothing about the distribution of the product or the nature and quality of the processes at work as they bear on the welfare of the poor. Even worse, conventional methods create no basis for understanding that poor people are not solely or even primarily guided by the capitalist concept of material efficiency. As Sandra Wallman (1977) and others have begun to show, poor people will sometimes prefer a greater degree of autonomy or power over their lives than an optimum degree of material success.

This leaves an independent analyst not only the task of differentiating what is real from what self-interested agencies say but also the invention of a new and far more defensible paradigm from which to make judgments. Without the funds or access to see the projects in operation, such an effort can at best be partially successful. However, if a project is manifestly designed without the participation of the poor or even without their interests in mind, and is implanted into a local economy extremely hostile to the welfare of the poor, one is justified in drawing at least some kinds of conclusions.

This chapter will first outline the basic intentions of international development efforts from a world system perspective. From that model the flaws in the system that now prevent aid from having a positive impact on the poor become instead logical constituent parts, processes, and values perpetuating the current patterns of growth and impoverization. The situation is by no means inevitable. An alternative model of participatory development will be advanced as the optimum way to reach and benefit the poor majority. A representative sample of eight projects from the World Bank and another sample of six from AID will be examined from this model and the perspective of Zaire's poor. UN agencies and France and Belgium are carrying out comparable aid programs, but their reports are even further from scholarly reach. Enough is at hand, however, to warrant some very sober conclusions about Zaire's future under the aegis of the world system and its present policies.

Until the early 1970s, virtually all foreign aid activities in Zaire, as elsewhere, pursued unapologetically the trickle-down technocratic development model. No historical basis was considered; poverty was there by act of God and nature or a colonial rape that ended with independence. Development constraints were finite, tangible things like bad roads or "traditional" man; there was no concept of processes at work creating and sustaining constraints. Project goals were production-centered and implementation was top-down and elitist in nature. Projects reflected the basic systemic interests of core societies: cheap primary commodities and labor, new investment possibilities, and ultimately new markets (Gran 1978).

The larger system's interest is manifest in the literature on each project. Project, sector, and country reports seek to guide the intellectual environment of Third World government officials concerned with development toward an open export-led model. No report ever mentions the unequal exchange inherent in trade between the First and Third worlds. Projects provide infrastructure and other facilities that remove basic impediments to profitable private investments. Projects support capital-intensive productive activities and tend to avoid support of basic means of production that would make a society more self-reliant. Project financing is designed to maximize profits of multinational corporate suppliers and to facilitate private international bank penetration of Third World economies. Projects in the last decade have been more supportive of agricultural and urban development that would diminish mass discontent that could be transformed into revolutionary politics.

Liberal supporters and participants in international development will react with horror to this portrayal of what conventional wisdom views through fogged and flawed humanitarian lenses. Recognizing to some degree the past failures, the U.S. Congress did legislate in 1973 what are termed "New Directions" for AID's activities. Aid is now intended to go as directly as possible to the poor majority and to encourage their participation in the process. The rhetoric of the World Bank soon followed suit. In the preface of recent annual reports, World Bank President Robert McNamara proclaimed that the bank will now place "greatly increased emphasis on investments which can directly affect the well-being of the masses of poor people of developing countries by making them more productive and by including them as active participants in the development process." Parenthetically, the actual semantic content of this statement is the reverse; it really means the better to tax them—which is what is happening.

Rhetoric aside, how does one judge whether aid actually helps the poor? Much of the conventional argument boils down to a simple assertion of costs and benefits. If a project takes place in a location where poor people are, they, as well as the wealthier and more entrepreneurial, will benefit in some reasonable proportion. This form of myopia represents not merely the arrogance born of years of nonaccountability but also a streak of utopianism about the goodness of people, which history does not support in Zaire or elsewhere. The World Bank (Squire and van der Tak 1975) has attempted to clothe the procedures used with pseudoscientific and mathematical garb. Commonest are the procedures of rate-of-return analysis and shadow pricing.

Mark Franco (in Amin 1975, pp. 35-301) in an important, albeit still obscure, work, has demonstrated the ideological basis of this methodology as one element serving ultimately to mystify the real working of the system and make operational its reinforcement and expansion. The complexities of the issues are many, and just a few points must suffice here. The bank's methodology presumes planning based on the continuation and extension of the existing social system; this reinforces established interests and helps to preclude the structural changes implicit in the concept of development.

This is demonstrated in multiple elements of ideology, theory, and technique. Conventional planning assumes maximum social harmony and production from the aggregation of micro cost-benefit decisions. The logically obvious reality in Zaire is, however, that a maldistribution of production factors means the decision making of unequals and far from optimal results, a situation that feeds on itself. The cost of or value accorded a given factor from the system's view is often not that from the individual's; this is especially true for an individual in a precapitalist mode dealing with the capitalist mode. The ideological basis for reference prices, for public goods, or the valuation of the environment and human life and health cannot be ignored as inconveniences. Quality of life and personal autonomy are alien for most in this paradigm. The uneven nature of capitalist development over time upsets the neat statistical graphs and tables of the World Bank designers and its kindred spirits. One is left with little more than an ill-constructed statement of the ability of a project to insert itself into a given economic structure.

While not denying that productivity (and a new method of its calculation) must play some role in assessing the value of international development activities, it is argued that the focus on material goals diminishes or destroys a far greater or more valuable potential for the aid recipient. This potential is that of becoming a more effective citizen in the broadest sense of the term. Occasional political voting is a minor activity. What matters most to the poor is that they develop the skills to participate in and take some control over the activities that affect their day-to-day lives. It is not simply that people are more productive in a participatory work environment, as Juan Espinosa and Andrew Zimbalist (1978) have painstakingly proved, but that by going through processes of economic participation one develops skills that can be used to mitigate social, political, and cultural oppression and powerlessness as well. Aid activities can be goal-oriented, transfer resources, and accomplish little. Or they can be process-oriented, create lifetime skills, and help to unleash transformations by which the poor themselves will overcome poverty.

The latter model of development is termed participatory development. Its intellectual heritage is diverse, but the work of the Inter-American Foundation and two Washington-based groups, Development Alternatives and, especially, the Development Group for Alternative Policies, deserves mention. The premise of the model is simple. If the poor participate in specific and tangible ways throughout the entire life of development projects, they will see the correlation between involvement and reward and simultaneously enjoy the tangible benefits. Also possible would be the enhancement of dignity that is inherent in autonomous behavior. This combination will result in optimum productivity and growth of human skills. Small transfers of material resources can thus have continuing social and economic benefits.

The participatory development model has not yet been refined into neat quantifiable terms but rests as a series of operational design principles. Perhaps it should remain at this level of generality to avoid rigidity of application. Even as general principles, they clearly reveal the chasm between conventional development design and what it really means to relate people to development. The author and several colleagues hold that:

1. A significant percentage of the specified group must participate in and control as many elements of project initiation, design, operation, and evaluation as possible.

2. The project design must include clearly defined and operational participatory mechanisms to guide administrative, productive, and distributive elements of the project.

3. The institutional linkages of the project with the larger economic and political system must be functional for those at the bottom; the aid inflow

and the productive gains must be protected. Thus the hostile development environment and prevailing confidence mechanisms (Elliott 1975) must be explicitly recognized in project design.

4. Technological and organizational aspects must be culturally feasible. If women are the farmers, it is counterproductive to train only male agricultural extension agents.

5. The project design must reach some reasonable standard of ecological soundness that reflects an empirically defensible analytical framework of the participants.

6. The project must show the potential for self-reliance; resources should serve a catalytic function, not a welfare function encouraging further dependency.

7. Comparable potential for self-sustainment must be evident; conventional aid activities often die when funding stops.

8. The project design must include enhancement of self-directed learning activities; intellectual dependency, as much as political and economic dependency, saps creativity and productivity.

To apply these development principles, or any other, requires an environment not totally inhospitable to the poor. In Zaire over the last 15 years, those agencies of the world system that have attempted to guide and facilitate its path toward capitalist modernization have found a political system and leadership concerned with power and its spoils, not development. Mobutu and the rest of his parasitic ruling class recognize the revolutionary pressures of desperate poverty and economic equality as they struggle with Zaire's have-nots for the same insufficient surplus. The same struggle for surplus is played out at the national, regional, and local levels, as well as between levels. There is some incentive for growth as this enlarges the spoils. There is little incentive for development and the improvement of the condition of human beings; this would diminish the individual share of spoils. To this, add the profoundly ingrained corruption of all economic and political activities (chronicled in other chapters) and the considerable hindrances of distance, terrain, climate, and disease. It is little wonder that peasants in many locales, when faced with the capricious and oppressive demands of both collectivity leadership and the larger system, have opted out, choosing to deny labor and goods if they cannot benefit from the effort.

Against this inimical setting AID and World Bank officials, as well as the rest of the international aid community, have chosen to work with the Zairian political and economic system and treat it as part of the potential solution instead of as the problem. On paper the system is said to have constraints that aid can overcome. In reality it is considered a major achievement if material actually reaches its destination and is in some measure applied to the intended activity. The result of this mixture of bureaucratic, political, and personal interests is very little activity that significantly helps or involves poor people.

An exploration of specific examples is now in order to demonstrate in detail the nature and depth of core country guidance, how the West employs not just its own public monies but also those of the Zairian government in the advancement of export-led growth to the advantage of private interests, and whether or how the poor majority in Zaire can hope to begin to work toward a more just and endurable future from their present predicament.

THE WORLD BANK IN ZAIRE

The World Bank has been the single largest foreign contributor to the economic path followed by President Mobutu between 1965 and 1979. After a $91.6 million infrastructure project in 1960 and the hiatus caused by the civil and revolutionary upheavals between 1960 and 1965, the World Bank was slow to return to Zaire. But the IMF-led restabilization effort in 1967 encouraged a perception of normalcy and stability. In November 1968, the bank issued the gray cover (last of four versions of most internal reports) of a three-volume report (AF-85a) on the economy of Zaire. Soon after in that fiscal year came the first of 18 Mobutu-era World Bank development projects approved between the fall of 1968 and the fall of 1978.

The bank's internal country reports, only rarely published (and never one on Zaire), deserve a comment for their historical role as guiders of the world system. The bank prepared gray-cover country reviews in March 1971, March 1973, July 1975 (the most exhaustive, in four volumes), and April 1977. Another can be expected in 1979. An agricultural sector survey was done in June 1972. Other shorter sector papers have been done for international meetings. The cumulative impact of these documents has been not only to provide the entire aid community, the U.S. State Department, and many others with the most complete and comprehensive factual and statistical portrait of Zairian economic data that was "available" but also to define what was valid and appropriate to consider in development analysis and how to conceptualize these topics.

Bureaucrats in national and international agencies, lacking time, resources, and motivation for independent research, have been cribbing from these reports for years. Indeed, the statistical material is quite useful if one keeps in mind the woeful caliber of the data in the first place. These reports (and comparable International Monetary Fund and UN Food and Agriculture Organization efforts) have served, however, far more important goals of miseducation. The rigid neoclassical economic orthodoxy of the bank's world model badly misconstrues historical reality, unfolding economic processes, human motivations, and much else. People rarely appear, and then only in the abstract mass. The bank's research consists of little more than two or three weeks of in-country discussions with top government officials and perusal of official documents. The research of others is often deemed irrelevant. Almost never are footnotes permitted; the result is a procedure by which reality can be shaded any way the writer wishes. Little wonder the reports mirror the institution as inherently elitist and concerned with maintaining the status quo.

The result of production-centered analyses is that the bank and those it influences do not know where the Zairian people are or how to relate development projects to them. Inhibited by the additional handicap that Zairian authorities must approve each report, the bank has avoided to this date any substantive discussion of corruption or underdevelopment administration. In the fall of 1978 some of its staff concerned with Zaire began to seek exposure to other forms of analyses. It is too soon to see if there will be any policy impact, but optimism is not in order; like any large bureaucracy, the bank has a tremendous ability to defend itself from new ideas.

Despite the sincere humanistic intentions of some of the international officials involved, the bank has thus legitimized, by its intellectual and material support, a development path that, by the bank's own data (chronicled in Chapter 1), consigns most Zairians to deprivation of elementary human rights for the indefinite future, if not permanently. It is to the more tangible aspects of this process, the design and operation of projects, that this chapter now turns. Valuable first impressions can be gained by a tabular summary of the bank's portfolio in Zaire (see Table 14.1).

Even before one begins to explore the technocratic implications of these projects, several points are obvious. Bank projects do not involve just the bank's money; they soak up significant amounts of local development funds and sometimes foreign exchange. Top government of Zaire officials partake of the decision making and the spoils. But the bank does so much of the coaching and project preparation that in most instances it is very much a relationship of unequals. A government official seeking an alternative development path thus finds powerful opponents both in government and in the international development community. Total foreign aid to Zaire ranged between $60 and $100 million a year from 1966 to 1973 (IBRD 1975a, vol. 3, Table 3.6), and apparently has not been coherently tabulated since. There are private voluntary agencies, church groups, and other bilateral aid activities in Zaire, but a Zairian government official cannot look to them for major funding or political support. The options for funding outside the world system are, in sum, minimal.

It is fitting to begin a more specific discussion of the bank's most recent development activities with the 1974 GECAMINES project, the expansion of the government's parastatal mining corporation described in detail in Chapter 7. This $435 million project is intended to raise copper production from 470,000 to 590,000 tons and cobalt from 16,000 to 20,000 tons per year. Money went to mine development, metallurgical and related facilities, industrial and administrative infrastructure, and employee housing and social facilities. Endless technical and statistical details fill two very long project papers (IBRD 1974). It was a stunning display of both government and bank priorities and a sure perpetuation of the skewed economy both are rhetorically opposed to. What will it do for people?

Very few Zairians participated in this choice of project. Unsurprisingly, very few benefit directly. The project paper promised the creation of 2,000 new jobs for local workers, an average cost of $160,000 per job. For a society of 26 to 27 million people, such a project makes little sense, as Chapter 1 argued. Ostensibly GECAMINES will earn further profits from the export of minerals, money that the government could then spend on social ser-

TABLE 15.1

World Bank Projects in Zaire, 1968-78
(millions of dollars)

Year	Purpose	Bank	Funding Local	Other
Fiscal year 1969	Highways, technical assistance	6.0	—	—
Fiscal year 1970	Development Finance Company (DFC)	5.0	n.a.	—
Fiscal year 1971	River transport	7.0	—	—
Fiscal year 1972	DFC II	10.0	n.a.	—
November 1971	Higher education	6.5	5.3	—
February 1972	Highways II	19.0	10.3	17.1
May 1973	Livestock	8.5	6.5	—
December 1973	DFC III	10.0	n.a.	—
December 1974	GECAMINES	100.0	215.0	120.0
January 1975	Highways III	26.0	12.8	1.5
May 1975	River Transport II	26.0	26.0	—
January 1976	Education II	21.0	27.5	—
March 1976	Water supply	21.5	31.0	17.7
September 1976	Cotton	8.0	3.5	3.1
March 1977	Livestock II	8.0	2.8	5.3
April 1977	DFC IV	10.0	n.a.	—
March 1978	Oil palm	9.0	23.0	15.4
Total		301.5	363.7	

n.a. = not available

Sources: Bank project and president reports.

vices and other people-related development. Nothing in the project design requires this, however, and it is not happening to any appreciable degree. Those officials who wanted more foreign exchange for their personal pleasure and political aggrandizement fared well, at least until the Shaba crises brought the economy to its knees. One can point to the training of Zairian personnel and their integration into the GECAMINES staff as a mild form of top-down participation. But most Zairians have not participated in any part of the project's process nor were any mechanisms designed so that they could.

The bank's design did provide certain linkages (enhanced transport and power capabilities) functional for GECAMINES, but paid little attention to the exploitative potential of further unequal distribution of resources in the project environment. The bank simply assumes (or hopes others will assume) that GECAMINES linkages with the larger world economy are mutually beneficial and compatible to each. Chapter 7 has demonstrated otherwise. Nothing is said of cultural feasibility; a requisite number of Zairians are presumed bribable to the appropriate capitalist norms. Ecological issues receive 1 page in 300; activities will mar the land, which is of little agricultural interest and is sparsely populated. Reclamation need not be undertaken now. Other pollution is asserted to be under control.

Does a mineral expansion project have a potential for self-reliance or self-sustainment? The world price of copper promptly fell far below the projected price per pound for the entire 1975-78 period. Rate of return has to have been lower than even the pessimistic 10 percent at 60¢ per pound. But the bank's analysis started from at least one false hypothesis. If additional power facilities are needed for additional mining operations, they are a cost that must be factored into a rate of return; they are not an item that can be termed a government expense to be borne by new GECAMINES tax revenues. This and other government tax expenditures are, in effect, Zairian subsidies of low international copper prices. Additionally destructive of self-reliant development are the diminished but still ongoing linkages to Belgian processing, marketing, and advisory services. Even in an optimally run mining venture, however, a Third World society without a monopoly or cartel possibility is ever in danger of unequal exchange, the debt trap, and other ills of powerlessness.

A word must be said about the ability of this project design to cushion its impact on the poor. Contributing to hospitals and schools is a liberal gesture. But the wage levels and other project spending cause local inflation and hardship. In the January 16, 1975, executive director's meeting of the bank, this was noted. The "dual economy" was admitted and other government and international programs were alleged to be attacking such issues. For the long-term sake of the poor, the project was thus designed to exacerbate and enlarge the enclave nature of the modern sector. It need not have been. Thus a project created for the maximum profit of government officials and multinational corporations unsurprisingly contains no real benefit to the Zairian poor or any mechanism by which the poor could seek to alter such processes. In many, many ways the GECAMINES expansion project is an archetypal demonstration of the world system in action.

There is wide agreement among conventional writings that the disintegration of Zaire's transportation system hurts both development and growth. The Zairian peasant, if asked, might be more ambivalent. Roads facilitate trade and the arrival of beer; but if roads got even worse, the central government might not be able to get agricultural monitors or military forces in to support the oppression of collectivity leadership, a situation raising the possibility of political change. The bank, like the government of Zaire, does not consult people, and views roads as a means to reach and exploit rural productivity. The bank's Third Highway Project, a $40.3 million effort begun in January 1975, is a typical example of the bank approach. Over three years it was intended to provide technical assistance to the Bureau of Roads, organize two pilot highway maintenance schemes and a countrywide logistic support system for maintenance, rehabilitate the 600-kilometer Kabinda-Kindu road, and carry out a highway traffic survey and feasibility studies (IBRD 1975b).

The bank did not explore the socioeconomic processes at work inhibiting the upkeep of roads. In a purely technocratic mode of reasoning, it argued instead that the Bureau of Roads was in charge, it did not have enough trained personnel, and the solution was to train more. Bureaucratic and political conflict caused frequent changes in the bureau's structure and scope of responsibilities, changes that the bank did not understand in any larger context. The bank simply found "no effective machinery for formulating transport policy or coordinating the operation and development of the respective transport mode" (IBRD 1975b, 567a-CK, p. 5). Why didn't the bank ask why? Similarly, the lack of knowledge of transport needs was merely accepted as a given. Despite the admittedly large element of chance, a government, aided by a phalanx of international consultants, would forge ahead.

Roads do not, however, exist in this sort of social vacuum. Without building a positive and participatory social contract between people and a regional government, there is little possibility of maintaining roads. The Mobutu government failed to do this. Its road development activities have been largely elitist, part of a spoils system in operation. The bank noticed one episode. In October 1973, the government began to contract aid to local operators for upkeep; by March 1974, costs visibly exceeded the budget and the contracts were ended (IBRD 1975b, 567a-CK, p. 11). In sum, an urban area such as Mbuji-Mayi may benefit from cheaper food, some plantations may have a renaissance, and some roads may be improved; but local and regional elites in Kasai Orientale and Kivu may prevent the poor from the most advantageous use of this improved factor of production.

In the mid-1970s, the bank and the Zairian government noticed that if agricultural production was going to improve, the quality of rural education had to improve. One result was the Second Education Project, begun in March 1976 and based on the analyses in reports 864-ZR and P-1715-ZR (IBRD 1976a). It allocated a total of $48.5 million in government and bank funds for rural primary teacher and agricultural technician training institutes and related technical assistance and studies. The ills of Zairian education have already been treated, but it is important here to understand the implications for rural areas of trickle-down educational development.

The bank properly notes the lack of incentive to become a rural teacher or civil servant. Low and uncertain pay, unpredictable delivery of materials, and perceived cultural deprivation are obvious. The best students seek better paying urban professions, and the average low quality of rural education re-creates itself. This noted, the bank project is conceptually ill-designed to break the vicious circle. These training institutes are government adjuncts over which collectivities have no say. David Ewert (1977), among others, found low education a common concern and a perceived barrier to money and advancement; given an opportunity, villagers would get involved. To get people to stay in a village and provide quality education over time, it is far more effective and less culturally conflictive if the teacher comes from the local area originally. If the village perceived that it was sponsoring one of its own for human resource training that would ultimately benefit the village, vertical bonds of support might be built. Instead, the project is designed and run as another exercise in political and cultural penetration of the village from above. Even worse, there is no apparent understanding that most agricultural work is done by women and to be effective the agricultural extension efforts have to involve women. Unless one begins with a participatory design, it is hard to see how either kind of rural education will have a very broad or deep impact, given the inequitable nature of local political economy and the government's disinterest in funding such social services.

The same inability to relate project to environment characterized the bank's approach to urban development in Zaire. The March 1976 Water Supply Project (IBRD 1976b) is a case in point. The bank quantifies with horror the extreme lack of piped water in urban areas and the health hazards it creates. In 1975 more than two-thirds of the urban population got water from pits, wells, springs, and streams; the 55 existing urban water supply systems served less than 3 percent of those in need. The bank's response was a $21.5 million credit to a $70 million project to be controlled by the parastatal REGIDESO, the National Electricity and Water Supply Corporation, which had presided over the creation of that human tragedy.

The Water Supply Project aims to improve availability of water for an additional 700,000 to 1 million people in six of Zaire's major cities. Of basic concern to the poor is the expansion of standpipes; by 1980 the entire population (1.5 million) of these cities is to have access to a standpipe not more than 5 minutes' walk away. The bank report does not break down the project expenditures clearly to show how much of the $70 million goes to the standpipes and how much to new treatment plants, reservoirs, supplies, training, and consultant services that would benefit primarily the urban elite.

It is difficult as well to determine if an intended one standpipe tap per 400 people is impractically too few; it does seem to be a reasonable effort to stretch the limited resources allowed to reach a maximum number of people. What is less pleasing is the method of distributing water; a contractor will control each standpipe, allotting water in exchange for tickets bought at REGIDESO offices. Many poor will not be able to pay, and the possibilities for new forms of corruption are significant. The government has, to be exact, created a new tax on the poor that they will have a hard time avoiding. In the bank report precisely opposite the page (Annex 12) describing this distribution system is Annex 13, the engineering consultant fees; a senior engineer of a German firm is getting $9,565 a month to supervise construction and a similar man in a French firm, $488 a day. One wonders what the thirsty Zairian would think of that.

The bank has sponsored urban development in Zaire primarily through the development finance company Société Financiere de Développement (SOFIDE), in which it has played a central financial and technical role since its inception in 1970. A fourth SOFIDE credit was granted in April 1977 (IBRD 1977b). The bank calls SOFIDE one of Zaire's best-run institutions and then criticizes its abilities to supervise the projects to which it loans. SOFIDE loans to medium and large business enterprises. SOFIDE's minimum loan is $11,500, which effectively precludes lending to small entrepreneurs. It is not surprising to find the World Bank, joined by the international banking community and the government of Zaire, lending scarce development capital to firms owned by the Zairian elite who also happen to run the country. What is sad is the myopic nature of the project reports, which ignore this dimension, and the lack of integrity of an international development community, which legitimizes subsidizing the elite as a way to help the Zairian poor.

In the late 1970s the bank has been driven by the economic disintegration, corruption, and political unrest to seek projects that are as economically isolated as possible. A production focus has led the bank to plantation activities. Cotton, livestock, and palm oil have been the targets. The Cotton Rehabilitation Project (IBRD 1976c) proposed a $14 million effort in September 1976 to improve the cotton buying, transporting, and ginning operations in the Equateur Region. The parastatal Office National des Fibres Textiles (ONAFITEX), which monopolizes these activities nationwide, would supervise a four-year effort with the aid of international consultants. The specific activities would center on the improvement of rural roads and agricultural extension, provision of trucks and support materials, and improvements in ONAFITEX's national and regional organization and performance.

Cotton has been a compulsory crop in Zaire since colonial days. It is thus a form of state tax. It is grown by an estimated 600,000 families; most of them devote one-third to one-half a hectare to this pursuit. Equateur, Mobutu's home region, is one of the five major areas. The bank report correctly speculates that bad roads, buying delays, low prices, market imperfections, and lack of extension advice all affect a farmer's productivity. But to presume without investigation that farmers can and will act as independent economic actors is to deny the parasitic reality of the collectivity administration, so ably painted by Michael Schatzberg (1977, pp. 170-86 passim). The peasant is faced with a very effective system of exploitation, oppression, and violence; in the general climate of scarcity and insecurity, there is a great probability that any surplus will be siphoned away by that system. The project's assistance to the field agents of ONAFITEX will simply make them more effective in harassing peasants to produce stated quotas. Prices remain fixed at the national level. The bank's Cotton Rehabilitation Project thus facilitates further and more complete exploitation of farm families in Equateur.

The bank's Ituri Livestock Project (IBRD 1977a), begun in March 1977, pursues the same preference that agricultural production can best be raised in the short run by rehabilitation. The bank contributed $8 million of a $16.1 million total effort to expand cattle production in the Ituri subregion of Haut-Zaire Region, the northeast corner of the country. The target is what the bank terms <u>small farmers</u>. Under the aegis of the parastatal National Ranching Development Authority (ONDE) and an Ituri Project Unit, funds would be applied to rehabilitate veterinary and animal production services, marketing, abattoirs, three existing ranches, and training and technical assistance. All of the milk and an estimated 55 percent of the increased meat production will be consumed in the region; the remaining 3,000 tons of meat will be shipped to urban markets, principally Kinshasa, to cut down current imports and foreign exchange loss.

Beef is a very cost-inefficient way to produce protein, if one were truly concerned with Zaire's poor. Looking deeply at the bank's analysis, one finds the honest admission that "data on which projections for all components have been made is weak . . . , although farmers and Government staff have considerable enthusiasm for the Project, there is no recent record of development in the area on which to base likely farmer response" (IBRD 1977a, 1305-ZR, p. 24). Of 170,000 families in the region, about 30,000 own some livestock and some 18,600 of these have cattle. The bank estimates 287,000 cattle in the project area, or about 15 per owner family. These herdsmen are very likely some of the richest Ituri farmers, with an average income three times the regional average (IBRD 1977a, 1305-ZR, p. 25). While subsidizing the diets of the pastoralists and the elite, who are the major meat consumers, the bank is also widening the income disparities in Ituri and enlarging the potential for exploitation. The government is happy to cooperate to gain further tax revenue, and the Ituri cattle owners may or may not be tempted by this revised form of confidence mechanism.

The Oil Palm Project, based on the analysis of Reports 1592-ZR and P-2296-ZR (IBRD 1978a), began in the spring of 1978 with no appreciable rhetoric about helping the poor. Palm oil production had been falling and local consumption rising throughout the decade; in 1975, 48,000 tons went for home use, 50,000 tons for industrial use, and 77,000 tons for export. About half was produced on plantations and half by smallholders. The government felt rehabilitation of existing plantations was the most cost-efficient way of increasing production, and the bank contributed $9 million to a $47.4 million effort. The project calls for a five-year program to provide planting, equipment renewal, workers' housing and social needs, vehicles, training, and technical aid. Three companies in Equateur and Haut-Zaire are involved; these companies represent two-thirds of Zaire's commercial oil palm industry.

Succinctly put, it is a supreme confusion of growth and development. The companies involved are subsidiaries of multinationals: Plantations Lever au Zaire (PLZ) is owned by Unilever, Ltd., and Busira and Compagnie de Commerce et de Plantations (CCP) are subsidiaries of the Belgian holding company Compagnie Générale. The project was prepared in 1976 by the companies involved (IBRD 1978a, P-2296-ZR, p. 14). It is very unlikely that any of the figures, including the profit margins, have been independently verified. The bank noted the endemic difficulty in attracting labor to the plantations, called for oversight on prices and work conditions, and then signed an agreement leaving final wage level authority in the hands of the companies. Such a project is not development, and further disadvantages Zairian smallholders in their relationship to the plantations and the market.

These are the eight World Bank projects in Zaire that have been prepared since bank president McNamara rhetorically redirected bank policy toward helping the poor. None of the eight projects is designed in a participatory fashion; a few elements of the Water Supply Project appear the most likely to have a positive benefit for the poor. Nor does the future look appreciably different. By a December 1978 listing (IBRD, 1978b) the 11 forthcoming projects are entitled Ports I, Highways IV, Smallholder Maize, Kwango-Kwilu Mixed Farming, Education III, Petrozaire Pipeline, Railways, DFC V, GECAMINES II, Agro-Industry I (sugar), and Fisheries. The dollar total would be about $184 million over the next three to five years. Can the Zairian poor turn in another direction?

AID IN ZAIRE

Between fiscal years 1962 and 1977, the United States, by AID figures (1978a, p. 133), allocated $588.9 million in loans and grants to Zaire. Development aid here, as for most other countries, has been imprisoned by the political, strategic, and ideological perspectives of the misnamed globalist view of the U.S. Department of State. Zaire is a large mineral-rich country (the world's leading cobalt producer) in a strategic central African location. Its government should be supported to solidify its allegiance to the West, less politely to keep Mobutu in power. Over a dozen years of such contraints, AID bureaucrats of various ilk have wrestled with (or ignored) the contradiction between supporting Mobutu and trying to help the poor in Zaire, especially after the explicit "New Directions" legislative mandate of 1973. A brief look at the several generations of policy formulation and some of the recent project initiatives will give indications whether U.S. bilateral assistance could be or could become more beneficial to the Zairian poor than have the efforts of the World Bank.

U.S. aid policy following the upheavals of 1960-65 was deeply conditioned by the perceived needs of security and stability. The AID Country Assistance Strategy Statement of September 1966 marked the rhetorical beginning of the move from emergency-oriented to development-oriented activities; the program became in reality little more than budget subsidies and police training to maintain national integrity. AID defines the actual shift from 1968 and points to 1968-74 as a definable period that saw small technical assistance projects in agriculture and education, but the vast bulk of funds going to transportation infrastructure and police training. AID expenditures from 1970 through 1974 averaged almost $8.5 million a year. The AID mission remained locked into the multidonor framework and program designed and led by the World Bank (AID 1974, p. 1).

In 1974 AID prepared its first major Development Assistance Program document for Zaire, in part to define how it would meet the new U.S. congressional mandate to help the poor. It was rapidly rendered obsolete by events in Zaire, but the nature of analysis is revealing. U.S. interests were baldly stated (AID 1975):

(1) to maintain U.S. accessibility to raw materials which are in abundant supply in Zaire;
(2) to foster U.S. investment in Zaire so that we will have access to the Zaire market; and
(3) to sustain our political interests in Central Africa, bearing in mind that Zaire is the "bellwether" for political stability in this part of the world. [P. 1]

Within these parameters, AID would develop a flexible strategy responsive in a realistic fashion to Zairian development needs and U.S. congressional concerns. It is truly verbiage designed to defend the writer rather than inform the reader.

Some samples are in order. Projects will support the IBRD consultative group approach, coordinate with Mobutu's planning team, provide top-level expertise, and yet serve as catalytic contributions to help the Zairian poor (AID 1975, pp. 2-3). The writers could report that in 1972 less than 5 percent of Mobutu's investment budget "was devoted to agriculture which determines the well-being of over 70 percent of the population" (AID 1975, p. 24) and, at the same time, still say that the government's greatest strength was Mobutu and the stability he provides. "There is also evidence that President Mobutu has a desire to use his power for the benefit of all Zairians" (AID 1975, p. 30). Further comments in the AID report oppose participation in development, support the creation of a new class of rural elite despite the social cost, applaud the Green Revolution's potential, define agricultural stagnation in purely technocratic terms, and admit that AID has no solutions —"any workable large-scale solution will have to be worked out by the Zairians" (AID 1975, p. 36).

Shorter versions of this intellectual cacophony have appeared each year thereafter in the Annual Budget Submission and the Congressional Presentation documents. AID has been caught in recent years among the political realities of Mobutu's interests, the State Department's world model, the need to appear competent before the Congress, and its own internal wars and bureaucratic needs. Occasionally through the resulting paper production and rhetoric is a glimmer of the impossibility of helping the poor by working through the system. Most striking is the June 1977 conclusion in the Annual Budget Submission document for fiscal year 1979: "It is unlikely that a development strategy based uniquely on the central government in Kinshasa and on the 'trickle-down' theory, will effectively reach the poor, especially in the rural areas where most of them are located" (AID 1977a, p. 3). On page 4 of the same document is the most coherent operational promise in all the AID documents this author surveyed:

> There is little consensus, knowledge, or experience with respect to how to carry out such programs. Therefore, each project activity will include R&D work in improving or creating institutions (technical, economic, administrative, social), determining the spatial requirements, selecting target groups, encouraging meaningful and effective citizen participation, ascertaining meaningful interventions and delivery systems, developing appropriate technology and establishing models to refine the processes.

Despite the elitist flavor (and contradictory strategy elements elsewhere in the document), one does get some sense of how AID projects in the latter half of the 1970s might be judged. Given the disintegrating economic and political situation in Zaire, the State Department sought higher levels of bilateral aid from an unenthusiastic U.S. Congress. After minimal $4-to-$5 million allocations in fiscal years 1974 and 1975, aid levels climbed to from $25 to $30 million a year the following four years. The amount for AID projects, as opposed to budgetary subsidies, has been much less, ranging between $5 million and $10 million. AID has focused more and more on rural development issues, particularly food and health. A review of six of AID's major projects in this period will indicate to what extent the agency has learned how to design and make operational development for poor people in an extremely hostile development environment.

In Endemic and Communicable Disease Control (AID 1976), a four-year effort begun in fiscal year 1976, AID is contributing $1,887,000 of a $6,144,000 project to enhance the Zairian government's ability to monitor and control such diseases. AID will work with the Zairian national Health Council, which was set up in November 1974, to try to bring some overall coherence to the previously unorchestrated development of health care that had short-changed preventive medicine and public health. The specific project, one of three in an integrated approach, will create a model malaria control program in the Kinshasa region, build a permanent measles immunization program in 16 urban regions, extend these programs into the health delivery systems of five development zones, and develop the human resources and skills needed.

This project design contains much beneficial potential and several impressive participatory elements. The intended emphasis on women as the communicators is very cogent. Some state-level capacity needs to be developed in these fields. Health care appears to be as corrupt as all other public services; the tardy and inadequate government response to the August 1978 cholera outbreak in Kivu and eastern Zaire, which had both political and financial motivations, may be, sadly, a reasonable measure of the National Health Council's abilities. The pronounced urban bias of the AID project feeds on the prevailing unequal situation; just because it is harder to reach rural villagers and they seem more resigned to disease is no reason (AID 1976b, p. 89) to term their immunization needs "less critical."

Basic Family Health Services (AID 1976a), scheduled to start in 1977 but delayed, is intended to aid in the creation of a graduated health delivery system administered through rural and urban health zones. The proposed institutional structure, patterned (unwittingly?) after the Vietnamese, is ideal for poor countries. It is a four-level pyramid providing maximum care at least cost; a village _animateur_ for basic and preventive medicine, a nurse or paraprofessional for every ten villages, a health center and maternity unit per subzone of 30,000 to 40,000, and a general hospital for every zone (50,000 to 250,000 people). With more financial support, a higher density and quality could be sought, and, indeed, AID wondered at the government's willingness or ability to apply such resources.

Two serious design flaws deserve comment. Health is to be treated in this system as a commodity and fees are to be collected. Because people will pay traditional healers does not mean they will accept, never mind pay for, Western medicine. Until the political economy evolves to afford people less corrupted social services and more remunerative productive activities, AID would be on better grounds simply to put pressure on the government to alter its budgetary priorities. A more serious flaw is in the recruitment of _animateurs_, or what are more widely called "health promoters." AID designers did not recognize the absolute necessity of local participation. If the promoter is going to stay any number of years in a locale, he or she should be recruited from the village. Without that, there is far less local acceptance or longevity of tenure. Health care then costs more and the system suffers more frequent disruption.

The bulk of AID projects has gone for aspects of agricultural development or growth. One is the 1978 grant of $3.35 million to a total $6.16 million to upgrade the abilities of INERA, the National Institute for Agricultural Research. The project paper (AID 1978c) reflects a far more sophisticated approach to development than in any of the IBRD projects. AID designers are far more willing (pp. 12, 61) to face the serious limitations of INERA in its present form and to seek multidisciplinary and participatory solutions. The summary of proposed curricula changes is apt. The assessment of the current agricultural extension effort is defensible:

> —farmers and merchants view extension work as a policing function of the forced cultivation of cotton and collection of license fees.
> —farmers contend that the agents knew little or nothing about farming and local conditions. [Pp. 17-18]

The multidisciplinary, participatory style of seeking new knowledge is refreshing. The willingness to consider women extension agents, having noticed that women contribute 60 percent of total farm labor, is not misplaced. It reflects a long overdue yet critical advance in cultural and social awareness. Most surprising, however, is recognition that research is not socially neutral and that research constituency groups must be identified. One must design explicitly for the major target, the small traditional farmer. "This will have to involve the researcher, extension agent and farmer in a continuous flow of information both ways" (p. 70).

Given this degree of excellence of design, several points remain uncertain. Obviously, political and budgetary constraints will impinge. Corruption will as well. One is not left with a feeling of exactly how extension agents will be transformed from monitors of the larger bureaucratic and tax systems to flexible and cooperative assistants aiding small farmers. How can bureaucratic incentives be altered and the obstacles of the local economic and political elite be surmounted? Finally, one would hope that the participatory design elements present here could be woven together in a more systematic and verifiable way, as suggested at the beginning of the chapter. All in all, however, this project is not a bad gamble in such a hostile development environment.

Cassava Outreach (AID 1978b) is a four-year $3.78 million grant to a total $9.11 million effort (1978-81) by the Zairian government's National Cassava Program (PRONAM). Cassava is Zaire's most important food, occupying about 50 percent of the cultivated land and supplying 70 percent of the people with some 60 percent of their caloric intake. Serious disease problems and insect infestations have cut production since 1974. AID will provide technical assistance, training, equipment, and vehicles to facilitate the transfer of new cassava technology to research substations around the country and several thousand farmers in surrounding areas. AID admitted this is a small effort with limited initial impact, but argued that the spread of new technology would benefit the poorest Zairians who cannot afford to have threatened their crop of last resort.

At the risk of sounding heretical, this author seriously questions the empirical basis of this effort as a top priority in helping the poor. Cassava should get some attention. While it is easy to grow and high in calories, it is, however, very low in protein. That it has become a predominant crop is a function of an extremely exploitative and parasitic rural economy. If the object is to feed people nutritionally, then structural and cultural changes are far more imperative than better strains of cassava. But what is most distressing about cassava and encouraging its use are some little-studied medical dimensions. It is common knowledge that the cyanogenic glucoside (HCN) in cassava is poison and must be cooked out; this means time- and fuel-consuming cooking procedures. But AID and the government have ignored the potential health hazards of microtraces of HCN, which are absorbed daily into the bloodstream from incompletely cooked cassava. In 1972 an AID-funded study (Slater et al. 1972) suggested that HCN combines with sulfur-bearing amino acids in ways especially harmful to young children:

Further, once the . . . HCN has bonded to a sulfur-bearing chemical, it is possible that the iodine in the system further binds with this thiocyanide. This may cause thyroid hormones imbalance, and possibly the HCN may prove to be goiterogenic. There is also an indication that HCN unbound by thio-chemicals may affect the central nervous system, causing advanced aging and deterioration of central nervous processes. [P. 6]

Given a cassava-consuming population with a short life-span and high incidence of goiter, more research, if not action, is certainly called for. New sources of protein could be sought among soybeans, fish, and various algae, especially spirulina. The recent discovery (To the Point, November 17, 1978, p. 36) by Belgian scientists in Zaire that an injection of iodine may counteract some effects of HCN does not diminish the need for safe, cheap, high-protein foods.

Agricultural Economic Development (AID 1977b), a five-year $3.53 million grant, intends to improve the ability of the Zairian Department of Agriculture to collect and analyze data to "identify, design, and evaluate development projects" (p. 3), and to plan, manage, and budget with greater effect. Between 1977 and 1981, AID will provide specialists to work in the department and train Zairians for specific needs in five areas. In a 100-page project paper eight basic constraints to agricultural development in Zaire are laid out in technocratic fashion and ameliorative steps are proposed. It is withal an unworldly project based on the assumption that the system is the solution. Political will and integrity are as important as enhanced technical skills; without the former the latter will have little positive impact on the Zairian poor.

AID's self-proclaimed show project in Zaire, and the last to be considered here, is the North Shaba Maize Production. It is scheduled to run from 1976 to 1982 and will cost AID $9.3 million. It also generated the longest project report (AID 1976c) and the most supporting literature in recent memory. This project is viewed as trying to develop a model for integrated rural development in Zaire that is both production-centered and participatory. It is in many ways a very sophisticated exercise and experiment for an international agency, made possible in large measure because two Americans on the design team had been doing anthropological fieldwork in the area the two prior years and because AID contracted with Development Alternatives to help design and run the project.

The production-centered dimensions come through at the onset of the project paper. The project purpose is defined as "to identify a rural development process for improving small farmer production and incomes for replication in other parts of Zaire" (p. 1). Project activities were divided into six components (AID 1976a): research and extension operations; encouragement of the creation of farmer groups or precooperatives based around farmers' centers; development and production of intermediate technology; improvements to marketing and credit "to facilitate the development of an expanded, more competitive private sector role in . . . grain marketing"; infrastructure development; and project monitoring and evaluation. The contradiction between trying to encourage more cooperative behavior for learning and productive activities and more competitive behavior for marketing does not seem to be squarely addressed in the mountain of documentation that follows.

Some of this project design and discussion is worth high praise. The level of factual and cross-cultural analyses is rare in Washington. The participatory research resulting in Annex I and the resulting litany of negative constraints to development as seen by the farmers appeared in no other AID or IBRD effort. Excellent commentary appears on women in development, complexities of defining farming units, protection of human rights, avoidance of social engineering, the need to think of the negative elements of modern technology, and much else. More of the elements of participatory development appear in some form here than any of the other projects examined.

Nevertheless there are several reasons, beyond the budgetary and staffing setbacks AID will admit to, why this project will not succeed in significantly improving the livelihood of most Zairians in the region. The failure to specify precisely local targets led to terms like "a representative sample" (pp. 77-78). Some idea of the dangers of the coalescing of a local male elite dominating the farmers' centers and the new factors of production is visible (pp. 91, 212, 229); but how will it be prevented in reality unless the focus is shifted to explicit encouragement of the participation of all farming units. A more complete sense of the conflictive nature of the situation would be visible if the anthropologists and others would adapt more of the multidisciplinary methodology of Schatzberg (1977), for example.

Worrisome as well is the role of GECAMINES and the project steering committee as a whole. Is the project really to provide more and cheaper maize to keep GECAMINES wages down? In terms of the government's political and pacification needs, it is a very useful place to have such a model project. The question of operationally dealing with corrupt local and regional officials is consistently skirted. What is to prevent regional officials from siphoning the harvest for profitable private uses? Finally, the presentation of a strategy to introduce new strains of maize and chemical inputs sounds like the Green Revolution, an exercise in dependency creation and world system penetration that has generated a mass of critical studies such as that of Biplab Dasgupta (1977) on India and that of Cynthia de Alcantara (1976) on Mexico.

These six AID projects reveal, in sum, a rather mixed performance. Unlike the IBRD, AID is willing to admit its limitations and ignorance on paper, encourage experimentation, seek more modern methodologies, consider participation more central, and try to maintain a more than rhetorical focus on the poor. Very limited resources and political conflicts both in Kinshasa and Washington limit results. So does the uneven nature of AID's human resources and the severe practical difficulties of doing any development of any sort in rural Zaire.

CONCLUSION

One could devote many more pages to other development efforts, especially hopeful ones of a small-scale participatory nature, such as AID's Bandundu Fishery Project, but enough is visible in this chapter and others to make some concluding judgments about Zaire's dilemma as a poor and peripheral nation in the world system on the eve of the 1980s.

Nominal political independence has not in the last two decades led to economic independence or the realization of elementary human rights for the Zairian poor. Instead, symbiosis of interests emerged between a new class of haves in Zaire and the core powers and their corporations still interested in cheap minerals and cheap labor. The balance between the two in the struggle to control the production of the Zairian poor has shifted over the ensuing years. The disintegration of Mobutu's ability to pay his international debts, beginning in 1976 and accelerating at the end of 1978, was met by the latest version of the systemic counterattack. During 1978 the IMF has been intruding or supervising the intrusion of more and more expatriate (European) financial technicians into top roles in appropriate government ministries (Financial Times, January 2, 1979) in order to recover resources for the payment of debts. Mobutu has traded another quantum of his partial sovereignty for the possibility of keeping the remaining amount and the spoils it implies. Several more rounds of this are possible, and mere coup d'etats are not likely to do more than re-create the symbiosis that preys upon and pauperizes the great majority of Zairians.

Sad conclusions remain. Zaire is one of the worst run, most inhumane economies on the globe. The Zairian poor, given only the voices of a few scholars, journalists, and bureaucrats in the world system, have no politically effective voice in this system. Indeed, the system has no use for them at this moment in history, needing these poor only marginally as either workers or consumers. At this writing, it has not proved possible even to engage the world system managers in a substantive dialogue about the creation of an alternative future wherein the Zairian people eat. Chase Manhattan is interested simply in its money. The U.S. State Department will not institutionalize new ideas. Nor will the World Bank. The IMF does not deign to recognize people, never mind ideas.

Without more citizens engaged in more participatory development the world over, there is but one clear certainty: 18 to 22 million Zairians, most of the society, will face the 1980s with a brief, hungry, and painful life as their only future. Human beings deserve more.

REFERENCES

Amin, Samir, et al. 1975. La planification du sous-développement. Paris: Ed. Anthropos-IDEP.

Dasgupta, Biplab. 1977. Agrarian Change and the New Technology in India. Geneva: United Nations Research Institute for Social Development.

de Alcantara, Cynthia H. 1976. Modernizing Mexican Agriculture: Socioeconomic Implications of Technological Change 1940-1970. Geneva: United Nations Research Institute for Social Development.

Elliott, Charles. 1975. Patterns of Poverty in the Third World. New York: Praeger.

Espinosa, Juan G., and Andrew S. Zimbalist. 1978. Economic Democracy: Workers Participation in Chilean Industry 1970-1973. New York: Academic Press.

Ewert, David M. 1977. "Freire's Concept of Critical Consciousness and Social Structure in Rural Zaire." Ph.D. dissertation, University of Wisconsin.

Gran, Guy. 1978." Development versus the World System: A Model Policy Planning Country Study of Peru." AID 1a-C-1245, March.

International Bank for Reconstruction and Development. 1978a. "Zaire Appraisal of the Oil Palm Project." Report nos. 1592-ZR and P-2296-ZR, March/April.

_____. 1978b. "Monthly Operational Summary of Bank and IDA Proposed Projects," sec. M75-903, December 12.

_____. 1977a. "Zaire Ituri Livestock Development Project Appraisal Report." Report nos. 1305-ZR and P-1964-ZR, February/March.

_____. 1977b. "Appraisal of: Société Financiere de Développement (SOFIDE) Zaire." Report nos. 1371a-ZR and P-2048-ZR, April.

_____. 1976a. "Appraisal of a Second Education Project in Zaire." Report nos. 864-ZR and P-1715-ZR, March.

_____. 1976b. "Appraisal of Water Supply Project." Report nos. 898-ZR and P-1700-ZR, March.

_____. 1976c. "Appraisal of the Zaire Cotton Rehabilitation Project." Report nos. 1179-ZR and P-1869-ZR, September.

_____. 1975a. "The Economy of Zaire." 4 vols. Report no. 821-ZR, July.

_____. 1975b. "Appraisal of the Third Highway Project Zaire." Report nos. 567-CK and P-1535a-CK, January.

_____. 1975c. "Appraisal of a Railway and River Transport Project Republic of Zaire." Report nos. 618a-ZR and P-1573a-ZR, May.

_____. 1974. "Appraisal of Gecamines Expansion Project Zaire." Report nos. 576a-CK and P-1551-CK, December and January.

Schatzberg, Michael G. 1977. "Bureaucracy, Business, Beer: The Political Dynamics of Class Formation in Lisala, Zaire." Ph.D. dissertation, University of Wisconsin.

Slater, Charles, et al. 1972. "The Bionomics of a Manioc-Dependent Culture Kinshasa, Zaire." University of Colorado, AID/CSD 3285.

Squire, Lyn, and Herman G. van der Tak. 1975. Economic Analysis of Projects. Baltimore: Johns Hopkins University Press.

U.S., Agency for International Development. 1978a. U.S. Overseas Loans and Grants and Assistance from International Organizations. Annual.

_____. 1978b. Cassava Outreach. Project paper no. 660-077.

_____. 1978c. INERA Support. Project paper no. 660-0064.

_____. 1977a. Annual Budget Submission FY 1979 USAID Zaire. June.

_____. 1977b. Agricultural Economic Development. Project paper no. 660-0052.

_____. 1976a. Basic Family Health Services. Project paper no. 660-0067. Zaire.

_____. 1976b. Endemic and Communicable Disease Control. Project paper no. 660-0058. Zaire.

_____. 1976c. Zaire-North Shaba Maize Production. Project paper no. 660-11-199-059.

_____. 1975. Draft Development Assistance Program (DAP) for Zaire, pt. 1, January.

_____. 1974. Field Budget Submission FY 1976 Zaire.

_____. 1970. Country Field Submission FY 1972 Congo (Kinshasa).

_____. 1968. Program Memorandum FY 1970 Congo (Kinshasa).

_____. 1966. Country Assistance Program FY 1968 Congo (Kinshasa), pt. 1, October.

Wallman, Sandra, ed. 1977. Perceptions of Development. Cambridge: At the University Press.

AN INTRODUCTORY BIBLIOGRAPHY FOR MODERN ZAIRIAN STUDIES

This bibliography is not intended as an exhaustive listing of works on modern Zaire. It is instead designed as a guide to the best, most recent, and most representative works on postcolonial Zaire, particularly Zaire of the 1970s. It does not duplicate the sum of chapter references but, rather, attempts to reflect the breadth of North American and European work in the social sciences. Material of Zairian origin, more difficult to obtain, is moderately slighted; CEDAF (1978) is the standard guide to much of it. Bustin (1972) is the most recent overall bibliographical work on Zaire. Researchers also will find valuable the Cambridge histories, Young (1965), and Vellut (1974) for initial investigation. As Jewsiewicki's bibliography (Chapter 2) suggests, no exhaustive treatment of specific authors was attempted; Verhaegen and Vansina, for instance, each merit far more bibliographic attention.

The section of unpublished works attempts to list the most useful works of an ideal literary universe. Multilateral organizations will not consciously release their material. The other works can be found in one or more Washington, D.C., libraries or the library of the university or author of origin. The researcher should know, however, what kinds and categories of studies exist for each Third World society.

PUBLISHED SOURCES

Abi-Saab, Georges. 1978. The United Nations Operation in the Congo, 1960–1964. London: Oxford University Press.

Adelman, Kenneth L. 1975a. "The Church-State Conflict in Zaire: 1969–1974." African Studies Review 18, no. 1:102-16.

_____. 1975b. "The Recourse to Authenticity and Negritude in Zaire." Journal of Modern African Studies 13, no. 1: 134-39.

Anderson, Barbara, and James McCabe. 1977. "Nutrition and the Fertility of Younger Women in Kinshasa, Zaire." Journal of Development Economics 4:343-63.

Anstey, Roger. 1966. King Leopold's Legacy: The Congo under Belgian Rule. London: Oxford University Press.

Bank of Zaire. 1975, 1976, 1977. Annual Report. Kinshasa.

Belliveau, Nancy. 1977. "Heading off Zaire's Default." Institutional Investor, March, pp. 23-28.

Biebuyck, Daniel. 1978. Hero and Chief: Epic Literature from the Banyanga (Zaire Republic). Berkeley: University of California Press.

_____. 1973. Lega Culture. Berkeley: University of California Press.

Bonehill, Daniel. 1978. "La dépendance et la fragilité." Monde diplomatique 291 (June): 1, 5.

Breitengross, J. P., ed. 1974. Planification et développement économique au Zaire. Hamburg: Deutches Institut für Afrika Forschung.

Bustin, Edouard. 1975. Lunda under Belgian Rule: The Politics of Ethnicity. Cambridge, Mass.: Harvard University Press.

_____. 1971. "Congo-Kinshasa. Guide bibliographique." Cahiers du CEDAF, no. 3-4.

Cambridge History of Africa. 1979-80. Vols. 6, 7, 8.

Centre d'Etude et de Documentation Africaine. 1978. Les périodique zairois (1970-1977). Brussels: CEDAF.

Centre de Recherche et d'Information Socio-Politiques. 1966a. Congo 1964: Political Documents of a Developing Nation. Princeton, N.J.: Princeton University Press.

_____. 1966b. Congo 1965. Brussels: CRISP.

_____. 1960. Congo 1959. Brussels: CRISP.

Chomé, Jules. 1974. L'ascension de Mobutu: Du Sergent Joseph Desiré au Général Sese Seko. Brussels: Complexe.

Ciamala Kanda. 1978. "Eléments de blocage du développement rural au Zaire (cas Luba du Kasai)." Cahiers économiques et sociaux 16, no. 3 (September): 334-71.

Ciparisse, Gérard. 1978. "An Anthropological Approach to Socioeconomic Factors of Development: The Case of Zaire." Current Anthropology 19, no. 1 (March): 37-41.

Comeliau, Christian. 1969. Conditions de la planification du développement: L'exemple du Congo. The Hague: Mouton.

Comité Zaire. 1978a. Zaire—Le dossier de la recolonisation. Paris: Editions l'Harmattan.

_____. 1978b. "Kolwezi '78." InfoZaire, vol. 5 (July/August).

Cornevin, Robert. 1974. "La politique interiéure du Zaire." Revue française d'études politiques africaines 108:30-48.

DeCraemer, Willy. 1977. The Jamaa and the Church: A Bantu Catholic
Movement in Zaire. London: Oxford University Press.

Demunter, Paul. 1972. "Structure de classe et luttes de classes dans le
Congo colonial." Contradictions 1:67-109.

Fetter, Bruce. 1976. The Creation of Elisabethville, 1910-1940. Stanford,
Calif.: Hoover Institution Press, Stanford University.

Gann, L. H., and P. Duignan. 1969-73. Colonialism in Africa. 5 vols.
Cambridge: At the University Press.

Gatarayiha Majinya, Kangafu Gudumbagana, and Didier de Lannoy. 1976.
"Aspects de la réforme administrative au Zaire." Cahiers du CEDAF,
no. 4-5.

Gerard-Libois, Jules. 1966. Katanga Secession. Madison: University of
Wisconsin Press.

Gould, David J. 1978. "From Development Administration to Underdevelopment Administration: Zairian Public Administration in the Perspective
of Paradigmatic Crisis." Cahiers du CEDAF, no. 6.

_____. 1977. "Local Administration in Zaire and Underdevelopment." Jour-
nal of Modern African Studies 15, no. 3:349-78.

Gould, David J., and Mwana Elas. 1979a. "Patrons, Clients and the Politics of Zairianization." In Political Patronage, Clientalism and Development, edited by S. N. Eisenstadt and René Lemarchand, forthcoming.

_____. 1979b. "Patrons, Clients and the Role of the Military in Zaire."
In The Performance of Soldiers as Governors: African Politics and
the African Military, edited by I. J. Mowe. Washington, D.C.: University Press of America, forthcoming.

Gouverneur, J. 1971. Productivity and Factor Proportions in Less Developed Countries: The Case of Industrial Firms in the Congo. London:
Oxford University Press.

Government of Zaire, Department of Agriculture. 1977a. Index No. 2, 0061-
1330, Agriculture, 1960-1976. Kinshasa, June.

_____. 1977b. Statistiques agricoles annuaire restrospectif 1970-1974. Kinshasa, May.

Government of Zaire, Département du Plan. 1978. Perspectives démographiques régionales, 1975-1985. Kinshasa.

Gran, Guy. 1979. "Zaire 1979: The IMF at Waterloo." In Foreign Assistance Legislation for Fiscal Years 1980-1981, Part 8, Foreign Affairs Committee, pp. 406-17. Washington, D.C.: U.S. Government Printing Office.

_____. 1978. "Zaire 1978: The Ethical and Intellectual Bankruptcy of the World System." Africa Today 25, no. 4:5-24.

House, Arthur H. 1978. The U.N. in the Congo: The Political and Civilian Efforts. Washington, D.C.: University Press of America.

Houyoux, Joseph. 1973. Budgets ménagers, nutrition et mode de vie à Kinshasa. Kinshasa: Presses Universitaires du Zaire.

Hull, Galen S. 1977. "Whose Victory in Shaba?" Africa Report, July-August, pp. 4-9.

_____. 1976. "L'université et état: l'UNAZA, Kisangani." Cahiers du CEDAF, no. 1/2.

Institut de Recherches Economiques et Sociales. 1968. Indépendance, inflation, développement. Paris: Editions Mouton.

International Bank for Reconstruction and Development. 1978a. World Development Report, 1978. IBRD and Oxford, August.

_____. 1978b. World Debt Tables—Supplements, EC-167/78/S-1, August 30.

International Monetary Fund. 1971. Surveys of African Economies—Volume 4. Washington, D.C.: IMF.

Janzen, John M. 1978. The Quest for Therapy in Lower Zaire. Berkeley: University of California Press.

Jewsiewicki, Bogumil. 1979. "Contributions to a History of Agriculture and Fishing in Central Africa." African Economic History. Special issue.

_____. 1978. "Histoire économique d'une ville coloniale. Kisangani 1877-1960." Cahiers du CEDAF, no. 5.

_____. 1977. "The Great Depression and the Making of the Colonial Economic System in the Belgian Congo." African Economic History 4:153-76.

_____. 1975. Agriculture nomade et économie capitaliste: Histoire des essais de modernisation de l'agriculture africaine au Zaire à l'époque coloniale. 2 vols. Lubumbashi: UNAZA.

Kabala Kabunda, M. K. K. 1976. "Multinational Corporations and the Installation of Externally-Oriented Economic Structures in Contemporary Africa: The Example of the Unilever-Zaire Group." In Multinational Corporations in Africa, edited by Carl Widstrand, pp. 303-22. New York: Africana.

Kamitatu-Massemba, Cléophas. 1977. Zaire, le pourvoir à la portée du peuple. Paris: Editions l'Harmattan.

Kankuenda Mbaya. 1977. "Les industries du pôle de Kinshasa: Réflexion sur la stratégie des pôles de croissance en pays africains." Cahiers du CEDAF, no. 1-2.

Kanza, Thomas. 1972. Conflict in the Congo. London: Penguin.

Kaplan, Irving, ed. 1979. Zaire, a Country Study. Washington, D.C.: American University and U.S. Government Printing Office.

Kashamura, Anicet. 1971. Culture et aliénation en Afrique. Paris: Edition du Cercle.

Klein, M., ed. 1979. Peasants in Africa: Historical and Contemporary Perspectives. Beverly Hills, Calif.: Sage.

Lacroix, Jean-Louis. 1967. Industrialisation au Congo: La transformation des structures économiques. Paris, The Hague: Mouton.

La Fontaine, Jean S. 1974. "The Free Women of Kinshasa: Prostitution in a City in Zaire." In Choice and Change: Essays in Honour of Lucy Mair, edited by J. Davis, pp. 89-113. New York: Humanities Press.

Lemarchand, René. 1964. Political Awakening in the Belgian Congo. Berkeley: University of California Press.

Lemarchand, René, ed. 1978. American Policy in Southern Africa: The Stakes and the Stance. Washington, D.C.: University Press of America.

Lutumbu-Lu-Vilu Na Wundu. 1976. De la Zairianisation à la rétrocession et au dialogue nord-sud. Brussels: Office International de Librairie.

MacGaffey, Wyatt. 1970. Custom and Government in the Lower Congo. Berkeley: University of California Press.

Mbuki Mwamufiya and James B. Fitch. 1976. "Maize Marketing and Distribution in Southern Zaire." Occasional paper. Mexico City: International Maize and Wheat Improvement Center.

Merlier, M. 1962. Le Congo de la colonisation belge à l'indépendance. Paris: Maspero.

Merriam, Alan P. 1974. An African World: The Basongye Village of Lupupa Ngye. Bloomington: Indiana University Press.

Monguya-Mbenga, Daniel. 1977. Histoire secrete du Zaire. Brussels: Editions de l'Espérance.

Mpinga-Kasenda and David Gould. 1975. Les réformes administratives au Zaire, 1972-73. Kinshasa: Presses Universitaires du Zaire.

Mulumba, Lukoji. 1976. "Investir au Zaire." Zaire-Afrique 103:141-52.

Naipul, V. S. 1975. "A New King for the Congo." New York Review of Books 22 (June 26):11.

Nkrumah, Kwame. 1967. Challenge of the Congo. New York: International Publishers.

Nzongola, Georges (Ntalaja). 1970. "The Bourgeoisie and Revolution in the Congo." Journal of Modern African Studies 8, no. 4:511-30.

O'Brien, Conor Cruise. 1962. To Katanga and Back. New York: Simon and Schuster.

Odier, Jeannick. 1975. "La politique étrangère de Mobutu." Revue française d'études politiques africaines 120 (December): 25-41.

Palmer, Robin, and Neil Parsons, eds. 1977. The Roots of Rural Poverty in Central and Southern Africa. Berkeley: University of California Press.

Peemans, J. Ph. 1975a. "The Social and Economic Development of Zaire since Independence: An Historical Outline." African Affairs 295:148-79.

_____. 1975b. "L'état fort et la croissance économique." Revue nouvelle (Brussels) 62, no. 12:515-27.

_____. 1974. The Political Economy of Zaire in the Seventies. Document 7406. Louvain, U.C.L.: Institut d'Etude des Pays en Voie de Développement.

Peerings, C. 1979. Black Mineworkers in Central Africa. London: Heine-mann.

Piret, Baudoin. 1978. "Le sous-développement du Zaire vu à travers la balance des paiements Belgique-Zaire." Contradictions 15-16: 187-205.

_____. 1972. "L'aide belge du Congo et le développement inégal du capitalisme monopoliste d'état." Contradictions 1: 111-37.

Popelier, G. H. 1977. "Nature et évolution de l'agriculture zairoise (1958-1975)." Cahiers du CEDAF, no. 6.

Radmann, Wolf. 1978. "The Nationalization of Zaire's Copper: From Union Minière to GECAMINES." Africa Today 25, no. 4: 25-47.

Rymenam, Jean. 1977. "Comment le régime Mobutu a sapé ses propres fondements." Monde diplomatique 278 (May): 8-9.

Schatzberg, Michael G. 1979. Politics and Class in Zaire: Bureaucracy, Business and Beer in Lisala. New York: Africana.

_____. 1978. "Fidélité au guide: The J. M. P. R. in Zairian Schools." Journal of Modern African Studies 16, no. 3: 417-31.

Schwarz, Alf. 1972. "Illusion d'une emancipation et aliénation réele de l'ouvrière zairoise." Canadian Journal of African Studies 6, no. 2: 183-212.

Tiker-Tiker. 1978. "Le concept du 'Développement Rural' dans le processus du développement économique du Zaire." Cahiers économiques et sociaux 16, no. 3 (September): 243-57.

Turner, Thomas. 1974. "Peasant Rebellion and Its Suppression in Sankuru, Zaire." Pan-African Journal 7, no. 3: 193-215.

_____. 1973. "La politique indigène du Congo belge: Le cas du Sankuru." Cahiers du CEDAF, no. 1.

Urbach, Alan. 1977. "Lessons to Be Learnt from Zaire Debt Settlement." New African Development, January, pp. 69-73.

U.S., Congress, Senate. Foreign Relations Committee. 1976. The Political and Economic Crisis in Southern Africa. Staff Report, September 1976.

_____. 1975. Security Supporting Assistance for Zaire, Hearing, October 24, 1975.

U.S., Department of Health, Education and Welfare. Office of International Health. 1975. Syncrisis: The Dynamics of Health—XIV Zaire. Washington, D.C.

Van Der Steen, Daniel. 1977. "Echanges économiques extérieurs du Zaire: Dépendance et développement." Cahiers du CEDAF, no. 4-5.

Vansina, Jan. 1978. The Children of Woot: A History of the Kuba Peoples. Madison: University of Wisconsin Press.

_____. 1966. Introduction à l'ethnographie du Congo. Brussels: Centre de Recherche et l'Information Socio-Politiques.

Vellut, J. L. 1975. "Le Zaire à la périphérie du capitalisme: Quelques perspectives historiques." Enquêtes et documents d'histoire africaine 1:114-51.

_____. 1974. Guide de l'étudiant en histoire du Zaire. Kinshasa.

Verhaegen, Benoît. 1978a. L'enseignement universitaire au Zaire de Lovanium à l'UNAZA 1958-1978. Paris: L'Harmattan.

_____. 1978b. "Impérialisme technologique et bourgeoisie nationale au Zaire." In Connaissance du Tiers Monde, edited by C. Coquery-Vidrovitch, pp. 347-80. Paris: Cahiers Jussieu 10/18.

_____. 1969. Rébellions au Congo, II. Brussels: Centre de Recherche et l'Information Socio-Politiques.

_____. 1966. Rébellions au Congo, I. Brussels: Centre de Recherche et l'Information Socio-Politiques.

Vieux, Serge A. 1974. L'administration zairoise. Paris: Berger-Levrault.

Weiss, Herbert F. 1967. Political Protest in the Congo: The Parti Solidaire Africaine during the Independence Struggle. Princeton, N.J.: Princeton University Press.

Weissman, Stephen R. 1974. American Foreign Policy in the Congo. Ithaca, N.Y.: Cornell University Press.

Willame, Jean-Claude. 1978. "La Second Guerre du Shaba." Enquêtes et documents d'histroire africaine (Leuven, Belgium), vol. 3.

_____. 1972. Patrimonialism and Political Change in the Congo. Stanford, Calif.: Stanford University Press.

_____. 1964-65. Les provinces du Congo: Structure et fonctionnement. Vol. 1: Kwilu-Luluabourg, Nord Katanga-Ubangi. Vol. 4: Lomani-Kivu Central. Leopoldville: Institut de Recherches Economiques and Sociales Lovanium.

Young, Crawford. 1978. "Zaire: The Unending Crisis." Foreign Affairs 57, no. 1:169-85.

_____. 1976. The Politics of Cultural Pluralism. Madison: University of Wisconsin Press.

_____. 1965. Politics in the Congo. Princeton, N.J.: Princeton University Press.

UNPUBLISHED SOURCES

Callaghy, Thomas M. 1976. "State Formation and Centralization of Power in Zaire: Mobutu's Pre-Eminent Public Policy." Presented at the African Studies Association Annual Meeting, Boston.

Depelchin, Jacques. 1974. "From Pre-Capitalism to Imperialism: A History of Social and Economic Formations in Eastern Zaire (Uvira Zone c. 1800-1965)." Ph.D. dissertation, Stanford University.

Ewert, David M. 1977. "Freire's Concept of Critical Consciousness and Social Structure in Rural Zaire." Ph.D. dissertation, University of Wisconsin.

Food and Agricultural Organization. 1976. "Zaire—Rapport de la mission de programmation, Mai-Juin," no. 22, Rome, September

Gould, David J. 1979. "The Problem of Seepage in International Development Assistance: Why United States Aid to Zaire Goes Astray." Presented at the American Society for Public Administration Annual Meeting, Baltimore.

_____. 1978. "Underdevelopment Administration: Systemic Corruption in the Public Bureaucracy of Mobutu's Zaire." Paper presented at the Conference on Political Clientelism, Patronage, and Development, Bellagio, Italy, August.

Government of Zaire. 1978a. "Programme de relances agricole (1978-1980)." Kinshasa, January.

_____. 1978b. Office de Gestion de la Dette Publique. "Rapport annuel 1977." Kinshasa, August.

_____. 1978c. "Synthese économique 1977." 2 vols. Kinshasa, July.

_____. 1971. "Politique, perspectives et moyens du développement." Kinshasa, July.

Hull, Galen S. 1978. "The French Connection in Africa: Zaire and South Africa." Presented at the African Studies Association Annual Meeting, Baltimore.

International Bank for Reconstruction and Development. 1978. "Zaire—Appraisal of the Oil Palm Project." Report nos. 1592-ZR and P-2296-ZR, March 29 and April 3.

_____. 1977. "Economic Conditions and Prospects of Zaire." Report no. 1407-ZR, April 13.

_____. 1975. "The Economy of Zaire." Report no. 821-ZR, July 23, 4 vols.

_____. 1974. "Appraisal of GECAMINES Expansion Project Zaire." Report nos. 576a-CK and P-1551-CK, December and January (1975).

_____. 1973. "Recent Economic Developments and Prospects of the Republic of Zaire." Report no. AE-31a, March 5, 2 vols.

_____. 1972. "Agricultural Sector Survey Republic of Zaire." Report no. PA-118a, June 19, 3 vols.

_____. 1968. "Democratic Republic of the Congo—The Congo's Economy: Evolution and Prospects." Report no. AF-85a, November 19, 3 vols.

International Monetary Fund. 1977a. "Zaire—Recent Economic Developments." SM/77/113, May 18.

_____. 1977b. "Consultative Group for Zaire. Papers and statements, ZA 77-5—77-9, May-August.

_____. 1977c. "Report on Zaire's Debt Renegotiation." SM/77/287, December 9.

_____. 1976. "Zaire—Use of Fund Resources—Stand-by Arrangement." EBS/76/129, March 13.

_____. 1975a. "Staff Report for the 1975 Article XIV Consultation." SM/75/189, July 17.

_____. 1975b. "Zaire—Recent Economic Developments." SM/75/225, August 26.

_____. 1972. "Zaire—Staff Report and Proposed Decision for the 1971 Article XIV Consultation." SM/72/45, February 17.

_____. 1968. "Democratic Republic of Congo." October, 2 vols.

Kabamba Nkamany, et al. 1978. "Investigation of Nutritional Consequences of the Drought in Bas-Zaire, 1978." Kinshasa: Zaire National Nutrition Planning Center, Report no. 8.

Kabwit, Ghislain C. 1978. "The Aftermath of Shaba I and II Crises: The Illusion of Political Changes and Reforms in Zaire." Presented at the African Studies Association Annual Meeting, Baltimore.

Kannyo, Edward. 1979. "Political Power and Class Formation in Zaire: The 'Zairianization Measures,' 1973-1975." Ph.D. dissertation, Yale University.

Katwala, Ghifem. 1979. "Bureaucracy, Dependency and Underdevelopment in Zaire." Ph.D. dissertation, University of California, Berkeley.

Mbuki Mwamufiya. 1977. "Maize Production and Marketing in Four Districts of Zaire: An Introductory Economic Analysis." Ph.D. dissertation, Oregon State University.

Nelson, Eric. 1976. "African Rural-Urban Migration: Economic Choice Theory and Kinshasa Evidence." Ph.D. dissertation, Yale University.

Nzongola Ntalaja. 1978. "The Continuing Struggle for National Liberation in Zaire." Presented at the African Studies Association Annual Meeting, Baltimore.

_____. 1975. "Urban Administration in Zaire: A Study of Kananga, 1971-73." Ph.D. dissertation, University of Wisconsin.

Regier, Fremont A. 1977. "Ownership: Participation in Planning, Administration, and Operation of a Rural Development Project Nyanga, Zaire." Ph.D. dissertation, University of Wisconsin.

Schatzberg, Michael G. 1979. "The State and the Economy: The 'Radicalization of the Revolution' in Mobutu's Zaire." Paper presented at the Canadian Political Science Association meeting, May.

_____. 1978. "Islands of Privilege: Small Cities in Africa and the Dynamics of Class Formation." Paper presented at the Conference on the Small City and Regional Community, Stevens Point, Wisconsin, March.

Sosne, Elinor D. 1974. "Kinship and Contract in Bushi, A Study in Village Level Politics." Ph.D. dissertation, University of Wisconsin.

Tollens, Eric F. 1975. "An Economic Analysis of Cotton Production, Marketing, and Processing in Northern Zaire." Ph.D. dissertation, Michigan State University.

Union Nationale des Traivailleurs Zairois. 1977. "Positions concernant la politique des salaires." Kinshasa.

United Nations Development Program. 1976. "Country Program for Zaire." DP/GC/ZAI/R.a, February 25, 1976.

United Nations Education, Science, and Cultural Organization. "Zaire: Etudes sectorielles de l'éducation." Paris, 2 vols.

U.S., Agency for International Development. 1979. "Zaire Country Strategy Statement." January (still classified).

_____. 1978. "Annual Budget Submission FY 1980 Zaire." June.

_____. 1977. "Annual Budget Submission FY 1979 USAID Zaire." June.

_____. 1976a. "Zaire—North Shaba Maize Production." Project paper no. 660-11-199-059.

_____. 1976b. "Fiscal Year 1977 Submission to the Congress—Security Supporting Assistance—Zaire, Zambia, Southern Africa." June 1976.

_____. 1976c. "Zaire Commodity Import Loan." Project paper, AID-DLC-2145/1, June 30, 1976.

_____. 1975. "Draft Development Assistance Program (DAP) for Zaire." Pt. 1, January.

_____. 1974. "Field Budget Submission FY 1976 Zaire."

_____. 1970. "Country Field Submission FY 1972 Congo (Kinshasa)."

_____. 1968. "Program Memorandum FY 1970 Congo (Kinshasa)."

_____. 1966. "Country Assistance Program FY 1968 Congo (Kinshasa)." Pt. 1, October.

U.S., Agency for International Development, Office of Housing. 1975. "Zaire Shelter Sector Analysis."

Young, Crawford. 1977. "Ethnic Politics in Zaire." Presented at the African Studies Association Annual Meeting, Houston.

PERIODICALS

AF Press Clips (Washington, D.C., Department of State).

Africa Confidential (London).

Africa News (Durham, N.C.).

Bulletin mensuel de la statistique (Kinshasa).

Cahiers du CEDAF (Brussels).

Cahiers économiques et sociaux (Kinshasa).

Contradictions (Brussels).

Demain L'Afrique (Paris).

Etudes zairoises (Kinshasa).

InfoZaire (Brussels).

Jeune Afrique (Paris).

Miso Gaa (Brussels).

Revue de la presse (Brussels, Belgian Foreign Ministry).

ABOUT THE EDITOR
AND CONTRIBUTORS

GUY GRAN is a freelance international development consultant in Washington, D.C. He taught history at North Carolina State University, testified many times before congressional committees on Vietnam War topics, and has written on the international development issues of three continents, including "Zaire 1978: The Ethical and Intellectual Bankruptcy of the World System," in Africa Today, October–December (1978). In 1975 he received his Ph.D. in comparative world history from the University of Wisconsin.

GALEN HULL, now with the Committee on Uganda, lived and traveled widely in Africa as a Peace Corps volunteer in Malawi and Associate Professor of Political Science at the National University of Zaire. He has published several articles on Zairian politics and education and earned a Ph.D. in political science from Northwestern University in 1974.

DAVID GOULD is an Associate Professor of the Graduate School of Public and International Affairs, University of Pittsburgh. He is the author of many articles on Zairian politics and five books—most recently, Law and the Administrative Process (Washington, D.C.: University Press of America, 1979). His J.D. and Ph.D. degrees were earned from New York University.

BOGUMIL JEWSIEWICKI is Professor of History at the University of Laval in Quebec and previously taught in Poland, Zaire, and Manitoba. He has published more than 20 works on varied themes in the colonial history of the Belgian Congo since 1972. He is currently coeditor of the Canadian Journal of African Studies. His Ph.D. was in economic history from the University of Lodz in Poland.

GHISLAIN KABWIT is an Assistant Professor of Political Science and International Relations at the University of Maryland, Eastern Shore. He has written several articles and conference papers on contemporary Zairian politics. He received his Ph.D. from the School of International Service at American University in 1975.

EDWARD KANNYO is an Ugandan national specializing in modern Zairian politics. He served as a research associate at the National University of Zaire at Lubumbashi and as acting instructor of politics at Yale. In 1979 he received a Ph.D. in political science from Yale.

GHIFEM J. KATWALA was an Assistant Professor of Political Science at the National University of Zaire at Lubumbashi and coauthored Les reformes administrative au Zaire 1972-73. In 1979 he earned a Ph.D. in political science from the University of California, Berkeley.

RENE LEMARCHAND is Professor of Political Science at the University of Florida (Gainesville). He has published multiple books and articles on the politics and history of Zaire, Rwanda, and Burundi and, most recently, edited American Policy in Southern Africa: The Stakes and the Stance (1978).

MAKALA-LIZUMU and MWANA ELAS are Zairians studying for their Ph.D.'s, or the equivalent, outside of Zaire.

ALLEN ROBERTS has traveled and worked in Africa for seven years, as a Peace Corps volunteer in Chad and anthropological researcher in Zaire. His Ph.D. in anthropology was received from the University of Chicago in 1979.

MICHAEL SCHATZBERG has taught at Dalhousie University and is now Assistant Professor of Political Science at Virginia Polytechnic Institute and State University. He is the author of several articles and Politics and Class in Zaire: Bureaucracy, Business, and Beer in Lisala (New York: Africana, 1979). He received his Ph.D. in political science from the University of Wisconsin in 1977.

ELINOR SOSNE has taught at Hollins College, Old Dominion University, and Western Michigan University. In 1974 she received a Ph.D. in anthropology from the University of Wisconsin.

THOMAS TURNER is Assistant Professor of Political Science at Wheeling College in West Virginia. He has taught at the National University of Zaire in Lubumbashi, published multiple articles on regional and national politics of colonial and modern Zaire, and is coauthor, with Crawford Young, of a forthcoming political history of modern Zaire. He received his Ph.D. in political science from the University of Wisconsin.